DØ146020

FRENCH PEASANTS IN REVOLT

French Peasants in Revolt

The Insurrection of 1851

by

TED W. MARGADANT

PRINCETON UNIVERSITY PRESS

PRINCETON, NEW JERSEY

To my Mother

Contents

List of Maps

List of Tables

Abbreviations

CG Clamecy	Conseil de Guerre judging suspects from Clamecy, archives in ADC
JM-1851	Justice Militaire, 1851 (archives of the military commission in the Yonne, located in AG)

Other abbreviations

arr.	*arrondissement*
CNSS	Congrès National des Sociétés Savantes
CP	Commissaire de Police
cult.	cultivator
D.E.S.	Diplôme d'Etudes Supérieures
Ins.	Insurrection
Int.	Interrogation
J. P.	Justice de la Paix
MC	Mixed Commission of a department in 1852
M. Int.	Minister of the Interior
M. Justice	Minister of Justice
M. War	Minister of War
P-G	Procureur-Général
Proc.	Procureur
S-P	Sous-Prefet
s.s.	secret societies
Tem.	Testimony

Preface

This book is about a series of provincial uprisings against the coup d'état of Louis Napoleon Bonaparte in December 1851. Its dramatis personae resided in country towns and villages whose placid landscapes offer unexpected charms for the contemporary tourist. It is hard to imagine such communities at the forefront of an insurrection, and in my travels to the sites of nineteenth-century rebellions, I often encountered surprise among local people who had never heard of the armed revolts that swept their areas in 1851. Only rarely did I visit a small town where the insurrection is still commemorated. A monument on the public square of Crest, in the Drôme—"From the Resistance Fighters of 1944 to the Insurgents of 1851"—comes closest to recalling this rebel heritage but, more commonly, the violent struggles of the Second Republic have been forgotten.

My purpose in this book is to recover the meaning of the insurrection of 1851 for the history of modern France. I began my research over a decade ago, when Charles Tilly encouraged me to investigate peasant resistance to the coup d'état in one or two departments. I chose the Drôme and the Hérault for my first research trip, aided by a fellowship from Harvard University. One rebel department led to another, and eventually I undertook research in thirteen departmental archives, assisted by research grants, fellowships, and sabbatical leave from the University of California (UC), Davis. In expanding the scope of my research, I benefited greatly from Tilly's suggestions and from the advice of David Landes, my mentor at Harvard University. They encouraged me to generalize from the specific events of 1851 to the broader movement of French society and politics in the nineteenth century. The result is a book of interest to historians and social scientists who may not have heard of the insurrection of 1851, but who are intrigued by the problem of peasant revolts in developing societies.

I have accumulated many other debts in preparing this book: to archivists and librarians in France who courteously guided me to relevant sources; to historians who read and criticized portions of my manuscript; to friends and colleagues at UC Davis who supported my long endeavor; to the staff of the UC Davis Department of History who typed my manuscript; and to the editors and readers of Princeton University Press who helped me turn a lengthy manuscript into a readable book. I am especially grateful to John Merriman, Roger Price, Tony Judt, Daniel Brower, and Dan Wick for reading and evaluating

xv

portions of my manuscript; to Nora and Eve Timm for their help in the early stages of my research; to Bobbie Figy for typing and proof-reading with great care the final version of the manuscript; to Julia Bastian, Arnold Bauer, Karen Gruetter, and Bill Hagen for their friend-ship all along the way; and to my wife, Joby, for her constant en-couragement, sympathy, and love.

Introduction

The French Second Republic began in Paris and ended in the provinces. Its first heroes were workers in the nation's capital, whose street barricades brought ruin upon the monarchy in February 1848; its last defenders were peasants and artisans in two dozen departments of the center and south, whose armed columns tried to oppose Louis Napoleon Bonaparte's coup d'état of December 2, 1851. The classic dialectic of modern French politics—urban revolutionaries versus rural conservatives—had somehow been reversed. In less than four years, the left-wing cause of a Democratic and Social Republic had gravitated from its Parisian epicenter to hundreds of small towns, bourgs, and villages on the periphery of the nation. When the president of the Republic overthrew the National Assembly, tens of thousands of men rebelled in the provinces, but less than 2,000 Republicans took arms in Paris. These provincial rebels proclaimed revolutionary commissions in over one hundred communes; they seized control of an entire department as well as a dozen *arrondissement* capitals; and they clashed violently with troops or gendarmes in thirty different localities. Although the army quickly restored order, the government recognized the extent of the danger by arresting thousands of suspects in the rebel zones. Indeed, the insurrection of December 1851 was the most serious provincial uprising in nineteenth-century France, and it provoked the largest political purge outside Paris between the Terror and Counter-Terror of the 1790s and the Resistance movement of the Second World War.

Despite the intriguing localization of Republican protest in the provinces, resistance to the coup d'état has generally been neglected by historians. As if to confirm E. H. Carr's observation that history is "inevitably a success story," the triumphant rise of Louis Napoleon, not the violent collapse of his Republican opponents, has been the central theme of most narrative accounts of mid-nineteenth-century France.[1] This bias toward the coup d'état rather than the insurrection

[1] Edward Hallet Carr, *What Is History?* (New York, Vintage Books, 1967), p. 167. Until recently, American and English historians have been especially inclined to focus their attention exclusively on Louis Napoleon's rise to power. Examples include Gordon Wright, *France in Modern Times*, 2nd ed. (Chicago, 1974), pp. 138-43; William L. Langer, *Political and Social Upheaval, 1832-1852* (New York, 1969), pp. 450-65; J.P.T. Bury, *France, 1814-1940* (London, 1949), 82-86; and Alfred Cobban, *A History of Modern France*, vol. II, *1799-1871* (London, 1961), pp. 146-57. By contrast, see the recent syntheses by Philippe Vigier,

has been favored by the assumption that Paris was the revolutionary center of France during the Second Republic. William L. Langer's concept of "urban revolutions" in 1848 is an especially influential statement of the view that authoritarian governments were endangered only by popular uprisings in the cities.[2] By implication, once military control over Paris had been restored in the civil war of June 1848, the threat of revolution was over. From the countryside would come only soldiers and votes for the counterrevolution. Thus, the populations of small towns and villages voted overwhelmingly for Louis Napoleon in December 1848, and they voted for him again by the millions when he held a plebiscite three weeks after the coup d'état. From the dual perspective of military control over Paris and electoral control over the provinces, the insurrection seems baffling and irrelevant. One noted historian, Alfred Cobban, has dismissed the entire crisis as mere stagecraft for the coup d'état. Louis Napoleon "had to begin with repression, not so much because the feeble resistance in Paris and a few minor movements in the provinces needed repressing, as because unless there were some repression there would hardly have seemed any reason for a coup d'état."[3] This interpretation of the revolt as a kind of "nonevent," fabricated in large part by Bonapartist administrators, is consistent with the fact that most districts of the nation remained calm in 1851. Furthermore, where provincial opposition to the government did exist, it had been exposed to severe repression before the coup d'état. According to Howard C. Payne, an authority on administrative repression from 1849 to 1852, "The backbone of organized opposition [to the government] was broken before December 1851 by the concerted efforts of the administration."[4] Even Philippe Vigier, a leading French scholar of the Republican movement in the provinces, has characterized the revolts as "pseudoresistance" by "pseudoinsurgents."[5] In the limelight of history stands the victorious Second Empire, casting a heavy shadow over the defeated Republican rebels of December 1851.

La Seconde République (Paris, 1967), pp. 69-118; Maurice Agulhon, *1848 ou l'apprentissage de la République* (Paris, 1973), pp. 88-197; and Roger Price, "Introduction," in Price, ed., *Revolution and Reaction* (London, 1975), pp. 1-72.

[2] Langer, "The Pattern of Urban Revolution in 1848," in Evelyn M. Acomb and Marvin L. Brown, Jr., eds., *French Society and Culture since the Old Regime* (New York, 1966), pp. 89-118.

[3] Cobban, *History*, II, 156.

[4] Payne, "Preparation of a Coup d'Etat: Administrative Centralization and Police Powers in France, 1849-1851," in Frederich J. Cox, et al., *Studies in Modern European History in Honor of Franklin Charles Palm* (New York, 1956), p. 186.

[5] Vigier, *La Seconde République*, p. 117.

This general consensus is diametrically opposed to the assertions of Bonapartist and Republican writers during the 1850s and 1860s, but their views have seemed tendentious or superficial to subsequent historians. Bonapartists defended the coup d'état as a decisive blow against "professional revolutionaries, anarchists of every sort, socialists, and especially secret societies."[6] At the same time, they claimed that the insurrection was nothing but a *Jacquerie*, a savage peasant revolt. For De Maupas, Paris prefect of police during the crisis, "Robbery, pillage, assasination, rape, arson, nothing was wanting to this mournful exhibition of the programme of 1852."[7] According to Quentin-Bauchart, *conseiller d'état* in the new regime, the rebels were motivated by "detestable greed" and they used the weapons of "pillage, fire, and murder."[8] M. de la Gueronnière, an Imperial senator in the 1860s, wrote excitedly in 1853: "Bands of murderers went through the countryside, marched on the towns, invaded private houses, pillaged, burned, killed, everywhere spreading horror of abominable crimes which take us back to the worst days of barbarism. It was no longer the fanaticism so unhappily present in party struggles. It was cannibalism such that even the boldest imaginations could scarcely suppose."[9] Filled with hatred of the rich, organized into terrifying secret societies, and bereft of political ideas, these new barbarians lashed out blindly against the social order. Had they been able to time their outburst for election day in May 1852, they might well have wrecked the nation. Through his coup d'état Louis Napoleon saved France from an impending disaster.

To this feigned hysteria of the Bonapartists, whose "Red Scare" helped mobilize public support for the Empire, Republicans countered with a sober narrative of rebel efforts to defend the Constitution. Their spokesman was Eugène Ténot, a Parisian journalist whose history of the insurrection, *La province en décembre 1851*, was first published in 1865.[10] In order to rehabilitate the Republicans and to denigrate the Bonapartists, Ténot emphasized the political objectives and military operations of the rebels, and he showed that they rarely attacked civilian lives or property. His careful reconstruction of the military clashes in each department only seemed to demonstrate, however, that

[6] Quentin-Bauchart, *Etudes et souvenirs sur la Deuxième République et le Second Empire (1848-1870)*, ed. by his son (Paris, 1901), I, 440-41.

[7] De Maupas, *The Story of the Coup d'Etat*, trans. Albert D. Vandam (New York, 1884), p. 408.

[8] Quentin-Bauchart, *Etudes*, I, 441.

[9] M. de la Gueronnière, *Biographies politiques, Napoleon III* (Paris, 1853), pp. 176-77.

[10] I have used the 9th edition, which contains valuable appendices (Paris, 1868), and the 13th edition (Paris, 1869).

the entire movement had been doomed from the start. If the insurrection of 1851 had been prolonged and bloody, it might have attained the kind of historical significance reserved for such spectacular though futile civil wars as the Vendée. Instead, resistance nearly always ceased as soon as troops arrived, if not before. Insofar as the major criterion for interpreting resistance to the coup d'état is its military efficacy, then the entire episode deserves little if any attention. Indeed, Ténot's book, which went through at least thirteen editions before the end of the Second Empire, was quietly forgotten during the Third Republic, and it still awaits its first reprinting in the twentieth century.

In recent years three historiographical trends have encouraged a new appraisal of the insurrection: analytical studies of social protest movements in Western Europe from 1750 to 1850; comprehensive investigations of particular regions of France during the Second Republic; and cultural studies of peasant life styles and forms of protest in preindustrial France. To begin with, the pioneering research of Eric J. Hobsbawm, George Rudé, Albert Soboul, E. P. Thompson, and Charles Tilly has shown that popular violence—"the crowd in history"—can be interpreted as a response to social change.[11] These scholars generally share the view that expanding markets in agriculture and manufacturing generated acute social tensions in the European countryside during the age of the French and the Industrial Revolutions. Specific forms of crowd protest—the food riot, the tax revolt, the destruction of machines, even the political uprising—reveal the determination of peasants, agricultural laborers, and rural artisans to defend their traditional way of life against the intrusion of capitalist exchange relationships, an urban social system, and a centralized state. From this perspective, protest movements have social significance regardless of whether they change the course of political history. By extension, insurgency in 1851 may have been a major event in French social history, despite its political failure. Soboul has made precisely this inference by linking the peasant rebels of December to an earlier wave of rural disorder in 1848; and Tilly has pursued this logic by relating the decline of rural industry in

---

[11] Hobsbawm, *Primitive Rebels* (New York, 1959); Hobsbawm and Rudé, *Captain Swing* (New York, 1968); Rudé, *The Crowd in History, 1730-1848* (New York, 1964); Soboul, *Paysans, sans-culottes et Jacobins* (Paris, 1966); Thompson, *The Making of the English Working Class* (New York, 1966); Thompson, "The Moral Economy of the English Crowd in the Eighteenth Century," *Past and Present*, 50 (1971), 76-136; Tilly, *The Vendée* (New York, 1967); Tilly, "The Changing Place of Collective Violence," in Melvin Richter, ed., *Essays in Theory and History* (Cambridge, Mass., 1970), pp. 139-64; and Tilly, "How Protest Modernized in France, 1845-1855," in W. Aydelotte, et al., *The Dimensions of Quantitative Research in History* (Princeton, 1972), pp. 192-255.

mid-nineteenth-century France to the heavy participation of rural artisans in resistance to the coup d'état.[12]

Meanwhile, detailed regional histories have brought into focus the socioeconomic, cultural, and political backgrounds of the insurrection. Thus, Philippe Vigier's doctoral dissertation on the "Alpine region" during the Second Republic interprets peasant radicalization as a consequence of agrarian depression and indebtedness. Vigier also presents evidence that Republican "secret societies" organized the insurrection in this region of southeastern France.[13] In a multivolume social history of the Var from the Old Régime to 1851, Maurice Agulhon shows how the social structure and cultural traditions of that Provençal department facilitated the diffusion of Republican ideals after the Revolution of 1848. He analyzes the insurrection as an interplay of traditional economic grievances and modernizing cultural influences within a political context of state repression and organized dissent.[14] Roger Price has synthesized the work of Vigier, Agulhon, and several other regional historians in his recently published *The French Second Republic*.[15] He identifies three factors that seem to have characterized the areas which resisted the coup d'état: economic distress, urban communications with the countryside, and secret societies. Motivated by social grievances and led by urban conspirators, the rural insurgents of 1851 protested against the rich and the privileged. Theirs was essentially a social revolt.[16]

The cultural dimension of peasant protest has received further attention recently from Alain Corbin, Eugen Weber, and Yves-Marie Bercé. These historians agree that economic backwardness and cultural isolation characterized widespread areas of rural France for much of the nineteenth century. Poverty and illiteracy fostered primitive emotions

[12] Soboul, *Paysans*, pp. 307-50; Tilly, "The Changing Place of Collective Violence," pp. 160-62.

[13] Vigier, *La Seconde République dans la région alpine*, 2 vols. (Paris, 1963), II, 33-34, 60-63, 163-64, 258-65, 285-99, 319-37.

[14] Agulhon, *La République au village* (Paris, 1970). I have published a review of Agulhon's work, "Peasant Protest in the Second Republic," *Journal of Interdisciplinary History*, 5 (Summer 1974), 119-30.

[15] Published in London, 1972. Foremost among the other regional studies are Leo Loubère, "The Emergence of the Extreme Left in Lower Languedoc, 1848-1851," *American Historical Review*, 73 (1968), 1019-51; Jean Dagnan, *Le Gers sous la Seconde République*, 2 vols. (Auch, 1928-29); and Christianne Marcilhacy, "Les caractères de la crise sociale et politique de 1846 à 1852 dans le département du Loiret," *Revue d'histoire moderne et contemporaine*, 6 (1959), 5-59. See also Claude Levy's brief economic interpretation of the insurrection, "Notes sur les fondements sociaux de l'insurrection de décembre 1851 en province," *Information historique*, 16 (1954), 142-45.

[16] Price, *The French Second Republic*, pp. 283-326.

in the countryside, and peasant violence flared up quickly against outsiders from the towns. The cultural horizons of rural life remained extremely narrow during the Second Republic, and peasants took advantage of their new political opportunities to vent local grievances against tax collectors, gendarmes, and usurers, rather than to join urban-based, national movements for social reform. Resistance to the coup d'état, like the tax revolts of preceding years, expressed age-old traditions of village solidarity and peasant violence. Only superficially did the insurrection resemble a modern defense of political democracy. In its deeper forms of collective expression, it harkened back to the "peasant furies" of the Old Régime.[17]

These social and cultural interpretations of radicalization and insurgency during the Second Republic have raised fundamental questions about the timing, direction, and political significance of social change in modern France. While some historians, such as Soboul, Tilly, and Vigier, have called attention to the disruptive impact of agrarian and industrial capitalism on rural society in the July Monarchy and the Second Republic, others, such as Bercé and Weber, have emphasized the persistence of primitive economic relationships and social habits within peasant communities still untouched by modern economic forces as late as the Second Empire or even the early Third Republic. Can peasant violence be explained as resistance to economic and social change if rural society remained immobile throughout much of the nineteenth century? How were socioeconomic and cultural factors transposed, in any case, into a Republican movement which had a strong following among urban workers, and which challenged the political and administrative traditions of the centralized French state? Among the recurrent cycles of revolution and counterrevolution in nineteenth-century France, that of the Second Republic found many peasants in the Republican camp. It is arguable whether this rural Republicanism can be reduced to the primitive outbursts of impoverished peasants, anymore than the Republican triumphs of the 1870s can be attributed to rural misery and ignorance. Social analysis needs to be integrated with politics in order to make intelligible the painful emergence of a democratic peasantry in modern France.

It is from this vantage point that the insurrection of 1851 can acquire its full historical significance: it marked the dramatic entry of tens of thousands of peasants into an urban-based movement for social democ-

[17] Corbin, *Archaïsme et modernité en Limousin au XIXᵉ siècle, 1848-1880*, vol. 1, *La rigidité des structures économiques, sociales et mentales* (Paris, 1975), especially pp. 485-516; Weber, *Peasants into Frenchmen* (Stanford, Calif., 1976), especially pp. 50-66, 93-114, 241-77; Bercé, *Croquants et nu-pieds* (Paris, 1974), pp. 165-91.

racy. This movement derived strength from the economic and social links between towns and villages, not from their mutual isolation; it acquired shape and direction through conspiratorial Republican organizations, which used traditional forms of culture for new political purposes; and it brought peasants into regional rebellions against the state, whose agents had been busily persecuting Republican militants before the coup d'état. In December 1851, as in July 1789 or May 1968, popular liberation meant different things to different people, but resistance to government repression was a keynote of the political left. This dialectic of repression and resistance deserves central attention in the history of social democracy during the Second Republic.

The argument of this book is organized accordingly. After a brief analysis in Chapter One of the main characteristics of the insurrection, Chapters Two, Three, and Four examine its economic and social foundations. Explanations that emphasize long-term economic backwardness or short-term economic decline are rejected in favor of more indirect social links between trends in the rural economy and peasant participation in resistance to the coup d'état. Most rebel districts experienced market development rather than market isolation during the years preceding the Second Republic, which helps explain urban-rural political cooperation in the Republican movement. So does the depression that characterized French agriculture from 1848 to 1851. While the economic effects of this depression were similar throughout the nation, its social and political repercussions favored the left wing in regions where towns and villages were cooperating rather than competing in the marketplace. Cash-crop zones of southeastern France were especially sensitive to Democratic-Socialist propaganda, just as they would provide rural audiences for Radical and Socialist politicians during the agrarian difficulties of the Third Republic. On balance, however, this section concludes that economic fluctuations were not closely related to either the geographical distribution or the social base of insurgency in 1851. Political organizations were the indispensable mediators between social forces and mass political action.

Chapters Five through Nine analyze the general features and particular contours of the political crisis that exploded into violence in December 1851. This central section of the book presents new evidence that "Montagnard" secret societies formed regional networks of political militants in all the regions where substantial numbers of peasants took arms after the coup d'état. The Montagnard underground, which originated in urban France, adapted itself to peasant economic grievances, forms of sociability, and political traditions. It also imparted a new dynamic to rural politics by recruiting peasant leaders, who organized village societies with the aid of professional men, merchants, and craftsmen from nearby towns and bourgs. Once the Montagnards succeeded in transforming Republican voters into conspiratorial militants, the governmental task of political repression became very difficult. The apparatus of centralized police controls did not operate efficiently in the countryside, where urban police agents rarely had good sources of information about Montagnard activities. Instead of eliminating dissent, arbitrary arrests of suspected conspirators only exacerbated tensions. Even the threat of military force proved counterproductive, unless it was backed by permanent troop garrisons in the countryside. Thus, the dialectic of repression and resistance undermined the legitimacy of the central government, and it enabled the Montagnards to merge their political cause with the popular issue of community defense against police repression.

This political analysis sets the stage for Chapters Ten, Eleven, and Twelve, which examine the armed mobilizations, violent clashes, and massive arrests after the coup d'état. The underlying theme of this final section is the anachronism of peasant uprisings against the state. In attempting to organize rural resistance to the coup d'état, Montagnards relied on a traditional form of protest, the armed demonstration, which could not withstand the firepower of the army. While crowds of townspeople and peasants succeeded in overwhelming small brigades of gendarmes, their military columns resembled village processions rather than army maneuvers. These columns were unprepared for serious fighting, and in nearly every encounter with units of the regular army, they dissolved into panic-stricken bands which took flight. Armed mobilizations only brought the wrath of the government down upon the Montagnards, and the police state of Louis Napoleon Bonaparte was built on the ruins of their movement. French peasants would have to wait another generation until the fall of the Second Empire enabled urban Republicans to mobilize them peacefully at the polls. Against the organized power of the state, conspiracy and revolt led peasants down a one-way street to jail.

FRENCH PEASANTS IN REVOLT

THE REGIONAL STRUCTURE OF REVOLT

At ten o'clock on the evening of December 3, 1851 a stranger entered the village of Boujan (Hérault) with a written message from the nearby town of Béziers: "The Commission at Béziers requests all the Montagnards to come at daybreak in arms, tomorrow, Thursday, December 4, to Béziers in order to hold a demonstration. The meeting place is the Old Cemetery." He gave the note, which bore several signatures, to a young vineyard laborer named Jean Baptiste Thibeyranc and vanished into the night.

Within four hours news of the impending demonstration had spread throughout the community, and dozens of men were gathered in a local café or huddled around bonfires in the village streets. Rumors circulated that "the Red Republic has arrived." At 4:00 a.m. Thibeyranc mustered everyone on the public square, assisted by a "communal delegate" named Castan who had been at Béziers during the night to confirm the orders. Many of the villagers wore blue shirts and red belts and carried rifles or farm tools as weapons. Leaving a rear guard of a few dozen older men in the commune, Thibeyranc commanded his column of around one hundred peasants to march. Descending a hill to the northeast of Béziers, they encountered a rebel post just above the first houses in town.

"Who goes there!" shouted the commander of the post.

"The People," replied Castan.

"Revolution," said the townsman, and he assigned them a guide to the Old Cemetery.[1]

Hundreds of men were already gathered in arms by the time the column from Boujan arrived. This was no surprise to Thibeyranc and his men. They were members of the "Society of the Montagnards," a secret organization with branches in all the communes near Béziers. First introduced in May 1850, this society had survived an initial wave of government repression, and it now contained over 1,300 members in the town and several thousand in bourgs and villages of the *arrondissement*. Other branches had been founded at the towns of Pézénas, Bédarieux, and St. Chinian, all within thirty miles of Béziers. The Montagnard recruits had taken oaths to defend the "Democratic and

---

[1] These events involving Boujan are described in Ints. Jn. Jq. Thibeyranc, Et. Bec, and Pr. Lévère, all cults. at Boujan; Urbain Lévère, cult. at Espondeilham; Pierre Counorgues, shepherd at Béziers; and Dossier Jean Cabrol, cult., at Boujan. ADH, 39M 144-60.

Social Republic" by force of arms, and some of them had procured weapons, munitions and a uniform—blue shirt and red belt—for the day of reckoning. When their leaders at Béziers responded to news of Louis Napoleon's coup d'état of December 2, 1851 by ordering an armed demonstration, Montagnards in town and countryside sprang into action. By sunrise on December 4, nearly 2,000 rebels from Béziers had been joined at the Old Cemetery by 1,000 men from twenty rural communes. Another 4,000 men from thirty-five other communes took arms later in the day. The coup d'état had provoked a general uprising of Montagnards throughout the region.[2]

Insurgents at Béziers sought to overthrow the Bonapartist subprefect, Collet-Meygret, and to install a Republican administration in the town. Their strategy was to mobilize such an imposing force of demonstrators that he would resign without a fight. When the Executive Commission of the Montagnard Society met on the evening of the third to debate its course of action, a few leaders advised against an *armed* mobilization, but they were outvoted. "We have to march in arms so we can use them if necessary," argued Casimir Peret, a wealthy merchant and former Republican mayor of the town, who presided over the meeting.[3] As a precautionary measure, the hard-liners did agree to send a deputation to the subprefecture in advance of the insurgents. They hoped that Collet-Meygret would resign. If not, he would be replaced by a show of force. As for the local troop garrison, nearly 1,000 strong, it would fraternize with the people. "Before commanding us to march," one Montagnard later testified, "we were told that the troops would not fire on us and would raise their gun barrels in the air. The authorities would cede their position without any resistance."[4]

Until shortly before their deputation appeared in the subprefect's office, the Montagnards enjoyed the advantage of secrecy. Collet-Meygret wrote at 9:00 p.m. on the third that the "demagogues" had decided to await news of events in Paris, and he confirmed "the same calm" at 5:15 a.m.[5] Not only the meeting at Peret's house but tumultuous gatherings at several cafés in town had escaped his attention. Yet a shoemaker named Baudoma had harangued a crowd from the top of a table at the café Palot that evening, announcing to everyone present, "The Constitution has been violated. It must be defended at the peril of our lives. Citizens, we must go tomorrow to the Old Cemetery."[6] Ac-

[2] Numerical estimates based on scattered Ints. and Tems. of Montagnards and eyewitnesses, in ADH, 39M 144-60; and CG Béziers, Bédarieux, and Capestang.

[3] Int. Jn. Galibert, cult. at Béziers, in CG Béziers.

[4] Int. Pr. Jalabert, cult. at Béziers, ADH, 39M 152.

[5] S-P Béziers, Dec. 3 and 4, in ADH, 39M 142.

[6] Int. Mathieu Coste, plasterer at Béziers, Int. Tournès, in dossier Paul Palot, and Int. Thourel, in dossier Jn. Lignon, ADH, 39M 148, 153, 156.

cording to one Montagnard decurion (commander of a ten-man section) who heard Baudoma's speech, "We decided that at 5:00 a.m. on the fourth we'd arrive with our men at the cemetery."[7] By midnight armed sentinels were posted throughout the *quartier* St. Jacques (in the southern part of town), and men were being mustered and led to the courtyard of a stonemason's house. At 4:00 a.m. they marched northward, numbering over 200.[8] Similar mobilizations were underway by the same hour elsewhere in town, having been preceded by house-to-house alerts. The mayor of Béziers later described the scene in his *quartier*, located near the cemetery:

> At 4:00 a.m. the street lamps went out. At that very moment all the doors of the houses in my neighborhood, mostly inhabited by cultivators, were opened. An unusual movement soon began as people hurried past. Soon I heard the appeal which the emissaries were making to the members as they went from house to house in every direction. Groups increased in size by the minute, all heading for the same point. . . . I heard a crowd forming not far from my house, on a piece of public property at the extreme end of town.
>
> . . . A band of over two hundred persons marching in step two-by-two passed under my window, keeping the most perfect silence, as ordered by the signal of a leader.[9]

Not one police agent, nor a single private citizen reported any of this agitation to the subprefect. It was 6:00 a.m. before the mayor finally arrived to inform him of the extraordinary turn of events.

Collet-Meygret had scarcely dispatched a request for troop reinforcements when he found himself confronted by three men. They carried a document which read:

> In the Name of the French People!
>
> The President of the Republic has violated the Constitution, so the People reclaim their rights. Consequently, your functions must cease. In our position as Delegates of the People, we have come to replace you.
>
> Deliberated publicly, December 4, 1851.
>
> (signed)   The People[10]

The group's spokesman announced that they had come to strip him of

---

[7] Tem. Claris, dossier Lignon, ADH, 39M 153.

[8] Ints. Julien Fillastre, shoemaker, Jn. Rouquette, cooper, and Ant. Rouquette, mason; and Tem. Pr. Burger, in dossier Raymond Dupy, ADH, 39M 149, 150, 157.

[9] Tem. Lognos, mayor of Béziers, in CG Béziers.

[10] Ténot, *La province*, p. 105.

his powers and to ask him to resign his post. Perhaps Collet-Meygret replied that he would never surrender to a mob; perhaps he temporized by denying the authority of the three men to represent anyone. In any case, he now had certain knowledge that a large number of "men of the people" would shortly arrive to demand his resignation. As soon as the deputation withdrew, he issued a call to arms, had the rifles of the forty-man post loaded, closed the courtyard door of the subprefecture, and sent an urgent message for the one hundred troops previously requested from the barracks. The subprefect was determined to resist force with force.[11]

Meanwhile, the insurgents at the Old Cemetery were organizing themselves into an imposing military column. Those from the town were assigned to units of around one hundred men—the *centuries* into which their Montagnard society was already divided. Those in the larger rural contingents marched as separate sections, while small bands of villagers were incorporated pell-mell into the ranks. Some of the sections were themselves based on ten-man units—the Montagnard *decuries*. According to one witness, "Every ten men had an individual placed outside the ranks who seemed to command them."[12] When the column set off for the subprefecture, it was headed by an elite unit of two-hundred rifle-bearing men from the *quartier* St. Jacques. The rebels in the next section had weapons of all sorts—scythes, staves, skewers, and pitchforks, as well as rifles—most of those in the third section had rifles, and so they continued, some units well-armed and some poorly armed. Generally speaking, the front sections were composed of townsmen, and villagers brought up the rear.[13]

It took twenty-five minutes for the long lines of men, three-abreast, to file out of the cemetery and into town. A red flag waved above one of the middle sections, and the men sang the Marseillaise as they advanced through the streets. They marched behind the Church of the Magdelaine, passed in front of the Fountain of Moses, crossed the wheat-market square, the Place St. Félix, and the Place St. Sauveur, and finally they reached the small square in front of the subprefecture.

Awaiting them with loaded weapons were the one hundred troops from the garrison. They had arrived just a few minutes earlier.

The insurgents entered the enclosure shouting, "Long live the troops of the line! You are free! We are brothers!"[14] They spread out to cover

[11] S-P Béziers, Dec. 4, in ADH, 39M 142, and Tem. S-P Béziers, CG Béziers, cited by Ténot, *La province*, p. 105.

[12] Tem. Frederic Bousquet, pharmacist, in CG Béziers.

[13] Tem. Pierre Gatelau, *commis-négociant*, in CG Béziers; and Ints. Jn. Thibeyranc, Ant. Dufour, window painter at St. Geniès-le-bas, Julien Filastre, Pr. Jalabert, A. Laussinot, stone quarrier, and Noël Puel, cult., in ADH, 39M 149-59.

[14] Tem. H. Lognos (n. 9) and letter from S-P Béziers (n. 11).

the narrow space as they moved forward. According to one rebel, "Those of us who were in the front ranks were pushed despite ourselves toward the troops, and we found ourselves only a few feet from them when the *sommations* were made."[15] The police commissioner only had time for two of the three legally required *sommations*. The troops were about to be disarmed when their commander, fearing for his own life, ordered them to open fire.[16]

They obeyed. One volley, fired point-blank, shattered the front ranks of the insurgents before a single shot could be fired in retaliation. Transformed by panic into a disorderly mob, the men ran for cover, leaving the soldiers in undisputed control of the subprefecture. Eight insurgents lay dead or dying on the pavement; another sixty were strewn about the square, some wounded, others stunned, still others trying to hide behind the fallen bodies, covered with blood and trembling fearfully. The army had delivered its reply to the Montagnards: No quarter.[17]

Some townsmen tried to rally their forces, retrieve their wounded comrades, and construct defensive barricades. They failed. At the sound of gunfire, the entire column had disintegrated, all the way from the subprefecture back to the Church of the Magdelaine. As one rebel later testified: "I heard a detonation of arms. Seized with terror, everyone fled. Several people remarked, 'The troops fired; that wasn't what we'd been led to believe would happen. We've been betrayed, we've been deceived. . . . The men from the villages only came to help.' Everyone disbanded."[18] In the midst of the disorder, a vengeful crowd assaulted two well-dressed pedestrians on the Place St. Felix, mortally wounding one and seriously injuring the other.[19] Cavalry promptly arrived to sweep clear the streets. A few insurgents who had taken cover in alleys and doorways near the subprefecture continued to direct sniper fire against the troops, killing two and wounding four. By 8:00 a.m. they, too, had been put to flight. Only abandoned weapons remained on the streets of Béziers as mute testimony to the armed demonstration of the Montagnards.

Revolts elsewhere in the region were a response to news of this

[15] Int. P. Jalabert (n. 4).

[16] Tem. Colonel Lehongre, CG Béziers.

[17] The S-P wrote that eight were killed (n. 11). Estimates of the wounded ranged from sixteen (military prosecutor, CG Béziers) to over eighty (letter from H. Giscard to his brother, Dec. 5, dossier Giscard, ADH, 39M 151). Sixteen wounded insurgents subsequently were arrested, including two who died soon thereafter.

[18] Int. Jn. Pr. Boulsier, *négociant* at Béziers, ADH, 39M 146.

[19] No reliable witnesses ever described this mob scene, although from testimony at CG Béziers it is clear that a crowd was present. Ténot minimizes the incident, *La province*, p. 108.

uprising. Map 1 shows the geographical distribution or insurgent activity throughout the *arrondissement*. Five classes of events can be distinguished, in addition to the march on the subprefecture. First, around 500 men from three bourgs (Servian, Montblanc, Nissan) began marching too late to join the rebels at the Old Cemetery and they dispersed enroute; so did a few hundred men from several villages. Second, Montagnard leaders at the cantonal seat of Capestang decided to seize local power instead of obeying the orders from Béziers. They mustered 400 men on the morning of the fourth and marched to the *mairie*, where a shoot-out with four gendarmes left one seriously wounded. This secondary revolt had repercussions in three other communes of the canton, where nearly 300 men gathered in arms. Third, several bourgs to the east of Béziers, including Marseillan and Bessan, had local demonstrations or abortive mobilizations on the same day, involving around 500 men. Fourth, Montagnards at Pézénas mobilized a partly armed crowd of several hundred townsmen and villagers at news from Béziers and tried to overthrow the municipal government. They succeeded in broadening the composition of the municipal council to include several "delegates of the people," but troops arrived on the morning of the fifth to restore order. As a result of this urban protest, over 1,000 men from ten nearby bourgs and villages either marched toward town or proclaimed local "revolutionary commissions." Finally, 400 armed rebels at the textile town of Bédarieux seized municipal power on the afternoon of the fourth, after emissaries returned with news of the insurrection at Béziers. That night a crowd of 1,000 assaulted the gendarmes, who were barricaded in the *caserne*, and killed three of them. Around 200 men from three other communes in the canton joined in this attack. The revolutionaries remained in power for several more days, but a mobile column of troops occupied the town without resistance on the tenth. The insurrection of December 1851 in the *arrondissement* of Béziers was over.[20]

These events in lower Languedoc had their counterparts in other regions of the nation. Indeed, Louis Napoleon's coup d'état generated the largest provincial uprising in nineteenth-century France. Nearly 100,000 men from around 900 communes participated in some form of protest against the coup d'état, and nearly 70,000, recruited from at least 775 communes, mobilized in arms against the government. Over 27,000 insurgents from around 270 communes participated in violent clashes with troops or gendarmes. Skirmishes, shoot-outs, and pitched

[20] These various mobilizations are described in detail in Margadant, "The Insurrection of 1851," pp. 243-91.

Map 1. *Arrondissement* of Béziers (Hérault)
Insurrection: December 3-5, 1851

LEGEND

- ◉ COMMUNE WHERE INSURGENTS CONFRONT TROOPS OR GENDARMES
- • COMMUNE WITH ARMED MOBILIZATION
- ○ COMMUNE WITHOUT ARMED MOBILIZATION
- ▶ COMMUNE WHERE MONTAGNARDS TRY TO SEIZE MUNICIPAL POWER
- ⟶ DIRECTION OF MANPOWER FLOWS
- ⊢⟶ MANPOWER FLOWS WHICH DISPERSE IN ROUTE
- SERVIAN CANTONAL SEAT

HERAULT

9

battles involved twenty-eight separate rebel formations and resulted in several hundred casualties. In retaliation, government officials launched a massive purge of suspected rebels and other political dissidents. A total of 26,884 persons (of whom 23,933 resided outside Paris) were judged by special commissions, and nearly 10,000 were sentenced to deportation. As measured by the scale of protest and repression, the transition from the Second Republic to the Second Empire was the most serious political upheaval in the French provinces between the Terror of the 1790s and the Resistance movement of the Second World War.[21]

Tables 1.1-1.3 present approximate measures of the scale of armed mobilizations, violent clashes, and unarmed demonstrations in three categories of departments.[22] The first category contains thirteen departments in each of which over 1,000 men were involved in armed mobilizations, with a median of 4,000 insurgents and 60 rebel communes per department. Map 2 shows that seven of these departments are located in southeastern France (Basses-Alpes, Ardèche, Drôme, Gard, Hérault, Pyrénées-Orientales, Var, and Vaucluse), two in the southwest (Gers and Lot-et-Garonne), and three in the center (Nièvre, Saône-et-Loire, and Yonne). A second category of seventeen departments includes all other cases of armed protest in the nation, with a median of 350 insurgents and four rebel communes per department. As the map illustrates, nine of these departments are located in central and southwestern France (Allier, Aveyron, Creuse, Haute-Loire, Loiret, Lozère, Puy-de-Dôme, Tarn, Haute-Vienne), and the rest are scattered elsewhere in the nation. In the third category are twenty-six departments which experienced only unarmed protest after the coup, with a median of 300 demonstrators and only one commune per de-

---

[21] These numerical estimates are necessarily approximate, but they provide orders of magnitude for comparative analysis. In the following thirteen departments, all calculations are based on the reports of *local* officials and on the interrogations and testimonies of local residents in rebel communes: Allier, Ardèche, Drôme, Gard, Hérault, Jura, Lot-et-Garonne, Nièvre, Saône-et-Loire, Var, Vaucluse, Yonne. Estimates for the Basses-Alpes are based on the register of suspects, drawn up by the "Mixed Commission" (prefect, public prosecutor, commanding general) of that department, in AN, BB[30] 398. Those for the Gers are based on Jean Dagnan, *Le Gers*, II. I am much obliged to Peter McPhee for sending me detailed information on the diffuse agitation that characterized events in the Pyrénées-Orientales (private letter, Aug. 13, 1974). I have scaled down his estimate of 5,000-10,000 men to exclude entirely localized, secret, and largely unarmed meetings. Concerning events in these and other departments, I have also used the following sources: (1) administrative reports from *procureurs-généraux* and registers of the Mixed Commissions, AN, BB[30] 395-402; (2) military reports from generals and gendarmes, AG, F[1] 51-54; (3) Ténot, *La province*; and (4) the secondary sources listed in the bibliography (Section 1).

[22] These and subsequent tables in this chapter are based on an exhaustive analysis of the sources described in n. 21.

TABLE 1.1

Departments with Major Armed Mobilizations in December 1851

Department	Scale of Armed Protest	Number of Communes Involved	Prefectures and Subprefectures Involved	Cantonal Seats Involved	Other Communes Involved
Basses-Alpes	10,000	90	Barcelonnette (SP) (Digne) (P) Forcalquier (SP) Sisteron (SP)	14	73
Ardèche	3,500	30	(Privas) (P) (Largentière) (SP)	4	26
Drôme	8,900	90	(Montélimar) (SP)	5	85
Gard	4,000	50	Alais (SP) (Nîmes) (P)	9	40
Gers	6,000	76	(Auch) (P) Condom (SP) Mirande (SP)	11	63
Hérault	8,000	60	Béziers (SP)	6	53
Lot-et-Garonne	5,000	60	(Agen) (P) Marmande (SP) (Nérac) (SP) Villeneuve-sur-Lot (SP)	4	54
Nièvre	3,400	28	Clamecy (SP)	2	25
Pyrénées-Orientales	3,000	72	(Prades) (SP)	3	69
Saône-et-Loire	1,200	20	(Mâcon) (P)	4	16
Var	6,300	68	Brignoles (SP) (Draguignan) (P)	14	53
Vaucluse	1,500	27	Apt (SP) (Avignon) (P) (Orange) (SP)	2	24
Yonne	2,200	29	(Auxerre) (P)	3	26
Totals	63,000	700		81	607

NOTE: Towns in parentheses are the objectives of armed marches but do not themselves rebel.

TABLE 1.2

Departments with Minor Armed Mobilizations in December 1851

Department	Scale of Armed Protest	Number of Communes Involved	Prefectures and Subprefectures Involved	Cantonal Seats Involved	Other Communes Involved
Ain	400	4		1	3
Allier	900	20	(La Palisse) (SP)	2	18
Hautes-Alpes	200	c. 5			
Aveyron	600	7	Millhau (SP) (Rodez) (P) Villefranche (SP)	3	2
Bouches-du-Rhône	100	3			
Creuse	250	3	(Bourganeuf) (SP)		3
Jura	600	10	Poligny (SP)		9
Haute-Loire	300	1		1	
Loiret	500	6			6
Lot	800	6	Figeac (SP)	2	3
Lozère	100	1			1
Nord	100	1			1
Puy-de-Dôme	400	6	Thiers (SP)	4	1
Basses-Pyrénées	100	2			2
Sarthe	250	1		1	
Tarn	200	1		1	
Haute-Vienne	400	5			5
Totals	6,200	82		15	67
All armed protest	69,200	782			

partment. The map indicates that these departments are clustered in the north, the east and the southwest. (Map 3 identifies the individual departments by name.)

The thirteen departments in the first category accounted for the bulk of the armed resistance to the coup d'état: 95 percent of all the rebels who fought against troops or gendarmes came from these departments, and so did 91 percent of those who took arms but who then dispersed without fighting. Similarly, nine-tenths (63/71) of the communes that had armed mobilizations of at least 200 men were located in these departments (see Table 1.4). So were over nine-tenths of all the communes where protesters took arms. By contrast, two-thirds of the unarmed demonstrators resided elsewhere in the nation; two-thirds (36/52) of the communes with at least 200 such nonviolent protesters were located elsewhere; and so were over three-fifths of all the communes that experienced unarmed protest against the coup.

These regional variations in patterns of protest correspond to variations in the types of communes from which demonstrators were recruited. Armed mobilizations usually originated in small towns or market bourgs and involved large numbers of rural communes, while unarmed crowds gathered mainly in cities and towns. The distinction between prefectures and subprefectures, which functioned as regional capitals, and cantonal seats or lesser communes provides a crude measure of this urban/rural contrast. As Table 1.5 shows, twenty-four prefectoral capitals had unarmed demonstrations, but none had armed revolts; a majority of the subprefectures that protested against the coup d'état did so without arms; but nearly all the smaller cantonal seats and rural communes that resisted the coup did so by taking arms.

Maps 4 and 5 illustrate this contrast between the regional character of most armed protest, involving substantial numbers of rural communes, and the localized pattern of unarmed demonstrations, confined in most cases to a few urban communes in each department. Map 6 marks the sites of violent clashes between insurgents and either troops or gendarmes. In most cases of violence, insurgents from regional clusters of communes were involved, as Tables 1.6 and 1.7 show in more detail.

The participation of large numbers of rural communes suggests that insurgency in 1851 was primarily a rural phenomenon. More precise analysis proves, however, that the dynamic centers of insurgency everywhere in France were not villages but towns or large bourgs which exercised administrative and market functions for nearby communes (see Map 7). To begin with, such towns and bourgs provided a disproportionate share of manpower to the revolt. The numerical weight of insurgents from urban centers can be inferred from the data in Table 1.4, which lists all communes where at least 200 local residents took arms. Fourteen subprefectures and thirty-four cantonal seats accounted for over one-quarter of all the participants in armed mobilizations (19,150/69,200 = 28%). Among these administrative and market centers, six subprefectures and eighteen cantonal seats supplied over two-fifths of all the rebels who participated in violent clashes with troops or gendarmes (11,750/27,500 = 43%). Such clashes were linked to especially large mobilizations at the subprefectures of Béziers (2,000 rebels), Clamecy (500), Forcalquier (400), and Marmande (1,000), and at the cantonal seats of Bédarieux (800), Bourdeaux (400), Cape-

TABLE 1.3
Unarmed Protest in December 1851

Departments	Commune	Size of Crowd	Objectives	Repression
With Major Revolts				
Basses-Alpes	Digne (P)	200	Release of prisoners	no
Drôme	Crest (CS)	200	Republican songs, riots against gendarmes	
Gard	Anduze (CS)	500	Republican demonstration	no
Gers	Auch (P)	500	Protest closing of Republican newspaper	T
Hérault	Clermont-l'Hérault (CS)	200	Republican songs	
	Florensac (CS)	100	Occupation of *mairie*	
	Montpellier (P)	300	Protest meeting	T,A
	Vias	200	Republican songs, slogans	
Lot-et-Garonne	Marmande (SP)	500	Pressure on CM	
	Villeneuve-sur-Lot (SP)	500	Pressure on CM	
	Port-St. Marie (CS)	200	Pressure on CM	
	Tonneins (CS)	800	Protest against coup and against CM	GN

P—Prefecture   CS—Cantonal Seat   CN—Garde Nationale   T—Troops
SP—Subprefecture   CM—Conseil Municipal   G—Gendarmes   A—Arrests

Pyrénées-Orientales	Collioures	200	Assault on CP	
	Estagel	500	Protest aided by CM, Attempt to rescue prisoners	T,A
	Prades (SP)	50	Protest coup	
	Perpignan (SP)	400	Seek news, protest coup	T
Saône-et-Loire	Louhans (SP)	200	Protest coup, oppose arrests	G,A
Var	Draguignan (SP)	500	Protest coup	
	Hyères (CS)	350	Protest coup, occupy *mairie*	T,A
	Toulon (SP)	500	Protest coup	T,A
Vaucluse	Apt (SP)	1,000	Protest arrival of conservative GN from rival commune	
	Bédariddes	200	Protest coup, form municipal committee	
	Caderousse	200	Protest coup, form municipal committee	A
	Mondragon	25	Attempt to occupy *mairie*	
	Mornas	50	Occupy *mairie*	A
	Orange (SP)	500	Attempt to occupy *mairie*	
	Pertuis (CS)	500	Demonstration against gendarmes	A
	La Tour-d'Aigues	50	Republican songs	
	Uchaux	60	Occupy *mairie*	
	Valréas (CS)	100	Occupy *mairie*	
Yonne	Bléneau (CS)	100	Protest against GN	
	St. Fargeau (CS)	500	Rescue political prisoners	A
Total in Major revolts	10,185			

Table 1.3 (*continued*)

Departments	Commune	Size of Crowd	Objectives	Repression
With minor armed mobilizations				
Ain	Belley (SP)	150	Seek news at *mairle*	
Aveyron	Rodez (P)	200	Demonstration against coup, protest arrests	T,A
	St. Affrique (SP)	200	Protest coup, support committee of resistance	
Bouches-du-Rhône	Aix (SP)	500	Protest coup, arrests	T,A
Haute-Loire	Brioude (SP)	150	Seek news	G
Loiret	Montargis (SP)	80	Protest demonstration	G,T,A
	Orléans (P)	800	Protest coup, attempt to occupy *mairie*	T,A
Lot	Cahors (P)	200	Protest coup	T,A
Nord	Douai (SP)	200		A
Puy-de-Dome	Clermont-Ferrand (P)	200	Seek news	T,A
Basses-Pyrénées	Bayonne (SP)	200	Pressure on CM	T
	Pau (P)	500	Protest coup	
Total with minor armed mobilizations	3,380			
With no armed gatherings				
Ardennes	Vouziers (SP)	50	Protest coup	GN
Ariège	Pamiers (SP)	300	Sing Marseillaise, throw stones at SP	A

Department	Town	Number	Action	Code
Aube	Bar-sur-Aube (SP)	500	Seek news, attempt to rescue prisoner	G
Aude	Chalabre (CS)	800	100 occupy *mairie*; 800 rescue prisoners	T
Cher	St. Amand (SP)	500	Protest murder of a Republican by the CP	T
Corrèze	Tulle (P)	100	Protest demonstration	
Côte-d'Or	Beaune (SP)	100	Occupy *mairie*	
	Châtillon-sur-Seine (CS)	100	Seek news, occupy *mairie*	G
	Dijon (P)	1,000	Seek news, attempt to demonstrate	T,A
Dordogne	Bergerac (SP)	100	Protest, rescue prisoner, occupy *mairie*	
Doubs	Besançon (P)	500	Protest coup	T
Eure-et-Loir	Chartres (P)	200	Seek news	T
Haute-Garonne	Toulouse (P)	1,500	Protest coup	T,A
Gironde	Bordeaux (P)	1,000	Protest coup	T
	La Réole (CS)	200	Support protest by CM	T
Ille-et-Vilaine	Rennes (P)	300	Demonstration	T,A
Indre-et-Loire	Tours (P)	300	Sing Marseillaise, protest at *mairie*	T,A
Isère	Grenoble (P)	300	Demonstration	T
Loire	St. Etienne (P)	200	Protest	T

Table 1.3 (continued)

Departments	Commune	Size of Crowd	Objectives	Repression
Maine-et-Loire	Angers (P)	1,200	Pressure on CM to protest coup	T,A
Marne	Reims (SP)	300	Protest demonstration	G,A
Meurthe-et-Moselle	Nancy (P)	200	Seek news	G
	Toul (SP)	300	Protest arrests	
Hautes-Pyrénées	Bagnères (SP)	200	Demonstration	T
Bas-Rhin	Strasbourg (P)	1,000	Demonstration	T
Rhône	Lyon (P)	600	Protest demonstration	T,A
Seine-Maritime	Elbeuf (CS)	300	Seek news, demonstrate	A
	Rouen (P)	150	Seek news	
Deux-Sèvres	Niort (P)	100	Attempt to occupy *mairie*	A
Tarn-et-Garonne	Castelsarrasin (SP)	200	Support protest by CM	
	Moissac (CS)	200	Attempt to occupy *mairie*	
Vienne	Poitiers (P)	200	Attempt to replace CM	
Total with no armed gatherings	13,000			
Combined total	76 communes	26,565	demonstrators	

TABLE 1.4
Communes with Large-Scale Armed Mobilizations

Department	Commune	Administrative Role	Approximate Population[a]	Scale of Mobilization	Violent Clash
Basses-Alpes	Barcelonnette	SP	2,100	500	
	Forcalquier	SP	3,000	400	yes
	Manosque	CS	5,900	500	yes
	Oraison		2,000	200	yes
	Riez	CS	2,400	200	yes
	Sisteron	SP	4,300	200	yes
	Valensole	CS	3,100	300	yes
Ardèche	Chomérac	CS	2,500	300	yes
	Lablachère		2,700	200	yes
	Vallon	CS	2,600	300	yes
Aveyron	Millhau	SP	12,600	200	
Drôme	Bourdeaux	CS	1,400	400	yes
	Dieulefit	CS	4,200	500	yes
	Grane		2,000	500	yes
	Mirmande-Saulce		2,500	800	
	Puy-St. Martin		900	200	yes
	Saou		1,000	200	yes
	Sauzet		1,500	200	yes
Gard	Lasalle	CS	2,500	300	
	Quissac	CS	1,600	200	
Gers	Barran		1,600	200	yes
	Condom	SP	8,200	500	
	Fleurance	CS	4,300	300	
	Jegun	CS	2,000	200	yes
	Masseube	CS	1,700	200	
	Mirande	SP	3,400	600	
	Vic-Fezensac	CS	4,200	500	yes
Hérault	Bédarieux	CS	9,100	800	yes
	Béziers	SP	24,300	2,000	yes
	Capestang	CS	2,700	400	yes
	Lespignan		1,500	200	yes
	Marseillan		3,900	200	
	Montblanc		1,300	200	
	Pézénas	CS	7,200	500	
	Servian	CS	2,300	250	
Jura	Poligny	SP	5,400	200	
Haute-Loire	Craponne	CS	2,600	300	
Loiret	Bonny-sur-Loire		2,600	400	yes

Table 1.4 (*continued*)

Department	Commune	Administrative Role	Approximate Population	Scale of Mobilization	Violent Clash
Lot	Figeac	SP	8,400	500	
Lot-et-Garonne	Barbaste		1,900	400	
	Bouglon	CS	900	200	
	Lavardac	CS	2,000	400	
	Marmande	SP	8,700	1,000	yes
	Mas-d'Agenais (Le)	CS	2,200	300	
	Villeneuve-sur-Lot	SP	12,800	300	
Nièvre	Clamecy	SP	5,600	500	yes
	Neuvy-sur-Loire		2,000	400	yes
Puy-de-Dôme	Thiers	SP	16,000	200	
Pyrénées-Orientales	Estagel		2,400	300	
	Laroque-des-Albères		1,200	200	
Saône-et-Loire	Cluny	SP	4,300	300	yes
	St. Gengoux	SP	1,800	250	yes
	Tournus	CS	5,600	300	
Sarthe	La Suze	CS	2,400	250	
Tarn	Mazamet	CS	11,000	200	
Var	Les Arcs		2,800	200	yes
	Barjols	CS	3,300	300	yes
	Brignoles	SP	6,100	300	
	Cuers	CS	4,300	500	yes
	La Garde Freinet		2,600	400	yes
	Le Luc	CS	3,800	700	yes
	Le Muy		2,400	300	yes
	St. Maximin	CS	3,600	200	
	Salernes	CS	3,000	500	yes
	Vidaubun		2,300	500	yes
Vaucluse	Apt	SP	5,800	250	yes
	Velleron		1,800	200	
Yonne	Moutiers		1,000	200	
	St. Sauveur	CS	1,800	200	yes
	Saints		1,300	200	
	St. Florentin	CS	2,600	200	
	71 Communes	Median Population = 2,600			

[a] Population in 1861, based on Joanne, *Dictionnaire des Communes de la France* (Paris, 1864).

TABLE 1.5

Types of Protest, by Administrative Role of Commune

	Prefecture	Subprefecture	Cantonal Seat	Commune Other
Number of communes with armed protest	0	17	96	674
Number of communes with unarmed protest	24	26	16	9
Total	24	43	112	683

TABLE 1.6

Armed Clashes with Gendarmes in 1851

Department	Site of clash	Date (December)	Communes Involved	Rebels Involved	Rebels Killed	Rebels Wounded	Troops Killed	Troops Wounded
Ain	St. André-de-Corcy	5-6	2	200				2
Allier	La Palisse	4th	7	300			1	
Basses-Alpes	Manosque	5th	1	500				2
	Volonne	5th	c.5	500				1
Gers	Monclar	4-5	3	300				1
Hérault	Bédarieux	4-5	4	1,000	2	c. 5	3	1
	Capestang	4th	2	400				1
Loiret	Bonny-sur-Loire	7th	1	400			1	
Lot-et-Garonne	Ste. Bazeille-Marmande	7-8	1	1,000				5
Nièvre	Clamecy	5th	1	200	1	5	2	2
	Clamecy[a]	6th	c.10	500			1	
Var	Cuers	5th	1	500			1	
Totals			37	5,600	3	c. 10	9	15
Departments with major armed mobilizations			27	4,500	3	c. 10	7	12

[a] Calculations count Clamecy only once (the incident on the sixth).

Map 2. Mobilizations, by Department, December 1851

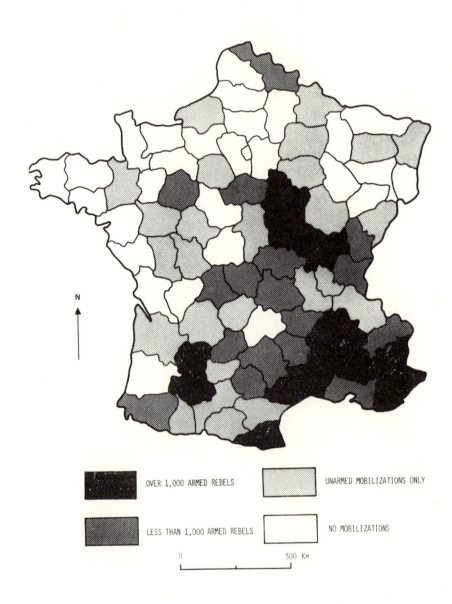

N

OVER 1,000 ARMED REBELS   UNARMED MOBILIZATIONS ONLY

LESS THAN 1,000 ARMED REBELS   NO MOBILIZATIONS

0   300 KM

Map 3. France, by Department, 1851

Map 4. Areas with Armed Mobilizations, December 1851

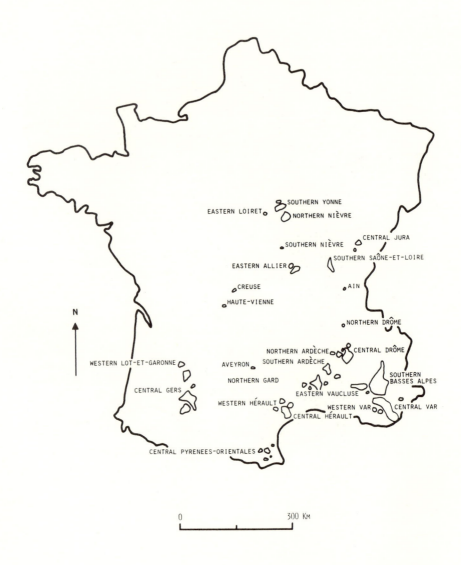

Map 5. Unarmed Demonstrations, December 1851

DOUAI

VOUZIERS

ROUEN
ELBEUF

REIMS

TOUL
NANCY
STRASBOURG

CHARTRES

BAR-S/AUBE

RENNES

MONTARGIS
ORLEANS BLÉNEAU
ST. FARGEAU
CHÂTILLON-S/SEINE

ANGERS TOURS

DIJON BESANÇON
BEAUNE
ST. AMAND
LOUHANS

POITIERS

NIORT

N

LYON BELLEY
CLERMONT-FERRAND
ST. ETIENNE

TULLE
BORDEAUX
BERGERAC
BRIOUDE GRENOBLE

CREST

LA RÉOLE
MARMANDE CAHORS
RODEZ
VALRÉAS
TONNEINS VILLENEUVE-SUR-LOT
MOISSAC ST. AFFRIQUE ORANGE
APT DIGNE
PORT-ST. MARIE CASTELSARASSIN
ANDUZE PERTUIS DRAGUIGNAN
BAYONNE AUCH TOULOUSE CLERMONT-L'HERAULT
PAU FLORENSAC AIX HYÈRES
CHALABRES TOULON
BAGNÈRES PAMIERS
PERPIGNAN
PRADES

0   300 Km

25

Map 6. Locations of Armed Clashes, December 1851

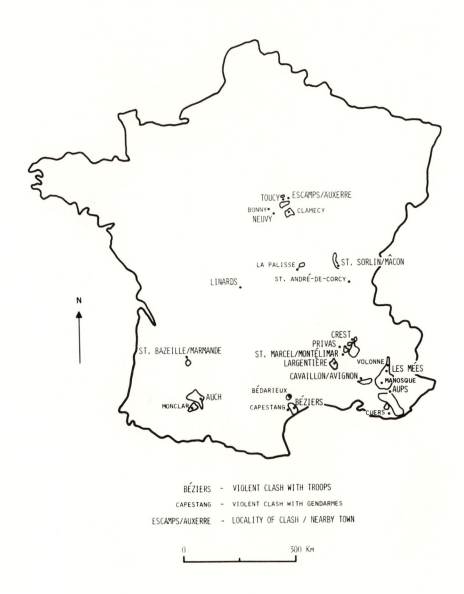

TOUCY● ●ESCAMPS/AUXERRE
BONNY● ● ●CLAMECY
NEUVY

LA PALISSE● ●ST. SORLIN/MÂCON
LINARDS● ST. ANDRÉ-DE-CORCY●

N

CREST
PRIVAS●
ST. BAZEILLE/MARMANDE● ST. MARCEL/MONTÉLIMAR
LARGENTIÈRE● VOLONNE● LES MÉES
CAVAILLON/AVIGNON● ●MANOSQUE
●AUPS
BÉDARIEUX●
MONCLAR● AUCH CAPESTANG● ●BÉZIERS
CUERS●

BÉZIERS – VIOLENT CLASH WITH TROOPS

CAPESTANG – VIOLENT CLASH WITH GENDARMES

ESCAMPS/AUXERRE – LOCALITY OF CLASH / NEARBY TOWN

0 300 KM

26

Map 7. Towns with Armed Mobilizations, December 1851

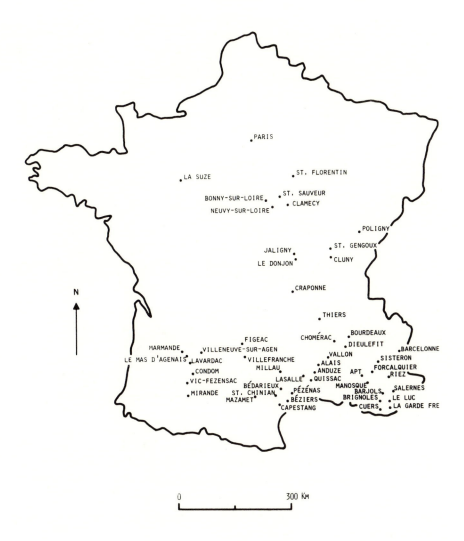

TABLE 1.7

Armed Clashes with Troops in 1851

Department	Site of Clash	Date (December)	Communes Involved	Rebels Involved	Rebels Killed	Rebels Wounded	Troops Killed	Troops Wounded
Basses-Alpes	Les Mées	9th	c. 40	4,000		c. 5		c. 5
Ardèche	Largentière	6-7	c. 15	1,500		2		
	Privas	4-5	5	500	2			
Drôme	Crest-Beaufort	6th	7	600			1	
	Crest-Grane	6th	2	600	2		1	
	Crest-Bourdeaux	7th	35	2,800	6	c.25	1	c. 5
	St. Marcel	6-7	13	800	2	c. 5		1
Gers	Auch	4th	30	2,200	1	5	3	20
Hérault	Béziers	4th	21	3,000	8	60	2	4
Nièvre	Neuvy-sur-Loire	8th	1	300	3			
Saône-et-Loire	St. Sorlin (Mâcon)	5-6	c. 6	600	2			
Var	Aups	10th	40	4,000	23-70	c.50	1	7
Vaucluse	Cavaillon	8-9	c. 5	c. 200	3			
Haute-Vienne	Linards	4-5	3	300		7		
Yonne	Escamps	6-7	c. 5	200	7			
	Toucy	6-7	c. 5	300	1	4		2
Totals			c.233	21,900	over 60	over 160	9	44
Departments with major armed mobilizations			c.230	21,600	over 60	over 150	9	44

stang (400), Dieulefit (500), Le Luc (700), Manosque (500), Salernes (500), and Vic-Fezensac (500). As for the twenty-four communes below the level of cantonal seats that mobilized at least 200 men, they were usually bourgs or *bourgades* with significant market functions and/or artisanal activities, rather than mere villages. Thus, La Garde Freinet (400 rebels), Neuvy-sur-Loire (400), and Bonny-sur-Loire

(400) were industrial centers with upwards of 2,000 agglomerated inhabitants, while Les Arcs (200), Barran (200), Oraison (200), Sauzet (200), and Vidaubun (500) were agricultural communities with considerably larger numbers of craftsmen and cultivators in the central agglomeration (around eight hundred or more) than the typical French rural commune contained (a few hundred agglomerated inhabitants).

Small towns and market bourgs also led the assault on municipal authorities. One of the most striking features of rebel activities in some departments was the proclamation of new mayors and/or committees of resistance, municipal commissions, etc. Over 100 communes experienced such changes in local officials, most of them located in six departments of the southeast and southwest. As Table 1.8 shows, two-fifths of these communes were subprefectures or cantonal seats (48/118). Only the departments of the Var, the Hérault, the Vaucluse, and the Lot-et-Garonne had significant numbers of municipal revolutions outside the cantonal seats. This was in part a reflection of the fact that many bourgs and agglomerated villages in southeastern France resembled small towns in their municipal traditions. The quest for public honor through local officeholding was an important cultural trait in Provence and lower Languedoc. At the same time, however, most rural seizures of power were a direct response to the revolutionary initiative of towns. Thus, Montagnard leaders at Brignoles (Var) urged their confreres in other communes of the *arrondissement* to follow their example by changing the local authorities. Their orders to this effect, sometimes sent directly to rural communes and sometimes relayed by cantonal seats, triggered changes in the composition of municipal governments in thirty-one other communes of the *arrondissement* (including four cantonal seats). Similar rural imitations of urban municipal revolutions occurred around Orange (Vaucluse), Pézénas, St. Chinian and Bédarieux (Hérault), and Marmande (Lot-et-Garonne). In only a handful of cases were local authorities changed in rural communes without such urban inspiration.

Furthermore, rebels in the towns and market bourgs planned the mobilizations of nearby rural communes and they organized regional gatherings in their own localities. The first stage in such regional mobilizations often involved the march of columns or bands of men from villages to the nearest subprefecture or cantonal seat. This centripetal pattern of rebel action involved at least 262 rural communes in thirty districts of the nation (see Table 1.9). Subprefectures exerted an especially strong pull on their rural hinterlands: the median number of communes that marched directly to a subprefecture was 13, as compared with a median of only 5 communes that marched first to a mere cantonal seat. This reflects the larger size and more diversified administrative and market functions of the subprefectures. All of them were unquestionably towns, while some of the cantonal seats were market bourgs with a predominantly agricultural labor force. In both kinds of administrative centers, Republicans sometimes circulated orders to meet at a specified rendezvous (at least seventeen cases), and sometimes they began the revolt and then urged their rural neighbors to contribute manpower (at least twelve cases). In either event, these subprefectures and cantonal seats usually supplied nearly as much manpower (median 300, total 11,450) as the combined rural forces which joined them (median 350, total 13,850). Such joint mobilizations of administrative centers and rural communes were especially characteristic of rebel forces that eventually fought troops or gendarmes: three-fifths of all those engaged in violent clashes with troops or gendarmes ($16,100/27,509 = 59\%$) were recruited from these districts, as compared with one-third of all participants in armed gatherings ($23,450/69,000 = 34\%$).

Finally, Republicans in towns and market bourgs played a key role in organizing marches toward major centers of political power, especially the prefectures. Such manpower flows generally involved step-

TABLE 1.8
Communes with Municipal Revolutions

Department	Subprefectures	Cantonal Seats	Bourgs and Villages
Allier		Le Donjon	
Basses-Alpes	Barcelonnette		
	Digne (P)	Les Mées	Thoard
	Forcalquier	St. Etienne-les-Orgues	Volx
	Sisteron	Volonne	
Aude		Chalabre	
Aveyron	Millhau		
Drôme			Rochegude
Gers	Condom	Fleurance	Gondrin
	Mirande	Jegun	L'Isle-de-Noé
		Masseube	
		Miélan	
		Vic-Fezensac	

Hérault		Bédarieux	Alignan-du-Vent
		Florensac	Caux
		Pézénas	Nézignan-l'Evêque
		Roujan	Quarante
		St. Chinian	St. Thibéry
		Servian	8 others
Jura	Poligny		
Loiret			Batilly
Lot	Figeac		
Lot-et-Garonne	Marmande	Bouglon	Burch
		Lavardac	Caumont
		Mas-d'Agenais	Longueville
		St. Livrade	Miramont
			Samazan
			Senestis
Nièvre	Clamecy		Neuvy-sur-Loire
Saône-et-Loire		Cluny	
		Tournus	
		St. Gengoux	
Deux-Sèvres	Niort (P) (abortive)		
Sarthe		La Suze	
Var	Brignoles	Aups	37 bourgs and
		Barjols	villages
		Collobrières	
		Cuers	
		Fayence	
		Grimaud	
		Le Luc	
		La Roque-brussanne	
		St. Maximin	
		Tavernes	
Vaucluse	Apt		Beaumont
	Orange (abortive)		Bédarrides
			Cabrières-d'Aigues
			Castellet
			Mirabeau
			Mornas
Yonne		St. Sauveur	Taingy

TABLE 1.9

Manpower Links between Administrative Centers and Rural Communes

Department	Cantonal Seat	Administrative Role	Rebel Role	Size of Mobilization	Rural Communes that March Directly to This Center	Combined Total of Their Forces	Rebels from this District who Clash with Troops or Gendarmes
Allier	Le Donjon	CS	I	100	6	200	400
	Jaligny	CS	P	100	4	200	
Basses-Alpes	Forcalquier	SP	P	400	24	1,000	1,400
	Manosque	CS	I	500	4	200	700
	Riez	CS	I	200	7	400	600
	Sisteron	SP	I	200	18	400	400
	Valensole	CS		300	3	200	500
Ardèche	Chomérac	CS	I	300	3	200	500
	Vallon	CS	P,I	300	6	500	800
Drôme	Bourdeaux	CS	P,I	400	7	500	900
	Dieulefit	CS	P,I	500	10	400	900
	Montélimar	SP	P	50	11	800	800
Gers	Jegun	CS	I	200	3	200	400
	Mirande	SP	I	600	17	700	
	Vic-Fezensac	CS	I	500	15	500	1,000
Hérault	Bédarieux	CS	I	800	3	200	1,000
	Béziers	SP	P,I	2,000	20	1,000	3,000
	Pézénas	CS	I	500	3	400	
Jura	Poligny	SP	P,I	200	6	200	
Lot-et-Garonne	Lavardac	CS	I	400	12	1,400	
	Marmande	SP	I	1,000	12	500	1,000
Nièvre	Clamecy	SP	P,I	500	15	1,000	500
Pyrénées-Orientales	Thuirs	CS	P	50	18	800	
Var	Aups	CS	P	50	5	350	
	Barjols	CS	I	300	6	300	600
	Brignoles	SP	P,I	300	4	300	100
	St. Maximin	CS	P	200	4	200	
Vaucluse	Apt	SP	I	250	8	250	200
Yonne	St. Sauveur	CS	I	200	3	300	200
	Toucy	CS	P	50	5	250	300
Totals				11,450	262	13,850	16,100

I—initiates revolt   P—plans rural mobilization first

linkage from one canton to another, and they resulted in several gatherings of over 2,000 insurgents. Thus, in the Basses-Alpes, Montagnards at Forcalquier, Sisteron, Manosque, Valensole, and Riez organized a march of at least 6,000 rebels from sixteen cantons on the prefectoral capital of Digne. In the neighboring department of the Var, around 2,000 rebels from Le Luc and several large bourgs marched toward the prefecture at Draguignan and then turned northwest to obtain reinforcements from the town of Salernes and the *arrondissement* of Brignoles. Eventually, over 4,000 men from forty different communes in nine cantons reached the market bourg of Aups, near the border with the Basses-Alpes. In the Gard, rebels descended the valley of the Gardon toward the prefecture at Nîmes, spearheaded by a small but active force from the subprefecture of Alais. Joined en route by contingents from the cantonal seats of St. Ambroix, Vézénobres, Lédignan and Anduze as well as by columns or bands from around twenty villages, they numbered over 1,500 when they approached Nîmes. Similar step-linkages occurred in seven other departments:

Ardèche	1,500 rebels marched to the subprefecture of Largentière from the cantons of Vallon, Joyeuse, and Les Vans (c. 15 communes).
Drôme	2,800 rebels marched to the town of Crest, en route to the prefecture at Valence, from the cantons of Dieulefit, Bourdeaux, and Crest-sud (35 communes).
Gers	2,200 rebels marched to the prefectoral capital of Auch, mainly from the cantons of Vic-Fezensac, Jegun, Valence, Montesquiou, and Auch-sud (30 communes).
Lot-et-Garonne	1,500 rebels marched toward the prefectoral capital of Agen, mainly from the cantons of Lavardac and Nérac (14 communes).
Saône-et-Loire	600 rebels marched to the prefectoral capital of Mâcon from the cantons of St. Gengoux and Cluny (c. 6 communes).
Vaucluse	1,000 rebels approached the prefectoral capital of Avignon, mainly from the cantons of Apt, Bonnieux, and Gordes (21 communes).
Yonne	Around 1,000 rebels marched toward the prefectoral capital of Auxerre in several bands from the cantons of St. Sauveur, Toucy, and Courson (c. 15 communes).

In four of the above departments a small town with several thousand inhabitants provided the main impetus for action (Apt, Cluny, Dieulefit, Vic-Fezensac). In the other three departments a comparable role was played by market bourgs serving as cantonal seats (Lavardac, St. Sauveur, Vallon).

Even below the level of cantonal seats, resistance to the coup d'état was more often characteristic of bourgs and *bourgades* than of primary rural communes. The former types of settlements shared some socioeconomic features with towns—a good-sized agglomeration, a differentiated labor force of craftsmen and shopkeepers as well as cultivators, periodic fairs, a resident notary or tax collector. The predominance of such semiurban communities can be measured at the national level by examining a 5% sample of all residents of rebel communes who were prosecuted in 1852. The sample contains 582 individuals who resided in 304 different communes.[23] Only 26% of these rebels came from primary communes, as compared with 31% from bourgs and *bourgades* below the level of cantonal seats, and 42% from towns and bourgs that functioned as administrative centers.[24] With respect to the communes themselves, 34% were primary villages, 37% were bourgs and *bourgades* below the cantonal level, and 29% were subprefectures or cantonal seats.

Although the typical insurgent resided in a semiurban agglomeration, this does not mean that he was detached from the soil. If we examine the occupational background of our sample of arrestees, we find that 44% were employed in agriculture, 48% in crafts and commerce, and 6% in liberal professions. Peasants were especially liable to prosecution in southeastern France, where 53% of the arrestees in our sample were cultivators. By contrast, only 24% of the arrestees from rebel communes of central and southwestern France were employed in agriculture. These regional variations reflect differences in settlement patterns: in southeastern France peasants tended to reside with the artisans in agglomerated settlements ranging in size from several hundred to several thousand inhabitants. In the center and southwest they usu-

[23] This sample was drawn from a register in the national archives, which lists all individuals in alphabetical order who were judged by the Mixed Commissions in 1852 (AN, F⁷ 2588-95). Every twentieth name was drawn, and information concerning place of residence, place of birth, age, occupation, marital status, and political role before and during the revolt was recorded. Systematic data concerning the political and socioeconomic characteristics of their communes of residence was then gathered from the sources in n. 21 and from Adolphe Joanne, *Dictionnaire des Communes de la France* (Paris, 1864).

[24] A "primary commune" is defined as any commune that lacked markets, notaries, tax collectors, or specialized industry, as reported by Joanne for the 1850s.

ally lived in dispersed hamlets and farmsteads, while many artisans lived in the bourgs and village-centers. Politicization before the coup d'état, voluntary participation in the revolt, and exposure to arrest thereafter were all correlated with an agglomerated settlement pattern. Consequently, artisans were arrested in large numbers from all rebel zones, peasants mainly from the southeast.

Republican political organizations were instrumental in linking various communes together within a regional movement of armed opposition to the state. Montagnard secret societies had been implanted before the coup d'état in all the districts where large numbers of peasants and village artisans participated in the insurrection. These associations functioned as a clandestine political party with a recognized hierarchy of leaders centered on the towns and with a mass base of membership. Republican efforts to maximize manpower during the insurrection naturally followed the preexisting lines of political influence which these organizations had created. Montagnard leaders and militants organized every armed mobilization that involved the convergence of substantial rural contingents on urban centers. They were especially active in the southeast (Basses-Alpes, Ardèche, Drôme, Gard, Hérault, Var, Vaucluse), but they also organized resistance to the coup d'état in several departments of the southwest and the center (Gers, Lot-et-Garonne, Nièvre, Yonne). This does not mean that Montagnard societies automatically generated revolt. Such clandestine organizations also existed in some districts which remained calm after the coup d'état—the Bouches-du-Rhône, the Cher, parts of the Hérault and the Yonne. Nonetheless, without the urban-rural linkage that they provided, insurgency rarely acquired much popular momentum, especially outside the towns.

The only apparent exceptions to this generalization were a few uprisings in central France (Allier, Jura, Saône-et-Loire). No Montagnard associations seem to have existed in the rebel canton of Le Donjon (Allier), where bourgeois Republican landlords relied instead on a small but devoted clientele of artisans, miners, and agricultural workers. They seized the bourg, mobilized support from several nearby communes, and marched with a few hundred men to the subprefecture of La Palisse. In the Jura, a longstanding secret society of Carbonari probably mediated between Republican leaders in the towns and those in some villages. Serious resistance to the coup d'état occurred at Poligny, where around 200 townsmen, aided by an equal number of peasants from several nearby villages, seized the municipality and overthrew the subprefect. As for the Saône-et-Loire, a substantial uprising occurred northwest of its prefectoral capital (Mâcon), although no Montagnard societies seem to have existed there. Yet very few villagers joined the several hundred men who marched from the town of Cluny and the market bourg of St. Gengoux toward Mâcon. The small scale of rural participation in these revolts at Le Donjon, Poligny, and Cluny confirms the view that Montagnard societies were at the basis of substantial regional opposition to the state.

Elsewhere in France, even small-scale linkage between towns, bourgs, and villages failed to take place. Either urban appeals for rural assistance went unheeded, or villagers took arms while the residents of administrative and market centers remained passive. Events in the Lot and the Aveyron typified the former pattern of urban isolation from the countryside. Republicans in several towns of these neighboring departments protested the coup d'état, but their efforts to organize armed mobilization elsewhere in the region were unsuccessful. At Figeac (Lot), for example, a crowd seized weapons at the *caserne* of the gendarmes on December 3 and helped a "commission of resistance" defy the subprefect and the municipal council. Yet emissaries from Figeac were unable to muster significant rural support, and only one other commune in the *arrondissement*, Gramat (a cantonal seat), had any serious protest, led by its Republican municipality. Similarly, political militants at the prefecture of the Lot (Cahors) sent messengers into the countryside on December 4 to recruit manpower, but no one answered their call to arms. At Villefranche (Aveyron), 100 men seized the weapons of the national guard on December 3 and marched toward the prefecture at Rodez, but they dispersed en route without recruiting any peasants. Comparable bands headed for Rodez from the cantonal seats of Marcillac and Sauveterre, led by their national-guard commanders, but only one rural commune joined their march and they turned back at news of calm in the town. Other cases in which townsmen appealed in vain for rural support include Thiers (Puy-de-Dôme), Niort (Deux-Sèvres), Beaune (Côte-d'Or), and Pau (Basses-Pyrénées).

Fragmentary rural mobilizations characterized events in several departments of the center and south. In the Haute-Vienne, for example, orders from Limoges sparked a chain reaction of armed gatherings at three bourgs to the southeast, but the 300 rebels from this area were prevented by troops from marching to their market center (the cantonal seat of Châteauneuf). A similar band of over 150 armed men from three villages near Bourganeuf (Creuse) was dispersed by gendarmes before reaching that town. Near the prefectoral capital of Lons-le-Saulnier (Jura) around 150 rebels from several villages also fled at the approach of troops. In the Pyrénées-Orientales, rural communes near the cantonal seat of Thuirs gathered secretly on the night of the seventh but they vanished without challenging the authorities. Bands of villagers remained even more isolated and conspiratorial in some districts of the Puy-de-Dôme (near Issoire), the Bouches-du-Rhône (near Auriol) and the Loiret (near Bonny-sur-Loire). In some cases these rural mobilizations were led by local Montagnards (Bouches-du-Rhône, Pyrénées-Orientales, Loiret), but they disintegrated for lack of any linkage with urban forces. Such fragmentary armed gatherings also occurred on the fringes of some major zones of insurgency. Examples include the cantons of Chabeuil (Drôme), Antraigues (Ardèche), Agde (Hérault), St. Amand (Nièvre), and Courson (Yonne). In all these cases, Montagnards gathered at orders or rumors of revolt, but they dispersed because nearby towns remained calm or because they encountered repressive forces.

If armed uprisings in 1851 often acquired regional momentum and nearly always had a regional orientation, unarmed demonstrations usually remained localized in cities and towns. Only a handful of the seventy-five crowds listed in Table 1.3 established any linkage with other communes, either during or after their demonstrations. Nonetheless, urban crowds did challenge the authority of the state in many cases. First, they involved relatively large numbers of participants. Although the median size of all unarmed gatherings was only 300, at least twenty-five towns and bourgs had 500 or more demonstrators and four cities had upwards of 1,000. One-quarter of all the Frenchmen who protested against the coup d'état were participants in unarmed crowds. Second, from the perspective of Louis Napoleon's government, many urban demonstrators had subversive political objectives. Crowds proclaimed revolutionary commissions (Chalabre, several bourgs in the Vaucluse); they tried to occupy town halls (Orléans, Hyères, Moissac); they pressured municipal councils into publicly denouncing the coup d'état (Marmande, Villeneuve-sur-Lot, Castelsarrasin, La Réole); they attacked agents of the state (Angers, Crest, Montargis, Pamiers, Pertuis); and they tried to rescue prisoners (St. Fargeau, Estagel, Rodez). Several of these incidents resulted in minor casualties and two ended in tragedy: one Republican and one gendarme were killed when an unarmed procession of sixty to eighty Republicans at Montargis (Loiret) collided with a brigade of gendarmes; and four peasants were killed and one wounded at Estagel (Pyrénées-Orientales) when a crowd tried to rescue a prisoner from troops. At the extreme, crowds precipitated full-scale urban insurrections (Apt, Marmande) or fostered armed mobilizations in nearby communes (Crest, Orange). The government showed its concern about urban protest by using troops to disperse crowds, even when their ostensible purpose was entirely pacific. At least twenty-nine crowd demonstrations were broken up by the army, and arrests were made in at least twenty-one cases. In the view of officials, the fact of protest was sufficient cause for repressive action, regardless of whether it was armed.

Yet most of these nonviolent crowd protests were too brief and disorganized to have any serious impact on the course of events. Despite their political content, they were usually spontaneous movements against a sudden turn of events rather than deliberate and well-organized efforts to thwart the coup. Even in the few cases where armed revolts followed nonviolent protests, this second phase of action was led by Montagnard leaders and militants rather than by the crowds themselves. Political organization and strategy, involving both urban and rural populations, was at the basis of the distinction between regional insurgency and localized crowd protest in 1851.

If Montagnards opted for insurgency in some small towns and rural communes, this was in part a reflection of the distribution of repressive forces on the eve of the coup d'état. The authorities in all the prefectoral capitals and the larger subprefectures had detachments of the army to help them control crowds; those in the smaller subprefectures and in the cantonal seats generally had only a handful of gendarmes at their disposal; and those in the rural communes usually lacked any military force at all. Inside the towns that had troops, armed opposition to the state was paralyzed in every case except Béziers. Either no protest occurred in such towns or it was nonviolent, even though nearby cantons might take arms (Draguignan, Digne, Auch). Outside these garrison towns, however, the balance of power was reversed. Here the brigades of gendarmes, each numbering only five or six men, were easily neutralized or overwhelmed by rebel forces. If we examine the twelve violent confrontations between insurgents and gendarmes (Table 1.5), we see that the rebels nearly always inflicted heavier casualties on the gendarmes than they themselves suffered. In ten of these incidents, not a single insurgent was killed or wounded, and in every case they remained undisputed masters of the terrain. So favorable was the equilibrium of forces to the rebels, that most units of gendarmes made no resistance at all: they surrendered, took refuge in their barracks, or fled.

Rebel fortunes quickly deteriorated, however, as soon as they collided with regular units of the army. While they gathered momentum only in districts that lacked troops (the single exception being Béziers), their political objective of overthrowing Bonapartist administrators led them ineluctably toward urban garrisons. In a few cases they turned back before disaster struck (Agen, Nîmes); elsewhere they fled at the first signs of military resistance (near Privas, Largentière, Montélimar, Auxerre, Avignon, Auch, at Linards and Toucy), or they dispersed in a few hours after an initial success against small numbers of troops (Crest-Bourdeaux). Only in the Basses-Alpes did rebels succeed in capturing a prefectoral town, and even they dispersed shortly after defeating a battalion of troops sent from Marseille to retake the town. The general fate of insurgents who confronted regular troops can be read in the casualty figures (Table 1.7): at least 58 rebels killed (perhaps 100 or more), and over 150 wounded, as compared with 9 soldiers killed and 44 wounded. The decisive riposte of the army ensured that insurgency was short-lived. Every violent clash occurred within the space of a single week (between the fourth and the tenth of December), and government authority was subsequently imposed without resistance throughout the zones that had rebelled.

In sum, the insurrection of 1851 was an impressive failure. Montagnards made a valiant effort to mobilize mass support against the coup d'état, but they abandoned hope as soon as they clashed with the army, if not before. Their movement had been founded on an illusion and was soon to be transformed into a fantasy. They had believed that the people in arms would sweep to victory, but the army proved them wrong. In the aftermath of defeat, their supreme defense of the Republic became a social myth of a *Jacquerie*, a mindless outburst of lower-class hatred against the rich and the well-educated. In fact, acts of social violence had been extremely rare, but the image of barbarian hordes, lusting after blood and rapine, helped Bonapartist propagandists consolidate public support for the new regime. The largest provincial uprising in nineteenth-century France entered historical memory as either a minor political incident in the rise of the Second Empire or as a major social crisis in the evolution of rural France. There it has largely remained until the present day.

THE ECONOMIC FOUNDATIONS OF
PEASANT MOBILIZATION

From the perspective of modern French history, the insurrection of 1851 seems paradoxically avant-garde in its political orientation and backward in its economic and social setting. However much Republicanism eventually acquired a rural following during the Third Republic, it is a commonplace of French historiography that left-wing opposition to the successive authoritarian regimes in nineteenth-century France was strongest in the cities and weakest in the countryside. Yet in 1851 the cities were generally calm, while small towns and rural communities in obscure corners of the land raised the standard of revolt. How can this curious localization of resistance to the coup d'état be explained? One solution to this problem consists in reinterpreting the political protest as an outburst of social discontent in backward regions of the nation. If it can be shown that areas of revolt in 1851 suffered from either chronic poverty or serious economic decline during the Second Republic, popular insurgency can be viewed as a displacement of economic grievances and social tensions into the realm of politics. Such an argument will be all the stronger if Republican resistance occurred in areas that had experienced riots and demonstrations against deteriorating economic conditions in previous years. Economic backwardness and endemic protest then become the underlying causes of popular violence in 1851.

The search for economic causes of popular rebellion during the Second Republic finds powerful inspiration in the earlier history of France. During the seventeenth century the insatiable fiscal demands of the Monarchy had provoked large-scale tax rebellions in many areas of the country.[1] Throughout the French Revolution, grave economic difficulties fueled protest and undermined public authority. Among the causes of revolutionary and counterrevolutionary mobilizations were the high price of grain and the difficulty of provisioning towns; the burden of seigneurial dues, tithes, and taxes; restrictions on communal rights of usage to common lands; and collapsing markets for

---

[1] Roland Mousnier, *Peasant Uprisings in Seventeenth-Century France, Russia, and China*, trans. Brian Pearce (New York, 1970), pp. 3-152; Boris Porchnev, *Les soulèvements populaires en France de 1623 à 1648* (Paris, 1963); Leon Bernard, "French Society and Popular Uprisings under Louis XIV," *French Historical Studies*, 3 (1964), 454-74.

rural textile goods.[2] Social antagonisms between rich and poor, town and countryside permeated the political life of France during the revolutionary epoch. Nor did economic protests cease with the reassertion of centralized authority. Every period of high grain prices from 1817 to 1847 was accompanied by extensive food riots, and the revolutionary upheavals of 1830 and 1848 were both followed by waves of tax riots and forest disorders. Direct action in defense of economic interests—cheaper food, lower taxes, free access to forests—culminated in the mid-century crisis from 1847 to 1849. Only in the second half of the century did such traditional forms of popular protest disappear almost entirely from the French countryside.[3]

When viewed against this background of frequent collective violence in redress of economic grievances, the insurrection of 1851 appears to fall into place as the last act in a long historical drama. The Marxist scholar Albert Soboul was the first to make such a connection explicit. In a series of articles entitled "The Agrarian Troubles of 1848," he presented a general view of rural protest during the Second Republic as a defense of the traditional peasant community against the intrusion of capitalist agriculture. The same areas of central, southwestern, and southeastern France that witnessed riots against enclosures, forest disorders, labor agitation, and tax revolts in 1848 were the zones of insurrection in 1851. The small farmers and sharecroppers of these areas adopted a variety of forms of struggle, but their aim remained the same: "There is an astonishing continuity of peasant reactions, always similar, in 1848 and 1851, as in 1789 and 1830: the traditional peasantry was defending the old collective rights which guaranteed its existence against the innovations of the new agriculture."[4] More recently, Le Roy Ladurie has called attention to the problems of underdevelopment rather than the tensions of modernization in explaining the rebellious tendencies of peasants in western, central, and southern France. Just as "primitive violence and monetary poverty went hand in hand," so "the political avant-garde of the nation sought its most massive support among the malcontents of underdevelop-

---

[2] Georges Lefebvre, *The Great Fear*, trans. Joan White (New York, 1973); Richard Cobb, *Les armées révolutionnaires*, 2 vols. (Paris, 1961-63); Tilly, *The Vendée*; Louise Tilly, "The Food Riot as a Form of Political Conflict in France," *Journal of Interdisciplinary History*, 2 (1971), 23-58; George Rudé, *The Crowd in the French Revolution, 1787-1795* (Oxford, 1959).

[3] Tilly, "The Changing Place of Collective Violence," pp. 139-64; Tilly, "How Protest Modernized in France, 1845-1855," pp. 192-255; Roger Price, "Popular Disturbances in the French Provinces after the July Revolution of 1830," *European Studies Review*, 1 (1971), 323-50.

[4] Soboul, *Paysans*, pp. 349-50.

ment."[5] Similarly, Yves-Marie Bercé and Eugen Weber have argued that economic backwardness fostered archaic mentalities and primitive forms of behavior in turbulent villages of southwestern and southern France.[6] From these several perspectives of capitalist expansion, under-development, or backwardness, the same geographical continuity would seem to confirm that economic hardship and peasant violence were interrelated throughout the Second Republic.

Precise geographical analysis shows, however, that peasant protest in 1848 and Republican insurgency in 1851 usually did *not* involve the same populations. At the level of departments, we can compare troop deployments against forest disorders (18,000 soldiers) and tax riots (15,000 soldiers) in the early months of the Republic with military and police repression after the coup d'état (26,884 prosecutions).[7] These two waves of repression struck different areas of the nation: the cor-relation coefficient between departmental measures of troop movements in 1848-49 and prosecutions in 1851-52 is slightly negative rather than strongly positive (−.11);[8] and none of the departments that received large numbers of troops to suppress tax and forest disorders also had large numbers of prosecutions for Republican insurgency.[9] At the level of cantons and communes, the same discontinuity can be confirmed: the agrarian troubles described by Soboul took place in 92 districts, all but 2 of which remained calm after the coup; incidents of protest against the 45-centimes tax spread to over 300 communes, only 9 of which lent any support to the insurrection; and forest disorders were most serious in 65 communes of the Pyrénées, not one of which re-belled in 1851.[10] Taking into account all reports of rural disorder, it is

---

[5] Emmanuel Le Roy Ladurie, *Le territoire de l'historien* (Paris, 1973), pp. 383-84.

[6] Weber, *Peasants into Frenchmen*, pp. 247-54; Bercé, *Croquants et nu-pieds*, pp. 163-221.

[7] The departmental distribution of troop deployments to suppress peasant dis-orders in 1848-49 is given by Suzanne Coquerelle, "L'armée et la répression dans les campagnes (1848)," *Société d'histoire de la Révolution de 1848, Etudes*, 18 (1955), 152-59. I have estimated a *bataillon* to mean 200 troops and a *compagnie* to mean 50 troops. For an estimate of repression after the coup d'état, I have used the numbers of persons sentenced by the Mixed Commissions in each depart-ment, tabulated by the "Statistique de l'insurrection de 1851," AN, BB[30] 424.

[8] Calculation of the mean square contingency coefficient phi.

[9] Maximum troop deployments in 1848: Haute-Garonne (4,985); Seine-Inféri-eure (2,420); Ariège (2,275); Hautes-Pyrénées (1,977); Moselle (1,958); Haut-Rhin (1,350). Maximum prosecutions in 1851-52: Var (3,147); Hérault (2,840); Basses-Alpes (1,699); Drôme (1,614); Nièvre (1,506); Yonne (1,167).

[10] Soboul, *Paysans*, pp. 307-50; R. Gossez, "La résistance à l'impôt: Les quarante-cinq centimes," *Société d'histoire de la Révolution de 1848, Etudes*, 15 (1953), 89-132; S. Coquerelle, "Les droits collectifs et les troubles agraires dans les Pyrénées en 1848," CNSS, 78 (1953), 345-64; judicial reports in AN, BB[18] 1460-61.

unlikely whether more than a dozen bourgs and villages participated heavily in both the economic protests of 1848 and the political uprisings of 1851, while several hundred joined the former but not the latter, and another several hundred joined the latter but not the former.

If we examine the peasant demonstrators of 1848 more closely, we find that they resisted local "capitalists" far less frequently than they opposed government forest guards or tax collectors. Class conflicts between the rural poor and wealthy landlords or tenant farmers, so common in early nineteenth century England, rarely took a violent form in France: Soboul describes only three riots against enclosures and one attack on a threshing machine in 1848, a paltry total in comparison with the hundreds of machine-breaking incidents during the English "Captain Swing" movement of 1830.[11] Of course, France had a much less extensive enclosure movement than England during the period of the classic agricultural revolution (1750-1850), and she lagged behind England in the adoption of labor-saving machinery throughout the nineteenth century. In northeastern France, where the three-field system of village agriculture prevailed, new crop rotations spread despite collective agricultural routines, and in western and central France, where enclosures had long been permitted, innovations in farming techniques depended on other factors, such as the supply of capital and the cost of transport. As for southern France, where conditions of soil and climate often favored labor-intensive methods of production, agricultural individualism operated through scattered plots of arable and horticultural land. Agrarian change in nineteenth-century France did not follow the English pattern of forcible enclosures and mechanization, so it is not surprising that French peasants rarely protested against the enclosure of open fields or the introduction of machinery.[12]

More characteristic of France were social tensions over peasant rights of usage to common lands. The rival jurisdiction of village communities and noble (or bourgeois) landlords over forests and wasteland was a

[11] Antienclosure riots at Ignol (Cher), Saléchan (Basses-Pyrénées), and Ville-Danet (Ille-et-Vilaine); destruction of a threshing machine at Mesnil-Amelot (Seine-et-Marne); other labor conflicts at Conques (Aude), Dolus (Charente-Inférieure), Lunel and Vic (Hérault). None of these communes participated in the insurrection. On English machine-breaking, see Hobsbawm and Rudé, *Captain Swing*.

[12] J. H. Clapham, *The Economic Development of France and Germany, 1815-1914*, 4th ed. (Cambridge, 1936), pp. 6-28, 158-94; Georges Duby, ed., *Histoire de la France rurale*, tome III, *Apogée et crise de la civilisation paysanne* (Paris, 1976), 183-305; Pierre Léon, et al., *Histoire économique et sociale de la France*, tome III, *L'avènement de l'ère industrielle (1789-années 1880)*, vol. 2 (Paris, 1976), pp. 619-735; and George Grantham, "Scale and Organization of French Farming, 1840-1880," in Wm. N. Parker and Eric L. Jones, eds., *European Peasants and their Markets: Essays in Agrarian Economic History* (Princeton, 1976), pp. 293-326.

major cause of peasant radicalization during the French Revolution.[13] Despite Jacobin efforts to disentangle communal and private-property rights, this problem persisted in some forested districts of the nation during the first half of the nineteenth century. Peasants demanded the right to gather wood or to pasture livestock in forests that were "private" in the eyes of the law, and sometimes they used violence to enforce their communal rights. Soboul mentions a dozen riots in 1848 against the sale or lease of common lands or against private forest owners, and Maurice Agulhon has proved that disputes between villages and private forest owners fostered left-wing extremism in the Var, a major area of insurgency.[14] It is important, however, to distinguish between the economic grievances that fostered local protests in 1848, and the generalized political consciousness that stimulated insurgency in 1851. Even in the Var, disputes over private forests led to only four demonstrations in 1848, while over sixty bourgs and villages took arms three years later.[15] None of the incidents described by Soboul occurred in communes that mobilized against the coup d'état, and near the rebel town of Clamecy (Nièvre), peasants from three nearby communes stayed home after having mustered 600 men in May 1848 to coerce a forest owner into recognizing their rights of usage.[16] Such localized efforts to wrest legal claims from the hands of recalcitrant proprietors had only a remote connection with Republican insurgency.[17]

Much more significant is the relationship between private forests and political consciousness during the Second Republic. Where peasants believed they had legitimate claims to customary rights of usage in private forests, they were often predisposed to accept the Republic with enthusiasm. Even where legal disputes had been resolved in favor of the villages, memories of their tenacious struggles against the seigneurs of the Old Régime and their noble heirs gave the populations of such areas a tradition of opposition to Legitimist landowners. Thus, nearly half (20/48) of the communes in the Var that had been en-

[13] Marc Bloch, "Le lutte pour l'individualisme agraire dans la France du XVIIIe siècle," reprinted in *Mélanges historiques* (Paris, 1963); Georges Lefebvre, "The French Revolution and the Peasants," in R. W. Greenlaw, ed., *The Economic Origins of the French Revolution* (Boston, 1958); A. Soboul, "The French Rural Community in the 18th and 19th Centuries," *Past and Present*, 10 (1956), 78-95.

[14] Agulhon, *La République au village*, pp. 49-92, 361-65.

[15] Ibid., pp. 361-62 (disorders at Baudinard, Montmeyan, Entrecastaux, Collobrières); register of MC Var, AN, BB[30] 398; Ints. rebels, AD Var, 4M 19-21, 26-28.

[16] P-G Bourges, Mar. 27, 1848, AN, BB[18] 1462.

[17] Outside the Var, the only documented examples of such continuity were at Aizac and La Bastide (Ardèche), and Anost and Roussillon (Saône-et-Loire), but none of these communes had major mobilizations after the coup. See P-G Nîmes, May 12, 1850, AN, BB[30] 382; and P-G Dijon, July 10, 1848, AN, BB[18] 1462.

gaged in legal disputes with forest owners in the generation before 1848 rebelled in 1851.[18] Similarly, insurgent villages in the Yonne had a history of antiseigneurial complaints involving forests. Unlike their counterparts in a few villages of the Var, no rebels in the Yonne expressed claims to forests during the revolt, but they were definitely hostile to resident noble families.[19] Elsewhere the relationship between rights of usage and insurgency is more tenuous, but it is noteworthy that some militant Republican villages in the Allier, the Drôme, and the Lot-et-Garonne also contained large private forests.[20] The issue of rights of usage facilitated the diffusion of Republican ideology into the countryside by undermining the patronage of Legitimist landowners. Not violent protest and economic desperation, but the ideological orientations of rural communities explain the connection between forests and rebellion in 1851.

The importance of the political context of economic protest can be seen even more clearly in the case of disturbances over rights of usage to *public* forests. Riots against the national forest administration in 1848 were far more persistent, extensive, and violent than conflicts with local forest owners. They revealed profound popular hostility to state controls on public grazing and wood-collecting in the forests. Crowds expelled state guardians of the public forests on pain of death; they cut down large quantities of wood in compensation for the fines they had suffered in earlier years; and they opposed the return of the guards by force of arms. Joint opposition to the state gave neighboring communes an incentive to coordinate their action, and several mobilizations of over 1,000 men challenged magistrates and troops in the Pyrénées. In such districts, mayors and national-guard officials sometimes marched at the head of their populations, flags flowing and drums beating in resolute and unanimous opposition to the restoration of public-conservation measures. Such calculated demonstrations rarely led to bloodshed, however, because either the villagers dispersed or the army retreated, depending on which side had mustered the more imposing numbers. Eventually arrests were made, suspects prosecuted, and the forest

[18] Agulhon, *La République au village*, pp. 50-73 (tabulation of legal disputes); and register of MC Var, AN, BB[30] 398.

[19] Claude Levy, "A propos du coup d'état de 1851 dans l'Yonne," *Annales de Bourgogne*, 25 (1953), 185; Louis Chevalier, "Les fondements économiques et sociaux de l'histoire politique de la région parisienne, 1848-1851," *Thèse*, University of Paris, 1951, pp. 594-95.

[20] Thus, at Le Donjon (Allier) the Legitimist mayor, M. de la Boutresse, who was "arrested" by the rebels on December 4, 1851, owned a large forest where *délits forestiers* were subsequently reported. CP Le Donjon, Mar. 3-6, 1865, AD Allier, M 1303.

guards reinstated. But the frequency of these disorders, their large scale, and their specific economic demands show that vital popular interests were at stake.[21]

Yet precisely because the source of repression in 1848 was the newly founded Republic, these disturbances generally had anti-Republican implications, and in no case did they lead to rebellion in 1851. For example, while hundreds of militants in the lowlands of the Pyrénées-Orientales mobilized secretly after the coup and suffered arrest and exile in 1852, the inhabitants of the canton of Montlouis, "violent, recalcitrant, inclined to resistance and rebellion," stayed in their mountain huts and evaded subsequent repression.[22] Similarly, in southeastern France the few cantons with serious disorders against forest guards in 1848 were quiescent in 1851, despite general insurrection in the plains and plateaus of the Basses-Alpes and the Drôme.[23] Here, too, ideology needs to be distinguished from collective action. Agulhon has shown that resentment at the forest administration was exploited by Republicans in the Var, but no disorders involving forest guards occurred in that department between 1848 and 1851. Indeed, the five communes that had protested in earlier years against state controls over public forests in the Var were all calm in 1851.[24] Physical assaults on forest guards did not prepare the way for insurgency against the government of Louis Napoleon Bonaparte.

Taxes have been a perennial source of popular discontent in French history, and the Provisional Republican government in 1848 shares with the kings of the Old Régime the distinction of having aroused violent opposition to its tax policy. Faced with an acute financial and industrial crisis in the cities, the new government imposed a temporary surcharge of 45 percent on the land tax. In northern France this policy worked: by July 13, 1848, over half the tax had already been collected in nearly all the departments north and east of the Loire river. Although

[21] Louis Clarenc, "Le Code forestier de 1827 et les troubles forestiers dans les Pyrénées centrales au milieu du XIXᵉ siècle," *Annales du Midi*, 77 (1965), 293-317; Clarenc, "Riches et pauvres dans le conflit forestier des Pyrénées centrales vers le milieu du XIXᵉ siècle," *Annales du Midi*, 69 (1967), 307-15; Coquerelle, "Les droits collectifs et les troubles agraires dans les Pyrénées en 1848"; John M. Merriman, "The Demoiselles of the Ariège, 1829-1831," in Merriman, ed., *1830 in France* (New York, 1975), pp. 87-118. See also the judicial reports in AN, BB^{18} 1460-61.

[22] P-G Montpellier, June 16, 1848, AN, BB^{18} 1460-61. On repression after the coup, see Horace Chauvet, *Histoire du parti républicain dans les Pyrénées-Orientales, 1830-1877* (Perpignan, 1909).

[23] Riots against forest guards occurred in the cantons of La Chapelle-en-Vercors (Drôme) and Seynes (Basses-Alpes), both calm in 1851. See Vigier, *La Seconde République*, I, 204-6; and P-G Aix, July 13, 1848, AN, BB^{18} 1460-61.

[24] Agulhon, *La République au village*, pp. 82-89; and register of MC Var, AN, BB^{30} 398.

over 30 public protests occurred in this region, troops had to be deployed in only 5 cases to restore order. Payment was slower in the southeast and along the Mediterranean coast: only one-third of the tax had been collected by July 13. Nonetheless, protest in this zone was extremely rare, and troops intervened only once. A veritable epidemic of tax disorders broke out, however, in the departments of the southwest, where less than one-fifth of the tax had been paid by July 13: nearly 150 demonstrations took place in this zone, and troops were involved in at least 52 of these incidents. The 45-centimes tax riots were essentially confined to the southwestern quadrant of the nation.[25]

Marketing networks in the turbulent districts of southwestern France consisted of rotating fairs in the countryside, and towns probably had less economic influence over villages here than in regions that had a larger scale of economic transactions. This combination of brisk local trade with weak long-distance commerce helps explain the sensitivity of peasants to falling prices and increasing taxes, and their willingness to defy the new Republican administrators in the towns. Indifference to national politics quickly became active hostility when bailiffs tried to seize the property of insolvent taxpayers, and when gendarmes carried tax registers away to town jails. It was the capture of prisoners that aroused the most popular indignation, and eight armed mobilizations of over 500 peasants tried to resist such arrests or to liberate prisoners. Like the forest disorders, these tax riots involved ritualistic confrontations between soldiers and peasants, who relied on threatening gestures and violent words rather than gunfire and physical assaults. Just as political organization rarely seems to have preceded the riots, so they usually ended without serious casualties, although panicky national guardsmen at the town of Gueret (Creuse) opened fire on peasant demonstrators, killing twelve of them. The government's swift mustering of troop reinforcements from urban garrisons persuaded peasants in most districts that violent resistance to the tax was futile.[26]

Neither the economic issues nor the political beliefs that generated these tax revolts were closely related to Republican insurgency. The controversy over the 45-centimes tax subsided in importance as Republican militants called for the abolition of the wine tax and the general reform of the fiscal system. Peasants who were embittered by government collection of the 45-centimes tax often became Bonapartists.[27]

---

[25] Numerical estimates based on the map published by Gossez, "La résistance à l'impôt," p. 132.

[26] Analysis based on the reports of magistrates in AN, BB[18] 1462. See also Gossez, "La résistance à l'impôt," pp. 39-132; Bercé, *Croquants et nu-pieds*, pp. 165-191; and Corbin, *Archaïsme et modernité en Limousin*, pp. 502-9.

[27] Bercé emphasizes the Bonapartist implications of tax riots, in *Croquants et nu-pieds*, pp. 208-14.

It is noteworthy that the rural populations did not join urban resistance to the coup d'état in riotous districts of the southwest. Thus, villagers at Malabat (Gers), where 3,000 men had gathered in June 1848 to protest fiscal coercion, turned a deaf ear to the call to arms that their cantonal seat, Miélan, issued on December 4, 1851; and so did villagers around Nay (Hautes-Pyrénées) and Marcillac (Aveyron), where protest against the 45-centimes tax had been widespread.[28] The internal dynamics of the tax revolts do suggest some parallels with the insurrection: village solidarity against government repression aided rural mobilizations in both movements; and peasant crowds held similar attitudes toward gendarmes, whom they hated, and soldiers, whom they respected. Yet the political discontinuities deserve to be emphasized. Tax riots in 1848-49 were essentially rural reactions against specific acts of repression, and they lacked any broader conception of political goals or any organizational bonds with urban militants. The tax rebels sought to retreat from the Republic, not to conquer it. In the words of one riotous population, "The commune of Villedieu does not recognize the Republic and owes it nothing."[29] Not with these beliefs did men rise in arms to defend the Republic in 1851.

Economic backwardness may still explain the basic geography of revolt in 1851, even if political factors mediated between poverty and protest. Perhaps insurgent districts of the nation suffered from a Malthusian dilemma of rising population, stagnant agricultural technology, and falling peasant incomes. Or perhaps they labored under the "Schumpeterian" fate reserved for regions with obsolescent technologies and routine entrepreneurs in a dynamic capitalist economy: the loss of markets to more efficient producers, and the agony of "deindustrialization."[30] In either event, economic decline may have heightened popular misery, sharpened social tensions, and created an explosive political atmosphere. Underdevelopment would then be a fundamental cause of revolt.

Alternatively, economic *expansion* may have created a basis in the countryside for militant Republicanism. The Marxian schema of popular immiserization and revolutionary upheaval has long been rivaled on the theoretical level by Alexis de Tocqueville's concept of a "revolution of rising expectations." Could de Tocqueville have been reflecting on the political consequences of economic growth during the July Monarchy when he perceived in the eighteenth century a gradual improve-

---

[28] On the tax riots in these districts, see AN, BB[18] 1462; on urban efforts to resist the coup, see AN, BB[30] 398, 401-2.

[29] P-G Poitiers, August 23, 1848, AN, BB[18] 1462.

[30] Tilly, "The Changing Place of Collective Violence," pp. 160-62.

ment in living standards, a widening popular aspiration toward economic equality—and a revolution?[31] Certainly such a theory might be more relevant to the disciplined rural contingents of 1851 than to their turbulent ancestors in 1789.

An emphasis on rising aspirations would also be consistent with the research of political scientists concerning the socioeconomic preconditions of citizen participation in politics. With respect to individuals, participation increases with income, education, and associational membership. With respect to societies, participation increases with urbanization and industrialization. Karl Deutsch has used the term "social mobilization" to characterize the attitudinal changes generated by rising per capita incomes, literacy levels, and rates of urbanization. Populations cease to be passive in relation to their governments, and they begin to demand public policies that will satisfy their new socioeconomic expectations. Deutsch further notes that rates of exposure to mass communications may increase more rapidly than rates of economic growth and social change. His theory implies that during the transitional phase to an urban-industrial society, peasants' aspirations will tend to outstrip their economic capabilities. Samuel P. Huntington has made this inference explicit in his discussion of rural political mobilization—the "green revolution." Indeed, he suggests that economic conditions in the countryside actually deteriorate during this transitional phase, while the peasants are increasingly exposed to "the enlightenment of the cities." The result is political instability and violence.[32]

But is economic decline a plausible correlate of rising peasant aspirations? Perhaps the "mass media" of the twentieth century permit urban politicians to leap directly into the huts of backward peasants, but in nineteenth-century Europe, expanding urban influence in the countryside presupposed economic growth and increasing peasant involvement in markets. The Norwegian scholar Stein Rokkan has shown, for example, that rural political mobilization in nineteenth-century Norway was a concomitant of peasant participation in an urban-centered economy and society. Between 1814 and 1870, Norwegian peasants entered an historical phase of "incipient mobilization" as monetization and urbanization broke down the "isolated pockets of subsistence communities in the countryside" and generated "complex systems of cross-local exchange and interdependence." By opening up the rural world

---

[31] Tocqueville, *The Old Regime and the French Revolution*, trans. Stuart Gilbert (New York, 1955), pp. 169-79; see also Richard Herr, *Tocqueville and the Old Regime* (Princeton, 1962).

[32] Deutsch, "Social Mobilization and Political Development," *American Political Science Review*, 55 (1961), 493-507; Huntington, *Political Order in Changing Societies* (New Haven, 1968), pp. 291-300.

to urban influences, market development created the social conditions for rapid and effective political mobilization: "a literate peasantry, a growing network of voluntary associations, increasing facilities for cross-local communication through the mails and the press, a steady increase in the spread of urban commodities and ideas toward the periphery, a growing flow of migrants at all levels of the social hierarchy from the rural areas to the cities." Upon these foundations of economic expansion and social development, urban radicals gained peasant support in Norway for a "decisive thrust toward power" in the 1870s.[33]

In sum, two divergent theories have been advanced by scholars to explain peasant involvement in urban revolutionary movements. For convenience they can be labelled the immiserization theory and the urbanization theory. The former emphasizes the unfavorable impact of economic trends on peasant living standards; some combination of population pressure, capitalist innovation, and market decline destroys the economic balance in the countryside and impoverishes the rural populations. From the grievances of destitute peasants, urban revolutionaries mount a violent challenge to the established regime. The urbanization theory focuses attention instead on the expanding economic and social horizons of the peasantry. While incomes may temporarily decline, the political significance of urbanization rests primarily in the social interactions it facilitates between peasants and townsmen. Furthermore, the basic trend of such a growth-oriented society is to improve living standards and raise popular expectations of even greater progress in the future. It is from the rising aspirations of urban-oriented peasants that revolutionaries fashion a mass movement in opposition to the existing government.

The starting point for an evaluation of these respective theories is the general evolution of the French rural economy in the first half of the nineteenth century. Was it expanding or declining, furthering urbanization or compounding the problems of subsistence-oriented peasants? Scholars are sharply divided on this question. For those who compare socioeconomic conditions in the countryside with a modern standard of high labor productivity and low population densities, the French agrarian economy appears to be backward in the 1840s. In most regions techniques of agricultural production were extremely labor-intensive, capital investments in machines or fertilizers were rare, and rural incomes were low. While the revolutionary land settlement had supposedly consolidated small peasant landowners as the dominant social type in the French countryside, relatively few families actually owned

---

[33] Rokkan, *Citizens, Elections, Parties* (New York, 1970), pp. 229-30.

enough land to subsist. Most peasants had to supplement their meager resources with low-wage labor in agriculture or "proto-industrial" activity (craft production for urban merchants, especially widespread in textiles). Such expedients were destined eventually to disappear, as agricultural laborers and rural craftsmen migrated to the cities in the later nineteenth and twentieth centuries. The future direction of the French rural economy—consolidation of medium-sized holdings, disappearance of nonagricultural activities, diffusion of more efficient techniques of production—is proof of its backwardness in the first half of the nineteenth century.[34]

An even more pessimistic outlook is shared by those scholars for whom population growth from 1801 to 1851 provoked a gradual but remorseless *decline* in rural incomes. Karl Marx was one of the first to adopt such a Malthusian perspective on the French peasantry of the July Monarchy. Noting that more and more "landowners" were appearing on the tax rolls, while an ever larger volume of debts entered the mortgage registers, Marx concluded that small-holding peasants were trying vainly to avoid the inevitable effect of population growth —land fragmentation—by going into debt. Farms were becoming smaller, techniques of production ever more retrogressive, and peasants languished in misery while urban usurers waxed fat off the interest payments on their loans.[35]

Among contemporary scholars who agree that rural population pressure could not be absorbed without a decline in peasant living standards, Jean Vidalenc is especially influential. His survey of the French countryside from 1815 to 1848 presents a bleak image of living conditions. At mid-century most peasants were still backward, illiterate, and impoverished. A dramatic population increase of 30 percent from 1801 to 1851 had created a vicious circle of land hunger, rising land prices, and usurious debts; industrial competition had reduced markets for rural handicrafts; and agricultural innovations had been monopolized by a small minority of large landowners. Vidalenc concludes that the "demographic push" in the countryside had grave, even tragic,

[34] Among scholars who emphasize the static qualities of French agriculture before 1850, see J. H. Clapham, *Economic Development*, pp. 6-28; and Michel Morineau, *Les faux-semblants d'un démarrage économique* (Paris, 1971), pp. 7-87. For a recent analysis of long-range trends in the nineteenth century, see P. Hohenberg, "Change in Rural France in the Period of Industrialization, 1830-1914," *Journal of Economic History*, 32 (1972), 219-40. Frank Mendels has elucidated the concept of a proto-industrial economy in "Proto-Industrialization: The First Phase of the Industrialization Process," *Journal of Economic History*, 32 (1972), 241-61.

[35] Marx, "The Class Struggles in France, 1848-1850," in Marx and Engels, *Selected Works*, 1 (Moscow, 1962), 215-17; Marx, "The Eighteenth Brumaire of Louis Bonaparte," ibid., pp. 336-37. See the recent critique of his views by Price, *The French Second Republic*, pp. 20-26.

consequences for the peasantry. In most of the nation, they suffered from "growing pauperisation."[36] After reading Vidalenc's book, a sympathetic reviewer asserted flatly: "There is no doubt that the first half of the nineteenth century is a somber period for the rural world— a demographic push not compensated for by economic development, hence a slow degradation in the living standards of the peasants almost everywhere in France."[37]

In a rural world where subsistence was the primary economic concern of most inhabitants, these Malthusian views have an implicit quantitative dimension: the population increased more rapidly than the food supply. Indeed, Albert Soboul, another member of this "pessimist" school, states bluntly that population growth exceeded the growth of agricultural output in the first half of the nineteenth century.[38] Yet most scholars who have examined statistical evidence concerning agricultural output during this period have reached the opposite conclusion —output grew considerably more rapidly than population. According to Emile Levasseur, the grain harvest increased by 34% between 1830 and 1847, while population grew by only 10%; David Landes has published French government statistics indicating that between 1815-24 and 1841-50 the wheat crop increased by over 50%, the potato crop by 150%, but population by only 21%; J. C. Toutain has calculated that agricultural output grew steadily from 1820 to 1870 at a rate of 1.2% per year, largely because of increases in labor productivity; and Levy-Leboyer has confirmed that annual growth rates in agriculture considerably exceeded the rate of growth of the population.[39]

Nor were agricultural improvements confined to northeastern France, where agricultural productivity was highest at the beginning of the nineteenth century. William H. Newell has calculated agricultural growth rates by department and by region for the period 1815-24 to 1865-74. His data, although admittedly based on incomplete sources, indicate that per capita agricultural productivity grew in every region of the nation. Agricultural labor productivity also increased substan-

[36] Vidalenc, *La société française de 1815 à 1848*, vol. 1, *Le peuple des campagnes* (Paris, 1970), 329-69.

[37] Daniel Ligou, review in *Revue d'histoire économique et sociale*, 48 (1970), 298-99. For a similar view of peasant poverty and backwardness as late as the 1870s, see Weber, *Peasants into Frenchmen*, pp. 3-166.

[38] Soboul, *Paysans*, p. 314.

[39] Emile Levasseur, *Histoire des classes ouvrières et de l'industrie en France de 1789 à 1870*, 2 vols., 2nd ed. (Paris, 1903-4), II, 277-78; Landes, *The Unbound Prometheus* (Cambridge, 1969), p. 154, citing *L'Annuaire statistique*, 25 (1905), Résumé retrospectif, 10*, 32*-33*; Toutain, *Le produit de l'agriculture française de 1700 à 1958*, vol II, *La croissance* (Paris, 1961); Maurice Levy-Leboyer, ".La croissance économique en France au XIXᵉ siècle," *Annales*, 23 (1968), 788-807.

tially throughout the nation, with the highest productivity gains in central and southwestern France. Newell concludes that France experienced a veritable agricultural revolution during the July Monarchy and the Second Empire. This revolution was based on two main innovations: (1) the cultivation of wheat on lands that had previously been confined to rye; (2) the introduction of fodder crops on previously fallow land, resulting in larger herds, more fertilizer, and higher wheat yields. It is noteworthy that Newell does not include specialized crops produced in Mediterranean France, such as wine, raw silk, olives, and fruit, in his estimates of agricultural output. The general increase in agricultural productivity from 1830 to 1870 was probably even greater than his research confirms, especially in the southeast.[40]

What about the fate of rural industry in the generation before 1848? All scholars are agreed that over the very long run, proto-industrial activity vanished from the French countryside, a process variously described as "deindustrialization" or "agriculturalization." Considerable evidence exists, however, that this decline was not only very slow; it had not yet begun in many areas of the nation by the mid-nineteenth century. Indeed, rural industry expanded substantially during the July Monarchy in precisely those regions where industrialization was most advanced—in the northeast and the center (Lyon-St.-Etienne).[41] As cotton and wool spinning was concentrated in factories, weaving was dispersed on an ever-wider scale in the countryside. Landes notes this expansion of the rural textile industry through the 1850s, and points to the tens of thousands of full-time rural workers in Normandy around 1860.[42] A similar diffusion of weaving into the countryside characterized the Lyon silk industry from the 1830s through the 1860s.[43] Comparable evidence could be presented for a host of other handicraft goods that peasants were producing for export in the 1840s —buttons and hats, locks and nails, pottery and wooden shoes, etc. A national inquiry into industrial and agricultural conditions in 1848 shows that nearly half the departments of the nation had significant

[40] Newell, "The Agricultural Revolution in Nineteenth Century France," *Journal of Economic History*, 33 (1973), 697-731. For the importance of cash crops such as silk and wine in the productivity increases of northern Italy during the same period, see Maurice Aymard, "Rendements et productivité agricole dans l'Italie moderne," *Annales*, 28 (1973), 492-97.
[41] For the distribution of the rural textile industry in the July Monarchy, see Levasseur, *Histoire des classes ouvrières*, II, 181-89; Arthur Dunham, *The Industrial Revolution in France, 1815-1848* (New York, 1955), pp. 181-90, 317-49.
[42] Landes, *Unbound Prometheus*, pp. 162-70, 188, 213. The rural linen industry in France was being ruined, however, by British competition, pp. 188-90.
[43] See the monograph on the department of the Rhône by G. Garrier, *Paysans du Beaujolais et du Lyonnais, 1800-1970*, 2 vols. (Grenoble, 1973), I., 202-14.

numbers of proto-industrial workers, with especially large concentrations in the villages of northern France.[44] Modernization and proto-industrial development were part and parcel of the same historical process.

The evidence concerning French agricultural and proto-industrial growth is impossible to reconcile with the Malthusian views of Marx, Vidalenc, and Soboul. Although inequalities in the distribution of wealth limited the peasant share of a larger national product, living conditions in the countryside were probably gradually improving rather than deteriorating during the July Monarchy. Certainly in some regions peasants were eating better food (some were even beginning to purchase meat), wearing better-quality clothing, and constructing more dwellings.[45] Mortality rates slowly declined in the 1830s and 1840s, and the demographic crises so characteristic of the *ancien regime* had largely disappeared from the countryside. That birth rates also fell is probably further evidence of rising expectations.[46] All of these trends were much more substantial after 1850, but the dramatic changes of the Second Empire and the Third Republic need not conceal the more gradual improvements of the July Monarchy.

This debate between pessimists and optimists concerns more than the income levels and employment opportunities of the peasantry. In a more fundamental sense it involves the meaning of urbanization in a nineteenth-century context. The "rural exodus" and urban growth after 1850 have misled some scholars into inferring that population growth in the earlier period reinforced the traditional, nonurban characteristics of French society. A small urban sector, admittedly expanding in size, was still overborne by the weight of a backward peasantry. In fact, the process of urbanization was taking place in the countryside itself. Not only cities, but small towns, bourgs, and agglomerated vil-

---

[44] See the cantonal census of proto-industrial and factory workers carried out in 1848, and published by Levasseur, *Histoire des classes ouvrières*, II, 300-334. Twenty-nine out of sixty-five departments included in his tables reported concentrations of industrial workers in at least eight cantons; of the ten departments reporting such concentrations in at least fifteen cantons, nine were in northern France.

[45] Evidence of improvement can be found in the monographs of social geographers, the publications of nineteenth-century observers, and a few works by historians. See, especially, Vigier, *La Seconde République*, I, 24-38; and Vigier, *La Monarchie de Juillet* (Paris, 1965), pp. 34-51; and Christopher H. Johnson, "Some Recent French Village Studies," *Peasant Studies Newsletter*, 2 (Oct. 1973), 9-16.

[46] On demographic trends, see Emile Levasseur, *La population française*, 3 vols. (Paris, 1889-92); Charles Pouthas, *La population française pendant la première moitié du XIXᵉ siècle* (Paris, 1956); and Charles Tilly, "The Modernization of Political Conflict in France," in Edward B. Harvey, ed., *Perspectives on Modernization* (Toronto, 1972).

lages were agents of urbanization in early nineteenth century France. Through these smaller centers of exchange, peasants were drawn into what might be characterized as a "proto-urban" society. They were not "urbanized" in the sense that they moved to cities. Instead, just as proto-industrial workers participated in an industrializing economy without themselves working in factories, so "proto-urban" craftsmen and cultivators participated in an urbanizing society without residing in cities. The transportation improvements of the Restoration and July Monarchies—more all-weather roads, more canals, the first railways— naturally played an important role in this proto-urban development. As market networks expanded, goods and manpower flowed from villages to towns and from towns to cities, preparing the way for a decisive shift toward a predominantly urban society. This second phase of urban development involved above all the transfer of proto-urban elements—craftsmen and laborers—from the countryside to the towns and onward to the cities. France did not move from a traditional rural society in the first half of the nineteenth century to a modern urban society in the second half; she passed through two distinct but closely related phases of urbanization.[47]

The political significance of proto-urbanization was twofold. First, large-scale markets for rural produce brought the peasantry into an economic system whose fluctuations were no longer determined primarily by local variations in the size of the harvest. The incomes generated by cash crops and craft exports now depended on regional, national, or even international market forces. Consequently, peasants had a direct interest in those aspects of national economic policy— tariffs, taxes, credit—that influenced the marketability of their produce and the terms of their employment. The more monetized the rural economy, the greater this interest became. Second, widening markets brought peasants into closer social contact with the residents of towns and market bourgs. The more the socioeconomic interaction between townsmen and villagers, the greater the range of urban political influences to which the rural populations were exposed. While neither market sensitivity nor urban-rural interactions guaranteed that *left-wing* politicians would capture a popular audience in the countryside, they did ensure that *urban* politicians, of whatever political persuasion, would be able to mobilize the peasantry more effectively.

[47] I am defining as proto-urbanization the process that Tilly and others have characterized as the "urbanization" of the countryside—the expansion of urban influence over rural communities. I would reserve the term *urbanization* for the process by which an increasing proportion of the entire population comes to reside in *cities*. This latter process, involving rapid growth rates of cities and negative growth rates in the countryside, did not generally begin in France until after 1850. See Tilly, *The Vendée*, pp. 16-37.

By contrast, subsistence farming implied social and political isolation from the towns. Marx recognized this in his famous caricature of social relationships in the French countryside:

> The small-holding peasants form a vast mass, the members of which live in similar conditions but without entering into manifold relations with one another. Their mode of production isolates them from one another instead of bringing them into mutual intercourse. . . . Each individual peasant family is almost self-sufficient; it itself directly produces the major part of its consumption and thus acquires its means of life more through exchange with nature than in intercourse with society. A small holding, a peasant and his family; alongside them another small holding, another peasant and another family. A few score of these make up a village, and a few score of villages make up a Department. In this way, the great mass of the French nation is formed by simple addition of homologous magnitudes, much as potatoes in a sack form a sack of potatoes.[48]

Of course, French peasants had never lived in such a state of extreme isolation. Not only was the village community a primary social unit during the Old Régime but many villages were linked through rotating fairs and periodic markets to a local town. The geographer Edward Fox has noted such clusters of town and hinterland in medieval France, and the anthropologist William Skinner has aptly described comparable socioeconomic units in imperial China as "standard market communities."[49] Nonetheless, in the absence of a substantial export market— "commerce" as opposed to mere "trade," in Fox's words—each of these standard market communities remained largely isolated in its subsistence economy.[50] External relationships were mediated through the political power structure—and over the heads of the peasantry—rather than through the marketplace. The crucial element of proto-urbanization— an expanding market for local cultivators and craftsmen—was still lacking.[51]

[48] Marx, "The Eighteenth Brumaire," p. 334.

[49] Edward Whiting Fox, *History in Geographic Perspective* (New York, 1971), pp. 24-25, 47; William G. Skinner, "Chinese Peasants and the Closed Community: An Open and Shut Case," *Comparative Studies in Society and History*, 13 (1971), 270-81; see also J. Jollivet and H. Mendras, eds., *Les collectivités rurales françaises* (Paris, 1971), I, 27-30. They adopt such a concept implicitly in discussing French rural society in the 1970s.

[50] Fox, *History*, pp. 37-45. Fox assumes that French towns in the interior were not engaged in substantial commerce during the early nineteenth century, and he admits being unable to explain why they increased in size during that period (ibid., pp. 113-14).

[51] For an eighteenth-century example of this, see Gabriel Bouchard, *Le village immobile* (Paris, 1972), pp. 125-206.

Between the Old Régime and the Second Republic, the spread of rural industry and cash-crop agriculture brought local marketing systems into regional circuits of exchange and rural populations into closer contact with townspeople. Neither trend occurred everywhere—peasant isolation persisted in rugged highland areas until the end of the nineteenth century—but on balance, the July Monarchy witnessed a substantial increase of market activity and proto-urban development in the countryside. More than ever before, small towns were channeling local produce into large-scale markets; bourgs and villages were participating in urban commercial networks; and specialized craftsmen were producing goods and services for local and extralocal consumption. Through the quickening pace of exchange between cities, towns, bourgs, and villages, the French countryside was entering Rokkan's historical phase of incipient mobilization. Its basic pattern of political mobilization would be influenced by economic growth and its social concomitant of urban-rural interaction.

An industrial and agricultural inquiry in 1848 called attention to the importance of exports in shaping the economic welfare of craftsmen, peasant producers, and agricultural laborers in many predominantly rural districts of the nation.[52] Especially noteworthy are the returns from cantons that contributed substantial manpower (over 200 men) to the insurrection. These returns, which include forty-eight cantons in the southeast, eight in the southwest, and four in the center, can also be compared with returns from a small sample of cantons drawn from calm areas of northern, western, and central France.[53] They confirm

[52] For the sorts of information provided by this Enquête, see P. Guillaume, "La situation économique et sociale du département de la Loire d'après l'enquête sur le travail . . . du mai 1848," *CNSS*, 86 (1961), 429-50; and J. Vidalenc, "La situation économique et sociale des Basses-Alpes en 1848," *Société d'histoire de la Révolution de 1848, Etudes*, 16 (1954), 121-59. For variations in its quality, which J. P.s sometimes completed alone and sometimes in consultation with "cantonal commissions" of employers and workers, see Agulhon, "L'enquête du Comité du travail de l'Assemblée constituante (1848)," *Annales du Midi*, 70 (1958), 73-85.

[53] Sample of rebel cantons based on ten cantons in the Basses-Alpes (Barcellonette, Forcalquier, Manosque, Les Mées, Peyruis, Reillanne, Riez, Sisteron, Valensole, Volonne); nine cantons in the Gard (Alais, Anduze, Lasalle, Lédignan, Lussan, Quissac, St. Ambroix, St. Chaptes, Vézénobres); eight cantons in the Hérault (Agde, Bédarieux, Béziers, Capestang, Murviel, Pézénas, Roujan, Servian); eight cantons in the Var (Barjols, Brignoles, Cuers, Grimaud, Le Luc, Rians, Roquebrussanne, Salernes); eight cantons in the Gers (Auch, Condom, Fleurance, Jegun, Masseube, Mirande, Montesquiou, Vic-Fezensac); six cantons in the Drôme (Bourdeaux, Chabeuil, Crest, Dieulefit, Loriol, Montélimar); four cantons in the Vaucluse (Apt, Bonnieux, Gordes, Pertuis); two cantons in the Ardèche (Chomérac, Vallon); one canton in the Jura (Poligny); one canton in the Yonne (St. Sauveur). Sample of nonrebel cantons based on two cantons each (chosen randomly) in the Ain (Bourg, Trévoux), the Aisne (Braine, Vermand), the Cantal (Laroquebroc, Ruines), the Corrèze (Larche, Trignac), the Eure-et-Loir (Brou,

that market involvement rather than economic autarchy characterized many districts of the nation at mid-century: in four-fifths of the rebel and nonrebel cantons alike, Justices of the Peace (J. P.s) reported that agricultural commodities or craft goods were being produced for export. Where the rebel cantons of the south differed from the quiescent cantons of the north was in the composition of their export sector. One-third of them produced silk thread (15/59 cases) rather than wool cloth (5 cases), another third sold distilled wine, or *eau de vie* (14 cases), and only one rebel canton exported enough grain and livestock to merit commentary in the J. P.'s report. By contrast, two-fifths of the nonrebel cantons in the sample (16/39 cases) marketed wool, linen, or cotton textiles, and nearly as many of them (15 cases) exported grain or livestock, while none of their J. P.s mentioned raw silk and only one referred to *eau de vie*.

The cash crops typical of rebel districts made rural producers sensitive to price fluctuations in export markets, and their J. P.s emphasized the depressing effect of low prices or poor sales on the local economy. Such complaints were universal in rebel cantons that exported raw silk or spirits (39 cases), and J. P.s often noted the relationship between low prices and contracting demand for labor in local markets. As the J. P. at Servian (Hérault) wrote, "When wine [for *eau de vie*] is selling at a good price, agricultural work is abundant, and when landowners are prosperous, other industries [local crafts] don't suffer." Similarly, the J. P. at Manosque (Basses-Alpes) explained, "Prosperity in agriculture depends on the price of crops, that of silk and tanning depends on commerce, and that of construction depends on good harvests and crop sales."[54] Two-fifths of the J. P.s from rebel cantons in the sample also blamed inadequate credit facilities for commercial difficulties and called for state banks or other forms of government credit to local producers.[55] In comparison with calm areas of the nation, J. P.s in rebel

La Ferté-Vidame), the Finistère (Bruc, St. Thégonne), the Maine-et-Loire (Cholet, Saumur), the Oise (Méru, Ressons), the Sarthe (Le Mans, Sablé), the Seine-et-Marne (Crécy, Moret), the Vendée (Noirmoutier, St. Falgent), the Vienne (Charroux, La Villedieu), the Haute-Vienne (Limoges, St. Laurent-sur-Gorre), and the Vosges (Châtel, Dorney); and one canton each (chosen randomly) in the Aube (Lusigny), the Calvados (Mézidon), the Charentes (Cognac), the Côtes-du-Nord (Broons), the Deux-Sèvres (Niort), the Eure (Etrepagny), the Indre-et-Loire (Châteaurenault), the Morbihan (Ploërmel), the Moselle (Sarralbe), the Pas-de-Calais (Parcq), and the Somme (St. Valery). Manuscript returns in AN, C 944-69.

[54] J. P. Servian, AN, C 954 (Hérault); J. P. Manosque, AN, C 944 (Basses-. Alpes).

[55] Only 28% of the J. P.s in the sample of nonrebel cantons called for credit reform.

districts were less concerned about industrial competition and less pessimistic about the basic living conditions of workers and peasants.[56] They reflected the outlook of rural populations whose cash crops seemed less exposed to long-term economic trends than the textile goods that proto-industrial workers in northern France were trying to market in competition with factory workers. In such districts, profits and agricultural wages seemed adequate in times of commercial prosperity. Indeed, field hands in southeastern France typically earned higher cash wages than their counterparts in other areas of the nation, although payments in kind reduced the impact of such regional variations.[57]

If the countryside of northern France was heavily engaged in industrial production for export, villages in the Midi were no less actively involved in cash-crop agriculture. A few small towns and bourgs in rebel districts did have some factory industry, including Dieulefit in the Drôme, and Bédarieux in the Hérault. Yet the industrial work force in rebel districts was usually much smaller than in calm areas of the north.[58] Craft specialists and their apprentices producing for local and regional markets were also less numerous in the south, but the differences in this regard were not so great.[59] Agricultural exports encouraged craft specialization in many rebel communes, whose social structure approached the ideal type of a "proto-urban" community. The marketing activities and differentiated labor force of such communes gave them the appearance of being urbanized villages or agricultural towns. Ranging in size from several hundred to several thousand inhabitants, they exercised some of the functions that a later age would attribute to cities: marketing and administration, craft production, shops and services. It is noteworthy that in a sample of 304 communes where armed mobilizations occurred, over one-quarter were subprefectures or cantonal seats, around half produced artisanal goods for export, three-

[56] While 74% of the J. P.s in the sample of nonrebel cantons complained about industrial competition, only 32% of those in the sample of rebel cantons did so. Similarly, 36% of the former and only 22% of the latter described the housing, food or clothing of workers as inadequate, mediocre or poor.

[57] In both samples, the median estimate of the annual income required by a family of four was 600 francs, but rebel cantons in southeastern France reported an average agricultural wage for male day laborers of 1.60 francs (summer), as compared with an average of 1.30 francs reported in nonrebel cantons.

[58] J. P.s estimated the size of the industrial and proto-industrial work force (concentrations of at least 100 workers in particular trades) in nineteen nonrebel cantons and twenty-eight rebel cantons. While the average of the former cases was 1,750, it was only 660 in the latter cases (medians of 1,100 and 538, respectively).

[59] Estimates from sixteen nonrebel cantons and twenty-four rebel cantons: average of 550 in the former cases and 440 in the latter (medians of 500 and 300, respectively).

fifths held agricultural markets or fairs, but only eight had over 10,000 inhabitants.[60] Such small towns and bourgs were neither burgeoning cities nor declining villages: they were proto-urban communities, midway between the rural isolation of the past and the urban-industrial society of the future.

[60] Sample drawn from 1/20 of the persons sentenced by the Mixed Commissions in 1852, as noted in Chapter One, n. 23.

· 3 ·

THE SOCIAL GEOGRAPHY OF REVOLT

Most rebel districts were actively engaged in market production, but their local economies varied widely from area to area, depending on natural resources and industrial aptitudes. In southeastern France, for example, silk, was the specialty of insurgent districts in the Drôme, the Ardèche, and the Gard; wine, olive oil, and cork stimulated exchange relationships in the insurrectionary zone of the Var; and *eau de vie* and wool textiles dominated the rebel economy in the Hérault. To the southwest, insurgent communities of the Gers tended to specialize in the production of wine and *eau de vie*, while those in the Lot-et-Garonne were more engaged in craft production for export. Finally, in central France rural participation in the revolt was most extensive where lumber and related products were being exported. The economic organization of these various regions needs to be explored more fully in order to confirm that market expansion was everywhere a significant force.

Nearly every rebel commune in the Drôme, the Ardèche, and the Gard was producing raw silk during the Second Republic as a cash crop.[1] Although mulberry trees and silkworms had been introduced to this region of France as early as the sixteenth century, the golden age of the rural silk industry was the first half of the nineteenth century. With its brief but intensive demand for labor—essentially in the month of May—silk raising could be well integrated into the economic cycle of small peasant households. A veritable "democratization" of this crop took place during the July Monarchy, as rising prices on the Lyon silk market stimulated an ever-larger volume of production. In the Gard, for example, the numbers of mulberry trees increased from 2.8 million in 1830 to 3.3 million in 1843 and over 4 million in 1853; in the Drôme the value of the harvest increased from 2.8 million francs in 1811 to 6 million francs in 1834, and around 15 million francs a year

[1] For the distribution of the silk industry in the Drôme, see Pierre Léon, *La naissance de la grande industrie en Dauphiné (fin du dix-septième siècle-1869)*, 2 vols. (Paris, 1954), II, 588-95; and Vigier, *La Seconde République*, I, 56-63, 69. For the Ardèche, see E. Reynier, *La Seconde République dans l'Ardèche* (Privas, 1948), pp. 13-14, 103; and Pierre Bozon, *La vie rurale en Vivarais* (Valence, 1961), pp. 130-37. For the Gard, see Raymond Dugrand, *Villes et campagnes en Bas-Languedoc* (Paris, 1963), pp. 388-90; and F. Rivoire, *Statistique du département du Gard*, 2 vols. (Nîmes, 1842), II, 20-21. See also the cantonal reports of the *Enquête* of 1848, AN, C 945 (Ardèche), 951 (Drôme), 953 (Gard).

in the 1840s.[2] Furthermore, peasant women and children could earn additional cash by working in the silk-spinning workshops and silk-twisting factories, which spread to all the major centers of production. Such small manufacturing firms were located in many of the bourgs that participated in the revolt. Thus, around one-quarter of the insurgent communes in the Drôme had silk-spinning or silk-twisting factories in 1849; this rebel zone employed 24 percent of the 7,300 silk workers in the department, with only 12 percent of the population.[3] Mulberry leaves and silkworms were at the basis of a rich and expanding industry, sensitive to price fluctuations in distant markets.

Silk was by no means the only crop produced in these districts of southern France, although contemporaries were most impressed by its broad diffusion of cash into the countryside. Each peasant family continued to grow as much of its own food as possible, and those who produced a surplus of grain and livestock sold it in local and regional markets. The social geographer Daniel Faucher has shown that in the plains and foothills of the Drôme, grain farmers succeeded in carrying out an "economic revolution" between 1800 and 1850. By planting the fallow fields with fodder crops, they increased fivefold or more their herds of horses, mules, and cattle, shifted completely from rye to wheat cultivation, and increased their grain output by 50 percent or more. Because these agricultural innovations were labor-intensive, the agricultural labor market also expanded, benefiting small peasant families. Many rebel communes in the Drôme were located in the southern portion of the region analyzed by Faucher, and their grain farmers participated in this general agricultural advance. Rural prosperity had a more solid foundation than silk alone.[4]

Wine was another cash crop in many communes of this zone, and lumber, pottery, building stone and tiles earned cash income for some localities. Diversified resources stimulated local exchange relationships, and a dense network of rotating fairs and weekly markets brought the rural populations into close contact with small towns such as Crest and Dieulefit in the Drôme, or Alais and Anduze in the Gard. The canton of Dieulefit provides an interesting example of how great an interdependency the combination of an export sector—"commerce"—and local exchange—"trade"—could create between these small towns and

---

[2] Dugrand, *Villes*, p. 389; Vigier, *La Seconde République*, I, 31; Daniel Faucher, *Plaines et bassins du Rhône moyen entre Bas-Dauphiné et Provence* (Paris, 1927), pp. 349-59, 456; and Raoul Blanchard, *Les Alpes occidentales*, tome IV, *Les préalpes françaises du sud* (Grenoble, 1945), pp. 358-60.

[3] "Statistique par communes de l'industrie de la soie, 1849," ADD, 56M 6.

[4] Faucher, *Plaines*, pp. 456-81. See also Blanchard, *Les préalpes*, 361-63, for similar agricultural improvements in rebel zones further east (Bourdeaux, Dieulefit).

their rural hinterlands. The commerce of Dieulefit was based on wool cloth, silk thread, and pottery. Like the town of Crest to the north, Dieulefit had once been the center of a putting-out industry for the spinning and weaving of wool. Many rebel communes in 1851 had worked up wool for merchant-manufacturers of these two towns back in the eighteenth century.[5] This putting-out system had been progressively abandoned, however, as the rural populations turned toward silk, improved their agricultural productivity, and ceased to be a reservoir of low-wage labor. By the 1830s nearly all the wool production had been concentrated at Dieulefit and Crest, and one manufacturing family, the Morins, dominated the industry at Dieulefit with their large-scale factory production.[6] In the meanwhile, silk spinning and twisting had been expanding to the point where by 1848 this industry employed the largest work force in the canton. As for pottery, it was produced for export in dozens of small workshops in the countryside, where excellent potter's clay and abundant wood fuel were available. According to the J. P. in 1848, the 300 workers in this artisanal industry were the most prosperous in the canton.[7]

How did this tripartite export sector benefit local peasants and craftsmen? If we consider a typical farm in the region, with a few fields planted in grain, vines, and mulberry trees, and with woods nearby, we find that some crops could be sold as raw materials for industry—silk and wood—while others—grain or wine—supplied local consumers. The farmer might also have a son working in a pottery kiln or a daughter in a textile factory, especially if the arable lands fell short of the family's needs. Or he might hire them out as farm-servants to larger farmers in the neighborhood. Extra cash would also be available at harvest time, when the commercial farmers took on additional labor. As for the local craftsmen—shoemakers, tailors, masons, etc.—their work depended on the general prosperity of the area. The more income was generated by exports and diffused throughout the town and countryside, the more buildings were constructed, the more clothing purchased, and so on. In sum, commerce was the essential support of trade within the canton of Dieulefit. This interdependency became especially obvious whenever the industries were depressed. As the J. P. reported

[5] Léon, *Naissance*, II, 28-31; Faucher, *Plaines*, pp. 429-36; Blanchard, *Les préalpes*, 409-13.

[6] Blanchard and Faucher agree that this concentration of wool textile production in the towns did not undermine peasant living standards, primarily because silk replaced wool as a source of cash in the villages. Blanchard, *Les préalpes*, p. 413; Faucher, *Plaines*, pp. 559-62.

[7] J. P. Dieulefit, AN, C 951 (silk, 700 workers; wool, 400 workers; pottery, 300 workers).

in 1848, "The importance of existing industries is such that when there is unemployment, for whatever reason, a general malaise is felt throughout the canton."[8] Few districts of the nation were more actively engaged in market relationships than the town and hinterland of Dieulefit; and few contributed as much manpower to the insurrection.

Further to the southeast were the small towns, bourgs, and villages of Provence. In this large zone of insurgency (the eastern Vaucluse, the southern Basses-Alpes, the central and northwestern Var), economic activities were even more diversified than in typical silk-producing districts of the Drôme or the Gard. Cash crops included olive oil and fruit as well as wheat, wine, livestock, and some silk; and proto-industrial exports ranged from bottle-cork, tanned hides, and shoes, to pottery, porcelain ware, and silk thread. Even in the eighteenth century the Provençal economy had been oriented toward Marseille, and with the rapid growth of that city and of Toulon (Var) during the July Monarchy, urban markets widened for olive oil, wine, livestock, fruit, and manufactured products. Exports to northern Italy and Africa were also channeled through these ports, and wheat shipments were imported to cover local grain deficits. The rhythm of agricultural and proto-industrial output in Provence was influenced to an increasing extent by far-flung commercial networks of exchange.[9]

All the leading centers of resistance to the coup d'état in Provence were engaged in cash-crop agriculture or craft production for expanding markets. In the Var and the Vaucluse, especially large-scale mobilizations took place in towns and bourgs with a significant proto-industrial sector. At La Garde Freinet, for example, a veritable industrial boom had transformed the social structure during the July Monarchy. Hundreds of peasants had been recruited as skilled workers in bottle-cork workshops, and they had acquired the high economic expectations and labor militancy of a prosperous industrial work force. Industrial expansion on a smaller scale also characterized Barjols, whose tanning industry had grown from 10 enterprises employing 100 workers in 1830 to fifteen enterprises employing 200 workers in 1848. Le Luc, another center of insurgency in the Var, was one of the most prosperous small towns of Provence during the same period. Among its exports were olive oil and chestnuts, tanned hides, lumber, distilled wine, bottle-cork,

[8] Ibid.
[9] On the economy of Provence, see Maurice Agulhon, *La vie sociale en Provence intérieure au lendemain de la Révolution* (Paris, 1970), pp. 13-50, 293-302; Agulhon, *La République au village*, pp. 28-32; P. Seignour, *La vie économique du Vaucluse de 1815 à 1848* (Aix-en-Provence, 1957); Pierre George, *La région du Bas-Rhône* (Paris, 1935); Blanchard, *Les préalpes*; and Vigier, *La Seconde République*, I, 44-70.

hats, and rope. The rebel subprefecture of Brignoles also had a significant industrial sector, in addition to its major commerce in wine and spirits. In 1848 the canton employed 200 workers as tanners, 100 as hat makers, 130 as sandal makers (for export), and 90 as silk spinners; another 450 craftsmen worked for local markets.[10] In the Vaucluse, the rebel subprefecture of Apt was a small industrial center. According to a contemporary account, it had "very active relations with Marseille." Candles and fruit preserves were manufactured "on a very large scale," its porcelains were "justly famous," and its hat making, wool preparation, and silk spinning employed "a large number of hands."[11] The J. P. in 1848 confirmed this industrial vitality: "The workshops of porcelain and pottery, silk and iron ore offer many resources for the canton of Apt; a crowd of workers are employed in them, and a large number of families depend on these various industries."[12]

Agricultural bourgs in the Var also participated in the insurrection and those in the Basses-Alpes played an even more dynamic role as rebel centers. This might seem paradoxical, because the Basses-Alpes had the reputation in the nineteenth century of being backward and impoverished. Aggregate measures of landed revenue would appear to confirm the meager resources of this largely mountainous department: in 1851 its estimated taxable net revenue per hectare of cultivated land was only 12 francs, as compared with a national average of 38 francs.[13] In fact, the department was divided into a low-density, subsistence-oriented zone in the Alpine cantons of the north and east, and a relatively high-density, cash-crop zone in the southwest, where the valley of the Durance, the hillsides of Forcalquier, and the plateau of Valensole were exposed to a Mediterranean climate. The irrigated sections of this latter zone were very fertile, and it is noteworthy that "superior quality" land in the department had an estimated taxable net revenue of 180 francs per hectare, as compared with a national average of 120 francs. Furthermore, grain farmers in the southwest had carried out an "agricultural revolution" in the early nineteenth cen-

[10] Agulhon, *La République*, pp. 31, 126-45, 380-81; Jacques Girault, "A la recherche du 'Var Rouge,' de l'insurrection de décembre 1851 au Front Populaire," *Cahiers de la Méditerranée*, 7 (Dec. 1973), 4-5; J. P.s Le Luc and Brignoles, AN, C 967 A (Var).

[11] *Annuaire indicateur du Vaucluse*, 1848, p. 69.

[12] J. P. Apt, AN, C 967 B (Vaucluse).

[13] Joseph Madier, *L'évolution du revenue net des propriétés non-bâties* (Paris, 1909), table for the years 1851-53, pp. 274-91. See also Vandal, "L'enquête de 1851 sur les revenus territoriaux de la France continentale," *Bulletin de statistique et de législation comparée*, 6 (Paris, 1879), 110-31, and Philippe Vigier, *Essai sur la répartition de la propriété foncière dans la région alpine son évolution des origines du cadastre à la fin du Second Empire* (Paris, 1963), pp. 141-55.

tury, along the same lines as those in the Rhône river valley: they had planted the fallow with artificial grasses, and they had replaced rye with wheat on the increasingly productive soil.[14]

It was in these relatively prosperous farming communities of the southwest rather than in the poorer villages of the mountains that the revolt was centered. This geographical contrast is shown clearly by Table 3.1. Communes noted for agricultural wealth, and those produc-

TABLE 3.1

Farming Wealth, Cash Crops, and Revolt (Basses-Alpes)

	Heavy Participation in the Revolt	Participation in the Revolt	No Revolt
Farming Wealth			
Commune with "rich" agriculture, "rich" soil, or "wealthy" inhabitants	23	46	23
Commune with poor agriculture, soil, or inhabitants	2	11	38
Cash crops			
Commune producing silk, olives, or good wine	31	31	10
Commune not producing silk or olives; only "mediocre" wine, if any	3	30	82

SOURCE: *Annuaire du département des Basses-Alpes, 1851* (Digne, 1851); Register of MC Basses-Alpes, AN, BB[30] 398.

ing labor-intensive cash crops such as silk, olives, or wine for export, were much more heavily involved in resistance to the coup d'état than other localities in the department.

The largest rebel force in the Basses-Alpes came from Manosque, a town of around 6,000 inhabitants in the valley of the Durance. Manosque had long been acknowledged as the terrestrial paradise of the department. The olive trees covering its hillsides produced an oil of excellent quality; the vineyards in its plain yielded abundant quantities

[14] Blanchard, *Les préalpes*, pp. 848-50.

of wine; irrigated portions grew vegetables and hand-sown grasses; and almond trees, walnut trees, and mulberry trees dotted the landscape. With all its agricultural resources, a majority of the labor force at Manosque were cultivators. In recent years, however, its commercial role had been expanding. Back in the eighteenth century it held only two fairs and a "mediocre" weekly market. By 1837 it had ten fairs a year and two weekly markets.[15] At the fairs, which were "very well attended" by consumers from the area and from surrounding regions, sales included the following commodities: "wool cloth, linens, colored fabrics, hardware, knives, ironware, jewelry, pottery, hats, leatherware, books; wheat and other grains, forage; sheep and lambs for fattening and for butchering; pigs, cattle for ploughing and for butchering; horses and mules, game, fowl, sausages, vegetables, herbs, and fruit."[16] In 1851 Manosque had twenty wholesale merchants and manufacturers, while the subprefecture of Forcalquier, its ancient rival, had only six, and the prefecture of Digne had only thirteen.[17] The political leadership exercised by Manosque throughout the Second Republic and during the insurrection was founded on its economic primacy in the department.

Proto-industrial and commercial expansion also had a favorable impact on the agricultural labor market, encouraging mobility aspirations within the peasantry. The J. P. at Le Luc noted in 1848 that many agricultural workers were quitting farming to undertake an industrial profession; once launched in their new careers, they were reluctant to return to the fields.[18] At Brignoles, the J. P. blamed the social pretensions of wealthy peasants for the growing labor shortage in agriculture. "A ridiculous pride, a mistaken self-esteem, are leading some of our cultivators to desert the fields in order to become workers in the towns. It isn't misery which pushes them toward this change, because we note that those leaving the land are the sons of our wealthiest farmers (*ménagers*). It is because of their contempt for the status of agriculture that they want to become artisans."[19] At Apt the J. P. expressed concern about a similar labor shortage and blamed socially ambitious fathers for the tendency of their sons to abandon farming, learn a craft, and emigrate to "large towns."[20] As for Manosque, there the main beneficiaries of expansion were the agricultural laborers themselves, whom the cantonal commission of 1848 regarded as more prosperous

[15] Blanchard, *Les préalpes*, pp. 878-79; municipal correspondence, 1830-48, AD B-A, 8M 59 (Manosque).

[16] Table of fairs, 1837, Manosque, AD B-A, 8M 59.

[17] *Annuaire du département des Basses-Alpes*, 1851.

[18] J. P. Le Luc, AN, C 967A.   [19] J. P. Brignoles, AN, C 967A.

[20] J. P. Apt, AN, C 967B.

than the artisans. One member wrote that agricultural wages had risen in the past few years to 2 francs a day in the summer, and 1.50 francs a day in the winter: "They increased after large projects were undertaken in the area, such as canals, factories, convents, public buildings, and the bridge over the Durance." The laborers naturally insisted on maintaining this higher wage, although the landlords were now the only employers of the "working class" in the area.[21]

Not all Provençal communities benefited equally from economic expansion. As noted in Chapter Two, some villages of the Var joined the revolt in hope of regaining traditional rights of usage to private forests. Others hoped to obtain a portion of the communal lands, an aspiration also reported from several insurgent districts of the Basses-Alpes.[22] A few bourgs were also beginning to suffer from industrial and commercial competition, especially those on the plateau of Valensole. Thus, only two pottery firms, employing nineteen workers, remained in the once-famous pottery bourg of Moustiers; and local merchants at the small town of Riez were threatened by "numerous bankruptcies," caused by "the concentration of commerce" and the technological backwardness of the local tanneries.[23] Where communities of marginal peasants or declining artisans did join the revolt, however, they were generally inside the socioeconomic orbits of more dynamic towns and bourgs. Regional trade was important for most rebel communes, as indicated by the fact that twenty of those in the Basses-Alpes alone requested the creation of additional local fairs in 1850.[24] Furthermore, regional labor markets were created by flows of seasonal migrants from the highland villages to the richer bourgs in the valleys. The juxtaposition of diverse economic aptitudes within the lands of Provence permitted the export-oriented communities to draw their less fortunate neighbors into significant exchange relationships.

To the west of Marseille the Mediterranean coastline passes the empty salt marshes of the Camargue and then sweeps in a southerly arc toward the Spanish frontier, passing the departments of the Gard, the Hérault, the Aude, and the Pyrénées-Orientales. The fertile plains of these departments were generally planted in grain during the eighteenth century, while their foothills further inland were covered with vineyards. The region had always been rich and densely populated in

[21] Dossier Manosque, AN, C 944 (Basses-Alpes).

[22] Agulhon, *La République*, p. 93, citing eleven cantons in the Var; AN, C 944 Basses-Alpes, cantons of Manosque and Riez.

[23] J. P.s Moustiers and Riez, AN, C 944.

[24] Report of Prefect, Basses-Alpes, to *Conseil général*, 1850, *Annuaire*, pp. 27-28. A total of thirty-four communes requested fairs that year, most of them located in the southwestern part of the department.

comparison with the mountainous interior of the Massif Central, and substantial towns such as Montpellier, Narbonne, and Peripignan had drawn wealth from the soil for generations. During the nineteenth century their urban exploitation of the land intensified, as wine markets expanded, and as wheat farms in the lowlands were converted into vineyards. For lower Languedoc as a whole, the period of most dramatic economic growth was the Second Empire, when the railroad permitted its high-yield, low-quality wines to undersell competitors in the Paris market. Earlier in the century, however, producers had reached distant markets by converting the cheap wine into *eau de vie*. This distilling industry, aided by technological progress, was slowly expanding during the July Monarchy, especially in the Hérault, where vineyards increased in area from 96,000 hectares in 1820 to 114,000 hectares in 1850.[25] Its most important center of production was the town of Béziers, whose merchants had the special advantage of being located on the Canal du Midi, permitting easy access to Bordeaux and the Atlantic trade. No town in these coastal departments was more commercially oriented; none had a closer trade relationship with nearby rural communities; and none reacted with such force against the coup d'état. From Béziers and its rural hinterland came the most massive uprising in lower Languedoc.

The economic power of the *eau de vie* industry in rebel districts around Béziers can be seen by examining their estimated revenues from *eau de vie*, wine, and wheat in 1852, *before* the expansion of the Second Empire. The seven wine-growing cantons of the *arrondissement* that were involved in the revolt earned around 10.2 million francs in 1852 from the sale of *eau de vie* and only 1.2 million francs from the export of wine; they also produced 2.9 million francs worth of wheat for local markets, but they had to pay an additional 2.2 million francs for wheat imports. The price of *eau de vie* regulated the incomes of all social classes—landlords (3,400) drawing profits from their vineyards, agricultural laborers (nearly 12,000) earning wages in the fields, and artisans dependent on local demand for their skills. The vineyard workers comprised a majority of the labor force in the bourgs and villages. They were four times as numerous as owner-farmers, and over ten times as numerous as tenant farmers.[26] According to the cantonal commissions in 1848, these wage earners were generally prosperous, espe-

[25] Dugrand, *Villes et campagnes*, p. 357; Loubère, "The Emergence of the Extreme Left in Lower Languedoc," pp. 1019-27; and J. Harvey Smith, "Work Routine and Social Structure in a French Village: Cruzy in the Nineteenth Century," *Journal of Interdisciplinary History*, 5 (1975), 358-64.
[26] Calculations based on quantities, prices, and labor-force data given in the quintennial agricultural and industrial *statistique*, 1852, by canton, ADH, M 10.

cially because they often owned a little land. Their living conditions were "fairly comfortable" at Béziers; they were "well fed and well clothed" at Servian; and the J. P. at Roujan reported that they had even been indulging in the luxury of drinking coffee for the past several years.[27] As for the artisans, they were more exposed to seasonal unemployment in some communities, but they often owned some land, and they could work for wages in the fields, too. No less than the agricultural laborers, their economic position depended on the vigor of the export sector. Around Béziers commerce determined the health of the entire economy.

Along the southern rim of the Massif Central were a string of small textile towns. While those in the Gard and the eastern Hérault had largely converted from wool fabrics to silk thread and silk stockings by the July Monarchy, those in the western Hérault and the Tarn continued to specialize in the production of wool cloth. The most technologically advanced wool towns were Lodève (Hérault) and Mazamet (Tarn), where large factories had been introduced; Bédarieux (Hérault) was also relatively progressive in its techniques of production, though weaving workshops were not yet mechanized. By contrast, peasants in some of the more isolated bourgs and villages of this zone continued to spin and weave with outmoded techniques for urban merchants. This juxtaposition of technological progress in the towns and backwardness in the countryside placed the rural textile workers in an increasingly difficult competitive position. Who rebelled in 1851, the "deindustrializing" villages or the modernizing towns? It was the textile towns of Bédarieux, St. Chinian, and Mazamet that resisted in arms the coup d'état, with little or no rural support. Industrial expansion coincided with militancy, rural decline with passivity.[28]

The most serious insurrection in this zone occurred at Bédarieux (Hérault), a town whose population had grown from under 6,000 to nearly 10,000 during the July Monarchy. A local surplus of births over deaths accounted for some of this increase, but the town attracted a strong flow of migrants to work in its expanding industries: its net rate of immigration was 6.3% from 1836 to 1840, 3.5% from 1841 to 1845, and 4.0% from 1846 to 1850.[29] In addition to the textile firms, which employed over 1,000 workers, Bédarieux had tanneries and a

[27] J. P. Roujan, AN, C 954 (Hérault).
[28] Concerning this textile sector, see Dugrand, *Villes et campagnes*, pp. 357-91; and André Armengaud, *Les populations de l'Est-Aquitain au début de l'époque contemporaine (1848-1871)* (Paris, 1961), pp. 230-42.
[29] Calculations based on the birth and death registers for the years 1836-50, and the population in 1836, 1841, 1846, 1851. Municipal Archives, Bédarieux.

large craft sector producing for local markets. Its labor force was generally assured of continuous employment, and even during the economic crisis of 1848 industrial output in the canton was worth 25 million francs.[30] Where economic conflicts did exist, they revealed the determination of upwardly mobile workers to defend their interests. This was especially true in that segment of the textile industry whose marketing was organized along capitalist lines, but whose system of production was still artisanal—the weaving of cloth. Strikes had erupted in the 1840s when the merchants tried to reduce the piece rates they were willing to pay the handloom weavers. Like the *canuts* (silk-weavers) at Lyon, the weavers at Bédarieux possessed some economic independence and considerable pride in their work.[31] They shared the mobility aspirations of other artisans in the town, with whom they intermarried frequently.[32] Rising literacy rates and sharply falling birth rates in the 1840s are proof that the traditional mentality of first-generation emigrants from the villages was changing rapidly.[33] On the eve of the Second Republic, the town of Bédarieux seemed to be an economic success, and its population, often just recently removed from the land, was determined to reap the benefits of progress.

As for those who had stayed behind in the countryside, they rarely participated in the political struggles of the Second Republic. The insurrection at Bédarieux did draw some support from workers at the nearby coal mines of Graissessac, but only one small band of textile workers marched to the aid of the town.[34] The bulk of the rural population in this region remained calm. Isolation, illiteracy, and perhaps a sense of rivalry with their higher-paid urban counterparts were ef-

[30] J. P. Bédarieux, AN, C 954 (Hérault). On the economic history of Bédarieux in the nineteenth century see Roger Allaire, *Histoire de la ville de Bédarieux* (Bédarieux, 1911).

[31] Concerning these strikes, see ADH, 39M 125; for comparisons with Lyon, see Robert Bezucha, "The 'Preindustrial' Worker Movement: The Canuts of Lyon," in Bezucha, ed., *Modern European Social History* (Lexington, Mass., 1972), pp. 93-123.

[32] Jo Burr Margadant, "The Sociology of an Insurrection: A Study of Social Mobility in Bédarieux 1846-1849," unpublished paper, UC Davis, 1972.

[33] Based on five-year moving averages, the birth rate at Bédarieux fell from 37.3 in 1841 to 31.3 in 1846 and 26.1 in 1851; the death rate fell from 32.5 to 28.8 and 26.0 during the same period; the marriage rate remained fairly constant (7.3, 7.0, 7.5).

[34] These workers were employed in a factory at Latour-d'Orb, near town; a band of rural spinners, weavers, and agricultural laborers at Colombières (valley of the Orb) did imitate the townsmen by proclaiming a local revolutionary commission, but they did not march. There was also some agitation at two textile bourgs near St. Pons, but no revolt. Republican conspiratorial organizations were just beginning to penetrate this isolated region in the fall of 1851. See the interrogations of suspects at Colombières, ADH, 39M 214.

fective obstacles to the radicalization of rural spinners and weavers. Nor was this pattern of conservatism among rural textile workers peculiar to the Hérault. In the Tarn, rebels at Mazamet failed to obtain any rural support, and throughout central and northern France rural weavers seem to have been immune to the radical appeals of textile workers in cities such as Lyon, Rouen, and Troyes.[35] It may well be that urban/rural competition in the textile labor market was a fundamental cause of conservatism in the French countryside during the Second Republic. The more the rural workers were experiencing industrial competition, the less willing they were to join a left-wing movement inspired by their urban competitors.

To the southwest of the Massif Central were the grain farms of the Toulousain, a region dominated by the city of Toulouse and oriented toward wheat production for distant markets. Through a rigid labor system of sharecroppers, annual farm servants, seasonal harvesters, and occasional laborers, the landlords in this region earned profits from their grain commerce, but the rural populations remained poor and isolated. Conditions in the labor market may have even deteriorated during the first half of the nineteenth century; only after 1850 did population pressure diminish appreciably, undermining the labor-intensive system of estate agriculture, and broadening the social base of landownership. Around Toulouse, where overpopulation seems to have been an acute social problem and a cause of agricultural stagnation, the coup d'état was greeted with utter calm.[36]

Further west, in the hill country of central Gascony, a series of small towns and bourgs stretched from north to south, just beyond the market radius of Toulouse. Several of them, including Condom, Vic-Fezensac, and Jegun specialized in the production of *eau de vie*, which they shipped through the entrepôt of Lavardac (Lot-et-Garonne) to the Garonne river and the port of Bordeaux. Several others, including Auch, Fleurance, and Mirande, had a more diversified, less productive agricultural hinterland whose traditional "polyculture" included wine,

[35] On the Tarn, see André Armengaud, "A propos d'un centenaire: Coup d'état et plebiscite dans le département du Tarn," *Annales du Midi*, 64 (1952), 41-49. There was agitation at one large textile bourg near Mazamet, but no revolt. For the conservatism of silk weavers near Lyon, see Garrier, *Paysans du Beaujolais*, 1, 322-28. For the clash between rural and urban textile workers in the Aube (Troyes), see Chevalier, "Fondements économiques et sociaux," 268-70.

[36] The two basic studies of this region around Toulouse are Armengaud, *Les populations de l'Est-Aquitain*; and Roger Brunet, *Les campagnes toulousaines* (Toulouse, 1965). Brunet includes the Gers in his analysis, but his evidence of overpopulation and deteriorating labor conditions is drawn from the eastern districts of that department, which were oriented toward Toulouse and calm in 1851. See Brunet, *Campagnes*, pp. 363-83.

grain, and livestock. Market relationships in central Gascony were active, and fairs grew in importance throughout the nineteenth century. Property was more widely distributed here than in districts further east, although a rigid social hierarchy, an unstable climate, and poor interregional transportation held back agricultural progress to the west of Auch and around Mirande.[37]

The broader diffusion of property encouraged peasant birth control, and the gradual expansion of commerce created mobility opportunities for peasants who acquired a craft skill and emigrated to the urban centers. The artisans in the bourgs earned consistently better wages and had higher economic expectations than the agricultural workers in the countryside. As a result, this region was experiencing significant demographic and social change in the 1840s. The rural communes were beginning to lose population, creating complaints among some landowners of a labor shortage, while the towns and bourgs were gaining artisans, causing complaints this time of a labor surplus. Unlike eastern Gascony, where artisans and agricultural workers were locked into the same authoritarian labor system, central Gascony had a superabundance of independent craftsmen, many of them recent migrants from the countryside. The J. P.s at Auch, Condom, Fleurance, and Jegun all complained that too many peasants were learning a trade and moving to town. No such complaints came from other districts of the Gers.[38] In December 1851 it was precisely this zone of central Gascony that rebelled against the government, led by the towns of Condom, Vic-Fezensac, Fleurance, and Mirande, and seconded by most of the bourgs. As for the villages, they generally remained calm, apart from those in close proximity to the towns of Vic-Fezensac and Mirande. The differentiation of artisans from cultivators, proto-urban bourgs from entirely rural communities, was at the basis of the social geography of revolt in the Gers.[39]

Immediately to the north was the wealthier department of the Lot-et-Garonne, whose fertile lowlands combined cash-crop agriculture with commerce and crafts. Many small towns and bourgs were located alongside the Garonne and the Lot rivers and their tributaries, and one-third of the labor force in the department was employed in

[37] In addition to Brunet, *Campagnes*, pp. 96-99, 243-48, 263-89, see the reports of the J. P.s in 1848, AN, C 953 (Gers).

[38] Reports of J. P.s in 1848, AN, C 953. These changes occurred later in the region around Toulouse. See Brunet, *Campagnes*, pp. 381-412; Armengaud, *L'Est-Aquitain*, pp. 296-323; and P. Feral, "La liquidation du prolétariat rural en Gascogne lectouroise," CNSS, 78 (1953), 425-39.

[39] On the role of small towns in the subsequent Republican movement of the Gers, see Guy Palmade, "Le département du Gers à la fin du Second Empire," *Société archéologique et historique du Gers*, 62 (1961), 83-86.

crafts, commerce, and the liberal professions. Although much of this nonagricultural sector was engaged in purely local trade, a few towns exported substantial craft goods to Bordeaux. Foremost among these industrial centers was Marmande, a subprefecture on the western edge of the department. Its population of 8,300 included over 1,000 artisans, producing hemp rope, hats, wine barrels, and tanned hides for export, as well as craft goods for regional consumption.[40] Outside the urban centers, however, sharecroppers continued to live within a semiclosed economy, producing grain for their "Masters" and employing an abundant labor force of poor peasants. Proto-industrial activity had been largely eliminated from the villages during the early nineteenth century.[41] In the Lot-et-Garonne, just as in the Gers, a sharp socio-economic cleavage existed between town and countryside. Not surprisingly, most insurrectionary activity was confined to the towns and bourgs. At Marmande, for example, rebel leaders mustered as many as 1,000 townsmen, but their call for rural support was rarely heeded. Only twelve other communes of the *arrondissement* turned out in force, and seven of these were bourgs with significant urban functions.[42]

One district of the department was an exception, however, to this pattern of rural deindustrialization, isolation, and political passivity. In the extreme south of the department, over 700 artisans were employed in bottle-cork workshops for the Bordeaux wine trade. The small town of Lavardac, already a port of transit for *eau de vie*, was the center of this expanding bottle-cork industry. The nearby bourg of Barbaste also produced bottle-cork, and so did the village of Xaintrailles. Vidalenc suspends his usual pessimism in describing this district of southwestern France: the regular employment these artisans enjoyed created a prosperity that was "exceptional for this region of miserable share-croppers."[43] In 1851, Lavardac, Barbaste, Xaintrailles, and adjacent villages mobilized over 1,000 insurgents. Nowhere else in the southwest was rural participation in the revolt so massive.

The largest rebel zone in central France covered the corners of three departments (Nièvre, Yonne, Loiret): the forest of the Morvan was to the southeast, and the forests of the Puisaye and the Gâtinais to the

[40] "Listes nominatives du recensement de 1851, Marmande," AD L-G, series M.
[41] Pierre Deffontaines, *Les hommes et leurs travaux dans les pays de la moyenne Garonne* (Lille, 1932), esp. pp. 280-87, 383, 414-15.
[42] Ints. and Tems. in AD L-G, 4U, 6U, Z.
[43] Vidalenc, *La société française*, II, 226-27. See also "Récapitulation, par arrondissement, des établissements industriels . . . à l'époque du 1 juin 1848," AD L-G, M, "Industrie, situation industrielle, 1850-1859," and the "Listes nominatives" for these communes, AD L-G, M, "Recensement de 1851."

northwest. Traversed by the valleys of the Yonne and the Loire rivers, this region contained a series of small towns and bourgs whose commerce in lumber or proto-industrial goods was of substantial importance. Foremost among these export-oriented communities was the subprefecture of Clamecy, a lumbering town of 6,000 on the Yonne river. Clamecy was the main transshipment point for lumber from the Morvan to the Paris market. Its several hundred lumberjacks, known locally as *flotteurs*, were entirely dependent on this wood trade, whose value for the *arrondissement* as a whole generally exceeded 6 million francs a year. Another several hundred artisans worked for local and regional demand, with shoemakers alone numbering nearly 100. The town also contained shopkeepers and merchants, who benefited from a brisk trade with the rural hinterland—two markets a week and six annual fairs.[44]

The *flotteurs* were the most distinctive component of the labor force at Clamecy. Their tasks were to sort out the logs that had been thrown helter-skelter into the river upstream, to stack them into separate piles for each lumbering merchant, and to construct log "trains," which were floated to ports in Paris. This commerce in logs, which fluctuated in accordance with Parisian demand for wood, was elaborately organized along capitalist (though *not* industrial) lines. A company of Parisian merchants, first created back in 1672, dominated the entire market. They purchased the wood directly from the forest owners and subcontracted to lumbering entrepreneurs who agreed to transport the wood at a fixed price per train. These entrepreneurs, who resided locally, then subcontracted in turn to skilled log-train builders, called *compagnons de rivière*. It was the *compagnons*, the equivalents in some sense to master artisans, who hired *flotteurs* in teams to help carry out the work. Like the master weavers at Lyon who led their apprentices in economic struggles against the silk merchants, the *compagnons* and their hired hands possessed a strong sense of their collective interests against the entrepreneurs and the wood merchants. They had a history of labor agitation, with violent peaks in 1709, 1763, 1792, 1824, and 1835, and they had a corporate organization. In 1848 the *flotteurs* of Clamecy presented a series of sophisticated labor demands to the commissioners of the canton: a wage scale, a labor exchange, regulation of piecework, a mutual benefit fund, a workers' association to dispense altogether with the entrepreneurs. As seasonal migrants to Paris in slack times, some of the *flotteurs* may have obtained their ideas about labor organization from militants in the capital.

[44] "Listes nominatives du recensement de 1851, Clamecy," Municipal Archive, Clamecy.

They were certainly as class-conscious and socialistic as workers anywhere in France.[45]

The lumbering industry at Clamecy faced two serious threats during the 1840s: competition from alternative suppliers of fuel to Paris, especially coal merchants; and competition from other points of transshipment along the river, especially ports downstream in the department of the Yonne. The *flotteurs* complained that wages were being reduced to starvation levels, and that fewer logs were being allocated to ports in the Nièvre (Clamecy and three nearby communes). During the same decade, however, occupational specialization in the canton of Clamecy was increasing, perhaps as a result of agricultural improvements. There was a gradual shift in the distribution of the labor force out of lumbering and into other occupations, as measured by the lists of young men, aged twenty, who comprised each year's class of potential military conscripts. Table 3.2 shows that between 1837-40 and 1847-50 fewer young men in the town and the rural communes were listed as lumbermen, and considerably more were listed as artisans, tradesmen, or professionals. Among occupational sectors that were re-

TABLE 3.2

Occupations of Twenty-Year-Old Men, Canton of Clamecy

	Town			*Rural Communes*		
	1837-40	*1847-50*	*% Change*	*1837-40*	*1847-50*	*% Change*
Craftsmen, shopkeepers, professionals	71	108	+52	41	94	+43
Lumbermen	51	29	−43	47	40	−15

SOURCE: Listes du tirage au sort, canton de Clamecy, 1837-40, 1847-50, ADN, série R.
NOTE: The results for the agricultural labor force are inconsistent: from 167 to 168 in the rural communes, from 23 to 46 at Clamecy.

cruiting larger numbers of youths in town were food (from six to fourteen), construction (from seventeen to thirty-three), and the liberal professions (from nine to nineteen); in the rural communes the food trades increased from 3 to 9 (no bakers in the earlier period, five in the latter), metals from five to ten, carpentry from four to eight, basket and wooden-shoe making from seven to thirteen. This evidence

[45] On the *flotteurs*, see Jean-Claude Martinet, *Clamecy et ses flotteurs* (La Charité-sur-Loire, 1975), pp. 17-56; and J. P. Clamecy, AN, C 960 (Nièvre).

of increasing craft specialization implies that despite the decline of the lumbering industry, the canton of Clamecy was benefiting from economic expansion.

In rebel communities of the Yonne, economic growth and increasing occupational differentiation were definitely interrelated. A sharp economic and social contrast existed between the villages in the interior of the forested region known as the Puisaye, and those along its eastern and southern edges.[46] The former were located in the "Basse Puisaye" (cantons of Bléneau and St. Fargeau), where population densities were low, land concentrated in the hands of large proprietors, and market opportunities very limited. At St. Fargeau, for example, the J. P. noted in 1833 that the lack of markets or commerce was preventing a middle class from developing in the area. Artisans were rare, and the very numerous day laborers were always on the verge of misery.[47] By contrast, the bourgs in the "Haute Puisaye" (cantons of St. Sauveur, Toucy, St. Amand), which surrounded this "anachronistic country," had better communications and more active exchange with the exterior. Thus, the J. P. at St. Sauveur reported in 1832 that agricultural productivity was growing, due to marling and artificial grasses; furthermore, pottery, wooden shoes, bricks, and tiles were being exported on a large scale.[48] In the Haute Puisaye and on the limestone plateau (*forterre*) further east, wages began to rise during the July Monarchy.[49] By 1848 landowners were complaining of a labor shortage in agriculture, and artisans of a glut in their labor market whenever the economy was depressed. In 1848 the J. P. at St. Sauveur lamented that "the young men who ought to work in farming prefer to learn a craft, though it doesn't benefit them as much."[50] Indeed, a substantial movement from agriculture to crafts had taken place in this canton during the previous generation: among potential conscripts, farmers and agricultural workers declined in numbers by 22 percent between the beginning of the Restoration Monarchy and the Second Empire, while artisans and tradesmen increased by 110 percent. As measured by these conscript lists, 29 percent of the labor force in the

[46] This distinction between "Haute" and "Basse" Puisaye is based on G. Goujon, *La Puisaye* (Paris, 1911). It is overlooked in the more general study by Jean-Paul Moreau, *La vie rurale dans le sud-est du bassin parisien* (Paris, 1958), and by Chevalier, "Fondements."

[47] J. P. St. Fargeau, Jan. 1, 1833, reprinted in Henri Forestier, *L'Yonne au XIX* siècle, 2ᵉ partie (1830-1848), (Auxerre, 1962), pp. 235-36.

[48] J. P. St. Sauveur, Dec. 12, 1832 and Sept. 30, 1833, in Forestier, *L'Yonne*, 2ᵉ partie, pp. 222-24. See also J. B. Robineau-Desvoidy, *Essai statistique sur le canton de St. Sauveur-en-Puisaye* (St. Sauveur, 1838).

[49] J. P. St. Sauveur, Nov. 14, 1847; J. P. Toucy, Nov. 21, 1847; J. P. Courson, Nov. 15, 1847, ADY, VI M 3-12.

[50] J. P. St. Sauveur, AN C 969 (Yonne).

canton was employed in crafts and commerce during the 1850s, as compared with only 13 percent around 1815.[51]

Resistance to the coup d'état took place in the bourgs that surrounded the Puisaye, rather than among the backwoodsmen of Bléneau and St. Fargeau. The insurrection in the Yonne originated at St. Sauveur and spread *eastward*, toward the richer bourgs of the Burgundian plateau, rather than westward, toward the Basse-Puisaye. Revolts also broke out in two bourgs to the south (St. Amand and Arquian), and in two small towns to the southwest (Neuvy-sur-Loire and Bonny-sur-Loire). These were all market centers for the Puisaye, and they all contained substantial concentrations of potters or other workers producing for export. As one authority has noted with respect to Neuvy and Bonny, they were located in an area of "great economic activity." There was much trade and circulation of merchandise along canals, rivers, and roads leading to neighboring departments and to Paris and Lyon.[52]

From Clamecy to St. Sauveur to Bonny-sur-Loire, this rebel zone was relatively urbanized, commercial, and proto-industrial in comparison with the "savage isolation" of the Basse-Puisaye. Deep in the forest, the impoverished laborers were supposedly ever ready to rebel, but they remained largely passive in 1851.[53]

This survey of the major regions of insurgency has shown that market expansion was, indeed, an underlying economic trend in rebel communities. The incomes of their populations were determined to a significant extent by production for export, either through the direct profits of such commerce or through the local trade that it stimulated. In some quiescent areas, on the contrary, peasants and rural artisans were either isolated from market forces, hostile to urban competitors, or subjugated by local landlords. Proto-urbanization was a general precondition for the regional mobilizations of 1851, with their urban inspiration and their rural support.

[51] Calculations based on the "listes du tirage au sort," 1814, 1816, 1854, 1860 (the only ones extant), ADY, R106-108.

[52] Marcilhacy, "La crise sociale et politique dans le département du Loiret," pp. 5-59.

[53] *Contra* Chevalier, "Fondements," p. 21, who emphasizes the backwardness of the Puisaye.

AGRARIAN DEPRESSION AND THE SOCIAL
BASES OF INSURGENCY

Production for the market implies exposure to price fluctuations. If most rebel districts of the nation benefited from the economic growth of the July Monarchy, did they suffer from contracting markets and falling prices during the Second Republic? On theoretical grounds, some political scientists would find ample cause for revolutionary discontent in such a combination of long-term expansion and short-term depression. During a phase of economic growth, people acquire higher expectations of well-being; during a phase of depression, these expectations persist in the face of declining living standards. The result is a widening discrepancy between economic expectations and achievements—a psychological state of "relative deprivation." The consequence, in turn, of relative deprivation is frustration, anger, and violence. By including both growth and decline as economic preconditions of revolutionary movements, this theory of relative deprivation reconciles de Tocqueville's emphasis on rising aspirations with Marx's emphasis on progressive immiserization. First formulated by James C. Davies, it has since been applied by "politimetricians" such as Ted Gurr to the quantitative analysis of collective violence in twentieth-century nation-states. With respect to the insurrection of 1851, it implies that the rebels were aspirants to prosperity made frustrated and violent by a sudden decline in their living standards.[1]

Indeed, Philippe Vigier has argued that an agricultural depression was the root cause of popular grievances and revolutionary tendencies in the French countryside from 1849 to 1851. The prices of most agricultural commodities were extremely low during these years, while markets for most industrial goods revived after a temporary paralysis in 1848. These divergent trends in the agricultural and industrial sectors of the economy explain the political contrast between a revolutionary peasantry and a quiescent urban working-class in 1851. According to Vigier, the agrarian depression had an especially severe impact in rebel districts of southeastern France, where numerous small farmers were heavily in debt to urban usurers. The prices of their cash crops

[1] Davies, "Toward a Theory of Revolution," *American Sociological Review*, 27 (1962), 5-19; T. R. Gurr, *Why Men Rebel* (Princeton, 1970); Gurr, "Psychological Factors in Civil Violence," *World Politics*, 20 (1968), 245-78.

fell to such low levels that these petty landowners could no longer meet their mortgage obligations. As a result, many of them suffered expropriation, and the rest feared the same fate. Vigier also notes the relationship between declining agricultural profits and (1) declining demand for construction and local crafts, and (2) declining demand for agricultural day labor. These secondary effects of the depression explain the participation of artisans and day laborers in a revolt dominated by small owner-farmers. As for sharecroppers, farm servants hired by the year, and industrial workers in the towns, they were much less exposed to the depression and much less involved in resistance to the coup d'état.[2]

This theory of agrarian depression and political revolt has been supported by other historians of the Second Republic, such as Claude Levy and Roger Price.[3] True, there is some disagreement concerning the specific social impact of declining agricultural prices. Thus, Levy places greater emphasis than does Vigier on the deteriorating market for agricultural labor, and he includes sharecroppers as a distressed and rebellious social category. Yet these scholars share Vigier's cataclysmic view of the relationship between economic trends and political insurgency. In the words of Price, "The most important factor in our explanation [of the revolt] is that of economic crisis and consequent social misery."[4]

If misery drove peasants to rebel in 1851, then presumably market conditions were considerably worse in rebel than in nonrebel districts. Similarly, if indebted owner-farmers were more exposed to economic ruin than other social groups, then presumably they were more actively involved in the revolt. With respect to both the geographical localization of insurgency and its social base, Vigier's theory can be tested. Did the "conjuncture" of price trends have an especially damaging impact on the economies of rebel districts? Were indebted owner-farmers in the forefront of resistance to the coup d'état? A careful review of the evidence concerning these problems shows that the relationship between economic fluctuations and insurgency is considerably more complicated than Vigier, Levy, or Price suggest. Market difficulties *everywhere* in France provided a focus for political issues

---

[2] Vigier, *La Seconde République dans la région alpine*, II, 10-88; for an extension of his interpretation to the nation as a whole, see Vigier, *La Seconde République* (Paris, 1967), pp. 92-96.

[3] Levy, "L'insurrection de décembre 1851 en province," pp. 142-45; Price, *The French Second Republic*, pp. 124-30, 203-204, 319-20; Loubère, "The Emergence of the Extreme Left in Lower Languedoc," pp. 1019-51; Marcilhacy, "La crise sociale et politique dans le département du Loiret," pp. 5-59.

[4] Price, *The French Second Republic*, p. 319.

during the Second Republic, but they did not determine whether local populations were pro- or anti-Republican, rebellious or quiescent, in 1851. Furthermore, low prices did not threaten entire social groups, such as owner-farmers, with economic disaster. Finally, the social base of participation in the revolt did not depend on the depth of "misery" among cultivators or artisans, the propertied or the propertyless. Whether specific communities and social groups rebelled in 1851 depended on their political experiences during the Second Republic, not their economic destinies.

There is no doubt that rebel districts of the nation experienced serious economic difficulties in 1848. The replies of their J. P.s to the industrial and agricultural enquiry of that year are nearly unanimous in their complaints of low prices and poor sales (*mévente*). The main cash crops that they produced had depreciated greatly in value since 1847. For example, silk cocoons at one major market of the Drôme sold for 4 francs a kilogram in 1847, but only 1.85 francs a kilo in 1848; *eau de vie* at Béziers sold in 1846 for 110 francs a barrel, in 1847 for 68 francs, and in 1848 for only 40 francs; wine in the Var declined in price by 50 percent between 1847 and 1848; the Paris market for wood "collapsed," etc.[5] Nor was the crisis confined to those directly engaged in the production of cash crops. Artisans working for local and regional markets suffered the repercussions of lower agricultural profits, and they complained of unemployment and price competition. As for industrial workers at small towns such as Dieulefit, Bédarieux, Apt, and Barjols, they also risked temporary layoffs, although their employers generally tried to stay in operation. The economies of rebel areas were generally depressed in 1848.

But nonrebel areas also suffered from declining markets after the February Revolution. J. P.s in northern and western France were gravely concerned about the suspension of activity among proto-industrial workers. For example, linen spinners at St. Valery (Somme) and Mézidon (Calvados) were being "ruined" by Belgian competition; the embroidery trade at Châtel (Vosges) was in profound decline, though no one knew why; the locksmiths at Charroux (Vienne) were being undersold by ready-made hardware; rural glovemakers near Sablé (Sarthe) were being hard-pressed by urban competitors, etc. In these regions a majority of the J. P.s also complained about low agri-

---

[5] Vigier, *La Seconde République*, I, graph on p. 75; *eau de vie* prices published by the local press at Montpellier (*Le Courrier du Midi*, *L'Echo du Midi*, *Le Messager du Midi*); Maurice Agulhon, "La crise dans un département méditerranéen: Le cas du Var," in E. Labrousse, ed., *Aspects de la crise et de la dépression de l'économie française au milieu du XIXe siècle, 1846-1851* (La-Roche-sur-Yon, 1956), p. 344; Chevalier, "Fondements," pp. 168, 368.

cultural prices, though a few did express satisfaction at recent progress. If rebel and nonrebel districts within southern France are compared, local reactions to the economic crisis are practically identical: seven out of eight rebel cantons in the Gers voiced concern about low agricultural prices, but so did twelve out of thirteen nonrebel cantons; silk-producing districts of the northern and the southern Drôme, the eastern Gard, and the eastern Hérault, all quiescent in 1851, had the same complaints about low silk prices and inadequate credit facilities as rebel districts; wine-producing cantons around Montpellier, calm in 1851, lamented the agrarian depression in the same terms as wine-producing cantons in the rebel zone of Béziers. The market crisis in 1848 was far more pervasive and general than the insurrection of 1851.[6]

Nor did the depression worsen in rebel areas from 1849 to 1851 while disappearing elsewhere in the nation. The agricultural commodities whose prices suffered the most depreciation throughout the Second Republic were wheat, wine, and *eau de vie*. All of them were produced in many districts that remained calm after the coup d'état. The case of wheat is especially interesting, because Vigier emphasizes the impact of low wheat prices on rural living standards. In fact, most areas of the nation that specialized in the export of wheat were bastions of political conservatism, regardless of their land-tenure patterns or property distributions. For example, the tenant farmers of the Paris basin, the owner-farmers of Champagne, and the sharecroppers of the Toulousain faced the same market situation of the lowest wheat prices in half a century. According to G. Désert, money-lease farmers around Caen (Normandy) were on the verge of a "catastrophe"; Chevalier asserts that in wheat-producing areas of Champagne numerous owner-farmers were forced to sell their lands in order to pay their debts; Armengaud cites testimony from near Toulouse that "all classes of society" were thrown into an "unparalleled discomfort" by the "continued decline in the price of grain." In all these areas low wheat prices persisted through 1851; in all of them the political result was hostility to the Republic and tacit or active support for the coup d'état.[7]

What about districts that exported wine or *eau de vie*? Unlike wheat, these were commodities which some rebel areas produced on a large scale for export—e.g. Béziers, Vic-Fezensac, Brignoles. There is no question but that the wine and spirits industries remained depressed in

[6] Reports of the J. P.s and cantonal commissions in 1848, AN, C 944-69.

[7] Désert, "Aspects agricoles de la crise: La région de Caen," in Labrousse, ed., *Aspects de la crise*, pp. 65-92; Chevalier, "Fondements," p. 542; Armengaud, *Les populations de l'Est-Aquitain*, p. 186. See also Paul Bois, "La crise dans un département de l'Ouest: La Sarthe," in Labrousse, ed., *Aspects*, pp. 272-315.

1849-51. At Béziers, the gross value of *eau de vie* sales declined by two-fifths between 1844-47 and 1848-51; and published series of wine prices in various areas of the nation all show a sharp decline during the Second Republic.[8] Yet many wine-producing areas greeted the coup d'état calmly: in Burgundy agitation was confined to a few towns; relatively few winegrowers participated in the revolts near Mâcon (Beaujolais) or Poligny (Jura); most wine-producing villages of the Rhône river valley remained passive; and no one protested in the vineyards near Bordeaux.[9] As for *eau de vie*, it was exported from the western Gers, the Charentes, and the Charentes-Maritimes, all quiet in 1851, as well as from rebel areas of the central Gers and the Biterrois. The political behavior of winegrowing areas cannot be predicted on the basis of their vulnerability to economic crises: they were *all* exposed to low prices, but relatively few rebelled.

Not only were many depressed areas conservative, but some relatively prosperous areas joined the insurrection. In the Var, for example, markets for bottle-cork, silk, and olive oil revived in 1849, and the economy of the department was basically prosperous in 1850-51.[10] Yet the fully employed bottle-cork workers of La Garde Freinet rebelled en masse, and so did the populations of silk- and olive-producing communities such as Le Luc. In the Vaucluse, exceptionally fine fruit harvests in 1850-51 stimulated the lucrative fruit-preservative industry at the rebel town of Apt; in the Drôme and the Hérault buoyant markets for silk and wool textiles ensured steady employment for the industrial labor force at the insurgent towns of Dieulefit and Bédarieux;

[8] For Béziers, calculations based on a bimonthly sample of prices and quantities exchanged from 1844 to 1851 (see Margadant, "Insurrection," pp. 25-26). Among the scattered series of wine prices, see, for example, François Convert, *Les ouvriers agricoles et les salaires en présence du phylloxera* (Montpellier, 1878); G. Thuillier, "La vigne en Nivernais au début du XIXe siècle," CNSS, 87 (1962), 587-88; and Pierre Goujon, "Le Vignoble de Saône-et-Loire au XIXe siècle (1815-1870)," *Thèse*, Lyon, 1968, pp. 188-89, and annex 1.

[9] On Burgundy, see A. Jacotin, "Notes sur le coup d'état du 2 décembre 1851 en Côte d'Or," *Annales de Bourgogne*, 13 (1941), 73-96; and "Rapport générale, Cour d'Appel de Dijon, 2 février 1852," AN, BB^{30} 396. In the canton of Poligny, rural participation came from the grain-producing plain of the Bresse, not the winegrowing communes of the "cote." See ADJ, MIV 45, Ins. Poligny. Near Mâcon, resistance was concentrated in the two small towns of Cluny and St. Gengoux-le-national, with artisans much more heavily involved than cultivators: at Cluny, 33% of the adult male labor force were employed in agriculture, as compared with only 11% of those prosecuted after the coup d'état; at St. Gengoux, the respective figures were 49% and 20%. See AD S-L, U, Ins. 1851, #1-2; and M, Census of 1851. Among winegrowing communes in the valley of the Rhône, small mobilizations occurred around Tain (Drôme) and in several bourgs near Orange (Vaucluse). See ADD, M 1353-55 and ADV M 48.

[10] Agulhon, "Le cas du Var," in Labrousse, ed., *Aspects de la crise*, pp. 316-56.

and throughout southeastern France, rising prices for raw silk brought a partial revival of the silk industry to rebel bourgs and villages.[11]

Three aspects of the relationship between market trends and political orientations help explain the absence of geographical "fit" between zones which suffered from low agricultural prices and those that rebelled in 1851. First, abundant harvests and low food prices benefited the mass of the population in many *rural* districts as well as in the towns. Next, market difficulties tended to divide rural and urban populations in northern France, while uniting them in the Midi. Finally, state economic policies were influential in strengthening or undermining public support for the status quo in various regions. While economic problems tended to polarize public opinion throughout the nation, they did not determine the political behavior of specific regions and communities.

It is obvious that industrial workers benefited from the abundant harvests and low food prices of the Second Republic, but less well known is the fact that so did many families in the countryside. Ernest Labrousse has developed a widely accepted theory of economic crises in the *ancien régime* that relates poor harvests and high food prices to rural unemployment and misery.[12] His model presupposes that the opposite condition of abundance and low prices generates prosperity. The model is not entirely adequate, for as David Landes has pointed out, farmers selling grain will generally benefit more from mediocre harvests and high prices than from excellent harvests and low prices.[13] Yet it can be applied to a socioeconomic situation in which only a small minority of landowners and tenant farmers realize profits from grain sales, while the bulk of the rural population have to buy their food in the marketplace. Such a situation was common in the French countryside during the first half of the nineteenth century. Labrousse has presented evidence that the average peasant holding was too small to produce a surplus of grain for sale.[14] Either these peasants specialized in the production of more labor-intensive cash crops, such as wine, or they worked part-time in rural industry, or they earned wages as agricultural laborers. However they made ends meet, they were con-

[11] Vigier, *La Seconde République*, II, 23-24, 28-30; police reports from Bédarieux, ADH, 39M 129-35.

[12] For his latest discussion of this model, see Labrousse, et al., *Histoire économique et sociale de la France*, vol. II, *1660-1789* (Paris, 1970), 529-63.

[13] Landes, "The Statistical Study of French Crises," *Journal of Economic History*, 10 (1950), 195-211.

[14] Labrousse, "The Evolution of Peasant Society in France from the Eighteenth Century to the Present," trans. David Landes, in Evelyn M. Acomb and Marvin L. Brown, Jr., eds., *French Society and Culture since the Old Regime* (New York, 1966), pp. 43-64.

sumers rather than sellers of grain. What was the direct impact of low food prices on such families? It could only be favorable, and Georges Dupeux has shown in considerable detail that in a typical wheat-producing area of north-central France, the bulk of the rural consumers—agricultural laborers and small family farmers—experienced a rise in their standard of living during the Second Republic.[15] Similar advantages accrued to cultivators who normally produced other crops and imported at least some of their grain. Excellent local harvests reduced their dependence on such imports, and low prices improved their purchasing power. Such was the case in most insurgent districts of the southeast. While they lost some revenue due to the low prices of other cash crops, such as wine and silk, they spent considerably less money during the Second Republic to purchase wheat.

This argument cuts more deeply into the theory that an agrarian depression caused misery and revolt in 1851. The fundamental economic problem of France in her proto-industrial and proto-urban phase of development was the provisioning of cheap food to her laboring population—artisans, agricultural workers, small farmers—all of whom had little or no land with which to feed their families. Until this problem was solved, the state was continually threatened by outbreaks of public disorder—riots against grain shipments (*entraves*), forcible public sales of grain below the market price (*taxation populaire*), mendacity, arson, etc. Here was a clear and present danger of "pillage" and "anarchy." The overwhelming importance of this economic issue in the French Revolution has been established by a host of scholars, and it was to remain a major public concern down to the end of the July Monarchy. Indeed, harvest shortages and high food prices in 1846-47 provoked a wave of food riots that helped undermine the prestige and authority of the regime. Yet during the Second Republic, when misery was supposedly widespread, there was only a handful of food riots, and no political protests were linked to the provisioning of food. The agrarian depression from 1848 to 1851 created a margin of subsistence, if not prosperity, which had rarely if ever before existed during a period of major political crisis in France. Memories of the *Jacqueries* of old abounded among fearful landlords, merchants, and officials, and they were astonished when in 1851 insurgents marched in arms without pillaging and burning in their wake. The lower orders were supposed to lash out in anger against the rich, as they had so often done in the past when their most vital economic interest—food—was threatened. But

---

[15] Georges Dupeux, "Aspects agricoles de la crise: Le département de Loir-et-Cher," in Labrousse, ed., *Aspects de la crise*, pp. 75-84. Among small peasants, only the *vignerons* of the Loir-et-Cher were hard-hit by the depression.

the politics of the Second Republic were not the politics of dearth and misery, and the men of December were not the Jacques of olden times. The adequate food supply of the period was an important precondition of their discipline, restraint, and orientation toward national political issues rather than merely local economic problems.[16]

This is not to say that classes and regions were insensitive to the commercial and industrial crisis of 1848 or to the persistence of low agricultural profits from 1849 to 1851. A major contrast existed, however, between northern and southern France with respect to the urban-rural impact of these economic difficulties. In the north, fluctuations in grain markets tended to place the countryside in an antagonistic relationship to the urban working class. Rural grain producers wanted high prices in export markets and adequate food supplies with which to feed their labor force; urban consumers wanted low prices and abundant imports, even at the risk of creating grain scarcities in the countryside. Conflict was especially acute whenever harvests were poor and prices high—many food riots were essentially defensive reactions of small townsmen and villagers against the export of grain to cities. The antiurban and anti-Parisian sentiment of the peasantry in northern France may well have been based in part on memories of such *crises d'ancien régime*. It is noteworthy that most of the food riots in 1846-47 were located in grain-exporting departments of the northwest that voted conservative during the Second Republic. Furthermore, rivalries of interest persisted during the inverse circumstances of abundance and low prices from 1848 to 1851. Although the laboring poor in the northern French countryside were assured of adequate food, the large landowners and tenant farmers in this region definitely experienced declining incomes. The more the conditions of the grain market benefited workers in the cities, the less they benefited rural elites. Furthermore, these notables were expected to support the unemployed rural textile workers so common in northern France in 1848-49, while at the same time financing unemployment relief to Parisian workers! Clashes of interest between rural grain producers and urban consumers, rural textile workers and urban competitors, made unlikely any political alliance between left-wing workers and the inhabitants of small towns or villages in this part of the nation.

In many districts of southern France such urban-rural antagonisms did not exist. Towns and rural communities were jointly dependent

[16] For a general discussion of food riots during the July Monarchy, see Tilly, "The Changing Place of Collective Violence," pp. 147-52. On the distribution of riots in 1846-47, see the map by R. Gossez, in Labrousse, *Aspects de la crise*, pp. 1-3. On the politics of dearth in the French Revolution, see especially Richard Cobb, *The Police and the People* (Oxford, 1970), pp. 246-324.

on wheat imports and cash-crop exports such as wine, silk, and *eau de vie*. Consequently, their economies moved in unison when prices fluctuated. In the plains and hillsides of Lower Languedoc, for example, Dugrand has noted that towns were "profoundly marked by the rhythms of rural life." They benefited from high prices of the main agricultural export, wine, just as they suffered from low wine prices. "Each depression in the price of wine is the signal for urban unemployment and numerous bankruptcy proceedings. A heavy atmosphere, combining pessimism and rancor, spreads through the town, reaching working-class households as well as bourgeois families."[17] Thus, low *eau de vie* prices from 1849 to 1851 were equally detrimental to townsmen at Béziers and to rural producers in nearby villages. Similar relationships of complementarity existed in silk-, wine-, and olive-producing districts of the southeast, *eau de vie* districts of the southwest, and lumbering districts of the center. As for the small industrial towns and bourgs in these regions, their exports also benefited the rural populations by stimulating local consumer demand for craft goods and agricultural produce. Commercial links with distant markets—Marseille, Lyon, Bordeaux, Paris—created a common economic dependency between town and countryside. The economic preconditions thereby existed for an urban-rural alliance on behalf of the same political cause.

The specific terms of such an alliance were influenced by regional opposition to national economic policies. Excessive wine taxes, a discriminatory tariff policy, and an inadequate credit system were widespread complaints of producers in the Midi. The system of indirect taxes on wine was extremely unpopular, both because of its vexatious mode of enforcement and because of its detrimental effect on consumer demand. Each political upheaval in early nineteenth century France had been accompanied by violent protest against the wine tax, and each time the old system had been forcibly restored. Conservative notables from the Midi again failed during the Second Republic to obtain a major reduction in this tax, while Republican politicians promised to abolish it.[18]

As for tariff policy, it had been biased toward wheat and textile producers during the July Monarchy. Here, too, anti-Republican notables made no revisions in favor of cash-crop exports from the Midi.[19] Finally, national credit policy was inadequate to the needs of

[17] Dugrand, *Villes et campagnes en Bas-Languedoc*, p. 83.

[18] For brief discussions of the wine tax in nineteenth-century France, see Gabriel Ardant, *Histoire de l'impôt*, vol. II, *XVIIIe au XXe siècle* (Paris, 1972), 295-319; and Robert Schnerb, "Les hommes de 1848 et l'impôt," *1848 et les Révolutions du XIXe siècle*, 38 (1948), 5-51.

[19] On French tariff policy during the July Monarchy and the Second Republic,

producers in southern France. Government discount banks existed for the use of industrialists, but cash-crop farmers also needed short-term credit facilities. This problem was especially serious in the silk zone of the southeast, where operating capital came largely from bankers at Lyon. The collapse of credit in 1848 placed silk producers in this region in serious straits, and they favored the creation of a national system of agricultural banks. Again the politicians from other regions, hostile to public credit, thwarted any such reform during the Second Republic.[20] The economic interests of southern France were often neglected by the anti-Republican "party of order," while left-wing Republicans embraced the cause of tax, tariff, and credit reform. Here was an important reason why the populations in some districts of the Midi responded more favorably to Republican propaganda than did those in northern France.

If low agricultural prices do not explain the geographical localization of revolt, does economic misery nonetheless explain the social base of political extremism within rebel zones? Which social groups in small towns, bourgs, and villages suffered the most economic deprivation during the Second Republic, and which of them participated most heavily in the revolt? With respect to the agricultural sector, historians such as Vigier and Levy have focused attention on the impact of low prices on owner-farmers, wage laborers, and sharecroppers. As for the craft sector, they have emphasized the plight of artisans threatened by outside competition, and those suffering from declining consumer demand in local markets. Insofar as misery determined revolt, the greater the impoverishment of these various social groups, the greater their numerical preponderance in the ranks of the insurgents.

The insurrection was supposedly localized in areas of small peasant properties.[21] In fact, the basic pattern of land distribution in rebel communities was hierarchical, not egalitarian. Large and small properties were juxtaposed side by side, creating an opportunity for those with an abundance of land to work it with the aid of the micro-proprietors.[22]

---

see Shephard B. Clough, *France: A History of National Economics, 1789-1939* (New York, 1939), pp. 91-132, 180-81; and Arthur L. Dunham, *The Anglo-French Treaty of Commerce of 1860 and the Progress of the Industrial Revolution in France* (Ann Arbor, 1930), pp. 3-27. For the political importance of this issue in Languedoc, see Loubère, "The Emergence of the Extreme Left," pp. 1026-27.

[20] In addition to Vigier, see Jeanne Gaillard, "La question du crédit et les almanachs autour de 1850," *La Société d'histoire de la Révolution de 1848, Etudes,* 16 (1954), 79-87. Concerning the special needs of silk producers, see Reynier, *La Seconde République dans l'Ardèche,* pp. 20-21.

[21] See, for example, Soboul, *Paysans,* p. 348; and Price, *The French Second Republic,* pp. 307-308, 312.

[22] For a refined typology of property distribution in southeastern France, see

The large landowners leased farms to sharecroppers for the production of grain and livestock, and they hired agricultural laborers to tend their vines, harvest their olives, cut their wood, and so on. While some peasants owned enough land to be completely independent of these landlords and their tenants, such "owner-farmers" were a minority in most leading centers of revolt. For example, they comprised less than two-fifths of the agricultural labor force around Lavardac and Marmande in the southwest, St. Sauveur and Le Donjon (Allier) in the center, and Béziers and Manosque in the southeast.[23] Even in the silk zone of the Drôme, where owner-farmers were more common than "day laborers," an agricultural census in 1852 indicated that only 40 percent of the farming population were self-sufficient peasant proprietors, while 36 percent also worked for others, 14 percent were landlords, and 9 percent were tenants.[24] Furthermore, the unmarried sons of peasant proprietors were generally counted as owner-farmers, regardless of whether they personally owned any land. The important social category of unmarried agricultural laborers, living with their parents but working part-time for other farmers, was often overlooked in the census records of the period.[25]

The social terminology used by contemporaries corresponds to the distinction between families with an excess supply of land and those with an excess supply of labor. The former comprised a small elite of "bourgeois" landlords, or "proprietors," while the latter formed a mass of "travailleurs de terre," or "cultivators." Between the proprietors and the cultivators were the artisans in the bourgs and some substantial peasant farmers in the countryside—*laboureurs* in central France, *ménagers* in Provence. These substantial peasants were more often than not tenants rather than proprietors, and their economic power was based on the size of their farms and the value of their livestock rather than the amount of land they owned. The crucial question was how many resources a family *controlled*, and in this respect a majority of the peasants in most rebel communities were mere cultivators, even

---

Vigier, *Essai sur la répartition de la propriété foncière.* His analysis shows that large or medium-sized properties were present in most of the rebel districts of the plains and foothills in the Drôme, the Vaucluse, and the Basses-Alpes, while small properties monopolized the soil only in (quiescent) areas of the high mountains.

[23] Calculations based on the census returns in 1851 for the rebel communes in the cantons of Lavardac, Mézin, Damazan, Nérac, Marmande, Mas-d'Agenais (Lot-et-Garonne); St. Sauveur, Toucy, Courson (Yonne); Le Donjon, Jaligny (Allier); Béziers, Capestang, Servian, Murviel (Hérault); Manosque (Basses-Alpes). Departmental archives, series M.

[24] Calculations based on the quintennial agriculture *statistique*, 1852, cantons of Crest-nord, Crest-sud, Bourdeaux, Dieulefit, Marsanne, Loriol, ADD, 42M 1.

[25] This generational contrast is mentioned in passing by Agulhon, *La République au village*, p. 30.

if they owned some land. Only rarely did such peasants use the hybrid term "proprietor-cultivator" to describe their own socioeconomic status.[26]

The wealth or poverty of these cultivators depended on the abundance of their harvests, the value of their cash crops, their income from supplementary activities as agricultural laborers, lumbermen, or artisans, and their burden of debts and taxes. Because their economic position was subject to a variety of influences, they tended to share a common fate with other social groups in the countryside: larger landowners who marketed crops, owed debts, and paid taxes; artisans who also produced goods for a market, borrowed money for commercial transactions, and paid taxes; agricultural laborers whose employment opportunities fluctuated in accordance with market demand. There is little reason to expect that low prices during the Second Republic were more ruinous for small peasant proprietors than for their richer or poorer neighbors. More important were regional differences in their basic economic strength or weakness. In central and southwestern France, owner-farmers were nearly as poor as agricultural laborers, while artisans generally had a higher standard of living; in southeastern France, all three groups shared in a more commercialized and urbanized economy, and they were on a more equal footing economically and socially.[27] In sum, rural misery encompassed small peasant proprietors and day laborers in the former regions; urban prosperity reached them more easily in the latter.

The plight of cultivators in rebel districts of the center and southwest is amply documented in the reports of the J. P.s for the cantonal commissions in 1848. The technical conditions of grain and livestock production favored tenant farmers in most of these districts, and agricultural wages were low. At Le Donjon (Allier), for example, only the large farmers could afford to temper the acid soils with chalk and obtain good wheat yields. According to the cantonal commission, most small owners and agricultural workers were equally impoverished.

> A single class of workers, those who work by the day and who are called day laborers, find themselves in a very precarious position, live from day to day, and in the event of the slightest unemployment or sickness, find themselves reduced to indigence. This situation is easily explained by the low value of their daily wage. The share-

[26] For social terminology in southeastern France, see Agulhon, *La vie sociale en Provence*, pp. 247-368.

[27] "Equality" was a question of degree. Artisans were still regarded as a superior social category in Provence, but the distance between them and cultivators was not so great as in the southwest. On artisans in Provence as a "middle class," see Agulhon, *La vie sociale en Provence*, pp. 123-37.

croppers are generally wealthy. The small owner-farmers, most of them burdened with debts at often usurious interest rates, can be classified with the day laborers. They may even furnish more recruits to indigence or mendicancy. The position of workers employed in (craft) industry is generally good.[28]

At Mirande (Gers) poor soil and harsh weather reduced even the sharecroppers to the miserable state of "the inferior class of owner-farmers," and low prices placed all landowners in difficult straits. Here, too, artisans earned higher incomes, while agricultural laborers were often indigent.[29] Other J. P.s from rebel districts of the Gers confirmed that workers on the land were considerably worse off in 1848 than craftsmen in the bourgs, though the latter were more vocal in their complaints of underemployment due to low market demand. If political discontent were a consequence of general misery, cultivators in these regions would be in the forefront of resistance to the coup d'état; if it were related to a temporary decline in incomes among those accustomed to a decent standard of living, artisans would be over-represented in the ranks of the insurgents.

In fact, cultivators were considerably less militant than artisans in all these districts. Nowhere did they comprise a majority of those prosecuted after the coup d'état for participating in the revolt: only 18 percent of those arrested for marching to Agen (Lot-et-Garonne) were employed in agriculture, 27 percent of those marching to Auch (Gers), 35 percent of those to Clamecy, 38 percent of those to La Palisse and Jaligny (Allier), and 42 percent of those to St. Sauveur and Auxerre (Yonne).[30] More precise measurement of the occupational base of insurgency confirms this political contrast between cultivators and artisans. By comparing the percentages of these two social categories prosecuted in 1852 with their respective percentages in the general population, it is possible to measure their relative numerical weight among all alleged rebels. If the ratio of these percentages is greater than 1.0, they were overrepresented in the revolt; if it is less than 1.0, they were underrepresented.[31] Table 4.1 presents the results of such analysis for three districts in central France, where larger per-

[28] J. P. Le Donjon, AN, C 944 (Allier).

[29] J. P. Mirande, AN, C 944 (Gers).

[30] Only the suspects who resided in communes that marched to these destinations are included in these calculations, based on the registers of the Mixed Commissions and the interrogations of suspects.

[31] This statistical measure—percentage of participants from a particular occupational sector divided by percentage of labor force employed in that sector—is based on William H. Sewell, "La classe ouvrière de Marseille sous la Seconde République: Structure sociale et comportement politique," *Le mouvement social*, 76 (July-Sept. 1971), 50.

TABLE 4.1

Ratios of Participation among Cultivators and Artisans
in the Insurrection

		Agricultural Labor Force	Artisans and Shopkeepers	Total Prosecuted
10 rebel bourgs and villages in the Yonne	Percentage of rebels	41%	55%	115
	Percentage of labor force	68%	21%	
	Ratio of participation	0.6	2.6	
9 rebel bourgs and villages in the Allier	Percentage of rebels	35%	54%	219
	Percentage of labor force	75%	21%	
	Ratio of participation	0.5	2.6	
9 rebel bourgs and villages in the Nièvre	Percentage of rebels	31%	45%	184
	Percentage of labor force	58%	25%	
	Ratio of participation	0.5	1.8	
flotteurs in the Nièvre	Percentage of rebels	24%		
	Percentage of labor force	15%		
	Ratio of participation	1.6		

SOURCES: For the Yonne, this analysis is based on the arrest lists and census returns in 1851 for the communes of St. Sauveur, Dracy, Escamps, Leugny, Moutiers, Ouanne, Saints, Taigny, Thury and Treigny. For the Allier, it is based on the same sources for the communes of Le Donjon, Bert, Jaligny, Luneau, Montcombreux, Neuilly-en-Donjon, St. Léon, Thionne, and Treateau. A. D. Yonne, III M¹ 156-65, and Census of 1851; A.D. Allier, series M census of 1851; register of the "Mixed Commission" of the Allier, A N. BB³⁰* 402¹ et². For the Nièvre, it is base on the rural communes in the canton of Clamecy. The census lists for 1851 are missing, so I have calculated the occupational distribution on the basis of the conscript lists for those communes, averaging the data from 1837-40 and 1847-50, A.D. Nièvre, series R. The register for the "Mixed Commission" is in A N, BB³⁰* 399.

centages of cultivators were arrested than in the southwest. Apart from the *flotteurs* near Clamecy, who were semiskilled laborers rather than cultivators, the farming population was far less heavily compromised in these districts than the artisans and shopkeepers. Of course, many rebels escaped prosecution, and the authorities probably treated insurgent farmers more leniently than craftsmen. This in itself is proof, however, that in central France cultivators were not the politically dangerous element in the population, despite their general state of poverty.

In southeastern France the monetary incomes of agricultural laborers and small peasant proprietors were higher in periods of prosperity but more sensitive to price fluctuations than those of comparable social groups in the center and southwest. Conditions in the labor market were of special importance to peasants in the winegrowing bourgs and villages of Languedoc and Provence. When prices were low, landlords had less capital with which to employ workers in their vineyards, and they tended to reduce their labor inputs, especially in the winter months. Agrarian depression thereby created a conflict of interest between the larger proprietors and the cultivators in these districts. At Béziers, for example, the subprefect wrote anxiously on the eve of the winter season in 1850:

> The harvests are inadequate, commercial orders are rare, and the produce of the vineyards is selling at a very low price. The farmers (*agriculteurs*) are in great distress, which leads one to fear that they will neglect to have their vineyards cultivated and thus leave unemployed a very large number of day laborers . . . (the *vignerons*) ordinarily only have a very short period of unemployment (*morte saison*), but the demand for their spade work will decline in proportion to the financial straits of the landowners.[32]

The threat of unemployment had as its counterpart lower wages, though cheaper food may have largely compensated vineyard workers near Béziers for declining nominal wages.[33] In any case, the low price of *eau de vie* sharpened social tensions between landlords and field laborers in this rebel district.

Similar reports of divergent interests between these two social classes came from some major centers of revolt in Provence. At Manosque

---

[32] S-P Béziers, Nov. 21, 1850, in ADH, unclassified, Industry, 1849-64.

[33] Wheat prices declined by approximately 20%, while fragmentary wage statistics from vineyards in the nearby *arrondissement* of Montpellier indicate a 15% decline during the Second Republic. For wheat prices, see ADH 123M 55; for wages, see Convert, *Les ouvriers agricoles*, p. 27; and Augé-Laribé, *Le problème agraire du socialisme* (Paris, 1907), p. 77.

one member of the cantonal commission in 1848 doubted whether employers could continue to pay high wages to the agricultural workers while prices and profits declined. He called for a public-works program to reduce the numbers of laborers whom the hard-pressed landlords were expected to employ.[34] Another advocate of landlord interests at Manosque proposed a profit-sharing plan to increase the efficiency and lower the cost of agricultural labor. He complained that the field hands were loudest to accuse the landowners of excess profits when the latter were operating in the red, and he voiced the hope that profit sharing would "destroy the unfortunate ideas of communism which are being spread among the workers."[35] At Cuers, another rebel "agrotown" in Provence, the cantonal commission was equally persuaded that agricultural workers were pushing their interests too far. While the landowners were suffering from low prices and heavy debts, the workers were "never unemployed," and refused to work over nine hours a day in the summer. "Custom doesn't permit the landowners to demand a longer working day, although the field hands have to agree that their health wouldn't suffer if they worked an hour longer, either in the winter or the summer, as they do in many other localities of the Var."[36] Nor were social tensions between proprietors and cultivators absent from silk-growing communities of the southeast. Just one week before the insurrection, Republican municipal councilors at Grane (Drôme) pleaded with the prefect to help finance public relief: "At this moment, because of the bad weather, the absence of silkworms for the past several years, and the disaster of the hailstorm which struck a large part of the commune this year, the landowners find themselves in such an embarrassed position that they can't employ the workers. Consequently, the commune is obliged to request special assistance from the higher administration so that, with its own small resources, it can occupy the indigent for a portion of the winter."[37] The economic repercussions of lower prices for cash crops were generally unfavorable to proprietors and cultivators in southeastern France, and where the social distance between them was great, the result was mutual resentment and hostility.

What about the problem of debts in rebel districts of the Midi? Low prices of cash crops unquestionably made it more difficult for proprietors to service past debts or to contract new ones. In three

[34] "Observation de François Lieutaud," dossier Manosque, AN, C 944.
[35] Eugène Robert, "Note sur une association entre patrons et ouvriers," dossier Manosque, AN, C 944.
[36] J. P. Cuers, AN, C 944.
[37] "Registre du Conseil Municipal de Grane," Nov. 30, 1851, Municipal Archives of Grane.

respects, however, the political impact of debts was less obvious than some scholars have suggested. First, in small towns and bourgs where indebted landowners employed agricultural workers, their sense of class solidarity against the claims of labor tempered any enthusiasm for the Republican program of credit reform. Second, in more egalitarian communities where proprietors relied mainly on family labor, the burden of old debts was far from being ruinous. Very few peasants were expropriated during the Second Republic, and they comprised only a minuscule portion of the insurgents in 1851. Finally, the basic issue for cash-crop farmers in the southeast was not urban usury, but the absence of *any* credit facilities for financing short-term commercial transactions. State agricultural banks would help remedy this deficiency in the marketing system of these districts, rather than save a horde of miserable peasants from bands of scheming usurers.

The evidence for deflating exaggerated views of peasant indebtedness is contained in local registers of expropriations, debts, and property sales. Vigier has used the data on expropriations in several *arrondissements* of southeastern France to argue that such forcible transfers of property increased to catastrophic levels during the Second Republic. Indeed, the annual rate of expropriations did double between 1840-47 and 1848-51.[38] Yet this increase looks rather small if these rates of expropriation are expressed in per capita terms: they rose from a rate of 1 per 2,000 inhabitants per year to 1 per 1,000 per year. More concretely, out of some 7,000 household heads in the district of Crest (Drôme), only around 100 were expropriated in the four years of the Second Republic.[39] These numbers are not negligible—a single expropriation could arouse fears of more to come—but they suggest that the immediate social impact of expropriations was confined to a few families. That impact was further mitigated by the fact that most victims had several creditors. Their failure to pay off their debts was a cause of considerable discomfort for their multiple creditors. Thus, in a sample of expropriations in the Drôme, nearly half involved 6 or more creditors, and four-fifths involved at least 2 creditors. When multiple debtors collapsed under the combined weight of their creditors, they resembled bankrupt businessmen whose borrowed funds had come home to roost, rather than marginal peasants who had been victimized by predatory usurers. Indeed, over one-quarter of the cases in the sample concern indebted merchants or artisans rather than proprie-

[38] Chart in Vigier, *La Seconde République*, I, 269; discussion in II, 32-35.

[39] Based on the registers of expropriations for the *arrondissement* of Die, Feb. 1848 to Sept. 1852 (six out of nine are extant, listing 69 expropriations in the rebel cantons of Crest-nord, Crest-sud, and Bourdeaux). ADD, unclassified *Procès-verbaux de saisie*.

tors or cultivators. An expropriation was certainly a disaster for whomever it befell, but more men probably benefited than suffered from such legal proceedings.[40]

This evidence contradicts the view that expropriated peasants were sufficiently numerous to constitute a mass base for revolt in 1851. Only at the leadership level could expropriations have a significant impact on Republican politics. This point emerges from a study of 154 expropriations that occurred from 1848 to 1852 in five rebel cantons of the central Drôme.[41] This region contributed nearly 6,000 men to the revolt and suffered 815 prosecutions afterward, among whom 19 can be located in the extant registers of expropriations. Even if all those who lost their lands also rebelled, they would account for only around 3.5 percent of the insurgents, and 3.3 percent of those prosecuted afterward.[42] Yet in the latter category were 9 rebel leaders, approximately 10 percent of all those exercising leadership responsibilities in this region. There was a pronounced tendency for the social base of political leadership to include men who had suffered financial ruin during the Second Republic.

For most peasant proprietors, however, the problem of debts was a cause for discontent rather than desperation. The bulk of the debts that were contracted through notaries and thereby liable to enforcement in the courts involved small sums of money and relatively short terms of repayment.[43] While some debts were contracted to buy land, this was probably the case in only a minority of land transactions.[44]

[40] Numbers of creditors and occupations of debtors are given in the registers of expropriations, cited in note 39. My analysis is based on the 10 extant registers out of 14 which originally existed for the *arrondissement* of Die, Apr. 1844–Sept. 1852.

[41] These 154 expropriations took place in rebel communes in the *arrondissements* of Die and Montélimar; 13 of the 18 registers of expropriations for these *arrondissements* from Feb. 1848 through Sept. 1852 are extant.

[42] Taking into account the missing registers, around 213 persons were expropriated during the Second Republic in this region (213/6000 = 3.5%); and around 27 of them were among those prosecuted (27/815 = 3.3%).

[43] In a 20% random sample of 2,600 notarized loans registered in the cantons of Crest-nord and Crest-sud from May 6, 1843, to Aug. 3, 1855, 78% were valued at less than 1,000 francs, and 71% were due in less than three years. ADD, 2C 25 236-51.

[44] The registers of notarial records note whether property sales were financed by the seller at interest, paid for in cash, or settled in other ways. In a 10% sample of around 7,500 property sales drawn from the same registers at Crest (n. 43), only 25% of the 744 cases involved loans at interest and 57% involved full cash payments. Vigier has cited administrative reports that speculative land sales on credit were extensive in the northern Drôme, but the notarial records from Crest suggest that this was not the case in the central Drôme. Yet mass resistance to the coup d'état came from the latter region, not the former. Vigier, *La Seconde République*, II, 62-63.

The primary purposes for borrowing money were probably (1) to finance expensive family transactions, such as inheritances, dowries, and weddings; and (2) to finance short-term commercial transactions. The family debts sometimes dragged on for years, but they were too deeply embedded in custom and property law to arouse public protest. The major problem of the credit market involved the high interest rates and general scarcity of loan funds for commercial operations, such as the purchase of livestock, the construction of a farm building, the payment of a servant, etc. Far from being concentrated in the hands of urban usurers, such loan capital tended to be scattered throughout the countryside in the hands of the larger landowners.[45] It was hard to locate and even more difficult to tap, especially for small producers. During the Second Republic the volume of loan transactions diminished appreciably, with short-term promissory notes especially sensitive to the declining profits of agriculture.[46] Peasants needed better credit facilities for commercial purposes, and this was the basic reason why some of them supported Republican proposals for state agricultural banks.

Just as cultivators in southeastern France were more sensitive to market fluctuations than their counterparts in the center and southwest, so they were more heavily involved in resistance to the coup d'état. They formed a majority of all those prosecuted for marching to Béziers (51%), Largentière, in the Ardèche (51%), and Digne, in the Basses-Alpes (50%); and they comprised nearly half of those pursued by magistrates for marching from Apt toward Avignon (47%), from Dieulefit to Crest (45%), and from the central and northwestern Var to Aups (43%).[47] In all these districts they formed a clear majority of the suspects who resided in agricultural bourgs and villages: 67% near Béziers, 62% near Largentière, 59% near Apt, 57% near Manosque and Forcalquier, 57% in the rebel zone of the Var, and 56% near

[45] In the sample of loans around the town of Crest, 72% were made by rural creditors; 74% were made by 486 individuals who appear only once in the sample; and only 12% were made by residents of Crest who appear more than twice in the sample. Yet moneylenders at Crest were supposedly exploiting peasants on a large scale, causing in large part the insurrection of 1851. See Vigier, *La Seconde République*, II, 163-64.

[46] In the same sample, notarized *obligations* in the canton of Crest increased from a base of 100 in 1844-45 to 113 in 1846-47, but then fell to 70 between 1848 and 1851. For *billets à payer*, the respective indices were 100, 108, and 55. For further analysis of the loan market around Crest, see Margadant, "Modernisation and Insurgency in December 1851: A Case Study of the Drôme," in R. Price, ed., *Revolution and Reaction* (London, 1975), pp. 261-65.

[47] Calculations based only on those suspects who resided in communes that sent contingents to these various destinations. Registers of the Mixed Commissions and Ints. of suspects.

Crest.[48] Their proportions among rebels in such rural communities were roughly equal to their proportions in the population as a whole. Table 4.2 shows this by comparing the ratios of participation among cultivators and artisans in three rebel districts of the southeast.

Among these cultivators, landowners were a distinct minority. In the southern Ardèche, for example, where magistrates provided in-

TABLE 4.2

Ratios of Participation in the Revolt (Southeast)

		Agricultural Labor Force	Artisans and Shopkeepers	Total Compromised
7 bourgs and villages near Béziers (Hérault)	Percentage of rebels	75%	19%	422
	Percentage of population	68%	19%	
	Ratio of participation	1.1	1.0	
12 bourgs and villages in the central Drôme	Percentage of rebels	65%	29%	413
	Percentage of population	75%	18%	
	Ratio of participation	0.9	1.6	
8 bourgs and villages near Apt (Vaucluse)	Percentage of rebels	63%	34%	245
	Percentage of population	82%	12%	
	Ratio of participation	0.8	2.8	

SOURCES: This table is based on the census lists and judicial investigations concerning rebels in the following communes: (*arrondissement* of Béziers) Capestang, Maraussan, Portiragnes, Roujan, St. Thibéry, Servian, and Vendres; (central Drôme), Autichamp, Beaufort, Bourdeaux, Lachamp, Mirmande, Puy-St. Martin, La-Roche-sur-Grane, Roynac, St. Gervais, Sauzet, Soyans, and Suze; (*arrondissement* of Apt) Bonnieux, Gargas, Gordes, Lacoste, Ménerbes, Roussillon, Rustrel, and St. Martin-de-Castillon. See the relevant dossiers (series M), AD Drôme, Hérault, and Vaucluse.

[48] Calculations based on the following districts: all communes except Béziers, which joined forces at that town; all communes except Largentière and Vallon in the southern Ardèche; all communes except Apt, which joined forces to march toward Avignon; all communes except the cantonal seats in the cantons of Manosque, Forcalquier, Riez, and Valensole (Basses-Alpes); all communes that marched to Aups (Var) except the cantonal seats and the industrial bourg of La Garde Freinet; all communes that marched via Dieulefit and Bourdeaux to Crest except the town of Dieulefit.

formation on the wealth of those prosecuted after the coup d'état, less than two-fifths of the cultivators possessed any land.[49] Census records for rural communes near Apt indicate that only one-quarter of the peasant rebels in that region were owner-farmers.[50] Similarly, land-tax registers for two important rural centers of insurgency near Crest show that less than one-third of the militant farmers owned any property, and less than one-fifth had a taxable income from land of over 50 francs a year.[51] By tracing rebels in the census returns for 1851 it is possible to confirm that peasant proprietors were less heavily represented in rebel ranks than agricultural laborers and the dependent sons of owner-farmers. Table 4.3 compares the ratios of participation among owner-farmers and day laborers in representative bourgs and villages of the Hérault and the central Drôme.[52] It shows that day laborers were generally overrepresented among insurgents; owner-farmers were more compromised where they formed the bulk of the agricultural labor force; but among families of peasant proprietors, dependent sons were consistently more militant than their landowning fathers. Class differences between landowners and agricultural laborers, and generational differences within the households of peasant proprietors, were reflected in higher ratios of participation among the young and the landless cultivators than among the older property-owning farmers.

While the political tendencies of cultivators varied regionally, artisans were everywhere in the forefront of insurgency. What was the economic context of their militancy? With few exceptions, machine industry did not threaten these rebel artisans with ruin. Most of them produced for local markets, which were not exposed to industrial competition. In a representative sample of 646 artisans and tradesmen who were prosecuted in rebel districts of the nation, only 7% were

---

[49] Such notations exist for seventy-four cultivators in the southern Ardèche, of whom twenty-eight (38%) owned some property. ADA, 5M 19.

[50] Calculation based on tracing all suspects in the census lists for the communes analyzed in Table 4.1.

[51] At Bourdeaux, 14/23 of the farmers compromised in the revolt were not on the land-tax rolls in 1846-51, and only 4 were taxed at an estimated annual income of over 50 francs. Tax roles for the four direct taxes, 1846-50, 1851-55, communal archives of Bourdeaux.

At Grane, 34/47 of the farmers who were compromised did not have any property listed in the *cadastre* (land-tax register) for the period, and only 8 had property listed with an estimated annual income of over 50 francs. *Cadastre*, commune of Grane, Municipal Archives of Grane.

[52] This analysis is based on a systematic tracing of all political suspects in the household census lists for the year 1851. The census distinguishes between *propriétaires-cultivateurs* (owners-farmers), *propriétaires-journaliers* (owner–day laborers), and *journaliers* (day laborers), as well as tenant farmers, farm servants, and farmers who are also craftsmen. Day laborers who own land are classified with other day laborers in Table 4.3.

TABLE 4.3

Ratios of Participation among Day Laborers and Owner-Farmers

		Day Laborers	Owner-Farmers and Sons	Owner-Farmers, Household Heads Only	Owner-Farmers, Dependents
I. 6 villages in the central Drôme	Percentage of participants	7%	69%	34%	35%
	Percentage of population	6%	70%	44%	26%
	Ratio of participation	1.2	1.0	0.8	1.4
II. 6 *bourgades* in the central Drôme	Percentage of participants	14%	31%	18%	13%
	Percentage of population	12%	41%	28%	13%
	Ratio of participation	1.2	0.8	0.6	1.0
III. 9 villages near Béziers	Percentage of participants	64%	8%		
	Percentage of population	38%	18%		
	Ratio of participation	1.7	0.4		
IV. 4 bourgs near Béziers	Percentage of participants	63%	7%		
	Percentage of population	42%	10%		
	Ratio of participation	1.6	0.6		

SOURCES: (I) Based on the villages of Autichamp, Lachamp, La-Roche-sur-Grane, Roynac, Soyans, and Suze, all with less than 15% of their labor force employed in the crafts; (II) based on the communes of Beaufort, Bourdeaux, Mirmande, Puy-St. Martin, St. Gervais, and Sauzet, all with from 15-30% of their labor force employed in the crafts, distinguishing them from more villages, hence the term *bourgade*; (III) based on the villages of Maraussan, Portiragnes, and Vendres; (IV) based on the cantonal seats of Capestang, Roujan, and Servian, and the relatively large agglomeration of St. Thibéry (pop. 1,750 in 1851).

employed in textiles, the main craft sector undergoing mechanization during the 1840s. The largest numbers of militant artisans were employed in construction (31%), followed by the food trades (21%), clothing (20%), and metalworking (13%). The ten crafts with the most prosecutions in these districts were stonemasons (57), shoemakers (57), blacksmiths (52), carpenters (39), stonecutters (35), weavers (34), joiners (32), tailors (28), clog makers (22), and bakers (22).[53] As skilled workers supplying local consumers, the practitioners of these traditional crafts generally operated singly or in small groups, and only in the region of Clamecy did any of them complain in 1848 of outside competition. Ready-made shoes, suits, and furniture, produced in urban workshops using semiskilled workers, were beginning to penetrate local markets in the Paris region.[54] Even this was not a case of mechanization but only of a somewhat more intensive division of labor among handworkers, and such rationalization of production methods does not yet seem to have posed any threat to tailors, shoemakers, and joiners in southern France.[55]

The major economic problem for these artisans was a saturated job market at the local level. If agriculture was prosperous, consumer demand for craft goods sustained a considerable labor force of artisans and tradesmen, especially in the bourgs and small towns. If agricultural profits then declined, and if farmers reduced their expenditures on construction, clothing, etc., the labor market for these artisans naturally contracted. Underemployment among craftsmen seems to have been widespread in rebel districts during the early months of the Second Republic. As the cantonal commission at Forcalquier (Basses-Alpes) wrote in 1848, "The stagnation of commercial affairs is the cause of the malaise felt by the workers (in local crafts)."[56] Although landownership gave some artisans a margin of security during such a period of underemployment, only a minority of those compromised after the

[53] The above analysis is based on all suspects from rebel communes in the districts of Clamecy; Le Donjon and Jaligny; Lavardac; Vic-Fezensac and Auch; Apt; Béziers; and Dieulefit-Crest. The towns of Clamecy, Vic-Fezensac, Auch, Apt, Béziers, Dieulefit, and Crest are not included. In addition to the sectors mentioned, 5% were employed in extraction, and 3% in miscellaneous trades.

[54] See the reports of the J. Ps for the cantonal commissions from Clamecy, St. Sauveur, and Toucy, AN, C 960 (Nièvre), 969 (Yonne). For the Parisian origins and impact of the ready-made clothing industry, see Christopher H. Johnson, "Economic Change and Artisan Discontent: The Tailors' History, 1800-48," in Price, ed., *Revolution and Reaction*, pp. 87-114.

[55] The only cantonal commissions in rebel districts of southern and southwestern France to complain of outside competition were at the towns of Béziers (Hérault) and Condom (Gers).

[56] J. P. Forcalquier, AN, C 944 (Basses-Alpes). Among the fifty-nine cantonal commissions from rebel districts analyzed in Chapter Three, twenty-seven mentioned the unfavorable impact of low export prices on local craftsmen.

coup d'état seem to have been in this relatively favorable position. For example, among the 212 artisans and tradesmen prosecuted in the Gers, 53 percent were described by magistrates as "poor," and only 28 percent had any "fortune" or "aisance";[57] among 74 prosecuted in the southern Ardèche, 62 percent were characterized as propertyless, entirely dependent on their labor, or poor;[58] and among those compromised in the middle Drôme, the census returns for 1851 indicate that two-thirds were not property-owners in addition to being artisans.[59] Low agricultural profits definitely had an impact on the incomes of such propertyless craftsmen, especially given the simultaneous tendency for the agricultural job market to contract.

But did underemployment remain a cause of serious discomfort for artisans in the months preceding the coup d'état? There is some evidence that the construction industry was depressed throughout the Second Republic, but some other craft sectors definitely revived after the temporary crisis of 1848.[60] At Clamecy, for example, the public prosecutor reported in 1850 that the artisans had enough work, while the *flotteurs* suffered from unemployment.[61] Yet the ratio of participation in the revolt was 1.4 among artisans and tradesmen at Clamecy, and only 0.6 among the *flotteurs*.[62] At Bédarieux the textile workers, who were also fully employed in 1851, had the highest ratio of participation in the revolt of any occupational sector in the town (textiles, 1.7; other crafts and commerce, 0.8; agriculture, 0.7).[63] The same pattern of full employment and political militancy characterized cork workers in the Var, porcelain workers at Apt, and textile workers at Dieulefit.[64] As for the more traditional crafts in the bourgs, their most marginal workers—young men employed as journeymen—were highly

[57] Notations published by Dagnan, *Le Gers*, II, 576-86. My analysis excludes the town of Auch, where local militants did not rebel in 1851.

[58] ADA, 5M 19.

[59] Based on a tracing of suspects in the census lists for communes in the cantons of Marsanne and Crest-sud. ADD, 35M.

[60] See Vigier, *La Seconde République*, II, 40-41; Chevalier, "Fondements," p. 544. This depression was nationwide. See, for example, G. Désert, "Aspects agricoles de la crise," in Labrousse, *Aspects de la crise*, pp. 57-63.

[61] P-G Bourges, Jan. 2, 1850, AN, BB[30] 374.

[62] Calculations based on the conscript lists for the town, 1837-40, 1847-50, and the registers of the Mixed Commission. ADN, series R; AN BB[30]* 399.

[63] Calculations based on a 20% sample of all adult males listed in the census of Bédarieux in 1851, and all those with dossiers in the archives of the military commission at Béziers, ADH, 39M 144-60.

[64] On the prosperity of cork workers at La Garde Freinet where labor conflicts were based on resistance to wage cuts preceding the Second Republic, see Agulhon, *La République au village*, pp. 305-12. At Apt, the porcelain workshops were in operation when the insurrection of December 1851 began (see dossier Jos. Martin, porcelain manufacturer, ADV, 4M 61). For Dieulefit, see Léon, *La grande industrie*, II, 800-804.

mobile and had the option of seeking work elsewhere if unemployment persisted in a particular locality. Insofar as commerce and industry revived in the towns from 1849 to 1851, the labor market for such journeymen artisans improved as well. The low food prices of the period were a further element which mitigated against any prolonged decline in the living standards of artisans. It seems reasonable to conclude that these workers and tradesmen experienced some decline in monetary incomes in 1848, recovered to a varying degree thereafter, and were earning a modest living, with adequate food, when the coup d'état took place.

The agrarian depression of the Second Republic encouraged Frenchmen to view political action as a means of defending their economic interests against unfavorable market trends. Those communities and social groups that rebelled in 1851 were generally sensitive to fluctuating prices, profits, and employment opportunities, and they did suffer some relative deprivation due to the low price of export commodities. Yet market conditions were not ruinous, nor were they strikingly different in rebel and nonrebel areas of the countryside. There is a remarkable discrepancy between the economic circumstances of France in 1851, and the political forces set in motion by the coup d'état. The former were grounds for discontent throughout the nation; the latter were evidence of an acute political crisis in particular towns and rural communities. Economic factors were preconditions, not determinants, of political action. The causality of insurgency in 1851 encompasses a variety of social and political forces without which the market trends of the period would have gone largely unnoticed in the transition from the Second Republic to the Second Empire.

· 5 ·

POLITICAL MODERNIZATION AND INSURGENCY

The insurrection of 1851 was a crisis in the political modernization rather than the economic development of nineteenth-century France. This is the fundamental proposition that explains the geographical and social localization of the revolt, its internal dynamics, and its historical fate. Concretely, insurgency was the outcome of a prolonged struggle between agents of the central bureaucracy and well-organized Republican militants, both claiming to support a vital element of political modernity. The bureaucrats stood for the rationalization of authority and the maintenance of national norms of social control; the Republicans stood for the democratization of authority and the creation of local forms of mass political participation. Socioeconomic factors influenced but did not determine the modalities of this struggle. It is in the political process itself that we must seek a coherent explanation of rebellion in 1851.

Political modernization can be analyzed as the expansion of two institutional spheres of government: the state and the polity. The state is that rational system of centralized authority whose agents claim a monopoly of the legitimate means of violence within a given territory. From the perspective of the social system, it is a superordinate entity, imposing its autonomous and sovereign will on social classes, families, and individuals. Its historical growth in France has involved the elaboration of complex bureaucratic and military hierarchies; the transformation or destruction of localized systems of authority (communal, seigneurial, etc.); and the exaction of revenues (taxes), services (military conscription), obedience, and loyalty from subjects of the monarchy or citizens of the Republic. By contrast, the polity is a rational system of centralized representation whose participants strive to mobilize voluntary public support. It is a subordinate entity with respect to the social system in the sense that it represents social forces vis-à-vis the state bureaucracy. Historically, the expansion of the polity in France has involved the creation of a representative national assembly and a competitive electoral system; the development of public associations such as political parties and special-interest groups; and the periodic or irregular mobilization of large numbers of citizens in electoral campaigns, public meetings, and nonviolent demonstrations. In sum, while the French state has been the domain of bureaucratic authority, legal unity, and compulsory obedience, the French polity has been the arena of representational authority, associational contention, and voluntary participation in public affairs.[1]

The fusion of a centralized state with a representative polity requires a delicate adjustment between the authority of bureaucrats and the rights of participants. In modern France such an adjustment was a long and painful historical process, extending from the 1780s to the 1880s. Frequent crises in the political system focused on two crucial aspects of the polity: its autonomy in relationship to the official apparatus of the state, and its scale in relationship to the entire society. In both respects, the French revolutionary experience caused enduring tensions between bureaucratic authority and popular rights. The postrevolutionary regimes of the First Empire, the Restoration Monarchy, and the July Monarchy feared unrestricted electoral competition—free elections would arm the enemies of the emperor, the king, or the ministry in power. At the same time, they welcomed the support of wealthy men, whose property and education gave them a natural ascendency over the mass of the population. By enfranchising the rich and mobilizing their votes on behalf of loyal candidates, these regimes hoped to subordinate the representatives of the polity—electorates and legislatures—to the agents of the state—ministers, prefects, magistrates, and gendarmes. This strategy of electoral manipulation led to government restraints on electoral organizations and propaganda, both to ensure government victories and to obstruct coalitions between defeated candidates and the disenfranchised mass of the population. In refusing to permit popular electoral participation, these regimes were equally determined to repress crowd demonstrations, riots, and conspiracies, which might otherwise proliferate as the only available channels of popular protest. Beneath the surface of liberal electoral institutions, the postrevolutionary state imposed rigid constraints on the polity.[2]

These constraints suddenly disappeared when Parisian crowds overthrew the July Monarchy in February 1848. By introducing universal

[1] In developing this general view of French political development, I have found especially helpful the work of Huntington, *Political Order in Changing Societies*; Tilly, "How Protest Modernized in France, 1845-1855," pp. 197-203; and Eugene and Pauline Anderson, *Political Institutions and Social Change in Continental Europe in the Nineteenth Century* (Berkeley, 1967).

[2] Among the many studies of administrative institutions and political conflict in postrevolutionary regimes, see, especially, Alan Spitzer, "The Bureaucrat as Proconsul: The Restoration Prefect and the *Police Générale*," *Comparative Studies in Society and History*, 7 (1965), 371-92; David Pinkney, *The French Revolution of 1830* (Princeton, 1972); Sherman Kent, *Electoral Procedure under Louis Philippe* (New Haven, 1937); and Howard C. Payne, *The Police State of Louis Napoleon Bonaparte, 1851-1860* (Seattle, 1966), pp. 3-26.

adult male suffrage, the Provisional Republican Government granted participatory rights to all Frenchmen, regardless of their social class. By guaranteeing freedom of press, speech, and assembly, it removed administrative barriers to the proliferation of independent political associations. During the subsequent electoral campaign to the Constituent Assembly (April 1848), France experienced an explosion of political energies as thousands of prospective candidates and their supporters founded committees, clubs, and newspapers. Political mobilization was especially intense in cities such as Paris, where economic difficulties polarized public opinion around social issues such as the "right to work." Throughout the nation, however, politicians competed for the prestige and power of legislative office. Having replaced the prefects of the monarchy with Republican commissioners, the new minister of the interior, Ledru-Rollin, tried in vain to ensure the election of bona fide Republicans. Although many commissioners headed lists of candidates, no single organization, no single ideology succeeded in dominating the electoral process. Political mobilization had outstripped the preexisting institutions of both the state and the polity.[3]

According to contemporary political scientists, such a disequilibrium between the pace of political mobilization and the development of political institutions is a major cause of violence and instability. In the words of Samuel Huntington, "Political violence and instability is caused primarily by the gap between the rapid pace of social change and the rapid mobilization of new groups into politics, on the one hand, and the slow development of political institutions, on the other hand."[4] The threat of anarchy is twofold. On the one hand, social groups that have hitherto been excluded from the polity may view the weakening of state authority as an opportunity to defend their local interests by force of arms. Eric Hobsbawm has pointed out, for example, that violent peasant protest becomes likely when a "firm, stable, and closed" structure of authority gives way to a "changing, shifting and open" one.[5] This is because peasants traditionally lack any modes of protest other than "relations of force—either real trials of strength or ritualised ones."[6] The rural disorders of 1848 can be interpreted as

[3] Among the studies of political life between February and June 1848, see Georges Duveau, *1848: The Making of a Revolution*, trans. Anne Carter (New York, 1968), pp. 53-181; Charles Seignobos, *La Révolution de 1848—Le Second Empire*, in E. Lavisse, ed., *Histoire de France contemporaine*, vol. VI (Paris, 1929), pp. 1-114; Peter Amann, *Revolution and Mass Democracy* (Princeton, 1975); and George Fasel, "The French Election of April 23, 1848: Suggestions for a Revision," *French Historical Studies*, 5 (1968), 285-98.

[4] Huntington, *Political Order*, p. 4.

[5] Hobsbawm, "Peasants and Politics," *Journal of Peasant Studies*, 1 (Oct. 1973), 13.

[6] Ibid., p. 16.

such localized peasant responses to a changing political conjuncture. On the other hand, social groups that are being newly mobilized into the polity may acquire heightened expectations and greater organizational skill without accepting the legitimacy of electoral leaders and representative institutions. Thus, many Parisians who were politicized during the electoral campaign of April 1848 subsequently rejected the legitimacy of the new Constituent Assembly. They demanded a "Democratic and Social Republic" and denounced as counterrevolutionary the conservative majority of the assembly, composed of provincial politicians. The situation became explosive when the antisocialist leaders of the Assembly's Provisional Executive Power decided in June 1848 to abolish the National Workshops, a large-scale system of unemployment relief for Parisian workers. Drawing strength from their national-guard units and inspired by the socialist ideology they had learned in political clubs, the populations of eastern and central Paris rose in arms. Only after four days of heavy street-fighting did the army and bourgeois national guard units succeed in crushing this violent challenge to an Assembly supported by a large majority of the nation's voters.[7]

How is political stability restored in such a transitional phase of modernization? As Samuel Huntington has shown, political-party development provides the basic solution to this problem in twentieth-century societies. The political party is "the distinctive institution of a modern polity" by virtue of its ability "to organize participation, to aggregate interests, to serve as a link between social forces and the government."[8] An alternative solution, however, is political demobilization through bureaucratic repression. Without necessarily changing the formal elements of a democratic polity—universal suffrage and representative assemblies—the centralized state imposes severe constraints on participants. Bureaucrats, police officials, and army officers treat opponents of the government as dangerous subversives, regardless of whether these dissidents seek victory in elections or revolution in the streets. Above all, advocates of demobilization strive to eliminate autonomous political organizations on grounds of national security and social defense. In other words, they systematically thwart political-party development. Huntington notes that "if a society has a reasonably highly developed and autonomous bureaucratic structure in its traditional phase, it will face acute problems in adapting to broader

[7] On the June Days, see especially Rémi Gossez, "Les antagonismes sociaux du XIX⁵ siècle," *Revue économique*, 1 (1956), 439-57; and Charles Tilly and Lynn Lees, "The People of June 1848," in Price, ed., *Revolution and Reaction*, pp. 170-209.

[8] Huntington, *Political Order*, p. 91.

political participation."[9] The existence of a centralized state with a tradition of political repression creates a strong likelihood that political demobilization rather than party development will be the preferred solution to a modernization crisis.

This was the case in France during the later months of the Second Republic. Ministers in Paris developed a coherent strategy of demobilization, and their eager subordinates in the departments imposed it on local populations. This strategy first emerged among conservative politicians in the aftermath of the June Days, became national policy shortly after Louis Napoleon was elected president of the Republic in December 1848, and achieved full implementation after the legislative elections of May 1849. Repression initially focused on crowd demonstrations and permanent agencies of political propaganda—clubs and newspapers. Demonstrations, confused with violent disorders, were prohibited; clubs, accused of plotting revolt, were restricted to public meetings at scheduled times; and newspapers, blamed for the spread of "subversive" ideas, were brought back under the jurisdiction of the courts. Subsequently, the clubs were prohibited, Republican newspapers were systematically prosecuted, and all other legal channels of Republican propaganda and organization were closed. Thus, administrators issued edicts to "dissolve" voluntary associations whose members were Republicans; they prohibited banquets and electoral meetings; and they prosecuted any displays of Republican symbolism in dress, song, or ritual. To carry out this policy of repression, agents of the state purged functionaries who were sympathetic to the Republic; revoked or suspended Republican mayors and deputies; dissolved Republican municipal councils; and reorganized, disarmed or abolished national-guard units that contained Republicans. By the first week of December 1851 Republicans had been almost completely excluded from the public realm. Their advocacy of socioeconomic reforms had been redefined as anarchy; their dissent as conspiracy; their opposition as revolution. In the minds of administrators, defenders of the Democratic and Social Republic were criminals.[10]

The ideological justification for this strategy was threefold. To begin with, unrestrained mass participation in politics was equated with street violence. It was to prevent a recurrence of the June Days that the Constituent Assembly empowered administrators to control po-

[9] Ibid., p. 87.
[10] For analyses of centralized political repression in 1849-51, see Payne, "Preparation of a Coup d'Etat," pp. 179-202; Payne, *The Police State of Louis Napoleon Bonaparte, 1851-1860* (Seattle, 1966), pp. 3-33; and John Merriman, *The Agony of the Republic* (New Haven, 1978).

litical associations in its "Decree on the Clubs" (July 28, 1848).[11] Next, organized political opposition was viewed as an intrinsic challenge to the authority of the state. Any national political organization, with regional and local branches, recognized leaders, and fund-raising procedures, would duplicate to some extent the state bureaucracy. Such an organization would supposedly be a permanent rival to the public authorities. Such were the categories of analysis used, for example, by the *procureur-général* at Aix in denouncing the *Solidarité Républicaine*, a national organization of left-wing Republicans founded in November 1848: "Here we find, inside the state, a rival organization, covering the surface of France and opposing to the departmental, *arrondissement*, and cantonal authorities its own departmental, *arrondissement*, and cantonal committees. It is a particular society in the general society; it is the disciplined and ultra-democratic party, exchanging correspondence from one end of France to the other, reaching agreements, cooperating together, ready to act as a single man by obeying the same orders."[12] Finally, the electoral movement of left-wing Republicans, whatever its mode of organization, was interpreted as an assault on the social order. Administrators became "soldiers of order" against "anarchists" and "demagogues" who threatened the very foundations of society. Commenting on a Republican victory in a local by-election, the *procureur-général* at Limoges typified this view in April 1850: "How can one fail to be impressed by the awesome and imminent peril! What more terrible threat than the revolt of the inferior classes, armed with universal suffrage, against the necessary conditions and the eternal laws of human society."[13] From violence in the streets, the focus of administrative attention had shifted to the electoral process. The main objective of political repression from 1849 to 1851 was to guarantee the electoral defeat of Republican candidates.

Electoral calculations became the primary concern of ministers, prefects, and public prosecutors shortly after Louis Napoleon Bonaparte took office as president of the Republic.[14] His consolidation of executive authority was marked by a substantial turnover in the prefectoral corps and by an official campaign against political clubs. The new minister of the interior, Leon Faucher, was determined to eliminate

---

[11] For a summary of this Decree, see Félix Ponteil, *Les institutions de la France de 1814 à 1870* (Paris, 1966), pp. 349-50.

[12] P-G Aix, Jan. 18, 1849, AN, BB[18] 1472[A]. Concerning the *Solidarité Républicaine*, see Marcel Dessal, *Charles Delescluze, 1809-1871* (Paris, 1952), pp. 93-120.

[13] P-G Limoges, Apr. 8, 1850. AN, BB[30] 378.

[14] On the comparative liberality of his predecessor, General Cavaignac, see Frederick A. De Luna, *The French Republic under Cavaignac, 1848* (Princeton, 1969).

left-wing, or "Socialist," organizations, and he introduced legislation on January 26, 1849, to abolish all public political meetings. Article One of his proposal, cosponsored by Louis Napoleon, read: "Clubs are forbidden. Any public meeting held periodically or at irregular intervals for the discussion of political affairs shall be considered a club."[15] When the *Solidarité Républicaine* protested this measure, Faucher had the police raid its Paris headquarters (January 29), and he arranged for the prosecution of twenty-nine of its national leaders as members of a "secret society."[16] Before obtaining a court verdict, he sent the prefects a peremptory circular (February 4): "I remind you that the *Solidarité Républicaine* is an association prohibited by the laws; wherever committees are established, the authorities are duty-bound to dissolve them and to help the magistrates prosecute their members."[17] Two weeks later he was back at the charge, this time denouncing the electoral committees of the "Socialist" party in another circular to the prefects. Posing the rhetorical question whether citizens had the right to create permanent electoral associations, he replied "No." On the pretext of elections, people would be able to "discuss every political question, pass in review every social problem, participate ardently in contemporary politics."[18] To cool such popular enthusiasm, Faucher ordered the prefects to suppress any such associations that existed in their departments.

Despite these ministerial instructions, officials in the departments generally tolerated Republican electoral committees during the campaign of April-May 1849 for the Legislative Assembly. These committees resembled the elitist electoral organizations tolerated during the July Monarchy: they rarely had either formal contacts with other departments, or a permanent organization, or a mass membership. This is not to say that prefects viewed Republican candidates with a benevolent neutrality. Career ambitions and social fears ensured their participation in the conservative and anti-Republican coalition known as the "party of order." The prefectoral style of electoral management was influenced less by commands from Paris, however, than by the traditions of the July Monarchy. Most prefects preferred discreet intrigue among conservative notables to official commitments and heavy-handed repression, which might be counterproductive among voters jealous of their independence. While closing down the clubs as

---

15 "Projet d'une loi sur les clubs," Jan. 26, 1849, in AN, BB18 1474A.

16 Dessal, *Delescluze*, pp. 103-4. See also Hippolyte Duboy, "Mémoire pour MM. Sarrut, et al.," [Men prosecuted as leaders or founders of the organization] undated (after Feb. 1, 1849), AN, BB18 1472.

17 Circular from M. Int. to Prefects, Feb. 4, 1849, copy in ADH, 39M 130.

18 Circular from M. Int. to Prefects, Feb. 17, 1849, copy in ADH, 39M 130.

forums of popular sedition, officials left open the main channels of electoral propaganda—newspapers, committees, and rallies.[19]

The results of the legislative elections were favorable to the party of order in the nation as a whole, but to left-wing Republicans, or "Montagnards," in only one-third of the departments.[20] This polarization of public opinion on a regional basis changed the political context of administration. Henceforth, where populations had elected conservatives, officials needed to guard against any weakening of the government's position. Where they had chosen Montagnards, officials needed to recover lost ground so that such bad examples would cease to contaminate the entire body politic. To assist them in this task, the conservative majority in the Legislative Assembly passed a law in July 1849 to close down any "clubs and other public meetings that might compromise public security."[21] The qualifying term "might" was nowhere to be seen in the orders which the minister of the interior promptly issued to the prefects: "The first use which you will make of this law, *M. le prefect*, will be to prohibit in the entire territory of your department and in an absolute manner any clubs or public meetings in which political affairs are discussed."[22] In a final tightening of control, administrators were empowered on June 6, 1850, to suppress electoral rallies.[23] For all practical purposes, public electioneering had become illegal.

While prefects helped royalist notables indirectly by repressing left-wing propaganda, their primary mission was to serve Louis Napoleon. This produced a latent conflict between the political orientation of the legislative assembly and that of the bureaucracy. For the royalist majority of the assembly, the main task of the state was to provide a protective shield for the notables against social revolution from below. In their view, the best way to accomplish this was to revive the *Censitaire* system of a class-based electorate. Thus, in May 1850 they passed an electoral law that made voter registration contingent on three years' residence within a single canton, as proved by the personal tax rolls. The mobile, the indigent, the young, and the dependent—nearly one-third of the electorate—were thereby disenfranchised.[24] From the per-

---

[19] On administrative electoral activity during the electoral campaign for the legislative assembly, see Theodore Zeldin, "Government Policy in the French General Elections of 1849," *English Historical Review*, 74 (1959), 240-48.

[20] Jacques Bouillon, "Les démocrates-socialistes aux élections de 1849," *Revue française de sciences politiques*, 6 (1956), 71-77.

[21] "Article One of the Law of the Clubs," June 19, 1849, AN, BB[18] 1474[A].

[22] Circular from M. Int. to Prefects, June 24, 1849, copy in ADD, M 1344.

[23] See the "Rapport par Jules de Lasteyrie," June 18, 1851, AN. BB[18] 1474[A].

[24] For a brief summary of this law and its effects, see Seignobos, *La Révolution de 1848*, pp. 153-54.

spective of administrators, however, the size of the electorate was less important than the effectiveness of political repression. If officials became strong enough to demobilize mass opposition, they would also be strong enough to *remobilize* the masses in support of the head of the state. Instead of reducing the scale of the polity, it sufficed to destroy autonomous electoral activity. The bureaucracy itself would take over the functions of a mass political party—selecting candidates, diffusing propaganda, and mobilizing voters. The more intense the struggle with Republicans, the more politicized the bureaucracy became. The end result was not destined to be another parliamentary oligarchy, but the plebiscitarian police state of the Second Empire, with its bureaucratic electoral managers, its "official candidates," and its rubber-stamp legislature.

In sum, bureaucratic opposition to left-wing Republicanism was the dynamic force behind the structural transformation of the French polity from an open, competitive system in 1848-49 to a closed, monopolistic system in 1850-52. The culminating event in this transformation was the insurrectionary upheaval at the end of 1851. Louis Napoleon's coup d'état of December 2 began as a power play against the National Assembly, whose deputies had failed to amend the Constitution on behalf of presidential ambitions for reelection. It was justified on populist grounds, and the president appealed for public support in a subsequent plebiscite, to be held on the basis of universal suffrage.[25] Once massive resistance to the coup emerged in the provinces, however, any pretence of governmental dependence on the will of the people was abandoned. Ministers in Paris jettisoned the few remaining restraints on political repression, declared thirty-one departments in a state of siege, and supervised a nationwide manhunt and purge of Republicans. Nearly 27,000 suspects were judged by summary administrative commissions, of whom over 10,000 were sentenced to deportation in Algeria. Naturally, all Republican newspapers were closed down. So were many private clubs, mutual-benefit societies, cafés, and inns, whose members were suspected of being Republicans. Meanwhile, the prefects arbitrarily revoked hundreds of municipal officials and deployed their administrative apparatus to mobilize voters in the plebiscite of December 20, 1851, and in the electoral campaign of February-March 1852 for a truncated "Legislative Body." Both efforts were unqualified successes: Louis Napoleon received 7 million yes votes and only 640,000 no votes in the plebiscite; and official candidates won all but eight seats to the legislature. A series of institutional changes ac-

[25] On the background and organization of the coup d'état, see Adrien Dansette, *Louis Napoleon à la conquête du pouvoir* (Paris, 1961), pp. 309-41, and Henri Guillemin, *Le coup du 2 décembre* (Paris, 1951).

companied these purges and elections, giving administrators nearly total power over public opinion in their departments. By terrorizing Republican opponents and by mobilizing the masses at the polls, the new regime had adapted the institution of universal suffrage to an authoritarian state. The modernization crisis of the Second Republic was over.[26]

If the coup d'état, purge, and plebiscitarian elections were a twofold process of demobilizing Republicans and remobilizing Bonapartists, the insurrection itself was a Republican countermobilization against the state. In its political dynamics, it was an abortive transformation of electoral power into insurrectionary strength. Populations that had already provided majority support for a "Democratic and Social Republic" tried through armed demonstrations to protest the coup, defend the Republic, punish repressive agents and collaborators of the government, and seize power immediately. Insurgency was most extensive where such populations had undergone intensive political socialization, first in the electoral campaigns of 1848-49, and then in secret societies that local militants had formed or consolidated thereafter. The shift from electoral to conspiratorial to insurrectionary action was the structural counterpart of bureaucratic efforts to exclude Republicans from the polity.

Such a shift was naturally far from automatic. It depended on two basic factors: (1) the organizational strategies and capabilities of leaders and militants in various districts of the nation; and (2) their maintenance of a local superiority of effective power despite the repressive zeal of bureaucrats and "men of order."

The organizational context of electoral and conspiratorial phases of mobilization differed considerably. Electoral successes in 1849 depended above all on the prestige and popularity of politicians at the level of entire departments. Voting was by *scrutin de liste*, i.e. each voter submitted a list of candidates for the department as whole, rather than a ballot for a single candidate. This system placed a premium on electoral alliances from town to town and *arrondissement* to *arrondissement*. The architects of such alliances were men of political reputation and skill, generally superior in social position, wealth, and education to the populace as a whole. Although few Republican leaders in 1849 belonged to the landed elite of the nation—the *grands notables* who paid over 1,000 francs in direct taxes—they generally exercised social influence over the residents of small towns and bourgs. In this respect, their departmental committees and congresses resembled the alliances of

[26] For a general survey of the consolidation of Bonapartist authority in 1852, see Payne, *Police State*, pp. 34-72; Pierre de la Gorce, *Histoire du Second Empire*, vol. 1 (Paris, 1894), 1-85; and Seignobos, *La Révolution de 1848*, pp. 222-44.

patrons, each of whom could guarantee the electoral discipline of his respective popular clientele. Of special importance in these alliances were politicians who had already been elected to the Constituent Assembly and who had mastered the art of public propaganda. It was Republican representatives such as Joigneaux, from the Nièvre, and Mathieu, from the Drôme, who fashioned the Democratic-Socialist program of political liberties and socioeconomic reforms that appealed to Republican voters in 1849. Their efforts were seconded by newspaper editors and electoral committee members in the towns of each department, who diffused propaganda and organized public rallies. As for local militants drawn from the artisanate and the peasantry, their contribution to Republican victories depended on the prior success of these regional and departmental leaders in creating a unified platform and a single slate of candidates. Victory also depended on whether anti-Republican politicians—Legitimists, Orleanists, and Bonapartists—succeeded in blending their respective political loyalties into a single list of candidates. The electoral strength of the Republicans in each department was inversely proportional to the cohesion of the party of order.[27]

In contrast, conspiratorial momentum in 1850-51 depended primarily on localized networks of mass organization. The clandestine associations of Republican militants, known as Montagnard societies, had a broad social base of membership, explicit procedures of affiliation, and precise obligations of loyalty and obedience. Exposed to severe administrative repression, they drew support more from horizontal relationships of social solidarity than from vertical relations of patronage. Recruitment was by word of mouth among trusted friends and neighbors, and subsequent political socialization was adapted to traditional social gatherings such as the neighborhood café, the social club, and the mutual benefit society. Although Montagnard activists moved easily across communal boundaries within standard market communities (small town or market bourg and surrounding villages), they had difficulty establishing close ties at higher levels of urban network—entire *arrondissements* or departments. Montagnard societies usually encompassed more "social space" within communities but less physical space within regions than the committees that preceded them.[28]

[27] The electoral organization of the Democratic-Socialists in 1849 has not been examined thoroughly in a national perspective. Among the regional and departmental monographs with useful details, see Vigier, *La Seconde République*, II, 183-209; Georges Dupeux, *Aspects de l'histoire sociale et politique du Loir-et-Cher, 1848-1914* (Paris, 1962), pp. 319-85; and Jean Dagnan, *Le Gers*, vol. I.

[28] For regional and local studies emphasizing the importance of Montagnard societies, see Vigier, *La Seconde République*, II, 285-98, 320-25; Marcilhacy, "La crise sociale et politique dans le département du Loiret," pp. 39-57; and Jean Dagnan, *Le Gers*, I, 436-73.

These variations in organizational influence are reflected in the relationship between Republicans' electoral strength in 1849 and Montagnard rebellions in 1851. As Maurice Agulhon has pointed out, resistance to the coup d'état "corresponds to the geographical differentiation of the 1849 election" at the national level: both phenomena were concentrated in central and southern France.[29] Among specific departments, however, the pattern is more complex. Resistance was generally no more extensive in departments where Republican candidates had obtained over 50 percent of the votes than in departments where they had received from 30 to 50 percent. Table 5.1 shows this by distin-

TABLE 5.1

Geographical Distribution of Republican Voters
in 1849 and Insurgents in 1851 (by Department)

% of Votes for "Democratic Socialist" Candidates in 1849	Scale of Insurgency		
	Major	Minor	None
Over 50	5	7	4
30-50	8	9	15
Under 30	0	0	37
Total	13	16	56

SOURCES: Departments with from 30% to 50% of the votes for Democratic-Socialist candidates and over 1,000 rebels were the Ardèche, the Gard, the Gers, the Hérault, the Lot-et-Garonne, the Var, the Vaucluse and the Yonne; those with over 50% of the votes for such candidates and with over 1,000 rebels were the Basses-Alpes, the Drôme, the Nièvre, the Pyrénées-Orientales, and the Saône-et-Loire. The percentage of voters for Democratic-Socialist candidates in 1849 is based on the map in Agulhon, "La Seconde République," p. 410.

guishing between departments with over 1,000 rebels, those with smaller numbers of insurgents, and those with no revolts. It is also noteworthy that only one of the sixteen departments where Republicans helped defeat all the *grands notables* had a major insurrection in 1851 (the Drôme).[30] The scale of resistance to the coup d'état was not a function of the effectiveness of Republican electoral organization at the departmental level.

Within rebel departments, however, electoral power and insurgency

[29] Agulhon, "La Seconde République, 1848-1852," in G. Duby, ed., *Histoire de la France*, vol. II (Paris, 1971), 417.
[30] André-Jean Tudesq, *Les grands notables en France*, 2 vols. (Paris, 1964), II, calculation based on map on p. 1216.

were strongly correlated. Indeed, rebel communities had typically been *more* left-wing than their departments as a whole. In all eight departments that had minority Republican electorates in 1849 but armed mobilizations of over 1,000 men in 1851, insurgent centers had given majority support to the left-wing candidates. This was true of Le Luc, La Garde Freinet, Barjols, Salernes, and Cuers in the Var; the cantons of Apt and Bonnieux in the Vaucluse; those of Vallon and Chomérac in the Ardèche; Anduze and Lédignan in the Gard; Béziers, Bédarieux, and Pézénas in the Hérault; St. Sauveur in the Yonne; Marmande, Mas-d'Agenais and Lavardac in the Lot-et-Garonne; and Vic-Fezensac, Jegun, and Mirande in the Gers.[31] As for the three departments with both majority Republican electorates and large-scale mobilizations, their revolts were also concentrated in Republican districts: the southwestern Basses-Alpes (as contrasted with the conservative east); the central Drôme (but not the conservative south); and the area of Clamecy (Nièvre).[32] The same was true of the smaller insurrections in majority Republican departments such as the Jura (Poligny), the Saône-et-Loire (Cluny, St. Gengoux), and the Allier (Le Donjon, La Palisse).[33]

The paradox of departments with minority Republican electorates and large-scale mobilizations disappears entirely when we turn to the conspiratorial phase of Republican dissidence. *Every* major zone of insurgency was covered by a network of Montagnard societies on the eve of the coup. This underground movement was most highly developed in rebel areas of Provence and Languedoc, where social conditions facilitated mass organizations among the peasantry (Var, Basses-Alpes, Vaucluse, Gard, Hérault, Pyrénées-Orientales, southern Ardèche), but it also existed in the other districts that mobilized over 1,000 insurgents (Clamecy, St. Sauveur, Dieulefit-Crest, Marmande, Lavardac, Vic-Fezensac, Mirande). By contrast, administrators uncovered evidence of Montagnards associations in only a few of the de-

---

[31] The returns have been published for the Ardèche (by canton), in Reynier, *La Seconde République dans l'Ardèche*, pp. 64-65; for the Gers, in Dagnan, *Le Gers*, I, 189-90; for the Var (by-election of 1850) in Agulhon, *La République au village*, p. 290; for the Vaucluse (by canton), in Vigier, *La Seconde République*, II, 211; and for the Yonne by Chevalier, *Fondements*, pp. 509-26. I have also examined the *procès-verbaux* for rebel electoral districts in the Gard, the Hérault, the Lot-et-Garonne, and the Var (AN, C 1502-46, 1525-78, 1571-135; and ADH, 15M 9).

[32] For the Basses-Alpes and the Drôme, see the map in Vigier, *La Seconde République*, II, 211; for the Nièvre, see AN, C 1534-92.

[33] On Cluny and St. Gengoux, see Goujon, "Le vignoble de Saône-et-Loire," II, 222-55; on Le Donjon and Jaligny, see Simone Derruau-Bonniol, "Le socialisme dans l'Allier de 1848 à 1914," *Cahiers d'histoire*, 2 (1957), 131-34; on Poligny, see P-G Besancon, Feb. 5, 1850, AN, BB[30] 373; on St. Sauveur (Yonne) see Louis Chevalier, *Fondements*, pp. 509-26.

partments with smaller uprisings (e.g., the Allier, the Bouches-du-Rhône, the Cher, the Loiret, and the Tarn).[34] In some of these other departments Republicans had been organized in a different manner before the coup. Thus, a Carbonari society existed at Poligny (Jura); a Republican mutual-benefit society at Cluny (Saône-et-Loire); and patron-client ties at Le Donjon (Allier).[35] Yet in the absence of the specialized associations of the Montagnards, armed resistance rarely extended into the countryside on a massive scale. The organizational shift from electoral committees providing bourgeois patronage to clandestine societies supplying popular leadership was the single most important precondition of mass uprisings in 1851.

If Montagnards succeeded in mobilizing large numbers of armed men, clearly the repressive policy of the state had been a partial failure. Despite a *national* balance of power overwhelmingly favorable to Louis Napoleon's government, Republican militants had maintained a *local* superiority of effective power in the areas that resisted the coup. In the absence of military force, administrative repression was more often than not counterproductive. National measures of the incidence of repression before the coup d'état show that repression and revolt were positively rather than negatively correlated. Thus, around half of the voluntary associations that prefects closed down by administrative decree between June 1850 and May 1851 were located in five departments which had major revolts (Basses-Alpes, Gard, Gers, Hérault, Var).[36] Furthermore, from 1848 to 1851 incidents of collective action that public prosecutors reported to the Ministry of Justice became increasingly localized in communes which subsequently rose in arms against the coup d'état. The inventories of judicial correspondence in series BB[18] and BB[30] of the National Archives mention specific communes in over 700 cases of riots, disorders, troubles, strikes, demonstrations, and seditious meetings described by the *procureurs-généraux* during the Second Republic.[37] If we calculate the proportion of these

[34] I have found many confessions of Montagnards among the documents of the military tribunals and Mixed Commissions of the Ardèche, the Drôme, the Gard, the Hérault, the Var, and the Yonne, and a few from the Lot-et-Garonne, the Nièvre, and the Vaucluse. Dagnan has published evidence of initiations in the Gers, Marcilhacy in the Loiret, and Cornillon in the Allier.

[35] On the Carbonari society at Poligny, see ADJ, MIV 40; the members of the mutual-benefit society at Cluny are listed in AD S-L, U, Ins. 1851, #2; for the role of bourgeois patrons in the revolt at Le Donjon, see AD Allier, M 1301-5 and Georges Rougeron, "La résistance au coup d'état dans le département de l'Allier," *La Révolution de 1848*, 32 (1935), 341-52.

[36] Calculations based on a tabulation of "clubs, dangerous meetings, political banquets, etc." prohibited by the prefects from June 19, 1850, to May 5, 1851, AN, BB[18] 1474.

[37] As noted below, these inventories list only a small fraction of the tax and

cases occurring in communes which rebelled in December 1851, we find that it rose from 6% in 1848 to 12% in 1849, 15% in 1850, and 28% in the first eleven months of 1851 (see Table 5.2). This data actually underestimates the trend, because most tax riots and forest disorders are not specifically included in the inventories. As we learned in Chapter Two, only a handful of these peasant protests in 1848 occurred in the rebel communes of 1851. Roughly speaking, insurgent communes probably had no greater share in *all* the collective incidents of 1848 reported to Paris (around 25/800 = 3%) than their numbers in the total population of French communes would warrant (775 rebel communes/35,000 communes = 2%). Yet in the last eleven months before the coup d'état, this small fraction of communes accounted for over one-quarter of all the collective incidents meriting repression in the eyes of the public prosecutors.

TABLE 5.2

Collective Protest, 1848-1851, and Armed
Resistance to the Coup D'Etat, by Commune

	1848	1849	1850	1851
Incidents Reported from Communes that Rebelled in 1851	17 (6%)	23 (12%)	21 (15%)	31 (28%)
Incidents Reported from Other Communes	265 (94%)	168 (88%)	117 (85%)	81 (72%)
Total	282	191	138	112

SOURCES: Inventories at the National Archives, BB[30] 333-35, 358-66, 391-94; BB[18] 1460-1501. All *émeutes* (riots), *désordres, rébellions, troubles, grèves* (strikes), *manifestations* (demonstrations), *entraves* (grain riots), *dévastations de forêts* (forest disorders), *pillages, rixes* (fights), *réunions séditieuses*, and *mascarades séditieuses* are included in the tabulation.

Administrators closed down visible though private associations only to face genuinely secret societies, and they repressed unarmed and largely symbolic demonstrations only to confront armed insurrections. Even military rule tended to exacerbate political tensions rather than to restore centralized authority: of the six departments declared in a state of siege before the coup, three had major insurrections (Drôme,

---

forest disorders in 1848, but they are reasonably complete for the last two years of the Second Republic. They are to be found at the National Archives, BB[18] 1460-1501 and BB[30] 333-94.

Ardèche, Nièvre).[38] For military force to be an effective political deterrent, it had to be deployed at the local level: almost no *commune* with a troop garrison rebelled in 1851 (the only major exception being Béziers). In the absence of local military superiority, administrative repression created martyrs to the Republican cause, strengthened the solidarity of local populations against the state, and guaranteed that if protest did occur after the coup, it would take a violent form.

To summarize our argument, two opposing forces clashed in 1851: a centralized state, determined to destroy all signs of left-wing dissent; and local populations of Republicans, organized within small areas along conspiratorial lines. The persistence of these "subversives" had increased the central trend toward a police state; the accentuation of repression had increased the local trend toward insurgency. With the coup d'état, this vicious circle reached the breaking point: in asserting their power by force of arms, Montagnards exposed themselves to a massive purge. No longer faced by an invisible enemy, no longer restrained by the law, administrators punished the rebel activists, dismantled their societies, and remobilized their erstwhile adherents in public electoral displays of repentance and loyalty. The state had restored order by destroying all organized opposition within the polity.

This argument derives theoretical support from the work of political scientists and sociologists who have analyzed the conditions of collective violence on a comparative basis. We have already noted Huntington's theory of political mobilization, institutional lag, and instability. In a more general theory of "internal wars," Harry Eckstein has developed an equilibrium analysis which also emphasizes political factors: "delegitimation," "subversion," "repression," and "elite inefficacy."[39] In his view, internal wars are "responses to political disorientation" within societies whose elites are divided and whose regimes are ineffectual.[40] Like Eckstein, Charles Tilly rejects theories linking popular protest movements directly to disorienting social processes or deteriorating living standards. It is changes in the conditions governing membership in the polity, not changes in rates of urbanization or economic growth, which are highly correlated with incidents of collective violence in modern France.[41] In Tilly's words, "The situations of gaining and losing political identity produce angry rebels with extraordinary fre-

[38] The Rhône, the Haute-Loire, and the Drôme were declared in a state of siege after an uprising at Lyon in June 1849, and the Ardèche, the Cher, and the Nièvre after local protests by Montagnards in October-November 1851.
[39] Eckstein, "On the Etiology of Internal Wars," in G. Nadel, ed., *Studies in the Philosophy of History* (New York, 1965), pp. 117-47.
[40] Ibid., p. 134.
[41] Tilly, "How Protest Modernized in France, 1845-1855," pp. 197-211.

quency."[42] Finally, the politimetrician Ted Gurr has developed a causal model of "civil strife" that is largely political in content, despite its origins in the psychological theory of relative economic deprivation. Gurr defines "deprivation" to include the loss or denial of "political goods" such as the right to vote and freedom of speech, and he correlates civil strife with specifically political intervening variables—"facilitation" (the organizational capabilities of dissidents), "legitimation," and "coercive potential."[43] Despite their varying emphases, all these theories are consistent with a political analysis of insurgency in 1851.

If our interpretation is sound, then the organizational capacity of local Republican militants was greater than the repressive skill of administrators in areas that experienced massive resistance to the coup d'état. To demonstrate this point, it is necessary to explore in depth the regional and local context of conspiracy: (1) How did Montagnard societies emerge in small towns and rural communes of southern and central France? (2) What socioeconomic and political conditions facilitated the solidarity of their membership? (3) What was the specific contribution of these organizations to the political struggle against the central bureaucracy? (4) What was the impact of administrative repression on their leaders and rank-and-file? The following four chapters are designed to answer these questions with evidence drawn from the several major areas of insurgency.

[42] Tilly, "The Changing Place of Collective Violence," p. 144.

[43] Gurr, "A Causal Model of Civil Strife: A Comparative Analysis Using New Indices," *American Political Science Review*, 62 (1968), 1104-24. He presents his multivariant model in much more detail in Gurr, *Why Men Rebel* (Princeton, 1970).

· 6 ·

BUILDING UNDERGROUND

"I swear on this iron to arm myself against all political and religious tyrannies, to combat them everywhere and always. I swear it, I swear it, I swear it." On the night of March 12, 1851, several young men from the bourg of Roujan (Hérault) were ordered to repeat this solemn oath. They knelt on the ground with their eyes blindfolded, their left hands on their chests, and their right hands on a dagger. Someone struck them three times on the head while a voice announced, "In the name of the sovereign people, by virtue of the rights which have been conferred on me by the Mountain, I dub you Montagnards." Several other voices muttered "Amen" and someone removed the blindfolds. Pistols were brandished before their eyes. "If you talk, your life will no longer depend on you," threatened the leader of the ceremonial, a local butcher named Higonenq. "If you reveal the secrets, you will meet with death, wherever you may try to flee." Then he showed them the signs of recognizance and taught them the password. The secret society of the Montagnards which they had just joined was not peculiar to Roujan. According to Higonenq, it existed everywhere in France.[1]

Few historical problems are more difficult to analyze than political conspiracies. By their very nature, "secret societies" operate outside normal channels of political activity and reportage—newspapers, pamphlets, brochures, etc. Often the only evidence of their existence is provided by police spies and administrators, whose information may be grossly exaggerated or completely false. Even where official sources can be corroborated by judicial evidence drawn from the testimony of conspirators, the central threads of such organizations are difficult to trace. This is especially true of the Montagnard societies during the Second Republic. The above account of a Montagnard initiation, provided by a plaster maker from Roujan named David Azema, was duplicated with minor variations by thousands of other men who confessed to magistrates after the coup d'état. They provided detailed information concerning Montagnard rituals, objectives, leadership, and organization in several hundred communes of the southeast, the southwest, and the center. Nearly all the historians who have consulted these judicial records have been struck by the importance of the Montagnard

[1] Int. D. Azema, plaster maker at Roujan, ADH, 39M 144.

121

movement within particular departments, such as the Drôme, the Gers, and the Nièvre. Indeed, some scholars, led by Philippe Vigier, have concluded that Montagnard societies were a major cause of resistance to the coup d'état. Yet the extent to which these various regional conspiracies formed a national political underground remains obscure. Despite their wide range of diffusion in at least fifteen departments of the nation, Montagnard societies appear from the judicial records as essentially regional, even local, phenomena. As a result, their political role in the history of the Second Republic has often been neglected by national historians.[2]

Yet Montagnard societies were definitely a national phenomenon in the sense that they provided a common organizational form and political orientation for Republican militants in geographically unrelated areas of the nation. Similar initiation ceremonies, leadership ranks, and political objectives characterized most of the ritualistic secret societies that spread into the French countryside during the months preceding the coup d'état. Separated from each other by hundreds of miles, men in bourgs and villages of departments such as the Yonne, the Gers, the Hérault, and the Var participated in the same basic movement of conspiratorial opposition to the government of Louis Napoleon Bonaparte.

The most distinctive feature of Montagnard societies was their ritual of affiliation. Each prospective member was blindfolded, presented with a weapon or weapons, and made to swear an oath of allegiance to the Republic. The blindfold was then removed and the initiate was threatened with death were he to betray the secrets of the society. Within this general format, used by all Montagnard initiators, the core element was the oath. Its terms varied from area to area and even from commune to commune in keeping with the changes which occur within any oral tradition. As one initiator from the Gard testified, "Because we never wrote anything down, the form of the initiation varied according to the person who received the members."[3] Nonetheless, some phrases of the *serment* were widely diffused in the nation. Thus, Azema's description of the oath he took at Roujan resembled some of those provided by Montagnards in other regions. The following examples are derived from the three geographical extremities of the

---

[2] Among secondary sources that discuss Montagnard societies, see Vigier, *La Seconde République*, ii, 183-92, 258-93, 320-26; Dagnan, *Le Gers*, i, 436-73; Marcilhacy, "La crise sociale et politique dans le département du Loiret," pp. 39-55; Agulhon, *La République au village*, pp. 366-67, 403; and Price, *The French Second Republic*, pp. 250, 265-67. The phenomenon is not mentioned by William Langer, for example, in his general study, *Upheaval*, pp. 450-65; or by Gordon Wright, *Times*, pp. 131-43.

[3] Int. V. Gascual, schoolteacher at Anduze, ADG, 3U 5/1.

Montagnard movement: the Nièvre (center), the Lot-et-Garonne (southwest), and the Var (southeast).[4]

> I swear to arm myself against tyranny, to defend the Democratic and Social Republic; I swear to kill a traitor if fate chooses me; I swear to die the most infamous death if I become a traitor or turncoat; I swear to help a brother in need. (Clamecy, Nièvre)

> I swear on this blade to rise up at the first signal and to arm myself to combat all political, religious, and social tyrannies, and to die if necessary for the triumph of the Republic. I swear it, I swear it, I swear it. (Gontaud, Lot-et-Garonne)

> I, freeman, in the name of the martyrs of liberty, I swear to arm myself against tyranny, whether political or religious. I swear to make propaganda for the Democratic and Social Republic. I swear to stab any traitors who reveal the secrets of the society. I swear to aid my brothers when they are in need. I swear to strike the traitors who would not be brothers like us. (Artignosc, Var)

Initiates in several departments (Nièvre, Gers, Drôme, Var) also promised to abandon their parents, wives, and children if ordered to march, and those throughout the southeast reported having been "constituted," "received," or "baptized" *frère* Montagnard.[5]

A second point of similarity between many Montagnard societies was their mode of organization. At the summit of local branches were presidents (Ardèche, Basses-Alpes, Drôme, Gard, Var) or commissions (Hérault, Lot-et-Garonne, Nièvre, Var), and at the base were ten-man units known as "decuries" or "sections." The rank of decurion existed in communes of the Drôme, the Gers, the Hérault, the Nièvre, and the Yonne; that of *chef de section* in communes of the Lot-et-Garonne, the Var, and the Vaucluse. Where the label of decurion was used, a further rank of centurion—the commander in theory of ten decuries— was sometimes created (Drôme, Hérault, Nièvre, Yonne). Above these local branches, *arrondissement* presidents or commissions and cantonal presidents or delegates were reported from the Ardèche, the Drôme, the Gard, the Hérault, and the Var. Especially in the southeast, Montagnards strove to create not only local paramilitary organizations but regional hierarchies of leadership.[6]

---

[4] Int. Jq. Fey, innkeeper at Clamecy, ADN, U, Ins. Clamecy; Tem. Roy, at Gontaud, AD L-G, 4U, Ins. 1851, *arr.* Marmande; Int. Jn. Bourges, cult. at Artignosc, AD Var, 4M 19-1.

[5] See, for example, Int. Edme Girault, at Clamecy, ADN, U, Ins. Clamecy; Dagnan, *Le Gers*, I, 448; Tem. Ant. Grontier, cult. at La-Roche-sur-Grane, ADD, M 1355; and dossier Brue-Auriac, AD Var, 4M 19.

[6] Multiple Ints. and Tems., analyzed more fully in Chapter Eight.

With respect to their political orientation, Montagnard societies combined a defensive posture with aggressive goals and tactics. On the one hand, leaders emphasized defense of the Republic, the Constitution, and universal suffrage as the central purposes of the organization. On the other hand, they promised recruits that if their cause triumphed, taxes would be lowered, wages raised, mortgage banks established, or popular living standards otherwise improved. Montagnards appealed to the legitimacy of the past—the Constitution of 1848—in order to found a new government in the future—the Democratic and Social Republic. Similarly, their tactics contained both a moderate element—electoral unity—and an extremist dimension—armed mobilization. Some Montagnards claimed ofter the coup d'état that their society had been founded solely for national (or local) elections, but their commitments under oath to take arms belie such assertions. In fact, they were prepared to attain power through the electoral process *or* to rise up in arms against the government. This dual strategy of electoral victory or armed insurgency was fused in the widespread belief that a new Republic would replace the government of Louis Napoleon Bonaparte in 1852—either at the polls or in the streets.

These shared traits of Montagnard ritual, organization, and strategy imply a common process of historical causation. To begin with, their ceremonials and paramilitary ranks were derived in large part from a preexisting culture of political conspiracy—the Republican secret societies of the July Monarchy. Of especial importance were Carbonari societies, which were implanted in several cities and towns of southeastern France (Marseille, Avignon, Cavaillon) in the 1830s.[7] It was in the plains of the Vaucluse that the first Montagnard societies emerged, using Carbonari initiation rites, in the winter of 1848. Next, these Montagnard societies were introduced elsewhere in France primarily as a result of left-wing Republican efforts to resist the electoral law of 1850, which sharply reduced their voting strength. An important role in this process of diffusion was played by a former Republican deputy from Avignon named Alphonse Gent, although not all areas of conspiracy were directly linked to his so-called Plot of Lyon. Finally, the spread of Montagnard societies within particular regions was a two-phase movement of urban and rural implantation. Once the organization had been established in a small town or market bourg, militants in that "central place" usually succeeded in helping the residents of smaller communes to found subordinate branches. This process of urban-rural political mobilization had already begun during

[7] On these Carbonari societies in the Vaucluse, see the "Acte d'accusation," P-G Aix, Sept. 15, 1841, AN, BB[18] 1472.

the electoral campaigns of 1848-49, and it gathered momentum in the months before the coup d'état. By December 1851, Montagnard societies existed in nearly all the communes of many districts in central and southern France.

The first half of the nineteenth century was the golden age of secret societies in France. Royalist Chevaliers du Roi conspired against the Empire, Carbonari plotted against the Restoration Monarchy, and obscure Republican and socialist societies—the Families, the Seasons, the Reformed Carbonari, the Voraces, the Communists, the Montagnards, Young Europe—burrowed underground during the July Monarchy. Oaths on daggers, secret gatherings of armed men, and rumors of impending massacres lent an aura of terror to these societies. For all the exaggeration of police spies and *agents provocateurs*, a conspiratorial tradition of Republicanism had taken form, mainly in the cities of Paris, Lyon, and Marseille, but also in towns and bourgs of the Vaucluse.[8]

This tradition combined a "primitive" cultural component—the initiation rite—with a relatively modern political orientation. The genuinely secret societies of the July Monarchy used initiation rites to impress upon recruits the solemnity of the combat in which they were engaged. Initiates were blindfolded, sworn to secrecy, and threatened with death to ensure their silence. Derived in most cases from the rituals of freemason societies, these ceremonials helped bridge the social distance between petit bourgeois leaders and lower-class recruits. They also reflected a popular taste for ritual characteristic of the journeymen artisans who belonged to secret associations known as *compagnonnages*. Initiation oaths represented both a rational response to police repression and an archaic tradition of verbal solidarity.

In their political objectives, Republican secret societies were heirs of the French Revolution. On the one hand, they sought to propagandize the cause of the Republic. Drawing inspiration from Gracchus Babeuf's Conspiracy of Equals (1797), some conspirators, led by Auguste Blanqui, also advocated the social ideal of absolute equality. In this respect they helped diffuse a left-wing ideology among urban workers, prefiguring the future direction of French socialism. On the other hand, these societies sought to overthrow the monarchy in a *coup de main*. For this purpose, they created military ranks, such as *chefs de sections*, urged recruits to procure weapons, and prepared to seize power. For lack of support within the French army, however,

---

[8] For studies of these various secret societies, see Gabriel Perreux, *Sociétés secrètes*; Lucien de la Hodde, *Histoire des sociétés secrètes et du mouvement républicain de 1830 à 1847* (Paris, 1850); Elizabeth Eisenstein, *The First Professional Revolutionary: Filippo Michele Bounarroti (1761-1838)* (Cambridge, Mass., 1959); and I. Tchernoff, *Le parti républicain sous la Monarchie de Juillet* (Paris, 1909).

their few attempts to foment revolt were complete failures. Thus, the uprising of the Society of Seasons in Paris (1839) was easily crushed and its leaders imprisoned for the duration of the monarchy; and armed gatherings of Carbonari in the Vaucluse (1841) dissolved into the night, merely precipitating a wave of repression. Secret societies were best equipped to indoctrinate men, not to seize power.[9]

With the Revolution of February 1848 the main justification for secret societies—protection against police repression—vanished overnight. Republicans now had a public forum, a mass audience, and an electoral avenue to power. Erstwhile conspirators founded public debating societies, known as clubs, and devoted their energies to the electoral campaign for the Constituent Assembly (April 1848). Although some militants were rapidly disillusioned with the results of universal suffrage, and others were embittered by the revival of police controls on the clubs, mass participation in the electoral process had transformed the conditions of political organization. When secret societies did reappear—in precisely the same areas where they had previously existed—their primary strategy was now electoral victory.

This was especially true of the Carbonari societies that Republicans revived in the towns of the Vaucluse during the winter of 1848-49. Threatened by a powerful Legitimist movement in this region, upper-class Republicans tried to ensure an electoral clientele by founding private social clubs, known as *cercles*, with secret political oaths. For example, the statutes of one such *Société de la Montagne*, dated 1848, described both a social club and a political organization. The society was supposed to have elected officers, a budget for mutual assistance, and a permanent meeting place with a concierge to serve drinks. At the same time, it was organized into ten-man groups, who had to obey their *chefs de section* blindly and to swear Republican oaths in secret initiations. The bourgeois *chef* of this particular society (at Gordes) tapped each recruit on the head during the ceremony, saying, "In the name of God, grand architect of the universe, I receive you *frère* Montagnard." Similar initiation rituals were diffused to bourgs near Orange early in 1849, and all these Montagnard societies participated actively in the electoral campaign for the legislative assembly (April-May 1849). They were vehicles for clandestine propaganda and political socialization rather than armed revolt.[10]

If the major purpose of Republican organization in 1849 was to win

[9] On the revolutionary ideology of Blanqui, see Alan Spitzer, *The Revolutionary Theories of Louis Auguste Blanqui* (New York, 1957). De La Hodde provides details on the paramilitary organization of these societies, *Histoire*, pp. 199-226.

[10] On the Montagnard society at Gordes, see Tem. C. Martin, shoemaker, and dossier Gordes, ADV, 4M 74; see Vigier for a general account of Montagnard societies in the Vaucluse, *La Seconde République*, II, 183-86.

elections, why introduce secret societies and paramilitary hierarchies at all? The answer was self-evident for most Republican leaders: secret societies were irrelevant to their cause. The only "Montagnard" societies which definitely existed at that time were in the Vaucluse and a few adjacent communes of the Drôme. Even the term *Montagnard* was rarely used. It referred primarily to a group of deputies in the Constituent Assembly who traced their political ancestry back to the extreme left—the "Mountain"—of the French Revolutionary Convention (1793). Politicians who supported these deputies generally called themselves Democrats, Democratic-Socialists, or simply Republicans. To wage a successful electoral campaign, they formed newspapers and committees, held rallies, and discussed politics in all manner of public and private settings, such as markets, *cercles*, and mutual-benefit societies. They did not need and they did not use ritualistic societies to mobilize Republican voters in May 1849.

The virtues of secrecy became increasingly apparent in the following months as prefects and public prosecutors closed off public channels of propaganda. Even before all permanent political associations were outlawed (in July 1849), Republicans had begun taking refuge in front organizations—*cercles, sociétés, chambrées*. This process of organizational camouflage was most advanced in towns and bourgs of southeastern France, where cultural traditions sustained a rich associational life in all classes of the population. Prefects soon began issuing edicts to "dissolve" Republican voluntary associations, as if to prove that only genuinely secret societies could hope to evade government repression. Nonetheless, the Montagnard model of organization probably remained peculiar to the Vaucluse and the southern Drôme (with one accidental transplant to Clamecy, in the Nièvre), until the winter of 1849-50.[11] It was the electoral law in May 1850 which precipitated a conspiratorial movement on a national scale. By disenfranchising many voters, that law threatened to exclude the Democratic-Socialists permanently from power. No longer could they expect electoral triumphs, especially in departments where they needed more votes in order to have a majority. It was to defend universal suffrage—by force of arms if necessary—that militants began organizing secret societies outside their original home in the Rhône river valley.

This transition from electoral to conspiratorial activity can be followed with especial clarity at the town of Béziers. Its first Montagnard organizer was a watchmaker named Eugène Relin, who had begun his revolutionary career on the Parisian barricades back in July 1830. Having gained and then lost a position in the gendarmerie, probably as a result of his Republican convictions, Relin moved to Béziers, where he

11 On Clamecy, see Int. Jean Mounier, ADN, U, Ins. Clamecy.

helped create a Freemasons' society in 1839. With the triumph of the Republic, he founded a political club in 1848, but he received only 592 votes in the department when he ran for the Constituent Assembly. In January 1849 he reduced his personal ambitions and joined with wealthier and more moderate Republicans in founding a private association named the *Société des Arts*. The members of this ostensibly nonpolitical society supported the Democratic-Socialist slate of candidates that a departmental congress chose in April, and their endeavors were crowned with local success: the Democratic-Socialists won a majority of votes at Béziers, though only one-third of the votes in the department as a whole.[12]

Relin and his friends already faced a hostile bureaucracy for whom electoral organization was subversive if its beneficiaries happened to be Republicans. In March 1849 they were raided by the police, who carried off their list of "democratic correspondents in the countryside."[13] The *procureur-général* at Montpellier denounced their electoral preparations as a conspiracy, though he lacked any legal grounds for prosecution.[14] When a by-election took place in July 1849, the legal situation had changed. Now the government had the Legislative Assembly's "Law on the Clubs" with which to harass the Republicans. The prefect published an edict on June 28 banning private as well as public gatherings where politics were discussed. On the very same day he had received an illuminating letter from the subprefect at Béziers:

> Before the elections are held, I believe it is indispensable to close down the nonpublic political gathering which exists at Béziers. This gathering is the center of action from which orders are diffused to all the enemies of order and public calm. If its members are left in peace to act, they will doubtless succeed in getting out the vote of their partisans, who are exhausted by the frequency of elections, and who, if left alone, would not be very inclined to leave work (in order to vote). Therefore, I think it is necessary to deprive them of this means of action by using the weapons which the Legislative Assembly has just given us.[15]

On July 1 the subprefect formally requested that the *Société des Arts* be dissolved, and on July 2 the prefect signed an edict to that effect.[16]

[12] The basic source on Relin's political career is the "Acte d'accusation" by P-G Aix, at his trial, AD B-R, 14U 53-54; on the Freemason society at Béziers, see ADH, 58M 17, dossier Béziers; on the *Société des Arts*, see S-P Béziers, Jan. 23, 1849, ADH, 39M 128.
[13] Letter from eleven members of the society to *L'Indépendant*, Mar. 30, 1849, published Apr. 4, 1849.
[14] P-G Montpellier, Apr. 13, 1849, AN, BB[18] 1474².
[15] S-P Béziers, June 28, 1849, and prefect's edict of the same day, in ADH, 58M
[16] S-P Béziers, July 1, 1849, and prefect's edict of July 2, 1849, ADH, 58M 17.

With the last remnants of Republican electoral organization out of the way, a right-wing candidate swept to victory.

Relin was undaunted. In December 1849 he created a new front organization called the *Société des Travailleurs*. Its sole declared aim was mutual benefit, but this time Relin took precautions to guard its political objectives from public view. Borrowing some Masonic rites, he had each prospective member swear a loyalty oath:

> I, equal peer of all, after having acquired knowledge of the statutes, of my own free will, obeying only the impulse of my will, do join in this respectable assembly which admits me as member and brother, in order to participate in the well-being of the association; I, democratic Republican, freeman, do swear in the presence of God and before all men to live as a good fellow-associate, to fulfill with love all the duties indicated by the statutes, in the measure of my abilities. May my oath be heard by all humanity! If I become a traitor, I consent to be driven from this meeting place forever. May my name be struck from the fraternal table and vowed to universal execration! Amen![17]

To no avail. The police commissioner knew that all the leaders of the *Société des Travailleurs*, "without exception," had belonged to the *Société des Arts*. He obtained an edict of dissolution from the prefect, raided the society, and even arrested Relin for "rebellion and insults."[18]

If front organizations could not survive, it remained to create a bona fide secret society. The threat to universal suffrage made Republican organization all the more imperative. Writing to a Parisian Democratic-Socialist on the eve of the parliamentary vote to restrict the suffrage, Relin called for extreme measures: "If the electoral law is passed, what will the people of Paris do, for example? Will they merely protest, or, reinforced by their rights, will they defend them, as we hope, even with arms? The provinces are admirably disposed; they will follow with enthusiasm a movement which they themselves cannot incite without exposing the Republic. I repeat: universal suffrage cannot be touched with impunity; not to defend it by every possible means is cowardly. The people would abdicate forever. . . . It is the moment; later it will be too late."[19] At this very time he was taking concrete steps to defend universal suffrage—he was organizing the Secret Society of the Mountain in the town and environs of Béziers. After the coup d'état, seventeen rural militants from nine different communes admitted having been personally initiated by Relin in April and May 1850. The

[17] Quoted in the "Acte d'accusation," cited in note 12.
[18] CP Béziers, Dec. 29, 1849, ADH, 58M 17; P-G Montpellier, Jan. 9, 1850, AN, BB¹⁸ 1474²; and P-G Montpellier, Jan. 28, 1850, AN BB³⁰ 362.
[19] Quoted in the "Acte d'accusation," cited in note 12.

oath that he used eventually spread throughout the region: "I swear on this iron, symbol of honor, to arm myself against all tyrannies, whether political or religious, and to combat them everywhere and always." So did his paramilitary organization of centurions and decurions. Although Relin himself was arrested on May 26, 1850, the movement he had launched continued to gather strength in the following months. Led by Casimir Peret, a wealthy distiller and former mayor of Béziers, the Montagnards in town numbered over 1,000 and those in around fifty other towns, bourgs and villages of the region exceeded 5,000 on the eve of the coup d'état.[20]

How did the Montagnard society reach Béziers? The rumored source was the city of Nîmes (Gard), but government prosecutors never acquired any certitude on this point. Indeed, not one single Montagnard organizer anywhere in France ever admitted diffusing the rituals from one department to another, or even from one town to another. Generally speaking, above the level of the *arrondissement* the conspiratorial activity of the Montagnards is shrouded in mystery.

Fragmentary evidence does suggest that political leaders in the cities of Lyon and Marseille played a central role in the Montagnard movement. Government officials themselves became convinced that Alphonse Gent, an ex-deputy from the Vaucluse who moved to Lyon in the summer of 1850, was the supreme leader of a conspiracy throughout southern France. When they arrested him in October, they discovered that he had been corresponding under a code name with several dozen political militants from fifteen departments of the southeast and the southwest. The case became a *cause célèbre*, and fifty-five Republicans were eventually prosecuted, most of them by a military tribunal at Lyon. Gent admitted at the trial that he had been trying to create a national organization of Republican defense. As a politician from the Vaucluse he was presumably familiar with the Carbonari rituals and the Montagnard societies prevalent in that area. From the city of Lyon, he was in a strategic position to diffuse such clandestine organizations to other departments, and some of his correspondents were definitely Montagnard initiators. That some interregional system of conspiratorial communications existed is shown by the fact that the first password of the Montagnard societies—"The Hour has Sounded / The Right to Work"—reached central and southwestern as well as southeastern France; and the second password—"Nouvelle Montagne"—appeared in both the center and the southeast while Gent was still in Lyon.[21]

[20] I have found 487 interrogations of confessed Montagnards in the *arrondissement* of Béziers, in ADH, 39M 144-60.

[21] For a general analysis of the "Plot of Lyon," see M. Dessal, "Le Complot de Lyon et la résistance au coup d'état dans les départements du sud-est," *Revue des révolutions contemporaines* (1951), 83-96; see also Vigier, *La Seconde Répu-*

Yet Gent seems to have had little contact with militants in the city itself, and some of his departmental correspondents were simply Republican electoral leaders, not Montagnard conspirators. He was creating a general movement to defend universal suffrage, within which the best organized societies were in southeastern France. Indeed, the "Nouvelle Montagne" which he was accused of founding may have originated at Marseille rather than Lyon. It was a public employee from Marseille named Joseph Lombard whose confession put the authorities on the track of a ritualistic society, and Lombard himself stated flatly that the "Nouvelle Montagne" was unknown at Lyon. He had been initiated at Marseille in March 1850—with the very same oath that Montagnards later used in the Var.[22] Furthermore, Republican journalists at Marseille succeeded in creating a network of correspondence with Montagnard leaders in the Var and the Basses-Alpes, and their newspaper, *La Voix du Peuple*, continued to circulate throughout the southeast until the coup d'état.[23] Especially after Gent's arrest, the main urban center for Montagnard societies may have been Marseille rather than Lyon. Consistent with this hypothesis is the fact that several Montagnard passwords in later 1850 and 1851—"Patience, Prudence, Perseverance" and "Ardeur, Action, Avenir"—reached from the Gard past Marseille to the Var, but never circulated in central or southwestern France.[24]

The key stage in the diffusion of Montagnard societies was everywhere the same: Republican militants in towns and market bourgs adopted the rituals and began initiating recruits in smaller communes. This process of urban-rural diffusion can sometimes be reconstructed in detail from the confessions of rural Montagnards after the coup d'état. Judicial records from the Hérault, the Drôme, and the Var show that Montagnards from Béziers initiated men from at least nineteen communes in that *arrondissement*; those from Montélimar and Dieulefit diffused the rituals to at least fourteen communes in the *arrondissement* of Montélimar; and those from Brignoles and Barjols made recruits in at least nine communes in the *arrondissement* of Brignoles. Less complete sources indicate that urban Montagnards played a similar role in founding rural societies around Apt and Orange (Vaucluse), Clamecy

---

blique, II, 286-88; and the judicial sources on the affair, in AN, BB[18] 1488, "Complot de Lyon," and ATML, "Affaire du complot de Lyon." The diffusion of these passwords can be inferred from scattered interrogations of Montagnards in the Yonne, the Gers, the Gard, etc.

[22] Tem. Joseph Lombard, employee in roads and bridges, Dec. 30, 1850, in AN, BB[18] 1488; many Ints. of Montagnards in AD Var, of which one was cited in note 4.

[23] See the list of correspondents from 27 communes of the Var to *Le Peuple*, in dossier Brignoles, AD Var 4M 19.

[24] Ints. of Montagnards, AD Gard, Var, Nièvre, Lot-et-Garonne.

and Nevers (Nièvre), Auch and Vic-Fezensac (Gers), Crest (Drôme), Pézénas (Hérault), Manosque (Basses-Alpes), St. Ambroix (Gard), and Toucy (Yonne). For example, two leaders from Apt attended an organizational meeting of fifteen villagers at Roussillon in the spring of 1850; Montagnards from Clamecy initiated "men from the country-side" whenever the latter attended markets in town; and those from Toucy used the occasion of a local fair in November 1851 to initiate several villagers from Merry-la-Vallée. Not only recruitment but sub-sequent Montagnard organization was generally centered on the *arron-dissement* capitals and cantonal seats. This was especially true in the Hérault (Béziers), the Var (Brignoles), the Gard (Alais, Anduze, Lédignan, and St. Ambroix), the Drôme (Dieulefit, Crest, Montélimar and Marsanne), and the Nièvre (Clamecy).

If Montagnard societies reached into the villages from small towns, this was the natural result of the routine channels of oral communica-tions that already existed at the district, or cantonal, level. Just as market transactions tended to focus on urban centers of periodic ex-change, so did administrative services, social hierarchies, marriage circles, and dialectical zones. Small market towns constituted "central places" around which villages were arrayed in regional systems of social communications. The existence of such central places in conspiratorial zones of the nation has recently been documented by social geogra-phers such as Dugrand, Brunet, and Barbier. Despite some confusion in vocabulary, these scholars agree that small towns, bourgs, or *bourgades* centralized economic and administrative activities for primary villages, or "peasant cells" in the departments of the Hérault, the Gard, the Basses-Alpes, and the Gers. Roughly speaking, the administrative unit of the canton combined a market center and a set of villages in a manner analogous to the standard market communities that the anthro-pologist Skinner has analyzed in nineteenth-century China.[25]

Joint social hierarchies, leisure activities, and speech patterns sus-tained urban-rural communications within such cantons. To begin with, large landowners tended to reside in the market centers rather than the primary villages. Unless they claimed descent from noble fam-ilies, such landlords comprised a "bourgeois" elite with an urban life style and a rural economic base. They were the traditional cultural brokers—the "notables"—between higher levels of administration and

[25] See Dugrand, *Villes et campagnes*, pp. 322-37, 431-64; Brunet, *Les campagnes toulousaines*, pp. 243-48; Barbier, *Villes et centres des Alpes du Sud* (Gap 1969), pp. 18-24. Skinner's general model is an elaboration of the "central place" theory first formulated by W. Christaller, whose classic study, *Central Places in Southern Germany*, has been translated by C. W. Baskin (Englewood Cliffs, New Jersey, 1966). For a useful introduction to this geographical literature, see Peter Haggett, *Locational Analysis in Human Geography* (London, 1965).

both local market centers and nearby villages.[26] Middling elements of the social hierarchy—merchants, shopkeepers, and prosperous craftsmen—also tended to cluster in the cantonal seats, while peasants were usually far more numerous than other social categories in the villages.[27] Through markets and fairs, these diverse social categories—bourgeois, artisans, and peasants—were integrated into a single social hierarchy with spatially distinct segments. Next, peasants visited the central places for news and entertainment as well as business. Markets and fairs were jovial occasions, sometimes accompanied by sporting contests and public dances. They enabled villagers to form friendships and marital alliances with the residents of other settlements in their market area. As one scholar has noted with respect to a northern French village, "People have regular contact with the inhabitants of non-adjacent villages only by frequenting the bourg (a cantonal seat). This is why their sphere of social relations tends to be the same as the zone of influence of the bourg which they frequent."[28] Finally, peasants within a given market area generally shared the same speech pattern. Those residing in the Midi conversed among themselves in a distinctive language (generally a variant of the *langue d'Oc*, or Occitan), but they could often speak French, too. Peasant bilingualism spread rapidly in the generation before 1848, in part because of greater market involvement and geographical mobility, in part because of greater exposure to the French language in government-sponsored primary schools. More and more peasants were able to communicate directly with those French-speaking elements of the urban population who were ignorant of the local dialect.[29]

The canton of Dieulefit (Drôme) provides an example of how such

[26] Concerning the concentration of rural properties in the hands of urban landlords, see Dugrand, *Villes et campagnes*, pp. 345, 352-53; and Brunet, *Les campagnes toulousaines*, pp. 268-89. The best analysis of this landed "bourgeoisie" in southern France is by Maurice Agulhon, *La vie sociale en Provence intérieure*, pp. 104-15, 358-60.

[27] This social contrast between towns and villages is less pronounced in southeastern France than in the center and southwest, due to the agglomerated settlement pattern, but it did exist. In the southern Basses-Alpes, for example, 54% of the labor force in the towns was employed in agriculture, as compared with 77% in the bourgs and 85% in the villages (census of 1851), data supplied by Barbier, *Villes et centres*, p. 21.

[28] Alain Morel, "L'espace social d'un village picard," *Etudes rurales*, 45 (1972), 63.

[29] Peasant bilingualism, a social phenomenon of fundamental importance, has been noted by very few historians. See, however, Agulhon, *La République au village*, pp. 192-95. For a contrary view, see Weber, *Peasants into Frenchmen*, pp. 67-94, who underestimates the extent and significance of bilingualism. His own statistical data show that by 1863, nine-tenths of all schoolchildren aged seven to thirteen could speak French, although only half of them could also write French (Appendix, p. 501).

communications networks were used for Republican electoral and conspiratorial purposes. To organize the electoral campaign of April–May 1849, a "Democratic Committee of the Town of Dieulefit" was formed by nine local residents, including the pharmacist Darier, the banker Defaysse-Soubeyran, the wood-turner Blancard, the watchmaker Benjamin Laurie, and the owner-farmer Blaise Prudant. The committee began its drive for votes with a thunderous proclamation: "People! Be on your guard! Rise up like a single man on election day and march to the defense of your threatened liberty." Addressing themselves to "inhabitants of the countryside, laborers in the towns," the Republican leaders of Dieulefit called for lower taxes, a smaller government budget, lower salaries for bureaucrats, state mortgage banks lending money at 3 percent, and free public education.[30] Having opened the campaign with this propaganda blast, they began organizing public meetings for townsmen and villagers: a rally of 200 at Dieulefit on April 14; banquets of 300 at the nearby village of Poët-Laval on the fifteenth and the seventeenth; a rousing popular farewell on the twenty-seventh for the town's delegates to a departmental conference of Republican leaders at Valence; and mass turnouts to greet three of the newly nominated candidates on May 4 and May 9.[31] On the latter day, all the surrounding villages were convoked by the Dieulefit leaders at least twenty-four hours in advance, and they sent "numerous contingents." At 10:00 a.m. a cannon shot announced the entry of the candidate, a deputy to the Constituent Assembly named Mathieu. An "immense crowd" awaited him along the road, shouting "Long live Mathieu! Long live our Representative!" At an indoor meeting, the pharmacist Darier opened the proceedings with an "eloquent speech" on the right to work, Mathieu gave a stirring defense of his legislative record, and the audience recited aloud the names of all the candidates on the Republican list. Mathieu left town triumphantly, accompanied by "a majority of the population."[32]

The Republican newspaper at Valence had boasted just before this electoral rally that "the enthusiasm of the population of Dieulefit is gaining more and more localities; propaganda is spreading without any effort."[33] The police commissioner in town agreed that the urban example had become contagious. As early as March 26 he had written, "They are recruiting proselytes in all the communes and the number is

[30] "Affiche: les membres du comité démocratique de la ville de Dieulefit aux électeurs de la Drôme," ADD, 11M 18.

[31] Letters from CP Dieulefit, Apr. 13, 14, 17, 23, and 28, May 4 and 5, 1849, ADD, M 1514.

[32] Letter from Gustave Meyer, secretary of the *comité démocratique* of Dieulefit, published in *La Constitution de 1848*, May 13, 1849.

[33] *La Constitution de 1848*, May 8, 1849.

continually growing." On April 28 he reiterated that the townsmen were finding adherants "among all the inhabitants of the countryside, where they are infiltrating their theories." Once the votes had been counted, he complained that their maneuvers among "the ignorant inhabitants of the countryside" had been successful. Furthermore, the political awakening of the peasantry seemed permanent. Even after the elections the police commissioner noted that "very active communications are taking place, not only among the cantonal committees, but even with the rural communes; there are groups in the villages these days which concern themselves with nothing but politics."[34] Indeed, it was so. During the next two years Montagnard societies spread throughout the canton, led by Darier, Defaysse-Soubeyran, and Blancard.[35] On December 6, 1851, these Montagnard *chefs* at Dieulefit mobilized nearly 1,000 men from the town and thirteen rural communes, and led them northward to the town of Crest in order to defend the "Democratic Republic."

Once momentum had been imparted by townsmen, leaders in the bourgs and villages extended the geographical range of recruitment by initiating men from neighboring communes. As a general rule, the Montagnard rituals were diffused from larger to smaller communes, and from agglomerated bourgs and villages to hamlets and farmsteads. Thus, three-quarters of the intercommunal initiations reported from the *arrondissement* of Béziers (excluding the town) involved an initiator from a larger commune than the initiate, and so did four-fifths of those reported from the central Drôme. Among the residents of bourgs who were especially active recruiters in the villages were a clerk at Bourdeaux (Drôme), a tax collector at Marsanne (Drôme), an owner-farmer, a *cafetier* and a day laborer at Servian (Hérault), a wood-merchant at St. Maximin (Var), and a carpenter at St. Sauveur (Yonne). These bourgs were all cantonal seats, but other agglomerations also hosted regional recruiters: a mason at Varages (Var), a farmer at Vesc (Drôme), a locksmith at Magalas (Hérault), a barber at Roussillon (Vaucluse), etc. Even the residents of small villages sometimes initiated men from other communes, aided by the rotating system of fairs and the annual cycle of festivals that existed at the village level.[36]

The final phase of Montagnard expansion occurred when local residents began initiating their friends and neighbors. The implantation of

---

[34] CP Dieulefit, Mar. 26, Apr. 28, May 4, 5, and 24, 1849, ADD, M 1514.

[35] See especially Ints. Jos. Archer, schoolteacher, L. Cordier, miller and deputy mayor, Ph. Morin, owner-farmer and municipal councilor, all residents of Montjoux, ADD, M 1357, 1359, 1366.

[36] Analysis based on interrogations of Montagnards from all these areas.

Montagnard societies in bourgs and villages depended above all on the energy of such leaders. Sometimes they were explicitly authorized by an outside organizer to perform initiations. For example, the Montagnard leader at Le Luc (Var) recruited the presidents of the societies at Flassans and Besse and assigned them the task of making initiations. Similarly, the leader at Grane (Drôme) persuaded two men from a neighboring village to become president and vice-president of their local society and to preside over all the initiations.[37] In the Hérault, Relin encouraged rural leaders to perform initiations, and so did the regional organizers who resided at Magalas and Boujan. In other cases the choice of a local initiator seems to have been left to the first recruits from a village, and in some communes anyone could make initiations. Whatever the procedures for selecting and controlling local *chefs*, these were the men who recruited the bulk of the Montagnards. Thus, three-quarters of the 503 initiations reported to magistrates in the *arrondissement* of Béziers were performed by local residents, and so were three-fifths of the 163 initiations reported in the central Drôme.[38] Mass recruitment at the base—the bourg, the village, the hamlet, the farmstead—was the work of local men.

The regional diffusion and local implantation of Montagnard societies was a slow process, extending from the spring of 1850 throughout the year 1851. By the eve of the coup d'état there were branches in over 700 communes of the nation. Southeastern France was the most well-organized region (around 500 societies), followed by the center (around 150 societies) and the southwest (from 50 to 100 societies). Departments with especially large numbers of branches include the Var (c. 90), the Nièvre (c. 85), the Drôme (c. 80), the Hérault (c. 70), and the Basses-Alpes (c. 65). Within each local society, the number of members varied from ten to several hundred or more, depending in part on the size of the population. Urban branches generally had at least 200-300 members (Clamecy, Apt, Dieulefit), with larger numbers at Bédarieux (around 400), Brignoles (550), and Béziers (over 1,000). Societies in the bourgs typically had 150 or 200 members, while those in the villages ranged in size from 10 to 100 members. For example, the bourg of Besse (Var) had 150 Montagnards, that of Capestang (Hérault) had 250, the *bourgade* of Ouanne (Yonne) had 50, the village of Artignosc (Var) had 50, that of Espondeilham (Hérault) had 20, and that of Fontenoy (Yonne) had 70. Generally speaking, Montagnards recruited only a minority of the adult male population, but their societies often included most of the young men, especially in the

[37] Ints. L. Bouis, butcher at Besse; and F. Turle, mayor at Flassans, in AD Var, 4M 19. Tems. Fr. Masseron, owner-farmer, and Jn. Jeune, day laborer, in ADD, M 1355, La-Roche-sur-Grane.
[38] Analysis based on all confessions from Montagnards in these areas.

villages. As a rough estimate, there were between 50,000 and 100,000 Montagnards in the nation as a whole. It was by far the largest conspiratorial movement in nineteenth-century France.[39]

[39] These estimates are based on the following sources:

Department	Number of Communes	Source
Southeast		
Basses-Alpes	65	Vigier, *La Seconde République*, II, map on p. 321.
Hautes-Alpes	9	Vigier, *Ibid.*
Ardèche	c. 50	Ints. of suspects, *arr.* Largentière, ADA, 5M 16, 18; statement of Jq. Froment, Montagnard leader at Assions, who named leaders in 35 communes of the department, ADH, 39M 138.
Bouches-du-Rhône	c. 25	Report of P-G Aix, Jan. 17, 1852, listing 27 communes where Montagnards confessed, AN, BB[30] 397.
Drôme	c. 80	Vigier; Ints. and Tems. in ADD, M 1353-71.
Gard	over 50	Tems. of Montagnards in *arrs.* Alais, Uzès, Le Vigan, ADG, 3U 5/1-3; letter from P-G Nîmes, Jan. 27, 1852, listing 23 communes with societies, AN, BB[30] 397.
Hérault	c. 70	Ints. and Tems. in *arr.* Béziers, ADH, 39M 144-60; register of MC Hérault, AN, BB[30] 401.
Pyrénées-Orientales	?	Only a few confessions, according to a personal communication from Peter McPhee, who has written a dissertation on the department during the Second Republic (University of Melbourne, Australia).
Var	c. 90	Ints. and Tems. in *arr.* Brignoles, AD Var, 4M 19 1-5 and 4M 26; Agulhon, *République*, pp. 366-67, 403; register of MC Var, AN, BB[30] 401.
Vaucluse	35	Vigier; Ints. and Tems. in ADV, M 11, 28-61.
Center		
Allier	c. 10	J. Cornillon, *Le coup d'état en Bourbonnais* (1903). Ints. and Tems. in AD Allier, M 1300-1305.
Cher	27	Michel H. Furet, "Le département du Cher sous la IIe République; étude politique (1851–début 1852)," (Diplôme d'Etudes Supérieures, Orléans–Tours, 1967).
Nièvre	85	Marc Autenzio, "La résistance au coup d'état du 2 décembre 1851 dans la Nièvre," (*Diplôme de Maîtrise*, Tours, 1970).
Yonne	over 25	Ints. and Tems. of suspects in the area of St. Sauveur, JM-1851, 251-59; letter from P-G Paris, Jan. 26, 1852, describing the societies in 14 other communes of the department, AN, BB[30] 396.
Southwest		
Gers	c. 40	Dagnan, *Le Gers*, I. 436-73.
Lot-et-Garonne	over 25	Ints. and Tems. in AD L-G, 4U, Ins. 1851; 6U, coup d'état; Z Victimes du coup d'état.
Tarn	2	Letter from P-G Toulouse, Dec. 11, 1851, AN, BB[30] 395.

7

SOURCES OF MONTAGNARD SOLIDARITY

Why did so many Frenchmen adhere to the Republican underground? This problem of popular motivation can be envisaged from three points of view. To begin with, peasants and craftsmen were attracted by the Montagnard program of socioeconomic reform. Leaders adapted their propaganda to the concrete grievances of local populations, and they promised that a "Democratic and Social Republic" would improve living standards. At a more subtle level, this propaganda acquired such popular resonance because it merged with preexisting political loyalties. Montagnards were the militant wing of the Republican movement, and they derived strength from historical traditions of loyalty to the Republic and opposition to the monarchy. The political experience of earlier regimes had left its mark on villagers as well as townsmen, especially where it had been influenced by deviant religious traditions (Protestantism, anticlericalism, religious "indifference"). Most fundamentally, membership in the underground was a social phenomenon. Montagnards operated through customary forms of sociability, such as voluntary associations and informal friendship groups. By politicizing this associational life, they transformed traditional loyalties to "brothers and friends" into a tenacious political movement.

The Montagnard ideal of a Democratic and Social Republic originated in 1848 as an urban ideology of social reform. A genuinely popular government would serve the interests of the poor, not the rich. Such was the basic propaganda line of Republican "socialists" immediately after the February Revolution. Preaching their doctrines in the clubs, these militants denounced "the exploitation of man by man," called upon the new government to guarantee "the right to work," and proposed various legislative reforms, including a state banking system and a graduated income tax. Low-interest public loans would enable workers to establish producer cooperatives, and a progressive tax would redistribute incomes in their favor. During the campaign for the Constituent Assembly, these socialist slogans and ideas filtered down to a few clubs and electoral committees in provincial towns such as Montpellier, but they rarely penetrated the countryside. The mass audience of left-wing Republicans seemed restricted to cities such as Paris, Lyon, and Limoges, where large concentrations of skilled workers were threatened by unemployment.

By May 1849 this situation had changed dramatically. Inspired by Montagnard representatives and provincial journalists, Republican militants in central and southern France mobilized a coalition of urban and rural voters around a program of economic reform. They applied the "socialistic" proposal of state banks to agriculture and called for a public system of low-interest loans to peasants; they supported the nationalization of railroads, canals, and insurance companies; they demanded a system of free and compulsory primary-school education; and they promised to reform the fiscal system. It was this latter issue of tax reform that had the widest circulation in the countryside, although cheap credit aroused peasant interest in some departments. Whether demanding the abolition of the wine tax (the *droits réunies*) and the urban sales taxes (the *octroi*), or proposing changes in the commercial license tax (the *patente*) and the land tax, Republican propagandists imparted a traditionalist concern for fiscal equality to their political alliance with urban workers. Henceforth, the Democratic and Social Republic was a rural as well as an urban ideal.

When Republicans began organizing secretly, they applied this same strategy of appealing to popular economic interests. According to Montagnard recruits, leaders of the underground made four kinds of economic promises to attract support: (1) they would abolish the wine tax and shift the general burden of taxation from the poor to the rich; (2) they would guarantee full employment and high wages; (3) they would provide low-interest loans through state banks; (4) they would satisfy popular demands concerning rights of usage to common lands. Which of these several issues militants emphasized depended on local perceptions of economic welfare. Thus, wine producers in the Hérault, the Gard, and the Var reported that abolition of the wine tax was a major objective of their Montagnard societies; silk producers in the Gard, the Ardèche, and the Var were enthusiastic about the prospects of cheap credit; journeymen artisans at towns such as Clamecy, textile workers at Bédarieux, and agricultural wage earners in vineyards of the Hérault and the Gard looked forward to higher wages; and peasants in some districts of Provence expected to regain their rights of usage to private forests or they planned to obtain a portion of the common lands.

Whatever specific interests Montagnard leaders promised to satisfy, their general approach to economic issues was the same: they tried to persuade the members of well-defined social categories, such as agricultural laborers or the village poor, that their common fate depended on the triumph of the Democratic and Social Republic. They offered economic incentives not to isolated individuals but to groups of men who already shared a sense of collective solidarity. This group consciousness appeared clearly in the testimonies of Montagnards after the coup d'état. According to a journeyman shoemaker at Clamecy, for example, "At all the meetings we were told that we had a great interest in belonging to the society because we would work less, we would earn more, and we'd no longer be under the yoke." An agricultural laborer from a bourg near Béziers echoed this class consciousness of wage earners in his testimony:

> I was recruited by Laurent Hermen (a shoemaker from a neighboring village), who told me that our position was very difficult, it only depended on us to make it better, and to reach this aim I must enter a secret society whose purpose was to unite the lower classes in the election. It was necessary to bring to power the leaders of the Red party (Republicans), with their government we would earn large daily wages and be perfectly well off. So I agreed.

In the Drôme it was the collective interests of "the people" to which Montagnards appealed in their promises of fiscal reform. For example, an initiator from the village of Grane announced to a group of recruits: "Citizens, there exists a society which you do not yet know about; this society has for its aim to change the government, to lower taxes, to make them fairer so that the tax on a small window will be less than that on a large window, to reduce the large government salaries, in a word, to improve the condition of the people." This class-conscious approach to the fiscal issue was echoed by a leader from the village of Crupies: "People said the aim of the association was to lower taxes and to distribute more equitably all the burdens which fall on the proletarians"; and another initiate from Crupies added that taxes would be shifted to "the capitalists." Montagnards in the Var also emphasized the solidarity of the village poor. "We wanted a good government which would suppress the indirect taxes and which would not place such heavy fiscal burdens on the poor," reported a wood-turner from the village of Tourves. "I was told that when we had the Republic we would be able to cultivate the communal lands and we would all be happy," testified a cultivator from the village of La Verdière. As for peasants in silk districts of the southeast, they, too, expected collective benefits from the Republic. One cultivator from a village in the Gard testified, "I was often told that if we had the real Republic, we would pay less taxes, only the rich would pay them, wages would be higher, and we'd have money at 3 percent at the mortgage bank." Similarly, Montagnards promised a villager in the southern Ardèche, "If they triumphed, they would give us the mortgage bank and the free school." In the minds of such recruits, not "I" but "we"— the workers, the people, the poor—would gain from the triumph of the Montagnard cause.[1]

Another feature of Montagnard propaganda was its tendency to short-circuit the connection between political change at the national level—the advent of the "real Republic"—and economic change at the local level. For example, one cultivator from the Gard was told that "at a given signal we would be masters of everything, we'd go take money at the mortgage bank at 3 percent, the Capitalists would have to pay taxes like everyone else, and there wouldn't be any more sales taxes (*octrois*) in the towns." This belief in instant progress was especially characteristic of peasants who felt victimized by external economic constraints. As another cultivator from the Gard testified, "We'd pay less taxes and we'd have more freedom. People added that we could yoke two draft animals to a small cart without being fined, we'd be able to sell our wine without being taxed, and we could go hunting and fishing whenever we pleased." Similarly, a cultivator from the southern Ardèche heard that "we wouldn't have any forest guard, any fishing guard, or any priest. We would lower taxes, we would divide the commons." According to a cultivator from one village in the Vaucluse, a local propagandist "gave us the hope that we'd no longer be bothered if we gathered wood on the mountain of the Luberon," and a neighbor testified that the same leader "preached politics to us and persuaded us that by conquering our rights we'd be free to hunt in the mountains behind our hamlet." Villagers in the northwestern Var also expected to reclaim their rights over common lands as soon as the Montagnards triumphed. One recruit reported that the society's aim was "to give us the right to go freely in the communal woods," and another testified, "Our aim was to obtain our rights of usage in the common lands." The more precise the economic demands of the Montagnards, the more they resembled the anarchist ideal of a free village community, emancipated overnight from the power of the state.[2]

This expectation of sudden change naturally influenced Montagnard perceptions of the way in which their cause would triumph. Many

[1] Int. Joannin, ADN, U, Ins. Clamecy; Int. Jn. Vidal, Lespignan, ADH, 39M 160; Tem. Ant. Grontier, La-Roche-sur-Grane, ADD, M 1355; Tem. Jn. Pr. Achard, ADD, M 1354; Int. E. Plèche, ADD, M 1368; Ints. A. Cival and Hip. Tassey, AD Var, 4M 19; Tem. Fr. Delbos, St. Victor, ADG, 3U 5/1; Tem. Jn. Roche, St. Genest, ADA, 5M 16.

[2] Tems. Et. Villaret and Jq. Virre, Maruéjols, ADG, 3U 5/1; Tem. S. Chabaud, Salavas, ADA, 5M 18; Ints. F. Peysson and L. Lambert, St. Martin-de-Castillon, ADV, 4M 76; Ints. A. Giraud, Carcès, and Jos. Dauphin, Montmeyan, AD Var, 4M 19.

peasants were told that they must vote together for Republican candidates, but they rarely viewed the electoral process as a long-range struggle for power. Instead, they expected a decisive victory in May 1852, a date that acquired millennial overtones in the minds of some recruits. It was but a short step from this conviction to preparations for direct action in the streets. Having committed themselves to take arms in defense of the Republic, recruits sometimes imagined that they would achieve their economic goals by force of arms. One flax worker and mason from a village in the Yonne testified that "the aim of this society was the overthrow of the government and the amelioration of the position of the poor and the fate of the workers"; and another mason from the same region reported that "it was a question of overthrowing the government of the Republic, after which the workers would be better paid." Similarly, a barber from Brignoles (Var) thought the Montagnard society would "lower the commercial license tax and suppress the tax on drinks, it would seize the communal governments and would replace the existing officials with its own nominees." In a few instances this belief in direct action even fostered rumors that the Montagnards would burn tax registers or mortgage registers. At the extreme point of psychological readiness to support the Democratic and Social Republic by force of arms, mob violence— the *Jacquerie*—might erupt.[3]

However much Montagnard societies functioned as trade unions for wage earners, defensive associations for taxpayers, or village syndicates for usagers of common lands, they were above all political organizations for the defense of the Republic. Some recruits promised to support the Constitution and universal suffrage, others agreed to oppose the restoration of kings, and they all swore allegiance to the Republic. Behind these political commitments was a deep-seated tradition of rivalry between the "Reds"—the Republicans of the Jacobin Terror —and the "Whites"—the Royalists of the Counter-Revolution. This factional rivalry often had a geographical base, depending on the religious orientations of local populations. For example, Protestant areas in southeastern France were traditionally Red by virtue of their hostility to the Catholic Church and its Royalist allies, the "Legitimists." Protestant peasants in the Gard, the Ardèche, and the Drôme had greeted the first French Revolution with enthusiasm, and they provided strong support for the Montagnards in 1851. Similarly, some Catholic populations in central and southern France were relatively

[3] Int. Pr. Charpey, Merry-la-Vallée, and Tem. Brunot, in dossier J. Fredouille, Ouanne, JM-1851, #252; Ints. M. Bremond and F. Brun, Brignoles, AD Var, 4M 19; Int. V. Fabre, Assions, ADA, 5M 16.

immune to clerical influences and hostile to the Legitimists. They had displayed their relative "indifference" in religious matters by support- ing the "dechristianization" measures of the "popular societies" during the French Revolution, and they constituted regional power bases for the Montagnards after the Revolution of 1848. By contrast, where de- vout Catholic populations had resisted dechristianization and had sup- ported the Whites, often violently, in the 1790s, they generally re- mained hostile to the Republicans from 1849 to 1851. Despite all the vicissitudes of Empire, Restoration, and July Monarchy, the Second Republic witnessed a resurgence of politico-religious loyalties dating from the First Republic.

Protestants were heavily involved in the Montagnards movements of the Gard, the Ardèche, and the Drôme. They voted overwhelmingly in favor of left-wing Republican candidates in 1849; they founded re- gional networks of clandestine societies around Alais, Nîmes, Largen- tière, Privas, and Dieulefit; and they spearheaded the armed mobiliza- tions in these areas. Although Catholics also joined the underground, especially in the Drôme, it was the Protestants who mustered the most manpower in defense of the Republic. Thus, seven of the thirteen ma- jority-Protestant cantons in the Gard participated actively in the in- surrection, as compared with three of the eighteen minority-Protestant cantons, and none of the entirely Catholic cantons. Half the sixty-odd communes of the Gard that took arms were over 80 percent Protes- tants, forty-six were over 50 percent Protestant, and only eight were entirely Catholic. Similarly, the foremost centers of insurgency in the Ardèche contained Protestant majorities (Chomérac, Vallon, Salavas). Even in the central Drôme, where four-fifths of the rebel communes were Catholic, Protestants were more unanimously engaged in the struggle than their Catholic neighbors. All fifteen Protestant com- munes of the area rebelled en masse, while two-thirds (39/59) of the Catholic communes mobilized only a minority of their able-bodied men.[4]

The Republican militancy of these Protestants reflected three aspects of their historical experience: massive adherence to the Jacobin phase of the French Revolution; persecution at the hands of the Bourbon dynasty and its Catholic allies; and secret resistance to the authority of the state. During the First Republic, the anticlerical and patriotic rhetoric of the Jacobins had reached a wide audience among Protes-

[4] For statistics on Protestants in these departments, see AN F^{19} 10031; ADD, 35M 9-370; Rivoire, *Gard*. Concerning the general connection between Protestantism and Republicanism, see Stuart Schramm, *Protestantism and Politics in France* (Alençon, 1954), and André Siegfried, *Géographie électorale de l'Ardèche sous la IIIe République* (Paris, 1949).

tants in regions such as the Diois (Drôme) and the Gardonnenque (Gard). For example, Protestant notables at Dieulefit and Crest had organized regional networks of popular societies in 1793, carrying dechristianization into precisely the same villages that sheltered Montagnard societies in 1851.[5] From this revolutionary experience many Protestants retained favorable memories. As one peasant from the Protestant commune of Anduze (Gard) later recalled, "If a majority of us were Republicans (in 1848), it was because we remembered our beautiful Revolution of 1793, whose principles our fathers had implanted in our hearts. We were, above all, the children of the Revolution."[6]

At the same time, Protestants remembered the religious wars of the Old Regime and the White Terror of the Restoration. The more they feared the triumph of their Legitimist enemies in 1849, the more firmly they supported the Republic. As for Louis Napoleon, his Roman Expedition to save the pope turned even conservative Protestants against him. As the police commissioner at Vallon reported:

Generally speaking, the wealthy Protestants don't support what are called socialist opinions, but most of them are left-wing Reds as a matter of principle. Some are only superficially on that side because they have been persuaded by propagandists for the Red and Social Republic that the Roman Expedition is a monstrosity. They have been led to believe that Henry V (the Bourbon pretender) has a chance of mounting the throne of his ancestors. Before their eyes has been unrolled the terrifying canvas of the old wars of religion. . . . This is what has carried them toward the idea of a pure and exalted Republicanism as a means of salvation and conservation for their religion.[7]

The police commissioner at Dieulefit agreed that "the events of Rome" and "religious fanaticism" had resulted in a massive Republican vote among Protestants in his area. There were even rumors that unless the Republican candidates won in May 1849, "the Catholic priests would force the pastors to take holy water and even to kneel." Similarly, the subprefect at Nyons (Drôme) wrote, "I am certain that many individuals in my *arrondissement* are Reds because, as Protestants, they are

[5] I am indebted to Richard Malby from Oxford University for this information. See also Jules Chevalier, *La Révolution à Die* (Valence, 1903).
[6] Memoirs of Jean Fontane, cult. at Anduze, published in Alfred Detrez, "Autour du coup d'état. Souvenirs d'un paysan," *La Revolution de 1848*, 32 (1909-10), 166.
[7] CP Vallon, cited by Reynier, *L'Ardèche*, p. 144.

enormously afraid of a Bourbon restoration and renewed clerical domination."[8]

If opposition to the Legitimist alliance of throne and altar motivated many Protestant voters, earlier traditions of secret worship may have encouraged their participation in the underground. The *procureur-général* at Grenoble suggested that conspiratorial activity was an intrinsic feature of Protestantism in the Drôme: "The character and the traditions, even religious, of a portion of the inhabitants in the Drôme predispose them to enter into affiliations whose mysteries, slogans, and nocturnal meetings in isolated places recall to the populations, notably those of the *Diois*, the *arrondissement* of Nyons and a portion of the *arrondissement* of Montélimar, the churches of the desert and the Protestant conventicles of earlier times."[9] Furthermore, Protestants rejected the confessional, and this cultural trait helped them conceal the existence of Montagnard societies from the police. Most Protestant suspects flatly refused to confess after the coup d'état, even in villages where nearly everyone was an initiate. For example, only the Montagnard leaders confessed in the entirely Protestant village of Crupies; the fifteen members who were interrogated all denied any knowledge of the society.[10] Magistrates obtained detailed information about Montagnard organizations in only two of the fifteen other Protestant-majority communes of the central Drôme where such societies probably existed (Montjoux and Cliousclat). They encountered the same reticence among most Protestant rebels in the southern Ardèche and the Gard. By contrast, Catholic recruits confessed by the hundreds in districts such as Béziers and Brignoles.[11]

Many Protestants were also devoted to the egalitarian ideals of the Montagnard movement. In some cases, they may have been motivated by a prophetic tradition of social justice. For example, a considerable crowd of Protestants sympathized with the Montagnard leader at Lasalle (Gard), a law student named Maurice Aubanel, when he preached the "Social Republic." "Soon it will come, and it will crush the houses, the roofs will become the foundation and the foundation the roofs," shouted Aubanel, whose father was the local pastor.[12] In religiously mixed areas, Protestant artisans and peasants shared the same economic

[8] CP Dieulefit, May 15 and 24, 1849, and S-P Nyons, Nov. 14, 1849, ADD, M 1514, M 1344.
[9] P-G Grenoble, Dec. 9, 1850, AN, BB[30] 391.
[10] Ints. E. Plèche, mayor, and Jn. Fr. Martin, rural guard, ADD, M 1365, 1368.
[11] Compare the few confessions of Protestant suspects in ADG, 3U 5/1-3 and ADA, 5M 16, 18, with the many confessions of Catholic rebels in ADH, 39M 144-60, and AD Var, 4M 19-21, 26-28.
[12] P-G Nîmes, report in 1850, AN, BB[30] 363.

concerns as their Catholic neighbors. Upper-class Protestants, who were generally more progressive than the Catholic notables, could fashion a political alliance on nonreligious grounds by promising social reforms. Thus, Darier, the Protestant pharmacist at Dieulefit, converted Catholic textile workers to the Montagnard cause.[13] Similarly, at Vallon the police commissioner reported that "working-class members of both religious groups are all imbued with subversive principles."[14] Protestant leaders were not always successful in creating such a religiously mixed movement, but social issues offered them their best hope of undercutting Catholic support for the Legitimists.

Just as Protestant populations who entered the Montagnard movement shared a political tradition favorable to the Republic, the same was true of many Catholic populations who supported the Montagnards. The historical origins of "left-wing" politics among Catholics in modern France can be traced to the French Revolution. According to Richard Cobb, the geography of "revolutionary extremism" in the 1790s curved in a "half-moon" from the Nièvre southwest through the Limousin to the valley of the Garonne, and southeast across the Allier and down the Saône and Rhône river valleys to the Mediterranean.[15] With the exception of the lower Rhône river valley (eastern Gard, southwestern Vaucluse, southern Drôme), where Royalists launched a White Terror during the Thermidorian reaction, these zones of dechristianization and Jacobin fervor voted Republican in 1849 and they continued to support left-wing politicians throughout the Third Republic. A more precise analysis of "ultrarevolutionary" districts in the 1790s would probably also reveal a close correlation with the areas of religious "detachment" or "indifference" which appear on twentieth-century maps of regional variations in Catholic religious practices. A direct line of geographical continuity can probably be traced from the dechristianization movement of the First Republic to the "Democratic-Socialist" vote in 1849, the Radical and Radical-Socialist vote in the late nineteenth century, and the religious behavior of Catholic populations after the Second World War.[16]

In any case, most of the districts that took arms in 1851 had definitely participated in the Jacobin phase of the French Revolution. For example, Clamecy had been the most revolutionary district of the Nièvre during the Jacobin Terror, and dechristianization had obtained

---

[13] Thirty of the fifty-one known insurgents whom I could locate in the census lists for 1851 at Dieulefit were Catholics (59%), in a population that was 61% Catholic.

[14] Report cited in n. 7.   [15] R. C. Cobb, *People*, pp. 127-28.

[16] See the maps of electoral behavior and religious practice in *Atlas historique de la France contemporaine, 1800-1965* (Paris, 1966), pp. 112-16, 147.

comparable support in neighboring districts of the Yonne that rebelled in 1851. Insurgent districts of the Allier had also been Jacobin strongholds during the First Republic.[17] With respect to revolutionary politics in Provence, Vovelle has constructed maps of the distribution of Republican societies and defrocked priests, which overlap to a remarkable extent with the distribution of Montagnard societies in 1851. He shows, for example, that the towns of Apt, Orange, Forcalquier, Manosque, and Sisteron all stimulated the movement of *déprêtisation* (abdication of priests) in their respective regions, eventually reaching over 100 communes. These same towns were Montagnard centers for the same bourgs and villages in 1851. By contrast, villages around Barcelonnette (eastern Basses-Alpes) had opposed Jacobin anticlericalism, and they remained right-wing during the Second Republic.[18] The case of the Var is more complex, but the most dynamic centers of insurgency in that department (Le Luc, La Garde Freinet, Vidaubun) had been strongly pro-Jacobin. Furthermore, popular societies had flourished in the agglomerated bourgs and villages of the Var, as elsewhere in the southeast.[19] In the southwest, the department of the Gers provides an especially clear example of political continuity. Its central districts (Condom, Vic-Fezensac, Auch, Mirande) had been overwhelmingly favorable to the Revolution and they rebelled in 1851; its eastern and western districts had resisted dechristianization, sometimes violently, and they supported the Legitimists during the Second Republic.[20] In sum, resistance to the coup d'état occurred primarily in areas of the nation that had already demonstrated their left-wing tendencies during the First Republic.

This long-range political continuity does not necessarily imply that Jacobinism led directly to "Democratic-Socialism." The First Republic was less the origin of a self-conscious revolutionary tradition in central and southern France than the precipitant of a Royalist reaction. It was opposition to this White Terror that defined the enduring factional alignments in these regions. Influential leaders of the Republican

---

[17] Jules Charrier, *La Révolution à Clamecy et dans les environs* (Clamart, 1922); Chevalier, "Fondements," pp. 585-87; Denys Bournatot, *Un chef-lieu de canton du Bourbonnais: Le Donjon, son histoire* (Moulins, 1963), pp. 132-40.

[18] Michel Vovelle, "Prêtres abdicataires et déchristianisation en Provence," CNSS, 89 (1964), I, 75-77; *Atlas historique de Provence* (Paris, A. Colin, 1970), pp. 166-68.

[19] Agulhon, *La République au village*, pp. 127-28, 296-98; Agulhon, *Pénitents et francs-maçons de l'ancienne Provence* (Paris, 1968), pp. 285-311.

[20] Mme. Septe, "Les suspects dans le district d'Auch," CNSS, 78 (1953), 185-94; P. Dieuzaidé, "L'Insurrection royaliste de l'an VII," *Revue Gascogne*, tome 22, pp. 199-210; G. Brégail, "L'Insurrection de l'an VII," *Bulletin de la société archéologique, historique, littéraire et scientifique du Gers*, 10 (1909), 235-50, 277-87.

electoral movement in 1848-49 were not always self-conscious Jacobins but they were invariably anti-Legitimists. As one justice of the peace in the *arrondissement* of Béziers wrote after the municipal elections of 1848, "At Thézan, as in all our rural communes, we know only two flags, that of revolution and that of counterrevolution, the tricolor flag and the white flag. Opinions are deeply divided: 1815, 1830 and 1848 found the same persons, the same families invariably under the same flag, and the friends of the revolution are in a great majority."[21] Similarly, popular support for the Republicans was often based on traditional hostility to the Bourbons. It was in these terms that the prefect of the Drôme explained why the Legitimist-Bonapartist electoral alliance in his department was overwhelmingly defeated: "Those who claim to be true Republicans cooperate with the Socialists, and call those who are opposed to them Whites or Royalists. Because in this department the Legitimists do not have the sympathies of the populations, many peasants and workers who had acclaimed Louis Napoleon (in December 1848) turned to the Republican-Socialists when they were told the government was leading them back to Legitimism."[22] In many districts of the nation where Republican leaders triumphed in 1849 and where Montagnards rebelled in 1851, Catholics had long opposed Legitimist politicians.

Factionalism was a widespread phenomenon in the local politics of nineteenth-century France. It was the natural counterpart of a stratified social system whose upper and lower layers were bound together in "vertical" patron-client relationships rather than opposed to each other in "horizontal" class relationships. Factional leadership was generally exercised by the members of prominent families—bourgeois landlords, professional men, merchants—who functioned as cultural brokers between local communities and the central bureaucracy. Through a combination of intrigue with state officials and services to local residents, these notables aspired to occupy appointive or elective positions in local administration—municipal councils, departmental councils, justices of the peace, etc. Naturally, the larger the number of potential competitors for these positions, the greater the likelihood of local factionalism. Generally speaking, enough elitist families were present in bourgs and large agglomerated villages to sustain well-defined factions. This helps explain why municipal power struggles were especially characteristic of the Midi, where many predominantly agricultural communities were large agglomerations—"urbanized villages" or "agro-towns." Thus, in 1848 over 70 percent of the local mayors' posts

[21] J. P. Murvièl, Aug. 24, 1848, ADH, 17M 32, dossier Thézan.
[22] Prefect, Drôme, Dec. 13, 1849, ADD, M 1344.

changed hands in departments such as the Var, the Vaucluse, and the Pyrénées-Orientales, as compared with a national average of only 50 percent.[23]

The relationship between local divisions and national politics was complex. For one thing, not all communes that possessed a factional style of politics were divided internally. Antagonisms between neighboring towns, bourgs, or villages sometimes generated what might be described as "spatial factions": all the residents of one social space, whatever their class position, opposed the residents of a neighboring social space. The same kinds of conflicts might also exist between neighboring *quartiers* within a town or sections within a rural commune. Spatial factions were especially characteristic of bourgs and large villages in Mediterranean France, where most marriage partners were coresidents of the agglomeration, and where young men consequently had a strong interest in defending their local territory against intruders from neighboring settlements.[24] The anthropologist Pitt-Rivers has described such agglomerations as "closed communities" by virtue of their distinctive sociocultural opposition to each other.[25] This concept needs to be applied cautiously to nineteenth-century France—market relationships, educational opportunities, and state centralization all created openness to external influences—but communal rivalries definitely shaped political divisions in some districts of the Midi. For example, most townsmen at Apt (Vaucluse) voted Republican, while their secular enemies at St. Saturnin-d'Apt voted Legitimist, and similar divisions between Red and White communes existed elsewhere in the Vaucluse, in the Var, and in the Gard.[26]

Furthermore, factional alignments shifted over time as new personalities and new issues arose. Each change of regime—1815, 1830, 1848—created fissions and fusions in the composition of local coteries. Although some families could trace their political lineage back to the First Empire or the July Revolution, others veered from one side to another as opportunity arose. For example, the dominant faction at Mézel (Basses-Alpes) during the July Monarchy had consisted of a bourgeois-popular alliance against the Fruhier family, whose claims to communal economic rights had given rise to a long series of trials. Yet

[23] Table in AN, C 977. On patrons and factions, see Tudesq, *Les grands notables*, II, 1117-37; Agulhon, *La République au village*, pp. 246-58; and Vigier, *La Seconde République*, II, 97-98, 388-439 *passim*.
[24] On village conflicts among youths, see Louis Mazoyer, "La jeunesse villageoise du Bas-Languedoc et des Cévennes en 1830," *Annales*, 10 (1938), 502-7.
[25] Julien A. Pitt-Rivers, "The Closed Community and Its Friends," *Kroeber Anthropological Society Papers*, 16 (1957), 5-15.
[26] See, especially, the reports of the P-Gs from Aix, Montpellier, and Nîmes, in AN, BB[30] 358-97.

who should emerge as the leader of the "party of Republican laborers" in 1848, denouncing the "party of the bourgeois" as reactionaries, but M. Fruhier's son-in-law, who was trying to restore the family's influence through ultra-Republicanism![27] Related to this instability of factional composition was the fact that local divisions between rival families, "clans," or neighborhoods has no *intrinsic* relationship to national politics. Wylie has shown in the case of the twentieth-century village in the Vaucluse how factional disputes can exist independently of the ideological and social divisions that supposedly motivate national political parties.[28] The same was all the more true in the nineteenth century, owing to the absence of mass political organizations at the national level. The disputes between rival notables during the July Monarchy often lacked any reference to national issues, and even after the February Revolution squabbles over municipal elections sometimes remained untouched by the political currents of the period. While some factional leaders accused their enemies of opposing the national government—as Royalists in 1848, or as "anarchists" or "demogogues" in 1849—others simply complained about the corruption, dishonesty, or strong-arm methods of their rivals.[29] The process of projecting communal divisions into national politics, which might be described as the "nationalization of factions," depended on the political consciousness of the local populations. It was not automatic.

It was the institutional context of extramunicipal politics that encouraged this nationalization of factions: a bureaucracy which sought to control local public opinion through the mayors and municipal councils, and politicians who tried to exploit local grievances in departmental electoral campaigns. Given the historical association between Legitimism and the Catholic church, religion easily became the symbolic issue around which national loyalties were grafted onto local factions. Where most artisans and peasants were strongly influenced by the clergy, Royalists had an advantage over Republicans. Where popular religious practice was infrequent or superficial, it was the Republicans who had the upper hand. There is no single explanation for why Catholics in predominantly Republican districts were less fervent than those in Legitimist areas. Among the factors which historians have emphasized are the following: (1) a deviant religious tradition within the landed elite, such as "crypto-Protestantism," "Jansenism,"

---

[27] P-G Aix, Aug. 30, 1848, AN, BB[30] 358.

[28] Laurence Wylie, *Village in the Vaucluse*, 2nd ed. (Cambridge, Mass., 1964), pp. 206-42.

[29] One-quarter of all the communes in the Drôme and the Hérault had disputed municipal elections in 1848. See the administrative correspondence in ADD, 11M 18, and ADH, 17M 40.

Freemasonry, or sheer indifference; (2) weak clerical influence over popular religiosity, linked to a variety of social conditions, such as strong municipal institutions, male/female role segregation in religious practice, Occitan monolingualism and illiteracy, and seasonal migration to cities; (3) direct conflicts with the clergy over many issues, including tithes and honorariums, sexual morality, municipal festivals, funeral ceremonies, and public schools.[30] Although anticlericalism was not a dominant theme of Montagnard propaganda, local Republican factions were generally indifferent if not hostile to the Catholic church. Indeed, men who attended religious services were sometimes ineligible for membership in the underground. As one cultivator from Béziers testified, "I wasn't in their society, they called me a *chapelet*, a *cul blanc*, because I go to church sometimes."[31]

At the leadership level, a factional style of politics ensured that Republicans had upper-class patronage in the market centers and the larger rural communes. These patrons provided services to lower-class clients, helped indoctrinate them in the virtues of the Republic, and vouched for the respectability of their cause. Despite Royalist claims that the Reds were all impoverished rebels against the notables, it was precisely landlords, professional men, and merchants who led Republican factions in many rebel communes. For example, seventeen landlords, three doctors, two surveyors, a retired functionary, a lawyer, a miller, a wine merchant, and an iron merchant were accused of patronizing the Montagnards in fifteen towns and bourgs of the southwestern Basses-Alpes; eight landlords, two retired notaries and a practicing notary, two pharmacists, a doctor, a health officer, and a miller were denounced in twelve towns and bourgs around Auch; and five landlords, a retired notary, a doctor, a surgeon, a veterinarian, a livestock merchant, and a wood merchant were compromised in six bourgs of the district of St. Sauveur. A similar pattern of upper-class patronage existed in at least twenty-two rebel communes around Béziers and eleven insurgent bourgs and *bourgades* of the central Drôme.[32] Indeed, bourgeois Republicans were considerably more exposed to repression after the coup d'état than were other social categories. Very few of them were as rich as the *grands notables* who led the Royalists, but they had sufficient wealth and education to exploit hierarchical social ties for political purposes. Thus, Nicholas Dautée, a landlord at St.

---

[30] Agulhon, *La République au village*, pp. 163-87; Gérard Cholvy, *Géographie réligieuse de l'Hérault contemporaine* (Paris, 1968); Christianne Marcilhacy, *Le Diocèse d'Orléans au milieu du XIXe siècle* (Paris, 1964).

[31] Tem. Pr. Burges, CG Béziers.

[32] Registers of MC Basses-Alpes, Drôme, Gers, and Hérault, AN, BB[30] 398, *400, 401; notes of MC Yonne, ADY, M[1]282.

Sauveur worth 160,000 francs, "made the greatest evil in his canton"; Garet, a retired notary at Leugny (Yonne), "exerted a pernicious influence over the inhabitants of the countryside, having a rather large fortune"; Jacques Espariot, a seventy-year-old landlord at Valensole (Basses-Alpes), exerted "a corrupting influence over the agricultural class, being irreligious, without morality"; Anselme Nougaret, a young landlord at Caux (Hérault), "began the perversion of public opinion by commenting on and explaining the newspapers to the lower classes"; and Defaysse-Soubeyran, a banker at Dieulefit, was "very dangerous" because he "dominated the countryside" by virtue of his profession.[33] These judicial comments could be duplicated for scores of other landlords and professional men who were prosecuted after the coup d'état for their role as Montagnard patrons.

Popular motivation was influenced in three respects by local factionalism. First, some recruits were directly obligated to their upper-class patrons. For example, a peasant at the village of Puissalicon (Hérault) testified that he had been recruited to the Montagnard society by a local doctor and distiller named Prosper Delhon, whose family had been persecuted by the Whites back in 1815: "I am in debt to Delhon. At the time of the elections in 1848, Delhon had given medical care to me and my daughters. To get me to vote his way, he told me that he would consider himself paid. I accepted and voted Red whenever he wanted. Later, his father loaned me one hundred francs, which I still owe him."[34] Second, recruits who were exposed to Legitimist denunciations of all Republicans as *canaille* viewed upper-class patrons as moral guarantees. Thus, a peasant at Artignosc (Var) was reassured to learn that "rich men, whose social position would serve as a guarantee, belonged to the society"; and recruits from Pourcieux (Var) were persuaded that "a society whose members included men who had received education and who possessed large fortunes couldn't have an evil end."[35] Finally, factional relationships created a strong sense of local political identity. In many communes popular consciousness of national politics was stimulated by the attraction or repulsion of local personalities, and by the strength or weakness of well-defined groups of Reds and Whites. Open conflict between local factions did not generally favor the Republicans, in part because it exposed them to state repression. Thus, armed resistance in 1851 occurred in only four of the thirty-three communes in the Gard and the Vaucluse whose

[33] Register of MC Basses-Alpes, AN, BB^{30} 398; notes of MC Yonne, ADY, III M^{1}282; dossier Nougaret, ADH, 39M 155; dossier Defaysse-Soubeyran, ADD, M 1360.
[34] Int. Jos. Mignonat, ADH, 39M 154; and dossier Delhon, ADH, 39M 149.
[35] Ints. Jos. Constant, Artignosc, and Ph. Boyer, Pourcieux, AD Var, 4M 19.

factional conflicts were reported to the Ministry of Justice.[36] It was subterranean conflict between a dominant population of Reds and a minority faction of Whites that created especially propitious local conditions for radicalization and insurgency. Through factional rivalries many men became Reds before they joined Montagnard societies, and they took arms as members of a Republican community of sentiment and opinion.

The process of politicization extended beyond factions to encompass a variety of solidary groups, such as private clubs, mutual-benefit societies, youth groups, and café clienteles. Montagnards were able to mobilize social loyalties for their political cause by either merging with such preexisting associations and friendship networks, or by imitating their patterns of sociability and solidarity. The basic strength and cohesion of the Montagnard movement was derived from the associational life of well-defined groups within local communities.

"Sociability" can be defined as a natural human inclination to derive enjoyment from conversation, play, and recreation. The history of sociability is thus coterminous with the changing forms through which men and women have participated in leisure activities. Of special importance for the political development of modern France has been the emergence of the voluntary association as an institutionalized expression of "sociability." Typical examples of such associations have included religious brotherhoods (*confrèries*), private social clubs (*cercles, chambrées, sociétés*), mutual-benefit societies (*mutuelles*), trade unions (*syndicats*), veterans' associations, athletic clubs, and musical societies. Although politics has rarely been an explicit purpose of these associations, the manner in which they have "organized" sociability has had several political consequences. First, they have often recruited their members from a single social class. Just as sociability within the home has generally been confined to relatives and friends with comparable incomes and life styles, the same has been true of extrafamilial institutions of sociability. By articulating the class structure of society, voluntary associations have comprised "action groups" for class-based political movements. Second, they have been *formal* organizations with explicit rules for the admission of members, the selection of officers, the collection and management of money, and the scheduling of meetings. Through participation in these associations, Frenchmen have acquired organizational experience, which they have applied to political parties. Third, voluntary associations have been corporate entities whose administrative "statutes" have been registered with local or na-

---

[36] Calculations based on incidents reported by P-Gs Aix and Nîmes, scattered dossiers in AN, BB[18] and BB[30].

tional authorities. Their official recognition has made them convenient shelters, or "front organizations," for political movements in periods of repressive government. Finally, the recreational and welfare activities of these associations have elicited popular loyalties, which political parties have tried to use for their own organizational purposes. Either through indirect affiliation or direct imitation, parties such as the Communists have incorporated formal patterns of leisure, recreation and welfare into their organizations. Indeed, as a *social* phenomenon the mass political party can be interpreted as a mobilization of sociability for political purposes.[37]

Associational development in modern France can be analyzed as a twofold process by which rational-legal modes of organization were first applied by the Church to customary spheres of leisure and welfare, and then extended under urban influence to new and increasingly secular forms of sociability. The religious phase of this process had been largely completed by the eighteenth century, when a variety of Catholic brotherhoods channeled elitist and popular sociability. The urban brotherhoods of landlords, merchants, and craftsmen were probably more elaborately organized and more stable than the rural brotherhoods of peasants, as predicted by the sociological theory that the rationalization of associational life is an aspect of the larger societal process of urbanization.[38] In any case, the shift from religious to secular associations definitely began in the towns, as Maurice Agulhon has demonstrated in his remarkably original study of penitential brotherhoods, freemason societies, *cercles*, and popular societies in eighteenth-century Provence. *Cercles* then proliferated in many towns during the first half of the nineteenth century, expressing the class consciousness of urban elites. Artisans and even peasants began imitating this bourgeois institution by introducing formal regulations to their customary social gatherings. Although religious brotherhoods continued to play a major role in the social life of urban artisans, secular mutual-benefit societies began to supplant them during the July Monarchy. Finally, the café or tavern became an increasingly important social institution

---

[37] On the politicization of French voluntary associations, see Maurice Agulhon, *Pénitents*, pp. 285-311; Agulhon, *La République au village*, pp. 207-45, 376-406; Robert T. and Gallatin Anderson, "The Indirect Social Structure of European Village Communities," *American Anthropologist*, 64 (1962), 1016-27; Robert P. Baker, "Socialism in the Nord, 1880-1914, a Regional View of the Socialist Movement," *International Review of Social History*, 12 (1967), 357-89; and Annie Kriegel, *Les Communistes français: Essai d'ethnographie politique* (Paris, 1968). See, also, the contrary analysis of how voluntary associations with economic goals can block party development, in Suzanne Berger, *Peasants against Politics: Rural Organization in Brittany, 1911-1967* (Cambridge, Mass. 1972).

[38] Compare Bouchard, *Le village immobile*, pp. 297-310, with Agulhon, *Pénitents*, pp. 86-160.

in the lives of workers and peasants. Stimulated by the gradual diffusion of new consumer tastes (coffee, beer, *eau de vie, limonade*), "public houses" multiplied extrafamilial and secular channels of sociability. They functioned as neighborhood social clubs, which supplemented or even replaced more traditional patterns of leisure based on kinship networks and religious institutions. The café, no less than the *cercle* or the *mutuelle*, expressed modernizing influences in small towns and rural communities.[39]

Formal voluntary associations were especially widespread in Mediterranean France during the July Monarchy, where all social classes shared a traditional preference for sexually segregated leisure activities, and where agglomerated settlements facilitated peasant imitation of urban-oriented elites. As landlords and professional men founded *cercles*, with written statutes, elected officers, membership dues, and rented premises, artisans and peasants in the bourgs and villages introduced new formalities to their customary drinking and eating clubs, which they called *chambrées* in Provence.[40] Market expansion and rising literacy encouraged this middle- and lower-class emulation of bourgeois sociability.[41] Peasant gatherings adopted fanciful names, such as *l'Apollon* or *Cercle de la Gaiété*; they wrote down rules and regulations; and they affirmed an ideal of calm, high-minded, and polite social behavior. For example, the statutes of one peasant *chambrée* near Apt contrasted rustic mores with bourgeois refinement by prohibiting loud noise, fights, thefts, calumnies, and obscene songs, drawings, or words.[42] Written rules also helped to regularize the position of the *chambrées* vis-à-vis the state, whose fiscal agents wanted to tax the consumption of wine in these private gatherings. Bourgeois associations and suspicious tax collectors were both characteristic of wine-producing communes in lower Provence and lower Languedoc, where administrators commonly detected *chambrées* and *sociétés* during the Second Republic. For example, a police commissioner in the canton of Pertuis (Vaucluse) reported in 1851 that small towns and bourgs in the lower valley of the Durance contained well-organized *cercles* and

[39] In addition to Agulhon, see Emmanuel Le Roy Ladurie's brief discussion of rural cafés as an aspect of modernization in eighteenth-century France, "Révoltes et contestations rurales en France de 1675 à 1788," *Annales*, 28 (1974), 14.

[40] For an ethnographic interpretation of these peasant *chambrées*, see Lucienne Roubin, *Chambrettes des Provençaux* (Paris, 1970), reviewed critically by Maurice Agulhon, "Les chambrées en Basse-Provence," *Revue historique*, 498 (1971), 337-68.

[41] For the connection between rising living standards and interclass imitation in Mediterranean villages, see Ernestine Friedl, "Lagging Emulation in Post-Peasant Society: A Greek Case," in Jean Peristiany, ed., *Contributions to Mediterranean Sociology* (Paris, 1968), pp. 93-106.

[42] Réglement of *La Société ou Chambrée* of Gargas, 1848, ADV, 4M 48.

chambrées, while villages and hamlets on the mountain of the Luberon had only customary gatherings, without names, officers, fixed meeting places or written rules.[43] Similarly, administrators observed associations more frequently in the large agglomerations of the coastal plains near Avignon, Nîmes, Montpellier, and Béziers than in the silk-producing villages of the Cévennes.[44]

With the advent of the Second Republic, some of these private clubs began to function as units of political solidarity and as media of political communications. The members of a *société* or *chambrée* usually belonged to the same social class (the bourgeoisie, the artisanate, or the peasantry), resided in the same neighborhood (a *quartier* of a town or bourg, an agglomerated village, or a hamlet), and shared the same age and marital status (the young, mainly unmarried men—*la jeunesse*—or the elderly married men—*les anciens*). This social conformity encouraged the *frères et amis* (brothers and friends) to support the same political cause. As one police commissioner reported in January 1849 from a bourg near Montpellier, "The inhabitants go to various societies every evening and especially on festival days. Each society has its own nuance, and the individuals belonging to it possess such a community of opinion that to know whether someone is a Legitimist, a moderate Republican, or a Montagnard, it is only necessary to know of which society he is a member."[45] Voluntary associations were all the more likely to acquire a uniform political coloration because they were such convenient settings for oral propaganda. By visiting the *chambrées*, Montagnard spokesmen succeeded in circumventing the police controls imposed on public meetings, much to the dismay of administrators. The *procureur-général* at Aix complained in February 1849 that "the *chambrées*, or private gatherings, have become a formidable instrument of agitation"; and his counterpart at Nîmes reported a year later that "the vast and ancient organization of the *chambrées* in the department of the Vaucluse is being exploited by socialist militants, who have converted them into veritable clubs."[46] Once the members of a *chambrée* had embraced the Democratic and Socialist cause, they could sustain their political fervor through oral recitations of Republican newspapers and through group singing. In addition to nationalist hymns such as the Marseillaise, enthusiasts could draw upon a widening

[43] CP La Tour D'Aigues, May 16, 1851, ADV, 4M 52.

[44] Reports of P-Gs Nîmes and Montpellier, describing some 300 *cercles* and *sociétés* that existed in towns and bourgs of the Gard and the Hérault in 1850, printed by I. Tchernoff, *Associations et sociétés secrèts sous la Seconde République* (Paris, 1905), pp. 59-76, 90-109.

[45] CP Pignan, Jan. 23, 1849, ADH, 39M 128.

[46] P-G Aix, Feb. 22, 1849, AN BB[18] 1474^A; and P-G Nîmes, Apr. 10, 1850, printed in Tchernoff, *Associations*.

repertoire of Republican songs, both French and dialectical, in praise of peasants and workers. Ribald jokes and boastful slogans—"Long live the Reds! Down with the Whites!"—could discourage the weak and the hesitant from opposing the dominant current of opinion among the *sociétaires*. Factional divisions might oppose Red and White *chambrées* within the same bourg, but behind the closed doors of each association, a single political orientation often reigned supreme.

While preexisting associations were politicized, new *cercles, sociétés*, and *chambrées* were organized for political purposes in Mediterranean France.[47] In founding social clubs with provisions for both leisure (a fixed meeting place) and mutual benefit (a treasury), politicians transferred familiar forms of sociability and welfare into the new domain of mass politics. Political *cercles* in the towns sometimes recruited scores or even hundreds of members from a cross section of occupational groups and educational levels. Such large front organizations, with their multiclass composition, precise leadership roles and systematic financial procedures, resembled the penitential brotherhoods so widespread in Provence and Languedoc during the Old Regime.[48] At the same time, the Republican *Cercles de Travailleurs* and *Cercles Démocratiques* that proliferated in urban centers of the Gard, the Hérault, and the Vaucluse derived their basic pattern of sociability—card playing, drinking, and conversation in a private clubhouse or the back room of a café—from the cultural model of the bourgeois *cercle*. They channeled the mobility aspirations of artisans and some peasants into political organizations that embodied elitist social values. As for the Republican societies which emerged in villages and hamlets around towns such as Apt (Vaucluse), Barjols (Var), and Alais (Gard), they were more homogeneous in class composition than their urban counterparts. These village *Sociétés des rouges*, as they were often known, had the same recognized status in the community as other *chambrées* or *sociétés*; their members gathered privately but not secretly to entertain themselves in the evenings. Here, political solidarity was based on the segmentation of leisure activities along generational and residential lines.[49]

Against this background of politicization and organizational innovation, the secret societies of the Mountain blended easily into the pre-

[47] The P-Gs at Nîmes and Montpellier noted around 100 *cercles* and *sociétés* founded after Feb. 1848 in the Gard and the Hérault, of which four-fifths were Republican (reports cited in n. 44).
[48] See, especially, the dossiers of Legitimist mutual-benefit societies at Bédarieux and Cette, ADH, 55M 23, 29.
[49] See the dossiers of Montagnard suspects from the villages of Varages (Var), Bonnieux (Vaucluse), and Cassagnoles (Gard), AD Var, 4M 19; ADV, 4M 74; ADG, 3U 5/1.

vailing sociocultural environment. Whether by infiltrating existing *chambrées* and *cercles* or by founding new ones, Montagnards could mobilize voluntary associations for conspiratorial purposes. Thus, *chambrées* overlapped with Montagnard societies in at least thirty-six communes in the *arrondissement* of Brignoles (Var) and twenty-one communes in the *arrondissement* of Apt. Similarly, Montagnard militants belonged to *cercles* and *sociétés* in several dozen communes of the Gard, ranging from industrial towns (e.g. Alais) to wine-producing bourgs (e.g. Vauvert) and silk-producing villages (e.g. canton of Anduze).[50]

These associations had two basic functions in the underground: concealment and solidarity. As private clubs, their premises could be used for conspiratorial activities without fear of police repression. Initiation ceremonies were held in the *chambrées*, and so were organizational meetings. As one villager from the Var testified, "We gathered at a meeting place which in appearance was occupied by a *Chambrée* with eighteen members, but which in reality served as a base for the members of the secret society. There we named the section leaders and the triumvirate of the society."[51] The customary privacy of the *chambrées* and *cercles* made them effective front organizations.

Even more important was the contribution of these clubs to the social cohesion of the Montagnards. Many recruits to the underground expected to receive assistance from their *frères et amis* in case of illness. Montagnard leaders throughout southeastern France fostered this expectation by promising that mutual benefit was a central objective of their organization. The prior cultural experience of religious brotherhoods and their secular derivatives, the *chambrées* and *sociétés*, helped give substance to these promises. For example, at the village of Carcès (Var), where the revolt originated in the *chambrées*, one Montagnard later testified that "each section used to gather separately to plan what must be done to provide the necessary labor services on the lands of members of the society who fell ill."[52] Monetary payments, labor services, and even burial rites were performed by Montagnards in some communities of the Midi, thereby extending into the political domain the welfare benefits customarily provided by the *confréries* and the

[50] Tabulations for the Var and the Vaucluse based on Ints, and Tems. of Montagnards, AD Var 4M 19, and ADV, 4M. Estimates for the Gard based on Tems. Montagnards in *arrs*. Alais, Le Vigan, and Uzes, ADG, 3U 5/1-3. See, also, R. Huard, "La défense du suffrage universel sous la Seconde République: Les réactions de l'opinion gardoise et le pétitionnement contre la loi du 31 mai 1850 (1850-1851)," *Annales du Midi*, 83 (1971), 315-36.

[51] Int. L. Feraud, dossier Ginasservis, AD Var, 4M 19.

[52] Int. A. Ambard, prop., dossier Carcès, AD Var, 4M 19. Montagnards from 29 other communes in *arr*. Brignoles said mutual assistance was an objective of their society.

chambrées. To the hope of collective assistance was added the desire to participate in the leisure activities of the Montagnards. Some recruits even claimed after the insurrection that they had been initiated in order to avoid the ostracism of their fellow club members. At Entrecasteux (Var), for example, where *chambrées* had existed "for a long time," the inhabitants told the justice of the peace that they had been under "moral pressure" to join the secret society. "The members of the *chambrées* stopped socializing with those who weren't on their side." A farmer from the nearby commune of Artignosc agreed that he had joined the underground in order to avoid the suspicion of the other members of "the society to which I belong."[53] The same social pressures existed in communes where a new club was founded by the Montagnards for recreational as well as political purposes. As one eighteen-year-old cultivator in the Gard testified, "A democratic society was founded at Maruéjols (a small village near Anduze); all the young men of the village were members, and I was obliged to live alone because they didn't want me with them. I finally decided to join in order not to be alone."[54] Although some *chambrées* and *sociétés* contained both initiates and noninitiates, the basic tendency was for Montagnard support to become unanimous in any club which they dominated. When that happened, their political solidarity as initiates became indistinguishable from their social cohesion as friends and drinking partners.

In some areas of southeastern France (the Bitterois, the central Drôme), male friendship networks were centered on public cafés rather than private clubs, and even in Provence, *cercles* and *chambrées* were sometimes abandoned under government pressure and replaced by cafés. Yet remarkably stable, well-structured, and exclusive clienteles generally frequented these cafés, which were easily transformed into political fronts for the Montagnards. Magistrates discovered after the coup d'état, for example, that public houses had been operating as Montagnard centers in at least twenty-one bourgs and villages in the *arrondissement* of Béziers and eighteen rural communes in the central Drôme.[55] In some cases the initiates had developed elaborate procedures to guard against outsiders. As one Montagnard from a bourg near Pézénas (Hérault) testified:

When the members were meeting together, they remained very silent in the presence of a stranger to the society. . . . As soon as a

[53] *Rapport* J. P. Cotignac, dossier Entrecastaux, and Int. E. Sappe, dossier Artignosc, AD Var, 4M 19.
[54] Tem. Et. Villaret, ADG, 3U 5/1.
[55] Tabulations based on Ints. and Tems. of Montagnards, ADH, 39M 144-60; ADD, M 1353-71.

stranger entered a café, or other public place, a member of the society would say, "It's raining," which meant everyone must stop talking for fear it was a police spy; the individual who was considered a stranger to the society would reply, "It's not raining," if he was a member, thus signifying that we could talk, and then we weren't bothered by him any more.[56]

Typically, the Montagnards monopolized a local café to the exclusion of the Whites, and they rarely had to worry about strangers. Business considerations encouraged many café owners and innkeepers to protect these politically subversive clients, and some publicans initiated recruits, collected dues, and otherwise aided the movement. They were subsequently arrested in large numbers, accounting for at least seventy prosecutions in the Drôme, fifty-four in the Basses-Alpes, forty-nine in the Hérault, and forty in the Vaucluse.[57] The severity of this reaction confirmed the importance of Montagnard cafés and inns in the southeast.

Montagnards also derived support from the contagion of example among urban artisans and rural youth groups. Artisans shared corporate traditions that implied common political orientations, and some of their mutual-benefit societies aided the Montagnard cause.[58] Furthermore, those who worked in teams experienced social pressures to imitate the political behavior of their comrades. According to one tanner at Béziers, "The tanners in my profession all belonged without exception to the secret society, so I was obliged to become initiated in order to avoid their ill treatment." Typically, imitation provided its own justification for action. As one stonemason at Montélimar (Drôme) put it, he joined the secret society because the other stonemasons belonged to it. Among the rural populations generational solidarity had a comparable effect. Thus, a rural stonemason near Montélimar testified: "For a long time I noticed that the young men of Sauzet seemed to despise me; I found out that it was because I didn't belong to their secret society; because everyone else was a member, my position was not tenable, so I resolved to join." In some of the smaller rural communes the young men—*la jeunesse*—entered the Montagnard move-

---

[56] Int. D. Azema, plaster maker, Roujan, ADH, 39M 144.

[57] Totals given in a general *statistique* of prosecutions after the coup d'état, AN, BB[30] 424. For particular examples, see Ints. J. Jullien, Donzère, and A. Camet, Chabeuil, ADD, M 1359, 1363.

[58] Examples include Bédarieux, Crest, Dieulefit, and La Garde Freinet. See the police correspondence about the textile workers' *Société de St. Etienne* at Bédarieux, founded in 1830 and dissolved by the prefect in 1850, ADH, 58M 16; police reports on mutual-benefit societies at Crest and Dieulefit, ADD, M 1348, 1510; and Agulhon's analysis of the cork workers' cooperative at La Garde Freinet, *La République au village*, pp. 330-60.

ment en masse, and one leader explained the socioeconomic pressures behind such recruitment in the Bitterois:

> For the rest, many men were affiliated to the society either in order to avoid the threats uttered against those who did not belong, or to avoid being ill-viewed by their comrades, the great majority of whom were members. What increased still more the number of affiliations was that in several localities the leaders of the work teams in charge of hiring the workers or the peasants wanted only members, or tried to enroll those who were not members. In certain villages, the members, who far outnumbered nonmembers, excluded the latter from their balls and their amusements; to avoid such exclusion even the recalcitrant ended up joining.

In the eyes of some young men, Montagnard societies were fraternities that they joined for social purposes; not to belong was tantamount to declaring oneself an antisocial being.[59]

If the culture of Mediterranean France prepared villagers as well as townsmen for membership in clandestine societies, that of southwestern France favored urban more than rural conspirators. Bourgeois *cercles* and artisanal *mutuelles* existed in many towns and market bourgs of the Gers and the Lot-et-Garonne, and they influenced Montagnard organization in a few cases (e.g. the *Cercle de Travailleurs* at Marmande, the *Association Mutuelle d'Assistance* at Lavardac). Cafés, inns, and shops hosted stable groups of Montagnard artisans in most of the market centers that rebelled in 1851. Outside these agglomerations, however, peasant sociability does not seem to have supported conspiratorial networks, although young men acquired some organizational experience through participation in the festive cycle of the rural community.[60] As for central France, there, too, the Montagnards were active mainly where they could rely on preexisting patterns of male sociability, above all, the cafés and shops in the bourgs. Although peasants who resided in hamlets sometimes developed their own nuclei of conspirators, membership in the underground was generally synonymous with participation in the social life of the bourgs.[61] The strength of Montagnard political allegiances throughout France was founded on the social consciousness of fraternal groups in the towns, bourgs, and rural agglomerations.

[59] Int. Et. Calvet, ADH, 39M 147; Int. P. Poize, ADD, M 1368; Tem. J. Jarrian, Sauzet, ADD, M 1355; Int. Jn. Jos. Thibeyranc, cult., Boujan, ADH, 39M 159.
[60] Dossier "Cercles et Sociétés," AD L-G, M2; Int. Ph. Lacroix, *bouchonnier* at Lavardac, AD L-G, 4U, Ins. 1851; S-P Marmande, Nov. 27, 1851, AD L-G, M3; S-P Nérac, Jan. 11, 1849, AD L-G, M2; Dagnan, *Le Gers*, I, 436-73.
[61] Ints. ADN U, Ins. Clamecy; JM-1851, #251-59.

8

THE PEOPLE'S LEADERSHIP

If Montagnard societies drew upon preexisting loyalties and aspirations in order to recruit members, they also imparted new elements of organizational dynamism to the Republican cause. Their initiation ceremonials and paramilitary hierarchies provided a democratic framework of political leadership. As a result, the Montagnards redirected popular loyalties away from upper-class politicians and official positions of power (e.g. mayors) toward party militants recruited from the mass of the population. Furthermore, in creating formal links and informal contacts between urban and rural societies, conspirators developed regional as well as local loyalties. Peasant recruits became devoted to their "brothers and friends" in the towns. The extension of political responsibilities from urban elites to the rural populations was especially characteristic of southeastern France, where substantial numbers of cultivators became decurions or section leaders in the underground. By participating in high-risk conspiratorial activities, lower-class peasants and craftsmen were able to acquire some of the political prestige hitherto monopolized by bourgeois patrons. For Montagnard militants, devotion to the cause of the Democratic and Social Republic became synonymous with new leadership opportunities and new organizational loyalties.

According to the French political scientist Duverger, the basic organizational trend in modern politics is from "cadre" parties, linking small committees ("caucuses") of notables during electoral campaigns, toward mass parties, coordinating the activities of local "branches," "cells," or "militias" throughout the calendar year. He views the mass party as a twentieth-century phenomenon and asserts flatly that "in 1850 no country in the world (except the United States) knew political parties in the modern sense of the word."[1] In fact, the trend toward mass parties had its abortive beginnings in France with the Montagnard movement of 1850-51. Unlike most of the Republican electoral committees that had sponsored candidates in the springtime campaigns of 1848 and 1849, the Montagnard societies were designed as permanent organizations with a mass base of membership, a substantial core of militants (as distinguished from more passive members), and a regional

[1] Maurice Duverger, *Political Parties*, trans. Barbara and Robert North, 2nd ed. (New York, 1959), pp. xxiii, 4-60.

network of branches. Each branch, which comprised all the members who resided in a particular commune, was responsible for local recruitment, indoctrination, fund raising and political mobilization. In these respects, the Montagnard societies resembled the Socialist party of the Third Republic, whose basic unit of mass political organization was the communal branch. At the same time, the small units into which Montagnard societies were generally subdivided (ten-man units known as *decuries* or sections) resembled Communist party cells in their concern for secrecy, and fascist squads in their military overtones. The leaders of these units could collect dues or circulate orders to rank-and-file "party members" without exposing the entire society to the risk of police informers. In the event of armed combat, they could muster their men secretly and deploy them in accordance with orders received from the higher-ranking leaders of their local societies (commissions, presidents, or centurions). To ensure coordinated mobilizations among these local societies, the Montagnards adopted another principle of modern party organization: vertical links subordinating branches, cells, or squads to leaders at higher levels of the urban administrative network (commissions or presidents at cantonal seats, *arrondissement*, and departmental headquarters). In principle, orders issued in cities such as Paris, Lyon, and Marseille could be transmitted down this leadership hierarchy to the rural base in the various conspiratorial zones of the nation. By articulating a formal organization with mass political objectives, the Montagnards foreshadowed twentieth-century party development to a significant degree.

The modernity of Montagnard organization should not, of course, be exaggerated. Apart from newspapers, no mass media of communication existed during the Second Republic, and the Republican press was severely hampered by Bonapartist administrators. Neither the state of publishing technology nor the extent of education favored a clandestine press and none existed, in sharp contrast to political conditions in repressive epochs of twentieth-century France (e.g. Vichy). Efforts to hold interdepartmental congresses in 1850 resulted in police prosecutions (the "Plot of Lyon"), and attempts to hold departmental meetings of cantonal leaders were rarely successful thereafter.[2] Unlike socialist and Communist party organizations, which have been able to link small towns to cities through such devices as the national congress and the departmental federation, the Montagnards were confined in large part to the oral-communications networks that encompassed single towns

[2] See, for example, Int. Jules Pierre Moyeux, describing an abortive effort to send delegates from Clamecy to a meeting at Nevers in October 1851, ADN, U, s.s., Clamecy.

and nearby rural communities. Not the nation or the department but the *arrondissement* and the canton comprised the effective boundaries of their leadership hierarchies.

Within each commune, Montagnard organizations also diverged from the ideal type of a well-articulated mass political party. The primary task of conspirators in 1850-51 was to recruit new members, but they did not use their paramilitary structure of *decuries* or sections for this purpose. Some societies relied on *parrains* or "godfathers" to sponsor the prospective initiates, others had special commissions to scrutinize their qualifications, and still others permitted anyone to recruit members.[3] The ceremonials themselves sometimes involved large numbers of recruits or a large audience of members.[4] The ten-man units were generally constituted at a later date without reference to the participants in these ceremonials. In some branches the leaders and members of these *decuries* were appointed by the local *chef*, elsewhere they were designated by an assembly of the entire society, while in still other cases groups of ten initiates were authorized to choose their own leaders.[5] The members of one section often knew the identity of fellow initiates in other sections, especially in the bourgs and villages, where secrecy was based less on specialized organizational devices than on shared social values. Although decurions and *chefs de section* were supposed to serve as subordinate military leaders, there is no evidence that any of them actually led military maneuvers before the coup d'état. These paramilitary organs atrophied for lack of use unless they were adapted to a second function, that of dues collection. Like twentieth-century mass parties, the Montagnards tried to raise funds by levying dues on their members. To introduce such a modern device of party financing, they justified membership dues as mutual assistance to "brothers and friends."[6] Insofar as rank-and-file members made regular

[3] For example, at Clamecy, meetings were held to select the *parrains* for prospective initiates (Int. Pr. Jouanin, journeyman shoemaker, CG Clamecy); at St. Thibéry (Hérault) a special commission examined the qualifications of persons who sought admission (Int. G. Gulerand, owner-farmer, ADH, 39M 150); and at Châteauneuf-de-Mazenc (Drôme), at least eighteen men, including several initiators, recruited members (dossiers of initiates in ADD, M 1356-71).

[4] Among many examples of collective ceremonials, see Ints. Jn. Pr. Béranger, shoemaker at Lachamp; and Jn. Jq. Morin, owner-farmer at Montjoux. ADD, M 1357, 1366.

[5] For example, at Puimisson (Hérault) the initiator, a mason named H. Granier, held a meeting of all the members and named six decurions and a centurion (Int. P. Pages, cult., ADH, 39M 156); at Lachamp (Drôme), the initiates met and elected their leaders (Int. Béranger, cited in n. 4); and at Barjols (Var) every ten initiates chose their own decurion. (Int. Louis Trotobas, tanner, AD Var 4M 19).

[6] Hundreds of Montagnards in southeastern France reported that mutual benefit was an objective of the society, and those in a few communes claimed that they

dues payments to their decurions or *chefs de section*, these leadership roles were well-defined elements of the local organization. In many communes, however, financial contributions were rare or nonexistent, and organizational subunits had at best symbolic significance. In such cases, the communal branch, not the *decurie*, was the only real channel of Montagnard activity.

The most well-articulated societies existed in Mediterranean France, where agglomerated settlements, cash-crop agriculture, hierarchial labor relationships, and associational traditions favored the sectional model of party organization. The *arrondissements* of Béziers (Hérault) and Brignoles (Var) led the nation in the financial operations and organizational complexity of their Montagnard societies. Initiates from at least fourteen societies in the former region and eight in the latter reported paying monthly dues of from 5 to 50 centimes to their section leaders, and some admitted that the money was collected for political purposes. As a decurion at Roujan (Hérault) confessed after the coup d'état, "The other nine members paid me one sou (5 centimes) a month to help the political prisoners."[7] The organizational hierarchy in the branches near Béziers consisted of executive commissions, centurions, and decurions; that near Brignoles had either triumvirates or presidents, seconded by vice-presidents and section leaders. Béziers probably had the largest society in France, with at least thirteen centurions, each commanding ten decurions; other large societies in that region existed at Capestang (four centurions, at least seventeen decurions), St. Thibéry (one centurion, at least thirteen decurions), Servian (two centurions, at least nine decurions), and Roujan (one centurion, at least eight decurions); seventeen other bourgs and villages near Béziers had two or more decurions.[8] Cantonal delegates were chosen in at least six branches to communicate with the urban leaders, and one rural centurion claimed that a threefold hierarchy of *arrondissement*, cantonal, and communal delegates existed for this purpose.[9] Montagnard organizations were equally elaborate in the *arrondissement* of Brignoles, where at least eight towns and bourgs had ten or more section leaders, headed by Brignoles (around thirty), Barjols (around twenty), St. Maximin (at least nineteen), and Besse (over fifteen). Another twenty-one bourgs and villages in the region had at least five section leaders,

---

had joined solely for this purpose. See, for example, the Ints. of suspects from Châteauneuf-de-Mazenc (Drôme), Neffiès (Hérault), and Camps (Var).

[7] Int. A. Montjeaux, cult., ADH, 39M 144-60.

[8] Tabulations based on the numbers of persons identified by initiates as centurions or decurions in these communes, ADH, 39M 144-60.

[9] Int. Jn. Jos. Thibeyranc, Boujan, ADH, 39M 159.

and seven more had at least two of them. Specialized organs—triumvirates or commissions—existed for regional communications between Brignoles and at least nine other communes, including the cantonal seats of Rians, Roquebrussanne, and St. Maximin, while presidents performed this function in other branches of the *arrondissement*.[10]

Elsewhere in southeastern France, Montagnard societies located in towns and bourgs sometimes had section leaders, and so did a few such societies in central France.[11] Yet in the foothills of the Alps, the Cévennes, the forests of central France, and the hills and valleys of the southwest, the rural populations often resided in small villages or dispersed hamlets and farmsteads. If peasants in these regions were recruited into Montagnard societies, they typically formed residential branches numbering at most twenty to thirty members. Their work patterns were usually individualistic, and only the lumbermen around Clamecy were familiar with the kinds of labor teams characteristic of large-scale Mediterranean viticulture. Cash wages were often less important than payments in kind, and cultivators were generally unaccustomed to the payment of dues for mutual benefit. Consequently, many Montagnards in villages around towns such as Apt (Vaucluse), Dieulefit (Drôme), Clamecy (Nièvre), and Marmande (Lot-et-Garonne) lacked both the need and the aptitude for sophisticated political organizations. A single leader, generally described as the president or the *chef*, often ran such a village society, perhaps seconded by a vice-president or a few other militants. Thus, in the cantons of Crest-nord, Crest-sud, Bourdeaux, and Dieulefit (central Drôme), nearly all the villages had a few Montagnard leaders, but only the town of Dieulefit, three bourgs, and four villages reportedly had decurions. Significantly, only two of these rural societies definitely had dues-paying members on a monthly basis.[12] The Montagnards at Crupies typified peasant reluctance to sustain a financial effort in this region. According to their president, "One month after the society's foundation, each member was asked to pay dues of a few centimes to help those who were being prosecuted or who were exposed to some personal ill. The offerings

[10] Tabulations based on Ints. and Tems. of initiates supplemented by the reports of J. P.s, AD Var 4M 19, 26.

[11] For example, the register of MC Basses-Alpes listed a few section leaders at Manosque, Volx, Riez, Forcalquier, and Puimoisson (AN, BB[30] 398); initiates at Clamecy named twenty of the decurions who formed a twenty-five-man executive commission governing that society (see, for example, Int. Jouanin, cited in n. 3); and an initiate at Ouanne (Yonne) described five ten-man sections, each with a *chef* (Tem. Barquet, JM-1851, #258, dossier Ouanne).

[12] Montoison, where the treasurer collected 21 francs from three decurions (Tem. Th. Bérard, innkeeper, ADD, M 1354), and Savasse, where one initiate admitted paying 25 centimes per month (Int. Eug. Reboul, cult., ADD, 1369).

were supposed to be renewed every month, but in reality they were levied only once, and the funds were deposited."[13] Such Montagnard societies had no use for decurions or section leaders. They were organized along communal lines under the leadership of an influential local resident, a small cluster of militants, or a conspiratorial chieftain from a nearby town.

Both of these types of organizational differentiation—multiple sections within communes and local branches within regions—provided new leadership opportunities for the peasantry. Generally speaking, branch leaders were recruited from social groups that had some extra-local contacts, but many subordinate ranks were filled by low-status cultivators. Thus, the social base of leadership widened most dramatically in communities where decurions or section leaders proliferated: nearly half of the known Montagnard leaders in the *arrondissement* of Béziers and Brignoles were cultivators, as compared with around one-quarter of those in the nation as a whole.[14] Of course, the most important leaders even in these regions were professional men, artisans, and tradesmen who resided in the market towns. To analyze the extent and limits of democraticization, we must distinguish between towns, bourgs, and villages, as well as between regions with elaborate Montagnard hierarchies and those with more simplified networks of local leaders. Yet at all echelons of the underground, the traditional leaders of the rural populations—middle-aged landlords and public officials—were supplanted by younger, less prestigious, and less well educated leaders. As historians such as Agulhon, Loubère, and Vigier have noted, democraticization was a general phenomenon in rural France from 1850 to 1851.[15]

Regional leaders of the Montagnards were usually townsmen whose occupations brought them into frequent contact with the surrounding rural populations. Their political role in coordinating village societies was facilitated by their strategic location in regional exchange relationships. As the historian Sabean has pointed out with respect to the role of townsmen in European peasant revolts, "The small town producer, merchant, or artisan is a part of the world of external commerce

---

[13] Tem. Jn. Pr. César Achard, innkeeper and adjoint, ADD, M 1354.

[14] In the national sample of political prisoners, described in Chapter One, n. 23, cultivators, day laborers, and other agricultural workers accounted for 24% (26/109) of those accused of being secret society leaders; they comprised 47% (135/286) of all those described by initiates as leaders in *arr.* Béziers; and they comprised 47% (102/216) of those similarly described in a sample of nineteen communes in *arr.* Brignoles.

[15] Agulhon, *La République au village*, pp. 422-26, 448-50; Vigier, *La Seconde République*, II, 258-61; Leo Loubère, *Radicalism in Mediterranean France, Its Rise and Decline, 1848-1914* (Albany, N.Y., 1974), pp. 73, 76.

and is an intermediary of the peasant with this world."[16] Villagers depended on such urban brokers when they joined regional movements against centralized political authority. Thus, the most important Montagnard leaders in rebel districts of the Drôme, the Gard, the Gers, the Hérault, the Nièvre, the Var, and the Yonne included eleven professional men, six merchants, and seven artisans and shopkeepers who resided in *arrondissement* capitals or cantonal seats.[17] Among the professional men were two pharmacists at Montélimar whose clientele included villagers, and one at Dieulefit; two former government officials with regional responsibilities at Brignoles and one at Auch; one school teacher at Crest and another at Anduze; a notarial clerk at Alais; and a landlord at Toucy. The six merchants in the sample all had rural clients: a distiller at Béziers who had wine-producing agents in nearby villages; a hardware merchant at Clamecy who sold tools to rural artisans; a banker at Dieulefit who discounted bills of exchange for farmers; a wood merchant at St. Maximin; a horse trader at Mirande; and a miller at Pézénas. By contrast, this sample contains only one retail tradesman with a predominantly local clientele, a café owner at Bédarieux. Several of the skilled artisans also produced specialized goods or services for regional markets: a watchmaker at Béziers, whose recruits from the villages "flocked to him on the pretext of having their watches repaired"; a metal-caster at Béziers; a tool-edge cutter at Barjols (Var); a wood-turner at Dieulefit; a piano tuner at Toucy, whose accounts covered thirty-three towns, bourgs, and villages in three departments; and a confectioner at Le Luc. Only two craftsmen in the sample may have worked exclusively for local markets: a shoemaker at Béziers, and a plasterer at Crest.[18]

[16] David Sabean, "Markets, Uprisings and Leadership in Peasant Societies: Western Europe, 1381-1789," *Peasant Studies Newsletter*, 2 (July 1973), 18.

[17] These twenty-four leaders were presidents or *chefs* of urban societies, presidents of cantons or *arrondissements*, or organizers of branches in rural communes.

[18] Alexis Breton, pres. at Montélimar; Jos. Peyron, 43, silk manufacturer and pharmacist, pres. of *arr.* Montélimar; Hippolyte Darier, 33, *chef* at Dieulefit and rural organizer; Constans, ex-*sous commissaire*, *chef* at Brignoles; Giraud, road engineer, member of town triumvirate at Brignoles and rural organizer; J.-B. Violet, 31, ex-lieutenant of gendarmes at Auch, rural organizer; Antoine Bouvier, 30, first rural organizer at Crest; Victorin Gascuel, 21, cantonal *chef* at Anduze; Ant. Delord, 36, pres. of *arr.* Alais; Louis Chauvot, cantonal *chef* at Toucy; Casimir Peret, 51, landlord and distiller, pres. of the *arr.* executive commission; Jn. Alex. Guerbet, member of the executive commission at Clamecy; Jn. Jq. Ant. Defaysse-Soubeyran, 36, landlord as well as banker at Dieulefit, a main rural organizer; Pr. Moulet, 52, cantonal *chef* at St. Maximin; Baptiste Lasserre, 32, rural organizer at Mirande; Lignière, *chef* at Pézénas and rural organizer; Fulerand Malaterre, 26, centurion and *chef*; Nicolas Relin, 43, first pres. of the Executive Commission at Béziers; Louis Chalon, 29, rural organizer at Béziers; Andre Louche, 32, rural organizer at Barjols; Louis Blancard, 44, rural organizer at Dieulefit; Jean Bouillard, 44, rural organizer at Toucy; Ch. Sigismond Meric, 36, regional

The diffusion of Montagnard societies from towns to bourgs and villages brought increasing numbers of individuals with predominantly local market functions into the top ranks of leadership. As Table 8.1 shows for 122 communes in four rebel zones of southeastern France, professional men, landlords, traders, and artisans presided over most of the branches located in bourgs and large rural communes (population over 1,000), while cultivators headed many branches in the villages.[19]

TABLE 8.1

Montagnard Presidents and *Chefs* in Bourgs and Villages

	Bourgs and Large Rural Communes (pop. over 1,000)	Villages (pop. under 1,000)	Totals
Professional men	10 (15%)	4 (5%)	14 (9%)
Landlords (*propriétaires*)	11 (16%)	5 (6%)	16 (11%)
Merchants, tradesmen, and artisans	37 (54%)	34 (41%)	71 (47%)
Farmers	10 (15%)	39 (48%)	49 (33%)
Totals	68	82	150

SOURCES: Interrogations and testimony of Montagnards in the *arrondissement* of Béziers, ADH 39M 144-60, *Le Messager du Midi* (Mar.-July 1852); interrogations and testimony of Montagnards in the cantons of Bourdeaux, Crest-*nord*, Crest-*sud*, Dieulefit, Loriol, Marsanne, Montélimar, ADD M 1353-71; register of the Mixed Commission of the Basses-Alpes, cantons of Forcalquier, Manosque, Riez, Valensole, AN BB³⁰ 398; interrogations and testimony of Montagnards in the *arrondissement* of Brignoles, AD Var, 4M 19, 26.
NOTE: For *arrondissement* of Béziers, *arrondissement* of Brignoles, central Drôme, southwestern Basses-Alpes.

Even within the fifty-two communes of the sample containing over 1,000 inhabitants, less than one-quarter of the high-ranking Montagnards practiced a trade or profession which gave them extensive regional contacts. Only three doctors, two functionaries, one notary, one surveyor, six merchants, and two manufacturers led Montagnard societies in the bourgs. Twice as many leaders in these communes were employed in a profession, trade, or craft whose market was mainly or entirely local. They include three schoolteachers, ten food or drink

organizer; Pierre Vié, rural organizer at Béziers; Jos. Seruty, pres. at Crest. All these men were accused by initiates of being conspiratorial leaders, not just Republican patrons.
[19] This analysis of high-ranking leaders is based on the interrogations and testimonies of Montagnard initiates concerning presidents, main initiators, and *chefs*, including a few centurions.

suppliers, and nineteen artisans. Alongside these professional men, shopkeepers, and artisans, were ten "proprietors," whose limited geographical range of influence is suggested by their places of residence: only two resided in a cantonal headquarters, while eight lived either in lesser bourgs or in predominantly rural communes. Whether they leased their modest properties to a tenant farmer or worked them with hired labor, their productive relationships were generally confined to a single commune. At the bottom of this occupational hierarchy of market influence were the ten cultivators who led Montagnard societies in communes with over 1,000 inhabitants. They resided mainly in bourgs of the Hérault (seven cases), with two cultivators in the forested region of the northwestern Var and one owner-farmer in a large village of the central Drôme.

As for the 69 communes with under 1,000 inhabitants, their top-ranking Montagnard leaders were almost all involved primarily in local relations of production. At this level of the market hierarchy were only one doctor, one surveyor, two merchants, and two manufacturers. Two more were schoolteachers by profession, neither of them employed by the state, and five were proprietors. The bulk of the village leaders in the sample were either traders and artisans dealing in local consumer goods (eleven in the food trades, twenty other artisans), or cultivators (forty cases).

Although documentary evidence for other rebel zones is usually less complete, shopkeepers, artisans, and farmers led rural societies in these districts, too. Around the town of Apt (Vaucluse), for example, the initiators, presidents or alleged *chefs* of Montagnard *chambrées* in five bourgs and villages included four owner-farmers, four cultivators, two craftsmen, two barbers, and a café owner.[20] Near Alais (Gard) the main leaders of six bourgs and villages were a schoolteacher, a building contractor, a *cafetier*, and three proprietors who may have also been farmers.[21] In five bourgs and villages near Largentière (Ardèche), men denounced as conspiratorial leaders included an insurance agent, a proprietor who formerly manufactured silk, an innkeeper, a joiner, and an owner-farmer.[22] The Montagnard initiators at the bourg of St. Sauveur (Yonne) were four artisans and two cultivators. Initiators and alleged *chefs* in eleven nearby bourgs and villages included a veterinarian, a proprietor, a retired tanner and proprietor, a livestock

[20] Ints. of initiates from Bonnieux, Ménerbes, Roussillon, Rustrel, and St. Martin-de-Castillon, in ADV, M11 52-61.

[21] Ints. and Tems. of initiates from Anduze, Cassagnoles, Lédignan, Canoules, Laval, and Maruéjols, in ADG 3U 5/1.

[22] Ints. and Tems. of Montagnards from Salavas, Lagorce, Assions, Vallon, and La-Bastide-de-Virac, in ADA, 5M 16, 18.

merchant, a gelder, four artisans, and seven farmers.[23] Montagnard organization near Clamecy is very obscure, but men who lead the insurrection had probably been activists in the underground. One leased out
land, one managed a stone quarry, two operated cafés, two practiced
a craft, one floated logs, and four worked in agriculture.[24] Only a few
Montagnard leaders in the Lot-et-Garonne can be identified on the
basis of scattered archival documents: two proprietors at the bourg of
Le Mas d'Agenais, a butcher at the bourg of Barbaste, two carpenters
at the villages of Réaup and Lisse, and a cultivator at the village of
Senestis.[25] As for the neighboring department of the Gers, its most
conspicuous Montagnard leaders in the countryside were professional
men, traders, and artisans. Dagnan refers to the following initiators in
bourgs and villages: two proprietors, a former notary, a notarial clerk,
a former publicist, a pharmacist, a former schoolteacher, a student, a
grain merchant, an innkeeper, two grocers, three weavers, a carpenter,
a tailor, a wood-turner, and a blacksmith's apprentice. To these initiators, all but three of whom resided in cantonal seats and other bourgs,
can probably be added several dozen of the artisans and cultivators
whom he names as Montagnard propagandists and rebel leaders in the
villages. These latter militants may not have held formal positions in
the Montagnard organization, but they fulfilled the functions of branch
leaders.[26]

Artisans and local tradesmen comprise the broad occupational category that contributed the largest number of high-ranking leaders in
the bourgs and villages. Their political influence was derived from four
characteristics of their socioeconomic position: independence, mobility, literacy, and strategic position in local exchange relationships.
To begin with, most rural artisans worked for their own account as
small-scale producers. The distinction between employers and wage-
earners, so characteristic of the artisanate in cities and large towns,
rarely existed in the bourgs and villages, and the above lists of leaders
include only three masters and one journeyman. Although rural crafts
were not always full-time occupations, they provided their practitioners with a margin of social independence lacking among agricultural
laborers. Viewed from this point of view, rural artisans possessed the
"tactical mobility" that the anthropologist Wolf has attributed to land-

[23] Ints. and Tems. of initiates in Dossiers St. Sauveur, Druyes, Fontenoy, Fon-
taines, Leugny, Merry-la-Vallée, Moutiers, Ouanne, Saints, Taingy, Thury, and
Villiers-St. Benoit, in JM-1851, #251, 252, 253, 255, 258.
[24] Ints. of suspects from Asnois, Billy, Brèves, Chevroches, Dornecy, Entrains,
La Maison Dieu, Oisy, Surgy, and Trucy-l'Orgueilleux, in ADN, U. Ins. Clamecy,
and s.s. Clamecy.
[25] Ints. of suspects, AD L-G, 4U, Ins. *arrs.* Marmande, Nerac.
[26] Dagnan, *Le Gers*, I, 443-73.

owning "middle peasants" in twentieth-century "peasant wars."[27] Their political commitments were not shaped by the class interests of local landlords.

Next, rural artisans tended to be more mobile than their farming neighbors. As young men, some of them acquired their training in nearby towns and a few embarked on the Tour de France, a national circuit of labor migration for members of the journeymen's associations known as *compagonnages*. Artisans were less likely to marry and settle in their commune of birth than were landowning peasants, although the extent of their marital mobility varied regionally. In the rural agglomerations of Mediterranean France, where communal endogamy was high, most *gens de métiers* (artisans and tradesmen) who led Montagnard societies were born in their commune of residence; in the more dispersed settlements of the central Drôme, a majority of artisanal leaders had been born in another commune, usually within the same canton.[28] Once settled, artisans and shopkeepers were likely to have business contacts with wholesale suppliers of tools and raw materials in the towns, while farmers probably purchased less than they sold in urban markets.[29] Just as local tradesmen funneled goods into the villages, so they were in a position to relay new political ideas.

Third, craftsmen and *commercants* tended to be more literate than their farming neighbors.[30] Literacy facilitated their dealings with urban merchants and heightened their awareness of urban values. Agulhon has shown that in Provençal bourgs and villages literate artisans transmitted elements of the national culture to the peasantry, and his analysis applies to other regions of the nation.[31] For artisans, political leader-

[27] Eric Wolf, *Peasant Wars of the Twentieth Century* (New York, 1969), pp. 276-302.

[28] Born in same commune: 14/18 cases in *arr.* Béziers; 11/12 cases in cantons of Forcalquier, Manosque, Riez, Valensole; 3/9 cases in central Drôme. Ints. ADH, 39M 144-60; register of MC Basses-Alpes, AN, BB[30] 398; Ints. ADD, M 1356-71.

[29] See, for example, the business loans *sous seing privé* contracted by artisans at Bourdeaux (Drôme) from bankers and merchants as far away as Lyon, ADD, 2C 268, 4-6 (1842-54).

[30] The higher literacy rate of artisans can be proved by examining the *listes du tirage au sort* of potential draftees, aged twenty, drawn up by canton each year. For example, in rural communes of the canton of Clamecy, 84% of the artisans and *commerçants* were literate (lists from 1847-50), as compared with 57% of the farmers and lumbermen; in the cantons of Crest-sud and Marsanne (Drôme), 57% of the nonfarming registrants were literate (lists of 1850), as compared with 45% of the farmers. ADN and ADD, series R.

[31] Agulhon, "Le rôle politique des artisans dans le département du Var de la Révolution à la deuxième République," *VIIIe colloque d'histoire sur l'artisanat et l'apprentissage* (Aix-en-Provence, 1965), pp. 83-101; and Agulhon, *La République au village*, pp. 188-206. On the skills, wealth, and prestige of craftsmen and shopkeepers vis-à-vis peasants in the bourgs, see Jean Vidalenc, *La société française*, II, 179-80, 241, 251, 258-59, 283-84, 302, 309.

ship was a natural extension of their previous role in this process of acculturation. As Republican written propaganda filtered into the countryside from 1848 to 1849, rural artisans and traders conveyed the new ideology of popular rights to the peasantry. In the apologetic words of a wheelwright near St. Sauveur, political subversion was caused by newspaper reading:

> If I talked about politics, it was only when I read the newspaper. I was a subscriber for only one month to *L'Union Républicain* (published at Auxerre). Certainly if I hadn't read that newspaper and others like it, I would not have done what I did (e.g. play an active role in the insurrection). . . . Biard, the grocer, subscribed to *La Feuille du Village* (written by the Republican publicist Joigneaux), and I read it when I went to get merchandise from him. I also read an issue of *Le Bien universel* (published in Paris) which Gibelin, the wooden-shoe maker, received.[32]

Because literacy often increased the rhetorical ability of prospective village leaders, the political influence of literate artisans survived government repression of written propaganda. At Marsanne (Drôme), for example, where all Republican printed material had been eliminated by 1851, the Montagnard "centurion" was a literate young joiner named Chabas. According to the mayor, he spoke rather fluently in French. This language skill must have impressed illiterate cultivators in the commune, because they placed their Xs on petitions that Chabas circulated against the electoral law of 1850.[33] Like Chabas, nearly all the artisans and tradesmen who headed Montagnard societies in southeastern France were literate, and many signed their interrogations with the flourishes of the well educated.[34] Literacy reflected their social aspirations and increased their political ambitions, a fact that some conservatives viewed with a mixture of fear and contempt. Thus, one hostile justice of the peace wrote that the foremost Montagnard leader at St. Sauveur, a "musician" named Amédée Patasson, "has no craft, or at least doesn't practice any, having failed in all the enterprises which he has tried." Patasson allegedly lived off subsidies from wealthy Republicans. "After having been a second-rate orator in the clubs, he remained

---

[32] Int. Alfred Terrain, 25, a rebel leader at Saints, JM-1851, #258, dossier Saints.

[33] Dossier Chabas, ADD, M 1359; and dossier "contre Joannin Chatelet," Sept. 1850, containing testimony from twenty-seven illiterate farmers and five illiterate artisans who "signed" the petition (several named Chabas as its circulator). ADD, 12U 33.

[34] The interrogations of thirty-three such leaders in *arrs*. Béziers and Brignoles and in the central Drôme have been examined for their signatures. All of them signed, and fourteen signed very well.

a secret agent of socialism and perverted the populations of St. Sauveur. . . . A man without education (i.e. secondary schooling), without talent, animated by a ridiculous ambition to command, he imagines that he is an important person, destined to occupy a high rank."[35] Ambitious craftsmen were often respected, however, by the rural populations. Thus, Prosper Chavanet, a youthful and literate shoemaker who served as vice-president of the Montagnards at St. Gervais (Drôme), received the full support of municipal officials after his arrest. They praised his family ("without fortune, but respectable and hard-working"), his morals ("habits of economy and work"), and his reputation ("enjoys the esteem of all the inhabitants of the commune"). Similarly, Auguste Valladier, a thirty-six-year-old joiner at Vallon (Ardèche), who admired the socialist deputy, Perdiguier, received high marks from the justice of the peace for his private morality—he was a "respectable man, laborious worker, loved and esteemed, incapable of an evil action."[36]

Whether denounced or admired, craftsmen and shopkeepers were *conspicuous* members of local communities. Therein lay the fourth and most important source of their political influence. Unlike the occupation of farming, which required long hours of solitary work in the fields, artisanal occupations either involved a fixed residence at a central point of exchange—a bakery, a café, a shoemaker's shop in an agglomerated settlement—or rotating visits to the farmsteads—itinerant tailoring, carpentry, construction work. In either case, artisans and tradesmen were in a strategic position to become more well known and more verbally skilled than the average cultivator. The food trades provide an especially good example of this locational advantage in rural communications networks. In the sample of Montagnard leaders from southeastern France, nearly half (11/21) of the suppliers of food or beverages also described themselves as proprietors, cultivators or day laborers. The most distinctive feature of their economic position was not their status vis-à-vis landed property; it was their central position in the exchange relationships of the village community. As a result, they were overrepresented in high leadership ranks, not only in comparison with cultivators but also in comparison with craftsmen who produced clothing and other goods. Around one-third of the artisans and shopkeepers in the sample of high-ranking leaders were employed in the food trades (21/60 cases), as compared with only one-fifth of all those arrested from various rebel zones. The workshops of shoemakers and other skilled artisans might foster leadership roles in like manner by attracting a rural clientele. Thus, a potter in a village near St. Sau-

---

[35] Dossier Patasson, JM-1851, #255, dossier St. Sauveur.
[36] Dossier Chavanet, ADD, M 1359; dossier Valladier, ADA, 5M 18.

veur tried to excuse his political activism by noting that "people came to warm themselves at my furnace, and they talked politics."[37] By December 1851 many villagers had, indeed, been talking politics, and none more so than the artisans, whose predilection for leadership was founded above all on their social role as communicators.

If artisans were more heavily represented in high leadership positions than their general numbers in the rural population would warrant, men employed exclusively in agriculture nonetheless headed many societies. Indeed, cultivators accounted for nearly half the village leaders in rebel zones of southeastern France, as Table 8.1 indicates. Their prominence can be explained by the fact that significant numbers of peasants shared some of the social traits which facilitated artisanal leadership. This was especially true of landowning peasants who produced a marketable surplus of grain, livestock, wine, or raw silk. "Owner-farmers" and their sons had more economic independence than peasants employed as sharecroppers, farm servants, or agricultural laborers; they had more frequent cause to attend markets and fairs; and they had more incentive to learn how to read and write. Within small villages and hamlets, their influence was accentuated by the leisure activities that bound peasant households together in "face-to-face" communities. If conspiratorial networks reached this far down the hierarchy of settlements, their foremost agents would often be landowning "middle peasants."

With respect to both landownership and literacy, evidence from several rebel zones supports this analysis. Although most peasant conspirators were loosely described by magistrates as "cultivators," their more precise status as owner-farmers, tenants, servants, or day laborers can sometimes be discovered in the communal census lists. Following this procedure, I have specified the property status of nine high-ranking peasants in the *arrondissement* of Béziers and twelve in the central Drôme. Around Béziers, where only one-tenth of the rural population were owner-farmers or their dependents, six out of the nine peasant leaders resided in such households (four as heads and two as dependent sons) and only three were day laborers.[38] In the central Drôme, where landowning peasants and their sons comprised around half the rural labor force, six of the twelve high-ranking cultivators were owner-farmers, five resided with their landowning fathers, and only one was a day laborer.[39] Many of the "cultivators" who led Montagnard socie-

---

[37] Int. Jq. Briot, at Moutiers, JM-1851, #258, dossier Moutiers.

[38] ADH, series M, census of 1851, Espondeilham, Lespignan, Portiragnes, Puimisson, Servian, St. Thibéry.

[39] ADD, series M, census of 1851, Autichamp, Cléon d'Andran, Montjoux, La-Roche-sur-Grane, St. Gervais, Souspierre, Suze, Les Tonils, Vesc.

ties elsewhere in southeastern France resided in upland villages where medium-sized or small peasant properties were common. In a few cases these Montagnard cultivators were even substantial landowners. Thus, Joseph Jean, a thirty-four-year-old cultivator at St. Martin-de-Castillon (Vaucluse), shared with his brother "a rather considerable fortune." According to the parish priest, this wealth aided Joseph in his "intrigues," and he was the most "intelligent" and "influential" conspirator in the commune.[40] Peasant leaders in central and southwestern France were also recruited in disproportionate numbers from middle strata of the rural population. Around Clamecy and St. Sauveur, where ploughmen (*laboureurs*) dominated the agricultural laborers (*manoeuvres*), five of the former and only two of the latter can be identified as village leaders. Futhermore, at least two of the cultivators who led rebel bands in this area were wealthy (*dans l'aisance*) and a third had some wealth (*quelque aisance*).[41] In the central Gers, where many peasants were poor sharecroppers or agricultural laborers, seven of the fourteen cultivators whom Dagnan identifies as village leaders were described by magistrates as wealthy (*aisé*), three as not very wealthy but presumably propertied (*peu aisé*), and only four as poor. Five of these twelve leaders were definitely owner-farmers, while other peasant suspects in the Gers, numbering forty-four, were never described as landowners, and three-quarters (thirty-three) of them were characterized as poor or very poor.[42]

Peasant literacy had been gradually expanding during the July Monarchy in conspiratorial zones of the nation, but substantial numbers of cultivators remained illiterate, especially among older men and dependent laborers. Furet and Sachs have shown that departments in southern France, which had relatively low rates of literacy at the end of the eighteenth century, experienced relatively high rates of growth in literacy from 1816-20 to 1866. In hitherto "backward" areas of the nation, "elementary acculturation" was reaching an ever greater proportion of the rural population. The thirteen departments with large-scale insurrections in 1851 had all participated in this historic growth of literacy.[43] Yet the literacy transition remained incomplete in rebel

---

[40] Tem. *curé*, affair of Lumières, ADV, 4M 74, canton of Pertuis.

[41] Judicial comments on Sévère Goubinat, 43, cult. at Taingy; Ant. Dessignole, 48, cult. at Taingy; and Léger Guidon, 34, cult. at Molesmes. AD Yonne, III M¹ 156-57.

[42] Judicial comments in the register of MC Gers, published by Dagnan, *Le Gers*, II, 576-86.

[43] Annual percentage rates of growth in the percentage of signatures in acts of marriage, 1816-20 to 1860, male only: median of 1.00 for thirteen rebel departments, as compared with 0.70 for all other departments. W. Furet and W. Sachs, "La croissance de l'alphabétisation en France (XVIIIᵉ-XIXᵉ siècle)," *Annales*, 29 (1974), Table 3, pp. 735-37.

areas, as cantonal data from the agricultural and industrial inquiry of 1848 suggests. All but two of fifty-seven commissions in rebel cantons reported literacy rates of less than 60 percent (generally male and female), with estimates ranging from 15 percent to one-third in twenty-eight cases, from 40 percent to 60 percent in fourteen cases, and under 15 percent in thirteen cases.[44] In such circumstances, the minority of peasants who had mastered the urban skills of reading and writing were more likely to assert independent political views than their illiterate neighbors. Like their counterparts within the artisanate, literate peasants would be in the front ranks of political leadership at the village level. Indeed, literacy data from the interrogations of twenty-six high-ranking peasants in Montagnard societies of the Hérault, the Var, and the Drôme confirm this hypothesis. Only two of these leaders were illiterate, sixteen signed their names legibly, and eight signed as fluently as their upper-class interrogators.

The entry of artisans and cultivators into leadership positions corresponded to a relative decline in the role of upper-class politicians. True, one-fifth of the high-ranking Montagnards in bourgs and villages of southeastern France can be classified as landlords or professional men. By the crude measure of occupation, they belonged to the traditional elite of "bourgeois" proprietors. Yet their share of political leadership was substantially lower than it had been before 1848, when functionaries and wealthy taxpayers had monopolized the political process. Furthermore, few of the Montagnard leaders who did describe themselves as "proprietors" had actually belonged to the *censitaire* elite of voters on the eve of the February Revolution. Out of 1,646 residents of the *arrondissement* of Béziers who paid direct taxes of over 200 francs in 1847 (thereby qualifying them to vote in national elections), only 2 led Montagnard societies in 1851; 3 more encouraged Montagnards to resist the coup d'état in arms; 2 were members but not leaders; and 8 were denounced as sympathizers In the central Drôme, not a single one of the 514 *censitaires* led a Montagnard branch and only 5 were accused of aiding the conspirators. With rare exceptions, the younger sons of such wealthy taxpayers also remained aloof from the movement: at most, 12 were compromised in the former region, of whom 2 were Montagnard *chefs*; and no more than 15 in the latter region, including only 2 leaders. Less than one out of five Montagnard societies in these two conspiratorial zones received any assistance from wealthy taxpayers or their sons, and less than one out of ten branches had such proprietors as leaders.[45]

[44] AN, C 944-69.
[45] See the *censitaire* lists for 1847-48, ADH, 9M 42-45, and ADD, 6M 37.

Fear, prudence, and pride were the motives underlying this bourgeois abstention from conspiracy. Class fear was a dominant theme of anti-Republican propaganda from 1849 to 1851, and many wealthy proprietors agreed that militant Republicans were "anarchists" bent on destroying society. Even bourgeois who sympathized with the Republic often agreed that preparations for the eventuality of armed revolt might encourage mob violence.[46] To this social fear was joined a prudent calculation that prominent opponents of the government must remain within the bounds of legality, however narrow, or risk arrest and prosecution. Indeed, several upper-class organizers of Montagnard societies in the central Drôme attracted the prefect's attention in 1850 and suffered arrest or exile.[47] Had they merely continued to patronize the Republicans without playing a direct role as Montagnard leaders, they would have been able to aid their political cause at less personal risk. Cautious intrigue rather than direct involvement in conspiracy was the preferred strategy of most bourgeois Republicans. Pride of social rank furthered this traditional strategy of patronage. To join a Montagnard society and to accept a formal position of leadership within its ranks was to enter a cultural world that most wealthy men considered beneath their personal dignity. As men of honor, they surely had no need of initiation ceremonials with oaths on daggers to confirm their political loyalty; and as men of high social rank, they had no need of leadership ranks such as "president" or "centurion" to sanction their political influence.[48] Their sense of social distance from "the people" discouraged activity within Montagnard societies. As a result, organizational power within the underground often passed out of their hands and into that of leaders drawn from less exalted social milieus.

Just as the Montagnards weakened the traditional links between private wealth and political influence, so they undermined the customary role of public officials as opinion leaders. In the eyes of the state, each commune was administered by a mayor, aided by a deputy and a municipal council. Appointive officials until the February Revolution, the mayors and deputies of small towns and rural communities (popula-

[46] See, for example, Int. Louis Gimié, 52, doctor at Béziers (landowner at Puimisson), who claimed he quit the society when he discovered that "all kinds of people" were being initiated and armed. ADH, 39M 151.

[47] Ernest de Saint-Prix, landlord at Mirmande; Joseph Benoit-Laroche, 46, doctor at Grane; and Joannin Chatelet, 39, tax collector (revoked in 1850) and *rentier* at Marsanne. See Ints. and Tems. of initiates from these communes, ADD, M 1353-71.

[48] See, for example, Int. Amédée Toutel, 56, retired school principal and landlord at Sauzet (Drôme), who did not submit to initiation because he was considered reliable. Although Toutel patronized the Montagnards and led the insurrection in 1851, he neither organized nor presided over the local society. ATML, Ins. 1851.

tion under 6,000) were chosen in 1848 by the municipal councils, themselves now elected by universal suffrage. Some served as Republican propagandists in 1849, but they retreated from oppositional activity thereafter or suffered revocation. Although few mayors or deputies took effective measures to halt conspiratorial activity in their communes (see Chapter Ten), few risked leading the Montagnards either. Under the cross-pressures of police agents and local constituents, they preferred neutrality to political commitment. Thus, in a sample of 272 communes, drawn from ten departments where Montagnards were operating in 1851, only nine mayors were accused of being conspiratorial leaders; another twenty were accused of patronizing the Republicans or aiding the rebels; and the overwhelming majority avoided governmental suspicion of disloyalty. In these same communes, deputies were only slightly more active in the Montagnard movement: sixteen were leaders and ten were patrons or members of the underground. As for ex-mayors who had previously been revoked on political grounds, they led conspirators or rebels in another 15 of these communes (of which 7 were in one district, the central Gers). A municipal official, past or present, led at most 41 of these 281 Montagnard branches (15 percent) and was compromised in another 23 of them (8 percent). In nearly four-fifths of the bourgs and villages, the initiative for conspiratorial activity came entirely from outside official channels of leadership.[49]

If many organizers and *chefs* of Montagnard branches were drawn from middle rather than upper levels of society, nearly all the cadres of the underground were recruited from the broad mass of the population. By "cadres" are meant subordinate leaders such as vice-presidents, centurions (where executive commissions or presidents also existed), treasurers, section leaders, and decurions. To these specific ranks can be added minor initiators who presided over a few ceremonials without assuming full responsibility for local recruitment. The tasks of cadres did not require the same specialized aptitudes for regional or local communications that influenced the selection of high-ranking leaders.

---

[49] This analysis is based on the following regions: 36 communes in the Ardèche; 26 in the Basses-Alpes (cantons of Forcalquier, Manosque, Riez, Valensole); 39 in the central Drôme; 19 in the Gard; 42 in the Gers; 33 in the Hérault (*arr.* Béziers); 15 in the Nièvre (vicinity of Clamecy); 39 in the Var (*arr.* Brignoles); 10 in the Vaucluse (vicinity of Apt); and 13 in the Yonne (area of St. Sauveur). The sources are the testimony of Montagnards in departmental archives (Drôme, Hérault, Nièvre, Var, Vaucluse) and in AG Vincennes (Yonne); the registers of MC Basses-Alpes, Gard, and Gers; Dagnan; and a statement by Jq. Froment, 46, ex-journalist and Montagnard *chef* at Assion (Ardèche), naming the leaders of 36 branches in the Ardèche, ADH, 39M 138 (unconfirmed by the fragmentary testimony of other Montagnards from the dept., in ADH, 5M 15-18).

In many communities the occupations of these subordinate leaders reflected the general distribution of the labor force: industrial workers and artisans in the towns, cultivators and artisans rather than professional men and tradesmen in the bourgs, more cultivators than artisans in the villages. At this level of party organization, the social forces of mass democracy often achieved full expression.

In the towns democratization implied the entry of wage earners as well as self-employed artisans into leadership positions. This was especially true in manufacturing centers such as Bédarieux, Dieulefit, and Barjols. Thus, 17 of the 29 known cadres at Bédarieux wove or spun wool in the town's weaving sheds and spinning mills; 3 of the 7 known centurions and decurions at Dieulefit were wool-weavers; and 4 of the 11 section leaders at Barjols were tanners. The coopers' workshops and tanneries at Béziers also supplied leaders for the Montagnards: 4 coopers and 3 tanners were among the 17 known centurions and subcenturions in the town. Cultivators also achieved leadership positions in some towns of the southeast, where agriculture employed a significant proportion of the labor force. They headed at least nine sections at Brignoles, nine at St. Maximin, three at Manosque, three at Bédarieux, two at Béziers, and two at Barjols. As for the other occupational groups that supplied urban cadres, some of them also included wage earners, especially those involving construction and clothing trades. In a sample of 113 cadres from six towns in the Drôme, the Hérault and the Var, 16 were masons and shoemakers, while only 8 were food and beverage dealers, and none were merchants or professional men.[50]

The social origins of Montagnard cadres in the bourgs and villages mirrored that of the general membership. Table 8.2 shows that just as most affiliates in conspirational zones of southeastern France were employed in agriculture and the crafts, so most vice-presidents, decurions, and section leaders were recruited from these same occupational sectors. Variations in the proportions of agricultural cadres from zone to zone are directly related to variations in the numbers of leadership positions available within the communal branches: there were six cadres per branch in the *arrondissement* of Béziers, six in the *arrondissement* of Brignoles, four in the central Drôme, and two in the southwestern Basses-Alpes. Artisans became correspondingly less important as cadres than they were as high-ranking leaders in regions where cadres were numerous; otherwise they increased their share of leadership at lower

[50] Another 13 were in woodworking, 20 in textiles, 9 in tanning, 3 in metals, and 5 in transport, alongside 27 in agriculture (towns of Barjols, Bédarieux, Béziers, Brignoles, Dieulefit, and St. Maximin). Cadres identified by initiates, in ADH, 39M 144-60; ADD, M 1353-71; AD Var, 4M 19, 26.

TABLE 8.2

Occupations of Montagnard Cadres (bourgs and villages)

	Agriculture		Crafts		Food Trades, Merchants		Liberal Professions, Proprietors		Total
	Arrondissement of Béziers								
High-ranking leaders	15	(36%)	12	(28%)	10	(24%)	5	(12%)	42
Cadres	108	(72%)	31	(21%)	8	(5%)	2	(2%)	149
Members	157	(78%)	25	(12%)	15	(8%)	3	(2%)	200
	Arrondissement of Brignoles								
High-ranking leaders	9	(25%)	12	(33%)	8	(22%)	7	(20%)	36
Cadres	25	(68%)	8	(22%)	1	(3%)	3	(8%)	37
Members	104	(69%)	30	(20%)	5	(3%)	11	(7%)	150
	Central Drôme								
High-ranking leaders	14	(35%)	7	(18%)	8	(20%)	11	(27%)	40
Cadres	34	(53%)	22	(34%)	7	(11%)	1	(2%)	64
Members	140	(63%)	56	(26%)	21	(9%)	5	(2%)	222
	Southwestern Basses-Alpes								
High-ranking leaders	6	(32%)	6	(32%)	3	(16%)	4	(21%)	19
Cadres	15	(47%)	14	(44%)	2	(6%)	1	(3%)	32
Members	59	(64%)	18	(20%)	8	(3%)	7	(8%)	92

SOURCES: (*Arrondissement* of Béziers) interrogations and testimonies concerning Montagnards in 26 bourgs and villages. AD Hérault, 39M 144-60; (*arrondissement* of Brignoles) interrogations and testimonies concerning high-ranking Montagnards in 34 bourgs and villages; those concerning cadres in 6 communes (Brue-Auriac, Entrecastaux, Flassans, Pignans, Pontèves, Régusse); lists of other suspects from these 6 communes. AD Var, 4M-19; and register of the Mixed Commission of the Var, AN BB[30] 398; (central Drôme) interrogations and testimonies concerning Montagnards in 23 bourgs and villages. AD Drôme, M 1353-71; (southwestern Basses-Alpes) notations of presidents (high-ranking leaders), vice-presidents, and section leaders (cadres), and affiliates in 15 villages (cantons of Forcalquier, Manosque, Riez, Valensole). Register of the Mixed Commission of the Basses-Alpes, AN BB[30] 398.

levels by supplanting professional men, proprietors, merchants, and food and beverage dealers. Irrespective of these regional variations, cultivators staffed a higher proportion of leadership positions in the villages than in the bourgs and large rural communes. They comprised 61 percent of the cadres in the dispersed rural settlements of the central Drôme, and 80 percent in the agglomerated villages around Béziers. This confirms that the heavier the social weight of the peasantry, the greater its leadership role in the underground. As for the propertied and commercial elements that played such a disproportionate role in high leadership ranks, they subsided in importance among cadres throughout southeastern France.

In reflecting the general distribution of the labor force, these rural cadres were not biased toward landowning peasants, as top-ranking positions had been. Agricultural laborers and small owners who worked part-time for wages played a substantial role as section leaders in southeastern France. By tracing Montagnard "cultivators" in the census lists for 1851, this entry of poor peasants into leadership ranks can be documented with especial clarity for bourgs in the *arrondissement* of Béziers. Out of forty-two peasant cadres whose property status can be determined, only six were owner-farmers, fifteen were day laborers who owned small plots of land (*journaliers-propriétaires*), and twenty-one were landless laborers (*journaliers*).[51] Among the bourgs with agricultural laborers as Montagnard leaders were Capestang, St. Thibéry, and Servian. At Capestang, where the three centurions were chosen by lot, one was a *journalier-propriétaire* and two were *journaliers*; among the subcenturions, decurions, and subdecurions, thirteen were *journaliers-propriétaires*, seven were *journaliers*, one was an owner-farmer, and five were artisans. Probably no other conspiratorial zone had such high proportions of agricultural laborers among its cadres, but many of the "cultivators" in Provençal bourgs who headed sections of the underground probably worked part-time for wages. Even in the central Drôme, half of the eighteen agricultural cadres who can be identified in a sample of nine communes were listed in the census lists as *journaliers* (three cases), *propriétaires-journaliers* (three), sharecroppers (two), or cultivators (one), rather than as owner-farmers (six) or the sons of owner-farmers (three).[52] Apart from the absence of farm servants, these proportions are roughly the same as those of all owner-farmers, tenants, and laborers in this region.

[51] Analysis based on the occupations of cadres as listed in the census of 1851 for the communes of Abeilhan, Capestang, Espondeilham, Portiragnes, Puimisson, Roujan, St. Thibéry, and Servian.

[52] Analysis based on the occupations of cadres as listed in the census of 1851 for the communes of Autichamp, Bonlieu, Manas, Marsanne, Mirmande, Montboucher, La-Roche-sur-Grane, Savasse, Suze.

A substantial shift in the balance of power between the generations accompanied this expansion in the social base of political leadership. During the later years of the July Monarchy, France had been governed not only by an oligarchy but by a gerontocracy. In a society where most landed property was transmitted through inheritance and where the life expectancy of wealthy landowners was relatively high, men under forty years of age rarely possessed large fortunes. A majority of the *censitaire* voters in 1847 were middle-aged, around one-third were over sixty years old, and less than one-fifth were under forty years old.[53] Once electoral rights were detached from property ownership and granted to all men aged twenty-one or more, a generational revolution in the age structure of political leadership became possible. By 1850, administrators in some districts of southern France were convinced that young, unmarried men could not be entrusted with the vote. These irresponsible hotheads spent too much time in the bars and *chambrées*, imbibing dangerous ideas along with copious quantities of wine.[54] In supporting the electoral reform of 1850, which effectively disenfranchised men in their early twenties, conservative officials exaggerated the contrast between unmarried "youths" and married men under the age of thirty-five or forty. Both groups belonged to a new generation whose political consciousness had not been formed by the July Monarchy. Young *celibataires* in their twenties and youthful married men in their thirties brought to the Republican cause all the enthusiasm of new converts. Their political socialization culminated in the Montagnard movement, whose dynamism owed much to their youthful vigor. Indeed, men under the age of forty dominated the cadres of the underground. For them, the politics of conspiracy was the politics of youth.

In the nation as a whole, three-quarters of the secret-society militants were less than forty years old, and nine-tenths were less than fifty.[55] In the southeast, where high-ranking leaders and cadres can be clearly distinguished, the latter were appreciably younger than the former. While the typical Montagnard president or *chef* was in his

[53] Although several scholars have examined the *censitaire* lists in various regions of the nation, they have not stressed the significance of age in the composition of this political elite. My generalization is based on a sample of several cantons in the Drôme and the Hérault (Crest, Montélimar, Béziers, Capestang), where men under the age of forty in 1847 accounted for from 14% to 22% of all the *censitaires*.

[54] For examples of such administrative fears, see S-P Apt, Mar. 15, 1850, in ADV, 4M 50; P-G Agen, Mar. 30, 1850, cited in Dagnan, *Le Gers*, I, 550; P-G Nîmes, Oct. 11, 1851, in AN, BB[30] 382.

[55] In my national sample of suspects (see Chapter Twelve), 128 persons were accused of being secret-society leaders, of whom 39 (30%) were under thirty, 54 (42%) were from thirty to thirty-nine, 26 (20%) were from forty to forty-nine, and 9 (7%) were fifty and over.

later thirties, the typical cadre was in his late twenties or early thirties.[56] Men under the age of thirty benefited especially from the proliferation of leadership roles. They comprised a larger proportion of the cadres than of the high-ranking leaders in all zones, and their share of subordinate positions was greatest in the well-articulated societies around Béziers. Despite this accent on youth, three-quarters of the Montagnard leaders were married. Indeed, societies in the bourgs and villages of the Hérault had a higher proportion of married cadres (77%) than those in the central Drôme (71%). This reflected a lower average age of marriage among agricultural laborers in Mediterranean vineyards than among the sons of owner-farmers in grain- and silk-producing areas. Not unruly *celibataires* but young men with family responsibilities were most likely to serve as cadres in the underground.[57]

Democratization also involved the entry of illiterate peasants into positions of political responsibility. The relationship between literacy levels and conspiratorial leadership was complicated, however, by the fact that young men tended to be considerably more literate than their elders. As beneficiaries of the primary-school reforms introduced by Guizot in 1833, young cultivators and artisans were in a better position to learn about politics than their illiterate fathers. Thus, the literacy transition implied a reversal of the customary pedagogical relationship between the generations in peasant communities: the young would teach the old about the new political ideals. In fact, artisans and cultivators who could read and write were disproportionately involved in the Montagnard movement: the literacy rate of all persons arrested after the insurrection was 57% in the rebel communes near Clamecy, 59% in bourgs and villages near Béziers, 71% in the cantons of Crest-sud and Marsanne (central Drôme), and 78% in the district of St. Sauveur (Yonne).[58] Yet contemporary estimates of literacy in these areas ranged from less than one-tenth to at most one-third of the population. Furthermore, the cadres of the underground had higher literacy rates than rank-and-file members. In the *arrondissement* of Béziers, for example, 71% of the urban cadres were literate, as compared with 45% of the other urban suspects, and 68% of the rural cadres were literate, as compared with 53% of the other affiliates. Simi-

[56] Average age of high-ranking Montagnards: 37.6 in *arr.* Béziers, 37.5 in central Drôme, 37.2 in *arr.* Brignoles, 37.2 in SW Basses-Alpes. Average age of cadres: 31.0, 32.4, 33.4, and 34.9, respectively. Calculations based on ages as given in Ints. and in registers of MCs.

[57] Loubère notes that over 85% of the married suspects in the Hérault were fathers, "the vast majority" with one or two children. Loubère, *Radicalism*, p. 79. This small family size may have reflected some birth control as well as the short length of time during which many suspects had been married.

[58] Calculations based on whether suspects could sign their interrogations.

larly, in the cantons of Crest-sud and Marsanne, the literacy rate of cadres was 89%, while that of other suspects was 67%. The association between youth, literacy, and political leadership was especially strong in the bourgs and villages near Béziers, where the cadres under thirty years of age had a literacy rate of 79% (versus 57% for older cadres). Nowhere else in France did the literacy transition have a greater impact on the transfer of political influence from *les anciens* (the old) to *la jeunesse* (the young).

At the same time, significant numbers of Montagnard cadres *were* illiterate, especially in Mediterranean France. Thus, around one-third of the rural cadres in the *arrondissements* of Béziers and Brignoles could not sign their names, nor could around one-quarter of the urban cadres in these regions. Cultivators who led sections in Provence were most likely to be illiterate: over half of those in the *arrondissement* of Brignoles were illiterate, including those under the age of thirty. Even cultivators who could sign their names well usually appeared ill-educated in the eyes of urban elites. Their involvement with written media of communication was intermittent rather than continuous, and their culture was still shaped primarily by the spoken word. Montagnard initiation ceremonies and oral propaganda responded effectively to the political needs of these semiliterate populations. By recruiting militants from both extremes of the literacy spectrum, the Montagnards brought to fruition the promise of mass democracy inherent in the ideal of a Democratic and Social Republic.

Wylie has pointed out that migratory peasants in western France were difficult to organize during the nineteenth century, while Sewell has shown that artisans who immigrated to Marseille were unusually active in the left-wing politics of that city during the Second Republic.[59] Neither of these relationships between mobility and political activism seems to account, however, for urban and rural variations in the proportions of Montagnard leaders who were migrants. Concerning the towns, evidence from Bédarieux and Béziers suggests that migratory artisans were no more likely to become political leaders than their general numbers in the population would warrant. At Bédarieux, where the population had doubled over the previous two decades, 38% (10/26) of the Montagnard leaders were migrants, but so were 47% (96/203) of the other arrestees, and 50% of all the grooms domiciled in town from 1846 to 1849. By contrast, at Béziers, where the population had remained steady during the July Monarchy, 82% (31/38) of the Montagnard leaders and 80% (148/184) of the other arrestees had

---

[59] Laurence Wylie, *Chanzeaux* (Cambridge, Mass., 1966), pp. 51-56: William Sewell, "La classe ouvrière de Marseille," pp. 39-48; see also Agulhon's discussion of the role of immigrant artisans at Le Luc, *La République au village*, pp. 401-3.

been born in town.[60] With respect to the countryside, migratory elements of the peasantry were no more or less likely to achieve leadership positions than their sedentary neighbors. Thus, in the cantons of Marsanne and Crest-sud (Drôme), where rural mobility across communal boundaries was high, 46% of the leaders and 40% of the other arrestees had been born outside their commune of residence; but in villages of the southwestern Basses-Alpes, where long distance emigration and communal endogamy limited short-distance mobility, 85% of the leaders and 82% of the affiliates resided in their commune of birth.[61] Montagnard leaders reproduced the migratory characteristics of their communities, one more sign of the broad social forces at work in the underground.

Through the obscure energies of ordinary Frenchmen in town and countryside alike, subversion had taken on the lineaments of a party organization with a mass base of membership. Henceforth, the impetus for political action would come from the lower depths of society. As the subprefect of Marmande wrote with foreboding on November 27, 1851, "Authority has passed into the hands of more violent men, belonging to the completely inferior classes of society."[62] Not all officials were persuaded that democratization increased the danger of a revolution. The *procureur-général* at Grenoble viewed with irony the situation in the Drôme just three months before the coup d'état: "I doubt very much whether the leaders who have any importance exert effective influence over the mass of their adherents or their coaffiliates. The power of initiative, if not the right of command, has passed to their subordinate officers. The democrats of the towns have more or less given way to the socialists of the villages, and the ideas of revolution to the instincts of subversion."[63] He implied that leaders recruited from the mass of the population lacked the influence and the experience to coordinate a serious movement of political opposition. Yet in the very process of building a grass-roots organization, Montagnard artisans and cultivators had developed confidence in their own political abilities. The participatory process of conspiratorial recruitment, indoctrination, and leadership had brought a new generation of militants into the political realm. They might fail to gain power, but they were prepared to muster their strength, with arms if necessary, in defense of the Republic.

[60] Birthplace of suspects is given in their interrogations and in the registers of the MCs; that of all grooms married at Bédarieux has been calculated by Jo Burr Margadant, "The Sociology of an Insurrection: A Study of Social Mobility in Bédarieux, 1846-1849," unpublished paper at UC Davis, 1972, p. 11, n. 28.

[61] Calculations for the Drôme are based on the interrogations of suspects; those for the Basses-Alpes are based on the register of the MC.

[62] AD L-G, M3 *Cercles* and societies.

[63] Letter dated Sept. 19, 1851, cited by Vigier, *La Seconde République*, II, 260, n. 196.

· 9 ·

PATTERNS OF REPRESSION

Administrative fears of political dissent became a self-fulfilling prophecy once Montagnard societies began spreading into the countryside. Prefects and public prosecutors were already beginning to view Republican associations as conspiratorial fronts and nonviolent protests as intolerable disorders. Now they faced a genuine threat of subversion and revolt. Yet their apparatus of coercive control was so poor that they failed almost entirely to halt the drift toward conspiracy. Most high-ranking leaders and nearly all the cadres of the Montagnards escaped detection, let alone arrest, in the months before the coup d'état. Efforts to improve the quality of political intelligence proved unavailing, and officials relied increasingly on force or the threat of force to maintain political loyalty. Their punitive actions against visible signs of opposition—customary social gatherings, symbolic demonstrations, hostile crowds—rarely weakened the invisible networks of the Montagnards. Instead, sporadic and arbitrary displays of coercive power stimulated hatred of the government. Repression was a direct cause of the insurrection it was supposed to prevent.

Police bureaucrats were naturally inclined to emphasize the virtues of repression, and they often blamed Republican agitators when their own actions provoked popular hostility. In the official mentality of the period, repression did not undermine public authority; it protected society from subversion. Some historians have reflected this optimistic view of police powers during the Second Republic, and they have interpreted the increasing severity of the government as proof of the decline of the Montagnard movement. Other historians have described cases, however, where heavy-handed police methods exacerbated political tensions and fostered insurgency in December 1851.[1] Behind these divergent scholarly views are theoretical and empirical problems inherent in the analysis of political repression. Theoretically, coercion can be viewed as both a deterrent and a stimulant of protest. It arouses fear but it also provokes anger among opponents of the government.

[1] Successful repression between 1849 and 1851 is emphasized by Payne, "Preparation of a Coup d'Etat," and John Merriman, *Republic*. For an opposing view that stresses the limits of repression, see Thomas Robert Forstenzer, "Bureaucrats under Stress: French Attorneys General and Prefects and the Fall of the Second Republic (10 December 1848–2 December 1851)," Ph.D. diss., Stanford University, 1973. For negative examples of repression, see Dagnan, *Le Gers*, 1, 530; and, especially, Agulhon, *La République au village*, pp. 346-60, 389-91, 423-25.

To reconcile these opposing effects, political scientists have argued that the relationship between repression and revolt is "curvilinear." The probability of political violence increases as negative sanctions and coercive instruments approach intermediate levels, but it falls again when sanctions become extreme and the forces of repression overwhelming.[2] This theory implies that sporadic repression is worse than none, while massive repression is an effective tool of authoritarian government. In the context of the Second Republic, it points to the gap between coercive objectives and performance as a crucial determinant of mass resistance to the coup d'état.

In verifying such a theory, however, it is often difficult to figure out whether repression was the cause of protest demonstrations or their effect. To resolve this problem, it is helpful to distinguish between the types of political opposition that officials tried to control, the strength or weakness of the sanctions available to them, and the concentration or dispersal of their coercive forces. To begin with, administrators had a much more difficult task dismantling secret societies than eliminating public propaganda. John Merriman has shown that they did succeed in paralyzing most legal opposition to the government before the coup d'état, especially in majority-Republican departments that did not develop an underground network in 1850-51.[3] It is in conspiratorial districts that a curvilinear relationship between repression and protest can be confirmed. If we distinguish between "high," "medium," and "low" levels of repression in such districts, we find that medium levels were most common and that even high levels rarely fulfilled government objectives before the coup. High levels of repression, which involved military operations against suspected conspirators, severe sanctions under the state of siege, and extensive deployments of soldiers in rural communities, were confined to a few districts of the nation before December 1851, and they succeeded in forestalling insurgency only where military forces remained conspicuous on the eve of the coup. Medium levels of repression involved sporadic attempts to control visible rather than conspiratorial forms of dissidence, preventive arrests followed by light jail sentences or acquittals, and concentrations of military forces in a few towns. This pattern existed in many conspiratorial districts, and it generated popular hostility to the government, especially in the towns and bourgs that spearheaded the insurrection. Low levels of repression, where political prosecutions and military forces were absent, characterized some rural communes that took arms in alliance with urban insurgents, but this pattern was more typical of areas which greeted news of the coup d'état calmly.

[2] Gurr, *Why Men Rebel*, pp. 232-73.
[3] Merriman, *The Agony of the Republic*, pp. 138-90.

The dialectic of coercion and protest can best be analyzed in a regional context. The first task is to analyze the failure of administrative efforts to dismantle Montagnard societies through arrests and prosecutions of suspected conspirators. Case studies of the central Drôme and the *arrondissement* of Béziers will show that even where some leaders were apprehended, the police powers of the state were too restricted for thorough repression to take place. Secondly, it is necessary to examine the impact of military operations in several "high-intensity" areas where the state of siege was imposed before the coup d'état. These include the central Drôme and the southern Ardèche, where troops first patrolled and then withdrew from rural communities, and the eastern Cher, where they continued to operate in the villages until the coup d'état. Only in the latter case did this policy of military intimidation actually deter insurgency in December 1851. The final order of business is to evaluate the efforts of civilian authorities to control the visible activities of conspirators. The ineffectual or counterproductive results of this policy will be illustrated with examples from several departments, including the Hérault, the Basses-Alpes, and the Gers.

The most obvious way to control subversion was to arrest the organizers of Montagnard societies. This was the national policy of the government, and wherever prefects or public prosecutors learned anything about conspiratorial activities, they tried to obtain juridical evidence against the leaders. Not only the so-called Plot of Lyon, but several other show trials in 1850-51—the Plot of Béziers, the Plot of the Southwest, and the Plot of Perpignan—were based on police surveillance of alleged conspirators.[4] The suspects in these *causes célèbres*, numbering around eighty, resided mainly in towns of southern France. Government prosecutors succeeded in convicting several dozen of them by referring the Lyon cases to a military court-martial and the Béziers cases to an outside tribunal (Aix). Yet these convictions involved only a few of the hundreds of Montagnards who were recruiting and initiating members of the underground. As police operations in the *arrondissement* of Béziers and the central Drôme show, Montagnard societies could not be broken up by prosecuting small numbers of leaders.

The Plot of Béziers began when rumors of "demagogic meetings" in the countryside reached the ears of the subprefect and the public prosecutor in March 1850. Despite their eagerness to arrest the "notorious" Republicans in town, these officials received orders from

---

[4] Concerning the Plot of Lyon, see Chapter Six, n. 21. The sources for the Plot of Béziers are in AD B-R, 14U, 53-54. For the Plot of the Southwest, see AN, BB[30] 392B; and for the Plot of Perpignan, see extracts of the reports of P-G Montpellier, published by J. Tchernoff, *Associations*, p. 357.

Montpellier to tighten their surveillance while awaiting military rein-forcements. It was over a month before they received any concrete leads: on May 18 the police commissioner arrested a loiterer who had pulled a knife on him, and a search of the culprit's house turned up three kilograms of contraband gunpowder, equipment for making more of the same, a few pistols, and a list of sixteen Republican mili-tants, including the Montagnard organizer, Relin. Four more men were arrested in the next few days for manufacturing gunpowder, and the subprefect wrote excitedly that a conspiracy was afoot in the land:

> There is a vast plot embracing this entire region, with ramifications perhaps extending to neighboring departments. It is clear to me that this organization has members in the smallest communes as well as the major ones. Our Reds have really drawn up plans to light great fires as a signal for the residents of the countryside to seize, even to eliminate, the civilian and military authorities, and then to pillage the town. They have been waiting for a favorable occasion to put this plan into action.[5]

By arresting the urban leaders of this extraordinary organization, the subprefect hoped to terrify their followers into submission: "We must strike with vigor, brilliantly, so the memory of their punishment will be lasting." Unfortunately, there was not enough evidence for "severe repression," but if the suspects were nonetheless "kidnapped" from the town and tried at Montpellier, "all thought of disorder or resistance will disappear, and calm will certainly be restored."[6]

The *procureur-général* at Montpellier opposed this strategy of pre-ventive arrests on the grounds that not enough evidence had yet been uncovered to prosecute any of the Republican leaders. His caution was quickly overborne by new police measures. On May 25 someone in the Montagnard society apparently confessed under the protection of anonymity, naming the five members of the Montagnard *commission d'initiation* and ten other leaders. Despite the doubtful legal validity of such a confession, the police rounded up seven of the suspects on the next day. As luck would have it, two of them were carrying notes that implicated all seven as leaders of a secret organization. Investigative magistrates issued search warrants elsewhere in the region, and they un-covered traces of secret meetings between the Béziers leaders and resi-dents of nine rural communes. Solid evidence was difficult to find, however, and they prosecuted only seven men outside the town, of

[5] S-P Béziers, May 21, 1850, ADH, 39M 134.
[6] Ibid. See, also, *Proc.* Béziers, Mar. 21, 1850, AN, BB[30] 319-P33; and letters from Garrison Commander Béziers, May 14, 1850, S-P Béziers, May 19 and May 20, 1850, and CP Béziers, May 19, 1850, in ADH, 39M 134.

whom only three were, in fact, Montagnard leaders. The Plot of Béziers was basically an urban police operation.[7]

Its results appeared at first to favor the government in two respects: the main leaders of conspiracy in the region had been removed from the scene; and their followers had been intimidated. The legal results of the case seemed to justify the former inference: ten suspects were jailed for over a year before being tried at Aix, and eight of them, including Relin, were convicted of belonging to a secret society and sentenced to prison for one or two years. True, they were acquitted on the main charge of conspiracy, but they were all still behind bars when the coup d'état took place. Writing on October 31, 1850, the subprefect concluded that the organization of the Montagnards had been paralyzed by their imprisonment: "Leadership no longer exists to maintain and direct the initial thrust of the movement, which by now must be exceedingly weak. If the rings of the chain still exist, no one can link them together. Since the arrest of the members of the *Comité Supérieur*, all concerted action has ceased. In particular, there is no longer any propaganda." With respect to the chastened attitude of the Republicans at Béziers, the *procureur-général* wrote on July 22, 1850: "As for the extremists, there are no more provocations, no more illegal weapons being carried, no more meetings in the countryside or the cafés, no more songs in the streets, no more red belts or ties. After having displayed so much audacity, they have been struck down by fear."[8]

Administrators gradually became aware, however, that they had failed either to halt the spread of conspiracy from Béziers to the countryside or to restore "moral order" in the town. By April 1851 the *procureur* was complaining desperately that he could not halt recruitment in the bourgs and villages. His superior at Montpellier responded with well-meaning but empty advice:

You ask, how can the growing recruitment of individuals be prevented? By noting it. Some of them must be willing to talk.

How can you find out in advance the day, the hour, the place of the demagogic meetings that are being held in the countryside? Watch everywhere, and find members who will talk.

Make arrests. Don't worry about the outcome of the trials. The faith of converts to demagogy is not so strong that they will heroically defy severe legal repression, even if it is only a threat.[9]

[7] P-G Montpellier, May 22, 1850, and *Proc.* Béziers, May 26, 1850, in AN, BB[30] 319; and "Acte d'accusation," P-G Aix, Feb. 22, 1851, in AD B-R, 14U 53-54.
[8] S-P Béziers, ADH, 39M 132; P-G Montpellier, AN, BB[30] 391.
[9] P-G Montpellier to *Proc.* Béziers, Apr. 19, 1850, quoted in a letter to M. Justice, Apr. 20, 1851, AN, BB[30] 392A.

In fact, magistrates obtained confessions in only two communes of the region during the eighteen months before the coup d'état. On this basis they were able to arrest most members of a branch at Berlou and a décurie at Villeneuve-les-Béziers.[10] Otherwise, they had only unsubstantiated rumors to guide their investigations, and many Montagnard branches in the *arrondissement* escaped detection altogether.[11] As for Béziers, its Montagnard leadership was reconstituted under the noses of the authorities, who learned nothing whatsoever about the urban society after having arrested Relin and his friends. What officials did know was that the mood of the "extremists" at Béziers remained hostile to the government. Already in August 1850 a crowd of 3,000 had gathered outside the local courtroom when thirteen "small fry" were being tried for illegal possession of gunpowder or weapons. After seven of the suspects had been sentenced to brief prison terms (a maximum of twelve months), a few of the spectators had shouted angrily at the authorities.[12] By October 31, the subprefect was convinced that "most of those who joined the Montagnard society still hope to realize their shameful projects"; and by April 1851 he was complaining that "our efforts are paralyzed, our action becomes null. . . . We are forced to admit . . . that to strike the perturbators they must reveal themselves by some act of reprehensible notoriety. Until then, we can only wait."[13] On the eve of the coup d'état he was still waiting, more ignorant than ever about the organization that would soon muster thousands of rebels against him.

While administrators in the Hérault were directing their attention at urban conspirators, those in the Drôme were trying to arrest rural as well as urban leaders of the underground. On May 13, 1850, the prefect of the Drôme sounded the alarm in a letter to the minister of the interior: "Secret societies are being organized in the department; they must be broken up and their leaders must be prosecuted."[14] During the previous several months he had been receiving anxious reports from the subprefects at Montélimar and Die, describing surreptitious agitation and rumors of conspiracy in bourgs and villages of the central and southern Drôme. Now the rumors involved the northern Drôme as well, and the prefect drew a stark portrait of the situation in a letter to the *procureur-général* at Grenoble, dated May 31: "There exists a

[10] P-G Montpellier, May 6, June 1, Sept. 9 and 30, Oct. 16 and 20, 1851, AN, BB[30] 392B, 393, 394.
[11] Out of thirty-six branches in *arr.* Béziers which were discovered after the coup, only fourteen had been reported in previous months, with prosecutions for conspiracy only at Béziers, Nissan, and Villeneuve-les-Béziers.
[12] P-G Montpellier, Aug. 10, 1850, AN, BB[30] 391.
[13] S-P Béziers, Oct. 31, 1850, Apr. 30, 1851, ADH, 39M 132.
[14] Draft from Prefect, ADD, M 1345.

vast plot against society and the government. The conspirators want to overthrow the status quo; their means of action are the refusal to pay taxes and armed insurrection. They are bound by an oath of terror to march at the first orders and to preserve the secrets of the society. Their rewards will be the abolition of taxes and the goods of the rich." Aided by an anonymous informer, he listed the names of fourteen alleged conspirators in six towns and five bourgs, and he claimed that secret societies also existed in another nineteen rural communes of the department. In his view the situation called for abrupt and decisive judicial action.[15]

The *procureur-général* argued that magistrates would not be able to obtain evidence against the suspects, and he doubted the accuracy of the prefect's revelations:

> These names of places and persons derive almost entirely from confidential sources, police reports, or public rumor, all unsubstantiated by witnesses or documentary evidence.
>
> Even if all the circumstances mentioned by the prefect could be demonstrated in court, still, in my opinion, they would only amount to the misdemeanor offense of belonging to a secret society. Most of them would escape any prosecution, either by their very nature, or by the way they have come to the attention of the authorities. By bringing them together somewhat arbitrarily, and by attributing a plausible but disputable significance to them, the prefect, in his just solicitude for maintaining and defending order, has perceived more than magistrates would be able to discover.
>
> I am also inclined to think that administrators have confused secret memberships, political meetings and an electoral organization.[16]

His objections were overruled, however, by the minister of justice, who ordered him to launch a "general investigation," encompassing "coordinated raids on all the persons allegedly involved in the plot, household searches, warrants for arrest."[17] Aided by military reinforcements from Lyon, the *procureur-général* had search warrants issued against thirty suspects, including all the persons denounced to the prefect.[18] Beginning on August 3, troops marched from the departmental capital of Valence to the central and southern Drôme, where they vis-

---

[15] Prefect, May 31, 1850, copy forwarded to M. Justice, AN, BB[30] 391. See, also, S-P Die, Apr. 25, May 6, 13, 15, 1850; and S-P Montélimar, Apr. 5 and 6, 1850, in ADD, M 1345.

[16] P-G Grenoble, June 22, 1850, AN, BB[30] 391.

[17] M. Justice to P-G Grenoble, which the latter quoted to General Castellane, July 18, 1850, AN, BB[30] 391.

[18] P-G Grenoble to General Castellane, July 18 and 20, 1850, in AN, BB[30] 391.

ited six towns and twelve rural communes in pursuit of subversives. By
the end of the year military and police operations had reached twenty-
nine communes in the department. The authorities could scarcely be
faulted for the scale of their investigations.[19]

Yet the *procureur-général* had been correct: the results of all this
coercive energy were paltry, especially in the central Drôme. The August raids yielded a grand total of one statue of Liberty, one rifle, and
one saber in the cantons of Crest-nord, Crest-sud, and Bourdeaux.
After five more months, only three political suspects from this area had
been arrested. The same disappointment greeted administrative efforts
in the cantons of Montélimar, Marsanne, and Dieulefit—a total of four
political arrests by the end of the year. Only in the canton of Loriol
had fourteen suspects been arrested, but the Montagnard leaders in this
area had fled, along with around fifteen other suspects. Further south,
officials succeeded in prosecuting twenty members of Republican mutual-benefit societies at Nyons and Le Buis, but these small towns were
Legitimist strongholds.[20] The conspiratorial preparations of Republican electorates in the central Drôme continued unabated into the year
1851. One further police operation—the "Plot of Grane" in June 1851
—did result in twenty-three prosecutions for conspiracy. Eleven of
these suspects were soldiers, however, and only two of the civilians
were Montagnard leaders. Again, most of the civilian suspects fled arrest.[21] Despite extensive military activity, magistrates obtained enough
evidence to prosecute only eleven Montagnard leaders in the central
Drôme before the coup d'état. They learned nothing about a majority
of the rural branches, and they prosecuted alleged conspirators in only
nine of the seventy-five communes in this region where Republicans
took arms in December 1851.[22]

If administrators in the Drôme and the Hérault were unable to acquire enough evidence for legal action against most conspirators, those
elsewhere in the nation were even less successful in controlling Montagnard societies. Often they neglected to distinguish at all between
electoral associations, social clubs, mutual-benefit societies, and genu-

[19] Tabulations of military and police operations based on scattered correspondence in ADD, M 1345.

[20] S-P Die, Aug. 7, 1850, and *Brigadier* Crest, Sept. 20, 1850, in ADD, M 1345;
ATML, s.s. Drôme, and "Plot of Lyon"; and P-G Grenoble, Dec. 9, 1850, in AN,
BB[30] 391.

[21] Transcript of the court martial, *La Gazette des Tribunaux*, June 6, 1852.

[22] Out of forty-seven communes in this region where magistrates uncovered
evidence of Montagnard societies after the coup, only nineteen had been mentioned in previous administrative reports of conspiracy. Leaders were arrested
from Bourdeaux (one), Crest (one), Manas (one), Marsanne (one), and Saou
(one); others fled arrest from Cliousclat, Grane, Marsanne, Mirmande, and Montélimar.

inely conspiratorial organizations. Officials in the Ministry of Justice admitted this when they drew up a report in December 1851 purporting to enumerate "the principal secret societies, or, what comes to the same thing, the unauthorized political societies that have been brought to the attention of the minister of justice."[23] They listed several hundred associations in around three hundred different communes, but only a few dozen were definitely Montagnard branches. Over half the Montagnard societies that had been detected were located in the departments of the Hérault and the Drôme.[24] Officials in most other conspiratorial districts had forwarded to Paris vague reports of clandestine activity before the coup d'état, but they had obtained enough evidence to arrest Montagnard leaders in only a handful of bourgs and villages.[25] Of course, alleged leaders from around thirty towns had been prosecuted in the Plot of Lyon, the Plot of Southwest, and the Plot of Perpignan, but where they had helped organize Montagnard societies, others generally replaced them. The strategy of halting subversion by gathering incriminating evidence against a few individuals nearly always failed.

Behind this failure were social and institutional obstacles to political surveillance. The authorities who were most responsive to national policy—prefects, subprefects, and public prosecutors—resided in the towns and socialized only with the propertied elite. Faced with a mass movement whose leaders were drawn from the middle or lower class, these high-ranking officials were unable to rely on their traditional source of political intelligence—the notables. Nor were they able to obtain much useful information from subordinate agents in the communes—mayors, rural guards, justices of the peace, police commissioners, or gendarmes. These officials were either too close to the local populations, in which case they were reluctant to "spy" for the government, or they were too distant, in which case they suffered from

[23] "Travail sur le mouvement démagogique avant le 2 décembre," Dec. 1, 1851, summary of judicial documents conserved in the archives of the criminal division, Ministry of Justice, published by Tchernoff, *Associations*, p. 280.

[24] The report mentioned only thirty-two Montagnard branches, of which thirteen were in the Hérault and five in the Drôme. Most of its examples of subversive associations were Republican mutual benefit societies or *cercles*. Ibid., pp. 279-387.

[25] Just before the coup, magistrates were investigating branches in the southwestern Yonne (*arr.* Joigny), the eastern Cher (esp. canton of Sancergues), the northern Nièvre (esp. canton of Cosne), the southeastern Loiret (canton of Briare), the southwestern Allier (Montluçon), the southwestern Lot-et-Garonne (canton of Mézin), and the northern Drôme (canton of Tain). Arrests were made in around ten communes of these districts, nearly all of which had armed resistance to the coup. See the correspondence of the P-Gs in AN, BB[18] 1485A, 1501, BB[30] 391, 392B, 394, as well as Tchernoff, *Associations*, pp. 279-387.

the same information gap as the prefects and prosecutors. Furthermore, Montagnard leaders consciously widened that gap by threatening traitors with death and by avoiding public meetings or written communications. Despite some efforts to improve their information-gathering techniques, police bureaucrats rarely learned anything specific about the underground. The difficulties that they encountered can be seen with especial clarity in the central Drôme and the *arrondissement* of Béziers, where police bureaucrats knew just enough about the Montagnards to fear them but not enough to destroy them.

Mayors were the most obvious instruments of political surveillance in the rural communes. As public authorities with law-enforcement responsibilities, they were supposed to exercise political police powers over their *administrés*. Yet now that they were elected by the municipal councils instead of being appointed by the state, they also had political responsibilities to their constituents. Instead of reporting what they knew about local militants, most of them adopted a neutral posture in the struggle between the state and the Montagnards: only six out of seventy-one mayors supplied the government with any written information about conspirators in rural communes of the central Drôme and the *arrondissement* of Béziers where Montagnard branches were discovered after the coup d'état; and only one mayor in these communes helped initiate any prosecutions for conspiracy.[26]

High-ranking administrators complained bitterly about this state of affairs. "Half the mayors are bad and the other half lack influence or energy," wrote one *procureur* at Béziers in April 1851. The new procedure for selecting rural mayors had "completely disarmed executive power," claimed the subprefect at Montélimar. "It makes effective surveillance of the rural communes almost impossible. Some mayors are pusillanimous and close their eyes; others, chosen by the masses, adhere to the principles of demagogy and socialism, and they don't exert any surveillance at all." The subprefect was convinced that "demagogic" propaganda had taken refuge in the countryside because the mayors refused to enforce the repressive policies of "higher authorities." The prefect of the Drôme agreed that administrative authority in the communes could not be restored as long as the mayors were elected by the municipal councils: "They think of themselves as independent men; they are pushed around too often by the municipal councils and policing is no longer possible. In a word, executive power has

[26] For the exceptional case of the mayor of Nissan (Hérault), see S-P Béziers, June 23, July 5 and 9, 1851, in ADH, 39M 134. No prosecutions resulted from the vague reports of the mayors at Montboucher, Puy-St. Martin, Saou, and Soyans (Drôme), and Pouzolles (Hérault), in ADD, M 1345-46, and ADH, 39M 134.

been annihilated and the unity of the government broken."[27] Although municipal officials could be suspended by the prefects and revoked by the Council of State, inaction against conspirators did not constitute sufficient grounds for such sanctions. In the seventy-one communes of the *arrondissement* of Béziers and the central Drôme where Montagnard branches definitely existed, nine mayors were suspended before the coup d'état, but only one of them had been accused of protecting conspirators.[28]

If municipal officials abstained from helping the government, this was not only because of their democratic mode of selection. Equally important was their sensitivity to social pressures. The mayors and deputy mayors viewed local conspirators "in the round"—as fathers and sons, peasants and craftsmen, friends and neighbors. If they helped the government prosecute its political enemies, they violated the confidence of men whom they had often known for years. To serve as a *mouchard* (police spy) for the state was to betray the social trust and to earn the lasting enmity of such men and their families. Prefects and subprefects did not have to live with the relatives and friends of those who might be hauled off to jail on charges of political conspiracy. The mayors did. Furthermore, if municipal officials in the bourgs and villages did collaborate with police bureaucrats in the prefectoral and *arrondissement* capitals, their own sources of political information became less reliable. Then they would be scarcely more helpful than the bumbling J. P. at Bourdeaux (Drôme), who wrote the prefect in March 1851, "I am trying to protect the respectable workers and laborious cultivators from conspiratorial recruitment, but the militants are avoiding me and preventing me from using my influence."[29] Even petty acts of repression could impair the quality of their political intelligence. As the deputy mayor at Puygiron (Drôme) explained to a patrol of gendarmes from Montélimar, he had failed to attend the local festival in January 1851—thereby missing an opportunity to punish some boisterous Montagnards—because "a rather large number of inhabitants are hostile to him for supposedly having arranged several (minor political) convictions."[30] Until the coup d'état shattered Republican hopes of victory in 1852, municipal officials would only make

[27] *Proc.* Béziers, cited in P-G Montpellier, Apr. 20, 1851, AN, BB[30] 392A; S-P Montélimar, Jan. and July 1850, ADD, M 1279; and Prefect Drôme, Oct. 2, 1849, ADD, M 1344.
[28] The mayor of Manas (Drôme), a Montagnard leader, was revoked, as were three of the six mayors in *arr.* Béziers whom the prefect suspended. ADD, M 1344-46, ADH, 17M 30-34, 40, ATML, s.s. Drôme.
[29] J. P. Bourdeaux, Mar. 31, 1851, ADD, M 1346.
[30] Gendarmerie Montélimar, Jan. 21, 1851, ADD, M 1346.

life unpleasant for themselves if they functioned as policemen for the state.

The auxiliary agents of these mayors, who were known as *gardes champêtres* in the rural communes, proved no more helpful to the government. Although they were theoretically subordinated to higher authorities, these rural guards depended for practical purposes on the municipal councils, which appointed and paid them. The prefects did retain the power of revocation over them, but they exercised this power only six times in the two regions.[31] Some rural guards joined the secret societies and only one definitely reported conspiratorial activity to centralized administrators.[32] The subprefect at Montélimar did propose their reorganization into cantonal "brigades" in order to provide "more direct and more rapid surveillance" of the countryside, but nothing came of this suggestion until after the coup d'état. In all his reports the subprefect only once alluded to the political role of a rural guard—some men "insulted" the guard of Bonlieu in April 1851 by telling him that soon the government would be overthrown and his throat would be slit.[33] Such predictions did not encourage rural guards to labor on behalf of the anti-Republican cause, whatever their personal beliefs.

Whether out of sympathy or fear, private citizens were equally reluctant to assist the government. "As for confessions, you know the pusillanimity of men in this area," wrote the subprefect of Béziers to the prefect in May 1850.[34] Even accurate revelations were of little use because informers demanded anonymity in order to avoid reprisals. In April–May 1850 the subprefect at Montélimar received the names of several Montagnard leaders in nearby villages, but in August his sources were "compromised" by the judicial investigation. Much to their anger and dismay, the denunciators were confronted with the suspects, and only one of them reiterated his story in court, helping convict two Montagnards.[35] Similarly, a noble who owned extensive properties to the northeast of Crest wrote several poison-pen letters to

[31] The guards at Cliouslat, Francillon, Grane, and Cliouslat (Drôme) were revoked for aiding the Montagnards; and those at Puisserguier and Florensac (Hérault) for failing to repress local disorders. ADD, M 1345-47; and ADH, 39M 128.

[32] Guards at Crupies, Espeluche, Teyssières, Vaunaveys, and Vesc, in the central Drôme, and those at Capestang, Castelnau-de-Guers, and Puissalicon in *arr.* Béziers were definitely initiates. (Ints. and Tems. in ADD and ADH). Guards at Laurens (Hérault), Marsanne, and Saou (Drôme) tried to help the central government. (ADH, 39M 132; ADD, M 1346-47).

[33] S-P Montélimar, Nov. 3, 1850, and Apr. 30, 1851, ADD, M 1345-46.

[34] S-P Béziers, May 21, 1850, in ADH, 39M 134.

[35] S-P Montélimar, Aug. 12, 1850, ADD, M 1345; and ATML, s.s. Drôme.

the police in 1850, denouncing some "Reds" in that area, but he refused even to sign his name. Subsequent police raids resulted in only two prosecutions, both for illegal possession of gunpowder.[36] From a commune to the west of Crest came another denunciation in 1850: "Justice absolutely must descend to Cliousclat with soldiers," scrawled a semiliterate and anonymous hand. "You'll find out everything . . . everything . . . you'll get the leaders, the biggest red bonnets." When this informer or a kindred spirit mustered enough courage to name a Montagnard leader at Cliousclat several months later, the gendarmes did find 360 bullets hidden in the man's house, but he had been in flight for several months and was nowhere to be found.[37] In the Hérault, anonymous sources gave the prefect and the *procureur-général* detailed and accurate information about the Montagnard leaders at Boujan and St. Thibéry, but no one could be prosecuted on the basis of such hearsay evidence.[38] In rare cases, informers might alert the authorities, but they almost never helped prosecute those whom they denounced.

Faced with the indifference, hostility, or fear of rural inhabitants, prefects and public prosecutors turned increasingly to centrally appointed officials—gendarmes and police commissioners—for political assistance. Yet these agents of the national government resided in the towns and large bourgs. They might patrol the countryside, but they could not spy upon the populations from day to day. Furthermore, their very loyalty to anti-Republican administrators reduced their value as sources of political information. They watched the "Reds" come and go, they reported rumors and they halted seditious demonstrations, but almost never did they penetrate the Montagnard societies. Gendarmes and police commissioners were "soldiers of order," not double agents.

At least the gendarmes were equipped and trained to police the countryside. Their small brigades of mounted horsemen were available for deployment from bases in the market towns and bourgs to nearby rural communities. Members of these special army units had an esprit de corps, a strong sense of authority, and some experience as investigative agents of the prefectoral corps and the public prosecutors. They did keep the Montagnards on the alert. Yet few of them took much political initiative: only four brigades in the two departments

---

[36] Four unsigned letters by La Bretonnière, *châtelain* at Montclar, named by S-P Die, Nov. 8, 1850, ADD, M 1345; ATML, s.s. Drôme.

[37] Anonymous letter, *circa* Oct. 1850, ADD, M 1345; Gendarmerie Loriol, Mar. 31, 1850, ADD, M 1346; P-G Grenoble, Apr. 23, 1851, AN, BB[30] 392A.

[38] P-G Montpellier, June 1, 1851, AN, BB[30] 393.

reported any conspiratorial meetings to the prefects or subprefects, and only three succeeded in gathering incriminating evidence against any Montagnard leaders.[39] Their main tasks were the preservation of order and the arrest of criminal suspects, not the exposure of elusive conspirators.

As for the police commissioners, they had rarely exercised any political responsibilities before 1848. By December 1851, however, they were the most important agents of centralized administration outside the *arrondissement* capitals. Their burgeoning political role was a direct consequence of the national struggle against the Montagnards, and it foreshadowed the police state of the Second Empire. Through the police commissioners, prefects and subprefects hoped to bypass the unreliable mayors and to establish direct political control over the populations. Police commissioners in the small market towns often made their first political reports in January 1849, responding to inquiries about Republican clubs; then during the electoral campaign of May 1849 they forwarded information about left-wing speeches and rallies. In the later months of 1849 they enforced administrative bans on political meetings and demonstrations; by the spring and summer of 1850 they were organizing raids on suspected Montagnards in the towns; and subsequently, they began patrolling the rural communes.[40]

Their new political role required a change in attitude and a change in legal jurisdiction. While their main function before 1848 had been to enforce local rules and regulations, now they needed to view themselves as front-line agents of the national government. Although some police commissioners were slow to recognize their new responsibilities, they either changed their ways or risked losing their jobs. Typical of the new-model police commissioners who emerged in 1850-51 was the agent at Bédarieux. "The eye of the police ought to penetrate into all corners of the town," he wrote in January 1850. According to this police commissioner, only the most rigorous action could preserve order in the town: "Bédarieux is composed of a working-class population, agitated, eager to rebel; a prompt and energetic example is almost always indispensable in such a situation to prevent the unleashing of a riot. . . . Therefore, I will strike hard and without pity against the guilty, whatever their faction. . . . I will redouble my blows to reach the agitators. . . . This is how a subordinate, a police commissioner,

---

[39] Three arrests by the brigade at Saulce-Mirmande, two at Tain, and two at Montélimar (Drôme); rumors investigated by the brigade at Affaniès (Hérault). ADD, M 1345-46, 1354 (dossier Mirmande); AN, BB[30] 394; ADH, 39M 132.

[40] Correspondence of CPs, in ADD, 1510, 1514, 1524, 1530; ADH, 39M 127-30, 132, 134-35.

must act in a canton deprived of a garrison or high-ranking administrators."[41]

If the ethos of the police changed, so did their jurisdictional authority. Previously, each commissioner had been paid by the municipal council of his commune of residence, and his legal responsibilities had been limited to that commune. With few exceptions only the larger cantonal seats had such commissioners. Now that subversives were operating in the countryside, administrators wanted "the eye of the police" to move accordingly—outward from the cantonal seats to the rural communes. Consequently, they requested and obtained permission to extend police powers throughout the cantons. For example, the subprefect at Die wrote on September 26, 1850: "Given the political situation at Grane, Puy-St.-Martin, Beaufort, and Plan-de-Baix (villages in the cantons of Crest-sud and Crest-nord), it is desirable to extend the powers of the police commissioner (at Crest) to both cantons." In June 1851 he confirmed that the commissioner had been empowered to visit "all the communes," not only in the two cantons of Crest but in the neighboring cantons of Loriol and Marsanne. He could travel "at any time to search the houses of any persons suspected of belonging to a secret society."[42] By the eve of the coup d'état, such rural authority had been delegated to the police commissioners in at least fifteen cantonal seats of the two departments.[43] The police were clearly following the Montagnards into the countryside.

They usually returned empty-handed. From January 1 to December 2, 1851, police commissioners in the *arrondissement* of Béziers helped gather evidence against only seven alleged conspirators, only two of whom resided outside the towns.[44] During the same period their counterparts in the central Drôme reported nothing but rumors about the leaders of the underground. Had the commissioners performed undercover work, they might have been more effective, but they lacked training in espionage techniques and received very little money to hire agents. In the entire department of the Drôme only 150 francs per month were available for espionage, and only one commissioner seems to have infiltrated a Montagnard branch.[45] As for espio-

[41] CP Bédarieux, Jan. 12, 1850, Dec. 31, 1849, ADH, 39M 132.

[42] S-P Die, Sept. 26, 1850, June 30, 1851, ADD, M 1345, 1279.

[43] Scattered correspondence in ADD, M 1510, 1279, 1247; ADH, 39M 128, 132, 134; AN, BB[30] 391, 392A.

[44] Two arrests each at Les Aires, Bédarieux, and Pézénas, one each at Béziers and Roujan. P-G Montpellier, Apr. 13, May 2, 3, June 9, 1851, AN, BB[30] 366, 392A, 393; CP Montpellier to P., May 3, 1851, and CP Béziers, Apr. 9, 1851, in ADH, 39M 132, 134.

[45] CP Montélimar, Dec. 5, 1851, S-P Montélimar, Dec. 4, 1851, and M. Int. to Prefect, Sept. 1, 1850, ADD, M 1347, 1345.

nage in the bourgs and villages, it scarcely existed. The one documented case of such undercover activity ended on a ludicrous note. Commissioner Pochard from Montélimar carried out a secret mission in July
1851, accompanied by a gendarme from Mirmande and a rural guard
from Saou. Disguised as political fugitives, the three men entered the
backwoods region around Bourdeaux in order to discover the where-
abouts of some men who had fled arrest several months earlier. They
arrived in the small Protestant village of Crupies and were promptly
greeted as heroes by a few dozen peasants at the local inn. They already suspected that the innkeeper was the president of a secret society. Now they feigned surprise when the rural guard appeared to
join in a round of drinks. Which side was *he* on? "Oh, don't be afraid
of the guard," the three soldiers of order were assured. "He's a brother,
he's our father, our leader. When he learns anything, he tells us—he
was initiated in this room and he's a decurion." Later, when the guard
himself became suspicious and took Pochard around back to ask for
the secret password of the society, the three spies hastily departed. Pochard wrote afterward to General Lapène that according to the peasants of Crupies, "The mayors and rural guards of these communes, except for the guard at Truinas, are all members of the secret societies."
Pochard did not know whether this was true, but he concluded:
"Whatever the case may be, I can assure you that the inhabitants of
the communes in the canton of Bourdeaux profess en masse the most
extreme opinions."[46] Meanwhile the police commissioner at Dieulefit
had received a hot tip that some political fugitives had just been seen
in the canton of Bourdeaux. Dashing to Crupies with two gendarmes,
he was surprised to find the brigade of gendarmes from Bourdeaux,
searching the assistant mayor's inn. As the police commissioner of
Dieulefit explained in a letter to the subprefect, "We learned that the
three persons whom we were chasing were none other than the police
commissioner at Montélimar, a gendarme from Loriol, and the rural
guard from Saou, all in disguise."[47] Such were the fruits of espionage in
the back country of the Drôme.

The failure of political intelligence was all the more glaring because
the existing legal system did not permit indefinite arrests without trial
or convictions in the absence of some evidence of wrongdoing. The
offense of belonging to a secret society ordinarily required a jury
trial, and from the government's point of view, juries were notoriously unreliable in political cases. If culprits were sent to lesser courts
for trial without a jury, they could not be punished by heavy fines or

[46] CP Montélimar, July 29, 1851, ADD, M 1346.
[47] CP Dieulefit, July 20, 1851, ADD, M 1346.

lengthy prison terms. Legal repression at this level simply made enemies who were usually out of prison again before the supreme political crisis of December 1851. Furthermore, judges at the misdemeanor and assize courts enjoyed life tenure, and they sometimes refused to convict political offenders or to reverse unfavorable jury verdicts on the basis of shaky evidence.

For these reasons, some prefects and public prosecutors began looking with favor on the legal framework of the state of siege. In departments under military jurisdiction, political cases could be referred to court martials, where penalties were severe and civilian juries absent. The *procureur-général* at Lyon was fully aware of these advantages, and he strained judicial procedure beyond reasonable limits in order to send political leaders from throughout southern France before the military authorities in the Rhône, where the state of siege had been in force since June 1849. Without the benefit of military justice, no convictions would probably have been obtained in the Plot of Lyon.[48] Officials in the Drôme, the Ardèche, the Cher, and the Nièvre also clamored successfully for the state of siege before the coup d'état. Not only did they hope to avoid jury trials in political cases, but they expected that displays of military force would bolster their authority. Nowhere else in France did administrators have such substantial coercive resources for defense against rural subversion. If the state of siege could guarantee order, these four departments would be among the most quiescent in the nation after Louis Napoleon overthrew the National Assembly.

In fact, the Drôme, the Ardèche, and the Nièvre all had major insurrections that were motivated in part by hostility to political repression. The case of the Drôme is especially interesting because its civilian authorities had relied on the state of siege ever since June 1849 to intimidate the Republicans. The prefect, Ferlay, had obtained military assistance at that time ostensibly in order to forestall a local revolt in imitation of the Lyon uprising of June 15. His deeper purpose had been to secure a right-wing electoral victory in a by-election, and he wrote to the minister of the interior shortly after the ballots had been counted:

> The introduction of the state of siege to the department has produced a very good effect. It has given courage to the moderate men, who are naturally very timid; it has disorganized the extremists, and has shown that they are definitely only a very small minority. Their influence is declining every day, and they are a matter of concern to

[48] *Rapport* of P-G Lyon, admitting the weakness of the prosecution's case, Mar. 31, 1851, AN, BB[18] 1488.

almost no one anymore. The men of order are today convinced of
the government's force. They dare admit aloud their sympathies. . . .
Moral order has been restored, and material order has not been seriously disturbed.[49]

"Moral order" meant anti-Republican opinion, and henceforth the prefect of the Drôme never wavered in his support of the state of siege. At
every suggestion that military controls be removed, he hastened to assure the central government of their beneficial results.

Although the initial shock of the state of siege appeared to favor
the government, the longer-term effects of military rule were counterproductive. In the absence of reliable political intelligence, the army
was a blunt and arbitrary instrument of coercion. It stimulated a cycle
of repression and resistance that thoroughly undermined governmental
authority, especially in the central Drôme. This region of the department, which mustered all 5,000 of the rebels who fought against troops
in December 1851, had experienced around half of the political prosecutions and three-fifths of the military and police operations reported
in the previous two years. From January through November 1851,
twenty-five of the thirty military raids and seventeen of the nineteen
political prosecutions in the department took place in bourgs and villages near Crest, Loriol, and Montélimar that rebelled en masse against
the coup d'état.[50] Nowhere else in the nation had troops been deployed
so frequently to repress subversives; and nowhere else had the rural
populations become so embittered as a result.

The political misuse of military power in the central Drôme began
near Montélimar, where the commander of the state of siege embraced
the anti-Republican cause with naive enthusiasm in July 1849. He had
scarcely arrived in town when a flood of visitors arrived at his door to
denounce their personal enemies as Reds. Drawing up a list of the
twelve "most dangerous men" in the area, the commander sent troop
columns into the canton of Marsanne to disarm several national guard
units. On one such operation soldiers arrested a rural mayor (at St.
Marcel) for allegedly insulting a notorious anti-Republican landowner
named Malgras. Placed on trial at Montélimar for this petty offense,
the mayor was acquitted after thirteen witnesses contradicted Malgras's

[49] Prefect, July 18, 1849, contrasting with his letters of June 16, 17, 1849, in ADD,
M 1344.
[50] Calculations based on judicial, administrative, and military correspondence in
1850-51, supplemented by a published list of persons convicted of political offenses
by the military tribunal at Lyon. AN, BB[18] 1485A, BB[30] 378, 389-94; AG, F[1] 46;
ADD, M 1345-47; L. Goudin, ed., *Livre d'Or des victimes du coup d'état de 1851*
. . . [Drôme] (Valence, 1883).

story.[51] Eighteen months later this factional infighting bore its fruits when all the villages that had been disarmed rose up with pitchforks and hunting rifles to march on Montélimar. Who should turn up in the mobilization of St. Marcel but the mayor, leading a crowd, which forcibly disarmed Malgras![52] Military force had comparable results at the village of St. Gervais, where 100 troops arrived at daybreak on January 18, 1850, to search various houses for arms and munitions. Behind this raid were false denunciations of the mayor by a Legitimist notary and his clerk. According to the *commissaire-générale* at Lyon, the expedition had produced an "excellent effect," although no compromising evidence had been found. Yet three weeks later a curious incident occurred at St. Gervais. A crowd paraded through the village streets, bearing a one-armed *mannequin*. At various crossroads, the *cortège* stopped and a proclamation was read aloud, sentencing the *mannequin* to death. This carnival masquerade was aimed at none other than the notarial clerk, a one-armed man! The general at Montélimar immediately dispatched gendarmes to "restore order" and to reprimand the mayor, but the subprefect now hinted that the political situation at St. Gervais had been jeopardized by the calumnies of the Legitimists and the threats of the army. "The local authorities, the municipal council, and almost all the inhabitants of the commune favor disorder," he wrote to the prefect. Indeed, when Montagnards at St. Gervais received orders to rebel nearly two years later, they had nearly unanimous public support. Only the notary and a local proprietor opposed the insurgents—and they were forced to march.[53]

These incidents in the canton of Marsanne were followed by much more serious political conflicts in the cantons of Loriol and Crest-sud. Trouble originated at the hamlet of Saulce (commune of Mirmande) on September 2, 1850, when a brigade of gendarmes tried to arrest a suspected Montagnard leader named Merlin. As the foreman of a small silk factory at Saulce, Merlin was responsible for the economic welfare of sixty women and children. Some of his workers feared that the factory would be closed if he were imprisoned, and others demanded payment of their wages. In the turmoil a few girls began demonstrating in the streets and someone rang the factory bell to mobilize popular support. A crowd of women and children, aided by several "men of disorder," gathered rapidly in front of the factory. They rescued Merlin from the gendarmes and carried him triumphantly to the village

---

[51] Undated *Rapport* by Lieutenant Houdeville, ADD, M 1344.

[52] Tems. Jn. Ant. Malgras and son, ADD, M 1355, dossier St. Marcel.

[53] Commissaire Lyon, Jan. 21, 1850, S-P Montélimar, Jan. 17, 20, Feb. 13, 1850, ADD, M 1345; Tem. Jos. Arsac, notary, ATML, Ins. St. Gervais.

square, where they sang the Marseillaise and danced the *farandole* around the liberty tree. The gendarmes retreated, Merlin and his friends took refuge across the Rhône river, and "strangers" demonstrated that night against "notable persons in the area" (probably suspected of being *mouchards*). The "affair" of Mirmande-Cliousclat had begun.[54]

While the military commander at Lyon dispatched reinforcements to the Drôme in response to news of this "revolt," Montagnards in the canton of Loriol tried to organize resistance to further arrests. They feared especially that Ernest de Saint-Prix, wealthy landlord, son of a revolutionary legislator (*Conventionnel*), and Montagnard organizer, would be the next victim of the government. On the afternoon of September 4, "agitators" began assembling in the cabarets of Cliousclat (a village near Mirmande); and at 6:00 p.m. the assistant mayor of the commune, a young owner-farmer named Jean François Garais, ordered the drummers of the national guard to beat the call to arms (*la générale*). Garais later admitted that in issuing this order he had been acting as a member of the local Montagnard society. While the drummers sounded the alarm, bands of men visited outlying farms to round up additional support, and soon a makeshift column of sixty to eighty farmers, artisans, and pottery workers headed for Mirmande. They were expecting a general mobilization throughout the canton in order to protect Saint-Prix, and they halted as soon as they learned that Mirmande was calm. Most of the armed demonstrators went home and the leaders fled during the night.[55]

This uprising, which prefigured the pattern of resistance to the coup d'état in rural communes of the Drôme, provoked a strong government reaction. Troops poured into the area to disarm all the national guard units and to arrest suspects. They captured six men without resistance but they could not find any of the leaders. Eventually, some thirty persons from Mirmande-Saulce and Cliousclat were tried by a military court martial at Lyon, but half of them remained in hiding until the coup d'état. Heavy prison terms helped turn these fugitives into guerrillas: on June 7, 1851, a band of them opened fire on a patrol of gendarmes in the forest of Grane (east of Cliousclat). Two gendarmes were wounded in this shoot-out.[56] The general in command of the state of siege was infuriated by the audacity of the rebels. Changing his previous strategy of using soldiers only for brief expeditions against rural populations, he now stationed several hundred soldiers indefinitely

---

[54] Tems. of witnesses, ATML, s.s. Drôme; P-G Grenoble, Sept. 13, 1850, AN, BB[30] 360.

[55] Int. Jn. Fr. Garais, ADD, M 1362; *Proc.* Valence to P-G Grenoble, forwarded to M. Justice on Sept. 21, 1850, AN, BB[18] 1474A; ATML, s.s. Drôme.

[56] P-G Grenoble, June 10 and Sept. 23, 1851, AN, BB[30] 393.

in the communes of Grane, Mirmande, and Marsanne. These troops raided nearby villages, searched several hundred houses, and seized a half-dozen men on suspicion of aiding the fugitives. Yet they did not turn up a single *contumace* (at least eighteen were in flight). The military unit at Grane was even accused of harboring Montagnard conspirators, and all the troops were hastily removed from the region at the beginning of July.[57]

The commanding general tried to justify this deployment of military force on the usual grounds that it had heartened the men of order and intimidated the "bands of evildoers, their adherents, and all men with evil passions."[58] In fact, the operation had been a total failure. The *procureur-général* at Grenoble, who had praised the state of siege back in July 1850 for inspiring fear in the Montagnards, wrote on August 10, 1851, that a dozen men "had compromised the moral authority of the state of siege by holding out successfully against a notable portion of the public forces." On September 19, he voiced even greater pessimism about the political situation in the central Drôme: "Subordinate officials do not always behave with moderation and justice in their investigations and police raids. Men who were harmless or undecided, men restrained by wise instinct or healthy opinions, find themselves treated as if they were dangerous and guilty. In their irritation they abandon caution and enter the general current (of opposition to the government)." The military dragnet in the cantons of Crest-sud, Loriol, and Marsanne had driven nearly everyone into the arms of the Montagnard activists. As the *procureur-général* recognized, the region had been "entirely lost to the cause of order," and "just about all the inhabitants share the most extreme opinions."[59] Three months later the political fugitives instigated uprisings at Grane, Cliousclat, and Marsanne, and Montagnard leaders mobilized majority support against the government in nearly all the bourgs and villages that had been raided by the army.

The dialectic of repression and resistance had a similar outcome in the neighboring department of the Ardèche, although military rule was not formally imposed here until September 12, 1851. Political tension became especially acute in the southern *arrondissement* of Largentière, where civilian authorities tried unsuccessfully to disrupt the Montagnards. In February 1850 the prefect had first reported conspiratorial activities in the religiously divided canton of Vallon, where the Protestant majority was overwhelmingly Republican in sentiment. It was not until October, however, that he obtained a specific lead: secret-

[57] General Lapène, *Exposé*, June 8, 1851, AG, F¹ 46; Prefect Drôme, June 6, 8, July 3, 1850, ADD, M 1346; P-G Grenoble, Aug. 10, 1851, AN, BB³⁰ 378.
[58] Lapène, report cited in n. 57.
[59] P-G Grenoble, Aug. 10, Sept. 19, 1851, AN, BB³⁰ 378.

society members were allegedly meeting on Sundays at the house of Henri Escoutay, an innkeeper at the village of Salavas. On October 27 three brigades of gendarmes raided Escoutay's inn, where they surprised the local Montagnard leader, Jacques Paulin, reading a "socialist text" to forty men. Everyone tried to flee, but when the gendarmes emerged with five suspects whom they had collared, a crowd of three hundred to four hundred assailed them with shouts of "Death." Overwhelmed by numbers, the forces of order released the prisoners and suffered insults all the way back to Vallon, where another angry crowd besieged their barracks.[60]

The prefect hoped to link this affair to the Plot of Lyon, which was just then unfolding, so magistrates tried to expand the case by issuing nineteen warrants to appear for questioning as well as twenty arrest warrants. This threat of legal action only antagonized the populations of Vallon and Salavas. Almost all the suspects went into hiding and then reappeared in arms at Vallon on November third, shouting "Down with the Tyrants! Down with the *Mouchards!*" After this demonstration, the mayor of Vallon pleaded with the subprefect that "in a country peopled by political and religious enemies, every act of military force causes anger and provokes threats." Even the "men of order," who feared for their properties and their lives, wanted the government to stop its investigation.[61] The subprefect tried instead to hire a secret agent, requested a military garrison at Largentière, and denounced the mayor of Salavas, whose son was in flight.[62] Throughout the winter the suspects received aid from the local populations, whose sense of justice was diametrically opposed to that of the subprefect and the gendarmes. In the bitter words of the mayor of Salavas, who wrote the subprefect on December 17 to resign his post rather than be fired: "It is possible that your position requires you to make every effort to arrest the fugitives in the affair of Salavas, but my position as a respectable man and as a Christian imposes on me the obligation to remain neutral and not to play the dastardly role of an informer."[63] This drama was finally resolved in the spring of 1851, when the "bandits of Salavas" stood trial on minor charges at the misdemeanor court of Largentière. As if to complete the government's embarrassment, all but two were acquitted, and the leader, Paulin, received only a fifteen-day jail term. He returned to Salavas and organized the insurrection in December.[64]

[60] Prefect, Feb. 17, Nov. 1, 1850, AN, BB³⁰ 394; S-P Largentière, Oct. 26, 1850, ADA, 5M 13.

[61] S-P Largentière, citing Mayor Vallon, Nov. 4, 1850, ADA, 5M 13.

[62] S-P Largentière, Nov. 14, Dec. 6, 1850, ADA, 5M 13.

[63] Mayor Salavas, Dec. 17, ADA, 5M 13.

[64] P-G Nîmes, Apr. 18, 1851, AN, BB³⁰ 392A; Tems. J. Eldon, at Lagorce, and A. Michel, at Vallon, ADA, 5M 18.

Another round of political conflict in the southern Ardèche centered on the *fêtes votives*, village festivals that customarily attracted large crowds during the summer months. Trouble began on August 3, 1851, when four gendarmes from Vallon tried to break up a café brawl at the festival of La-Bastide-de-Virac. Two hundred "Protestant democrats" put them to flight, and the eight leading suspects in this affair disappeared. "Here we are again in this miserable canton of Vallon," wrote the subprefect despairingly, "with a numerous band of suspects who are going to roam about and ransom our countryside just as the criminals of Salavas did all winter long. A profound political demoralization was caused in certain communes by the presence of those bandits."[65] He had scarcely finished reporting this incident when a more serious clash occurred on August 10 at the festival of Laurac, near Largentière. This time two brigades of gendarmes provoked a riot by trying to break up a "banquet" of fifty or sixty Reds who were singing "demagogic songs" in defiance of a recent prefectoral edict. Shouting "Death to the gendarmes!" a crowd of several hundred young men threw bottles and rocks at the forces of order, wounding all eight of them slightly. The gendarmes fought back with firearms and sabers, possibly inflicting a few casualties. They soon took refuge in the *mairie*, where the subprefect and fifty national guardsmen from town eventually rescued them.[66] A final outbreak of violence took place on August 31 at Vinezac, another village near Largentière. By this time the prefect had banned all further *fêtes votives*, and troops had arrived at Largentière to enforce his edict. One hundred and fifty inhabitants of Vinezac, who were prevented by a detachment of fifty soldiers from holding their festival, threw some stones at a patrol of gendarmes who were enforcing new closing hours in the cafés. They were forcibly dispersed by the troops, who allegedly opened fire and made six arrests.[67]

Although these three disorders were spontaneous protests against government repression, the subprefect interpreted them as evidence of a widespread conspiracy. On August 11 he speculated that by insulting the gendarmes at the village festivals the Reds hoped to reduce the force and prestige of "authority" before the elections of 1852. On the thirteenth he reported a confession by a Montagnard recruit that the leaders of the Reds were plotting to invade Largentière, murder the authorities (including the subprefect), and pillage the town. He voiced concern on the nineteenth that "it will be difficult to prove that a plot

[65] S-P Largentière, Aug. 5, 6, 1851, ADA, 5M 13.
[66] S-P Largentière, Aug. 11, 1851, ADA, 5M 13; P-G Nîmes, Aug. 14, 1851, AN, BB³⁰ 382.
[67] S-P Largentière, Sept. 1, 1851, ADA, 5M 13; P-G Nîmes, letter cited in n. 66.

preceded the riot at Laurac, compromising all the demagogic leaders," but on the twenty-third he exulted that "some compromising papers" had been seized by the police in several rural communes. "It's about time to get some proof of the existence of secret societies," he commented. Meanwhile, the subprefect had been calling for troops to help make political arrests. Once three hundred soldiers did arrive at Largentière, he wanted them to have full powers of coercion. "The state of siege expresses the prayers of all our populations," he wrote on August 28. For the subprefect, only the army could restore "moral" as well as "physical" order.[68]

The *procureur-général* at Nîmes was not at all convinced that arbitrary displays of military power would further the cause of authority. "I consider it very dangerous to use public force on the slightest pretext," he wrote to the minister of justice after the crowd demonstration at Vinezac. If small numbers of gendarmes or soldiers continued to fight with entire populations over seditious demonstrations or local police regulations, people would acquire the habit of engaging them in combat. "Once accustomed to fighting, and having on their side the immense superiority of numbers, they will end up getting the upper hand." The *fêtes votives* were a traditional institution, and "unless the country were placed under the regime of the state of siege, to prohibit them is to incite disobedience or to bloody the soil of all the communes in an *arrondissement*."[69] The minister of justice replied sternly on September 10: "Under normal times and conditions, the reflections which you suggest concerning the frequent use of public force to prevent seditious demonstrations could be correct. But the state of the *arrondissement* of Largentière is entirely exceptional—secret societies and sedition are organized there on a permanent basis. It is absolutely essential that force remain on the side of the law and authority."[70] If the state of siege was necessary to enforce this policy, so be it. Two days later, Louis Napoleon signed the decree that placed the department of the Ardèche under military rule.

The subprefect quickly learned that his troubles were far from over. He wrote the prefect on September 16 that the commanding general of the state of siege at Largentière had asked him scornfully, "Do you think we can keep sending detachments to the *fêtes votives*? It isn't possible." The general had a simple solution to the political crisis—"arrest all the Reds." Of course, it was up to the subprefect to find them. "You have troops, use them! Get Mazon (a Montagnard *chef*

68 S-P Largentière, Aug. 11, 13, 19, 23, 28, 1851, ADA, 5M 13.
69 P-G Nîmes, Sept. 4, 1851, AN, BB³⁰ 394.
70 M. Justice to P-G Nîmes, Sept. 10, 1851, AN, BB³⁰ 394.

who had fled arrest back on August 12), etc. Otherwise, you'll have a bad record."[71] The general also insisted on keeping all 300 of his troops at Largentière instead of stationing some in the cantons of Vallon and Vans. For the subprefect, there was nothing to do but renew his plea for secret agents and hope the general would change his mind. Gendarmes and police did succeed in arresting a few suspects in October, but by the end of the month only 120 troops were left at Largentière, and the subprefect had to abandon his plans for additional garrisons in the region. The political situation remained unchanged in November: no more seditious demonstrations, but no more revelations of Montagnard activity either. The government now controlled the town of Largentière with the army, but its authority in the countryside remained negligible.[72] On December 6 nearly 1,000 insurgents poured over the Pont-d'Arc from the canton of Vallon, heading for Largentière; they were joined enroute by hundreds of rebels from Lablachère, Les Assions, and other rural communes that had been targeted by the police for house searches and political arrests in earlier months.[73] Officials at Largentière could console themselves that they had one advantage not shared by most police bureaucrats in the nation: they had the state of siege.

The one department where military commanders did preserve order in the countryside was the Cher. Their mission began less than two months before the coup d'état, and they had a clear objective, adequate numbers of troops, and a ruthless disposition. Civilian authorities in the Cher first learned in September 1851 that secret oaths were being administered to workers and peasants in the eastern zone of the department, bordering the Nièvre. The *procureur-général* at Bourges wrote on September 23 that his subordinate at St. Amand had begun to arrest "a rather large number of the members" in the cantons of Nérondes and La Guerche. In fact, only a dozen suspects had been apprehended on the basis of vague oral revelations. The *procureur-général* gave free rein to his political imagination and wrote on October 4 that the aim of the secret societies was "destruction and pillage." One week later his prophecy seemed fulfilled. Several villages in the canton of Sancergues rose up in arms on the night of October 12-13 and marched toward the town of Sancerre. For the *procureur-général* this was a premeditated conspiracy, which revealed "the frightening instincts of an insurrection of riff-raff (*gueux*) and rabble (*jacques*)." The time had come for massive repression—"unhindered by an unreliable jury"—and

[71] S-P Largentière, Sept. 16, 1851, ADA, 5M 13.
[72] Correspondence of S-P Largentière, Oct.–Nov. 1851, ADA, 5M 13.
[73] Tems. and Ints. in ADA, 5M 16, 18.

the *procureur-général* called on October 20 for a declaration of the state of siege. On the following day Louis Napoleon issued a decree to that effect, placing both the Cher and the Nièvre under military rule.[74]

The "insurrection of the valley of the Loire" was actually a popular protest against political repression, improvised in the heat of the moment. Its origins were a police raid on the village of Précy, "the center of radicalism" in the canton of Sancergues. Arriving at daybreak on October 12 with mounted gendarmes, the *procureur* of Sancerre arrested three "demagogues," including the former mayor of the village, and spirited them away to the town jail. After long discussion, the inhabitants of Précy decided to rescue the prisoners. At the sound of the tocsin, bands gathered that night with makeshift weapons, formed themselves into a military column, and marched northward. En route they were joined by most of the men from the neighboring village of Jussy, forming a total contingent of around 300-400 men. Approaching Sancerre, they heard rumors that troops were coming and fled in disarray. A second armed mobilization occurred on the following night, this time in response to further arrests that soldiers were making at Précy. The tocsin rang at St. Léger, Beffès, and Argenvières, three small villages along the canal of the Loire. Around 200-300 men gathered at St. Léger and marched westward toward Précy, recruiting additional manpower by force in isolated farms. They, too, dispersed at the mere rumor of troop reinforcements.[75]

This abortive protest movement triggered a flow of several hundred cavalry, artillery, and infantry into the eastern Cher. Gendarmes had already arrested some of the participants in the first uprising, and 200 soldiers occupied the rebel villages on the fourteenth without a fight. "The repression is total," the magistrate in charge of the military expedition wired on October 15 to the minister of justice. "I have made a *razzia* of weapons and men. The *misérables* are finally trembling. I will have a fist of iron."[76] Major Forgeat, the military commander of the operation, wrote on the same day that his troops were hunting down all the participants in this "incredible movement." He had only praise for a subordinate officer who had murdered one of the prisoners—"a good example."[77] This military occupation of the countryside continued indefinitely: troops still guarded the villages of Précy and St. Léger on December 4. Furthermore, one arrest led to another, and

---

[74] P-G Bourges, Sept. 23, Oct. 14, 20, AN, BB³⁰ 394; AG, G⁸ 186-87, Ins. Nièvre, 1851-52.

[75] P-G Bourges, Nov. 22, 1851, AN, BB³⁰ 394; Major Forgeat, army commander at Précy, Oct. 15, 1851, AG, G⁸ 186-87; Furet, "Le département du Cher," p. 92.

[76] Telegraph from A. Fay to M. Justice, AN, BB³⁰ 394.

[77] Letter cited in n. 75.

magistrates began unravelling the threads of Montagnard organization in the eastern Cher.[78] Between the army's rural garrisons, the mass arrests (74 suspects from the five rebel villages), and the magistrates' investigations, the rural populations were very much on the defensive when news of the coup d'état reached the area. Only at the town of St. Amand did Republicans try to demonstrate—without arms—against the government. Elsewhere, there were no rebels, only victims in the Cher: nearly 1,000 men were eventually swept into prison during the mass purge that military and civilian authorities launched after the coup d'état.[79]

Across the Loire river, General Pellion, commander of the state of siege in the Nièvre, was trying to achieve a comparable success. He obtained troop reinforcements at Nevers, established a garrison at the *arrondissement* capital of Cosnes, and sent mobile columns of troops into the *arrondissement* of Château-Chinon. Everywhere their purpose was to intimidate the Reds and to organize the "men of order" into paramilitary defense units. These measures were probably effective because none of the towns visited by the general's troops had revolts after the coup d'état. As for the *arrondissement* of Clamecy, the general explained that he had left it until last because it was not as "bad" as the others. "I expect no delay in arriving there," he added in a letter dated November 16. Yet ten days later he complained that the "men of order" in the *arrondissement* of Clamecy were refusing to organize themselves. He did issue edicts to close down five Red cafés in the canton of Clamecy, but he had not yet given the town the benefit of his salutary presence when the coup d'état occurred.[80] Meanwhile, the *procureur* at Clamecy was trying single-handedly to punish the Reds. He had eleven suspected Montagnards from nearby cantons imprisoned at Clamecy during the second half of November, and he had the town's leading Republican (and Montagnard), Guerbet, convicted and sentenced to a minor jail term for the second time in a row.[81] This petty repression, unaccompanied by military force, created an explosive atmosphere in the town. As one militant wrote on November 24, referring to Guerbet's prosecution: "These tyrants! These executioners! Their turn will come, and then we'll take vengeance, thank God! Here in town and nearby they are committing injustices every day; they are

---

[78] Letter from commander of the state of siege, Dec. 4, 1851, AG, G⁸ 186-87; P-G Bourges, Dec. 1, 1851, quoted in Tchernoff, *Associations*, p. 294.

[79] Furet, "Le département du Cher"; Ferdinand Pelloille, "Le procès des Mariannes du département du Cher (1851-1852)," *Union des Sociétés Savantes de Bourges, Mémoires*, 8 (1959-60), 122-58.

[80] General Pellion, Oct. 21, 31, Nov. 3, 16, 24, 25, 1851, AG, G⁸ 186-87.

[81] Autenzio, "La résistance dans la Nièvre," p. 127; *Gazette des Tribunaux*, Feb. 2-3, 1852; Ténot, *La province*, p. 28.

stuffing the prisons with our men."[82] Yet according to the *procureur*, repression had scarcely begun. On December 4 he wrote, "This is the town of the Nièvre where the demagogic faction is the strongest, yet not a single arrest has been made, the mobile column hasn't visited the town, the subprefect's request for a garrison of 120 troops has remained unanswered, and there are only 6 gendarmes."[83] It was a situation ripe for disaster, and two days later the *procureur* fled Clamecy in the face of 1,500 rebels.

In most conspiratorial zones, civilian authorities retained full responsibility for political surveillance and repression until the coup d'état. Despite their failure to penetrate and dismantle Montagnard societies, these police bureaucrats had several means at their disposal to limit the influence of Republican militants. They could try to disrupt written propaganda by prosecuting Republican newspapers; they could obtain the revocation of unreliable functionaries, including mayors and deputy mayors; they could "dissolve" voluntary associations, especially Republican mutual-benefit societies, *cercles*, and *chambrées*; and they could impose legal sanctions on public "disorders." In all four respects, coercive policy was national in outline but regional or local in application, depending on the strategies of *procureurs-généraux* in the appellate court jurisdictions (usually covering four departments), prefects in the departments, and subprefects and *procureurs* in the *arrondissements*. Everywhere officials were ordered to halt left-wing propaganda, to purge opponents of the government from administrative ranks, to eliminate "political" societies, and to repress disorders. How they conformed with these directives depended on their varying appraisals of the political danger they confronted. Generally speaking, administrators who suspected the presence of clandestine organizations were especially determined to suppress visible associations, however nonpolitical their basic functions, and to punish Republican disorders, however innocuous their content. As a result, they often accelerated the very trends toward clandestine organization, disciplined protest, and mass opposition that they were trying to reverse.

The *procureurs-généraux* and their subordinates used every legal device to destroy Republican newspapers, but their limited success in this domain had little impact on the underground. According to a special register of newspaper prosecutions from December 12, 1848, through December 1850, there were 335 court cases against 185 Re-

---

[82] A. Lenoir, *limonadier*, to Mayer, Nov. 24, 1851, ADN, U, Ins. Clamecy, dossier Lenoir.

[83] Letter quoted by Autenzio, "La résistance dans la Nièvre," pp. 121-22.

publican newspapers published in seventy-seven cities and towns; yet only 12 of these cases took place in departments that subsequently had major resistance to the coup d'état. The register lists 95 prosecutions of Republican newspapers at Paris, 21 at Lyon, 15 at Toulouse, 13 at Dijon, 11 at Metz, and 9 at Bordeaux, as compared with 3 at Montpellier, 2 each at Auch, Avignon, Mâcon, and Nîmes, 1 each at Agen, Toulon, and Valence, and none at Auxerre, Digne, Nevers, Privas, or Perpignan (all prefectoral capitals in departments with major uprisings).[84] The outcome of the prosecutions is not noted systematically in the register, but Forstenzer has concluded from court cases in several departments that government prosecutors rarely attained their objective of eliminating the Republican press.[85] What seems to have happened is that big-city journalists, already favored by larger circulations, weathered the storm of prosecutions more easily than small-town publishers and editors. By the time Montagnard societies began spreading into the countryside, this weeding-out process was already far advanced. Conspirators did not rely in any case on newspaper propaganda to make recruits, although they stood to benefit from the regional communications networks that journalists were able to establish. Ironically, the two newspapers which definitely performed this function in 1851—*La Voix du Peuple*, at Marseille, and *l'Egalité*, at Auch—both survived until the coup d'état, despite government prosecutions.[86] At best, press controls prevented Montagnards in other areas from creating similar regional networks of communications; at worst, they merely encouraged the trend toward conspiracy.

Administrators had little difficulty purging their ranks of Republicans who owed their appointment to the national government, but they had to find legal pretexts in order to remove from office small-town and rural mayors and deputy mayors, who were supposed to be chosen by democratically elected municipal councils. Some prefects did suspend large numbers of municipal officials on political grounds, and the Conseil d'Etat revoked 848 mayors and deputy mayors and dissolved 276 municipal councils between April 18, 1849, and February 28, 1851.[87] These administrative sanctions were supposed to discipline municipal authorities, but they sometimes had the opposite effect of provoking hostility toward the government. Indeed, if we examine the eighteen departments with the largest numbers of such revocations and dissolutions, we find that eight of them had major uprisings against

---

[84] AN, BB[18] 1470.
[85] Forstenzer, "Bureaucrats under Stress," pp. 375-411.
[86] Ténot, *La province*, p. 133; Degnan, *Le Gers*, 1, 381-403.
[87] Statistical *Résumé* by department of decisions made by the Conseil d'Etat between these two dates, AN, C 977.

the coup d'état.[88] Municipal purges tended to produce a popular back-lash in the Republican districts of politically divided departments such as the Gers, the Vaucluse, and the Var, where Montagnards faced strong opposition from police bureaucrats despite the support of some municipal officials in the bourgs and villages. For example, the central Gers and the eastern Vaucluse, where Republican electorates and Montagnard rebels were concentrated, bore the brunt of the municipal purge in these departments.[89] Within such districts, resistance to the coup d'état was more rather than less likely in communes that had been subjected to prefectoral interference in municipal politics. Thus, in the *arrondissement* of Béziers, armed mobilizations occurred in nearly three-quarters (11/15) of the communes whose mayor or deputy mayor had been revoked or suspended for political reasons, as compared with only half (43/84) of the other communes.[90] The political history of specific communes, such as Le Donjon in the Allier and Cuers in the Var, confirms that administrative sanctions against Republican municipal officials worked more often to undermine than to consolidate habits of popular submission to authority.[91]

There were two reasons for this. For one thing, if a Republican mayor or deputy was replaced by an anti-Republican, factional divisions within the commune were more often than not intensified. The subprefect at Apt was convinced that "revolutionary" administrators increased the influence of "demagogy," but he also argued that talk of insurrection became more frequent as a result of municipal purges: "Each time that a mayor or any other functionary was removed from office, people said, 'They won't always be the masters, we won't have to wait long.' "[92] Tensions became especially acute in small towns and bourgs where this kind of "counterrevolutionary coup" took place, as Agulhon has shown in the case of La Garde Freinet. In May–June 1851, the prefect of the Var obtained the revocation of the acting mayor and the dissolution of the municipal council at this large cork-producing bourg. He promptly installed in office a reactionary clique of cork manufacturers and their allies, who hired a police commissioner and

[88] At least 30 revocations and dissolutions: eight departments, including the Gers, the Hérault, the Pyrénées-Orientales, and the Saône-et-Loire; 20-29 revocations and dissolutions: ten departments, including the Nièvre, the Var, the Vaucluse, and the Yonne.

[89] Table of mayors and *adjoints* suspended or revoked in the Vaucluse, 1849-69, and S-P Apt, July 7, 1850, in ADV, 3M 28, 4M 49; Dagnan, *Le Gers*, I, 307-67.

[90] Calculations based on correspondence in ADH, 17M 30-34, 40.

[91] Georges Rougeron, "De la Révolution de février au 2 décembre," in *La Révolution de 1848 à Moulins et dans le département de l'Allier*, Rougeron et al. (Moulins, 1950), pp. 36-37; Agulhon, *La République au village*, pp. 423-24.

[92] S-P Apt, May 7, 1850, ADV, 4M 50; Tem. Grave, ex-S-P Apt, Aug. 21, 1851, AN, BB[18] 1485.

proceeded to harass the Republican cork-workers. Their repression culminated on October 21-22, 1851, with the dissolution of a Republican cooperative for the production of bottle-cork, followed by the arrest of eight Republican leaders on trumped-up charges of rebellion. By the eve of the coup d'état, the new authorities were universally hated at La Garde Freinet, and they were seized, imprisoned, and forced to march by the insurgents, who brought the old municipality back into power again.[93]

In some cases, however, municipal purges simply brought other Republicans into office, while stimulating more opposition among those who had been arbitrarily revoked. This happened at Manosque, for example, where the government revoked a *liquoriste* named Buisson in 1849 and subsequently prosecuted him unsuccessfully at the assize court of Digne. Buisson's replacement, a landlord named Barthélemy, was also a Republican. In 1850 Barthélemy reportedly gave a speech to a crowd of 500, urging them to reelect Buisson to his seat on the *Conseil Général*: "The reelection by a large majority of this good citizen will prove to his judges that a man who enjoys such public esteem cannot be guilty. In the early days of Christianity, the martyrs were sanctified; today they are made representatives."[94] Barthélemy remained in office until the coup d'état, presumably because he was more reliable than the next in line for office, a shoemaker whose workshop was a Republican center. Both men were arrested for complicity in the insurrection, as were thirty-four other mayors and deputy mayors in the Basses-Alpes.[95]

Administrative and legal sanctions against voluntary associations were especially frequent in Mediterranean France, where politically active *cercles*, *chambrées*, and mutual-benefit societies were so common. The prefects in this region issued decrees to close down over two hundred "private" associations, nearly all of them Republican.[96] Whatever their ostensible purpose, these social clubs and philanthropic societies functioned as centers of political propaganda for "democrats," "socialists," "anarchists," and "demagogues," as administrators were accustomed to describing Republicans. Their dissolution would hopefully restrict if not altogether eliminate the influence of such opponents of the government. Thus, the subprefect of Apt predicted that once the inhabitants of the town of Pertuis were prevented from meeting together in the *chambrées*—"those centers of fanaticism"—they would

---

[93] Agulhon, *La République au village*, pp. 346-60.
[94] P-G Aix, Apr. 13, 1850, AN, BB[30] 370.
[95] Register of MC Basses-Alpes, AN, BB[30] 398.
[96] Estimates based primarily on the correspondence of P-Gs Aix, Montpellier, and Nîmes, much of which Tchernoff reprints, *Associations*, pp. 59-123, 279-387.

gradually calm down. "Thus, we can hope to have seen the last of that column of 1,200 electors, all voting like a single man," he wrote in November 1849. Similarly, the *procureur-général* at Nîmes informed the minister of justice in May 1850 that it was necessary to close down all the political societies. Otherwise, "citizens would become accustomed to acting with such unison that they would eventually triumph over all the efforts of authority."[97] Officials also argued that Republican associations were dangerous because they encouraged "disorder." Thus, when the police commissioner at Bédarieux reported that "most members" of a longstanding mutual-benefit society of spinners "belong to the Socialist Party," the subprefect obtained its dissolution on the following grounds: "This society, evidently political, is the cadre in which all the forces of socialism have been organized at Bédarieux. It is important to destroy such a center immediately; it is a permanent threat of disorder in the town."[98] Finally, administrators sometimes claimed that private associations were "secret societies" whose aim was the overthrow of the government. In such cases, edicts of dissolution would presumably help forestall the threat of insurrection.

This campaign against Republican associations increased the probability of conspiracy and insurgency in 1851. The prefects of the Gard, the Hérault, the Pyrénées-Orientales, and the Vaucluse all issued over twenty edicts against Republican *cercles*, yet half of the communes affected by these sanctions protested against the coup d'état (50/96 cases), as compared with only one-fifth of the other communes in these departments (178/870 cases). The correlation between administrative sanctions against Republican societies and resistance to the coup d'état is especially strong in the Hérault and the Vaucluse, two departments where nearly all visible associations of Republicans were closed down in some *arrondissements* but not others. Thus, every Republican *cercle* in the *arrondissement* of Orange had been dissolved by early 1851, and so had the Republican *chambrées* in all but three communes of the *arrondissement* of Apt; by contrast, such associations continued to exist with administrative forebearance in at least fourteen communes of the *arrondissements* of Avignon and Carpentras. Montagnard societies in the former two regions protested against the coup d'état, while the tolerated associations in the latter two regions remained calm. Similarly, all the Republican front organizations that came to the attention of the authorities at Béziers were closed down, while those in at least thirteen communes of the *arrondissement* of Montpellier remained

[97] S-P Apt, Nov. 22, 1849, ADV, 4M 49; P-G Nîmes, May 12, 1850, AN, BB[30] 382.
[98] S-P Béziers, July 2, 4, 1851, ADH, 39M 134.

tolerated until the coup d'état. While the secret society of the Montagnards spread throughout the former *arrondissement* and took arms in December 1851, none of the Republican societies in the latter *arrondissement* tried to resist the coup.[99]

Administrators sometimes did succeed in controlling organized Republican opposition in the towns, but their sanctions against associations rarely worked in the bourgs and villages. The larger towns in Mediterranean France not only had better police surveillance and much larger military forces than the small towns and rural communities, but they often had patron-client associations of Legitimists, too. Through tacit alliances with these Legitimist mutual-benefit societies, some prefects and subprefects managed to counterbalance rather than to destroy Republican associations. This was generally the case, for example, at Avignon, Montpellier, and Nîmes, three prefectoral capitals that were dominated by the Legitimists.[100] In many small towns and rural communities, however, political surveillance was poor, troops absent, and Legitimist associations weak or nonexistent. Fearing Republican organization in such underpoliced communes, administrators tried to "dissolve" whatever associations they did discover. This only drove the militants underground. They gathered discretely in the back rooms of cafés, they formed new societies or *chambrées* under a different guise, and they organized bona fide secret societies. The more prefectoral edicts rained down upon the bourgs and villages, the more Republican opposition was monopolized by the Montagnards. In the Var and the Vaucluse, for example, many of the *chambrées* that the government tried to close down in 1850-51 persisted under Montagnard sponsorship.[101] Attempts to prosecute violations of administrative edicts on association rarely succeeded, and even favorable courtroom verdicts entailed only derisory penalties of a few days in prison or small fines. As the *procureur-général* at Aix learned with chagrin in April 1850, political trials involving the law on associations could backfire against the government. He had six Republican leaders from Vidaubun and a visiting politician from Marseille prosecuted for holding an electoral rally at a private society, but the suspects turned the trial into a political victory. Over 1,000 villagers from the region flocked to Draguignan

---

[99] Analysis based on prefectoral edicts and administrative reports in ADV, 4M 52; and dossiers of banned societies in ADH, 58M 16-24.

[100] The subject of Legitimist associations in these and other Mediterranean towns merits study. On their role in 1848, see the report of the prefect of the Hérault, July 4, 1848, in ADH, 39M 126.

[101] Agulhon, *La République au village*, p. 389, n. 46; Ints. of Montagnards from Artignosc, Besse, Bras, Brignoles, Entrecastaux, St. Maximin, Sillon, Varages, AD Var, 4M 19.

for the proceedings, and all seven men were acquitted.[102] Instead of preventing conspiracy, attempts to close down private associations usually stimulated the ardor of the Republicans and encouraged their participation in the Montagnard movement.

Suppression of "disorder" was the last and most important weapon in the hands of anti-Republican administrators. "Disorder" was an elastic term that police bureaucrats applied to any unusual public incident, be it a riot, a street brawl, a peaceful demonstration, a drunken celebration, etc. From the perspective of the struggle against opponents of the government, these irregular events threatened public order whenever they revealed left-wing political tendencies, regardless of whether violence occurred. Symbolic demonstrations of Republican sentiment—songs, slogans, emblems with the color red—aroused the most administrative concern and generated the most repressive energy from 1849 to 1851. Increasingly, the campaign against disorder focused on politicized elements of popular culture: songs, dances, banquets, parades, masquerades, *charivaris*, and funeral processions, in which groups of Republicans displayed their solidarity and defied the Whites or the authorities. The visibility of these customary forms of collective behavior made them convenient targets for police bureaucrats. Every appearance of the Reds in public became both a symbol of moral disorder and a pretext for political repression. The conspiratorial preparation of the Montagnards might escape the attention of the police, but their "anarchist" demonstrations would surely bring the swift hand of justice down upon their heads.

The mobilization of Republican forces in electoral campaigns and clandestine organizations did encourage the diffusion of political symbols into traditional elements of popular culture. The process of politicization produced three types of disorder, depending on whether collective action involved factional rivalries, protests against agents of the state, or demonstrations of solidarity. This threefold classification is analogous to the Tillys' distinction between "competitive," "reactive," and "proactive" modes of collective action. Using their terminology, café brawls and street fights (*rixes*) between Reds and Whites were competitive disorders; rebellions and insults against police commissioners, gendarmes, or other "authorities" were reactive disorders; and political banquets, songfests, and funeral processions were proactive disorders. Underlying all these forms of collective action was a basic shift from local to national symbols of group identity. Apart from reactive protests against enforcement of the hunting laws, and proactive demands for higher wages, most of the provincial disorders in 1850-51

[102] P-G Aix, Apr. 15, 22, 29, May 8, 1851, AN, BB[18] 1474A.

were "ideological" in orientation. The "reactionary" peasant protests of 1848-49 had been replaced by collective actions with a distinctively modern component of national political ideology.[103]

These ideological disorders were especially characteristic of southeastern France, where exuberant public displays of factional, communal, and generational solidarity characterized the traditional culture. The Mediterranean appellate court districts of Aix and Montpellier accounted for nearly one-third of the several hundred collective incidents listed in national judicial inventories for the years 1849-51. Local sources indicate that in the department of the Hérault alone officials reported around 200 ideological disorders from January 1, 1850, until the eve of the coup d'état.[104] Within the *arrondissement* of Béziers, demonstrations of solidarity were reported most frequently during this period (26 cases), followed by protests against repression (14 cases), and factional conflicts (9 cases). Similarly, in the department of the Vaucluse, funeral processions and other expressions of solidarity accounted for 29 of the ideological incidents reported in 1850-51, as compared with 7 reactive disorders and 8 factional fights.[105] Just as Montagnard societies were oriented toward regional and national centers of power, so their recruits participated more often in demonstrations of associational power than in fights with local rivals.

Yet official reports of ideological disorders cannot be taken at face value. They reflect not only objective trends in political agitation but subjective changes in administrative perceptions of the subversive threat to public order. If urban and rural populations were incorporating political symbols into their traditional culture, officials were becoming increasingly anxious about every sign, however trivial, of "anarchist" opinion. Serious public challenges to government authority, as measured by the extent of violence and the numbers of participants, declined sharply in frequency between 1848-49 and 1850–November 1851. Not a single incident of large-scale collective violence (over 1,000 participants) occurred in conspiratorial districts of the nation during the last eleven months before the coup d'état; and only a hand-

[103] Charles, Louise, and Richard Tilly, *The Rebellious Century, 1830-1930* (Cambridge, Mass., 1975), pp. 48-55, 248-54; C. Tilly, "How Protest Modernized in France," p. 215.

[104] I have tabulated 202 ideological disorders in the Hérault during this period (197 of which involved Republicans), using the following sources: reports of the gendarmerie, summarized in a "List of riots, serious disorders, seditious cries and emblems, threats, violence, March 1848—September 30, 1851," ADH, 39M 132; reports of S-Ps and CPs, in ADH, 39M 126-30, 132, 134-35; reports of P-G Montpellier, esp. in AN, BB[30] 362, 380, 391-97.

[105] Analysis based on correspondence of S-Ps, CPs, and gendarmes, in ADV, 4M 50-52 bis; and P-G Nîmes, esp. AN, BB[30] 363, 382, 391-97.

ful of small-scale ideological disorders resulted in any casualties to public agents or civilians.[106] Yet police bureaucrats continued to report
examples of sedition, not because crowds were becoming larger and
more violent, but because these bureaucrats were extending the geographical range and definitional criteria of their observations. For example, the administrative campaign against Republican songs, symbols,
and emblems began in the towns and then reached into the countryside. As police commissioners and gendarmes began applying national
policy toward sedition to rural communities, their reports of ideological disorder increased. The result was an apparent rise in the volume of rural sedition.[107] Similarly, administrators began to focus attention on funeral processions after they had succeeded in eliminating
more obvious public demonstrations, such as banquets. Religious so-
lemnities may well have acquired political overtones early in the Second Republic, but nearly all the reports of this phenomenon date from
1850-51.[108] The very discipline and calm of participants in funeral processions aroused official anxiety. How could the "men of disorder" be
at the same time orderly—unless some diabolical organization were the
secret cause of their public appearances?[109]

Montagnard societies probably were behind some of the covert demonstrations of political solidarity that occurred in 1850-51, but their
very success in maintaining discipline undercut administrative policy.
Montagnard leaders were rarely compromised in disorders, and their
recruits generally risked only minor penalties if they defied the authorities in boisterous songfests, dances, *charivaris*, or *cortèges*. Most
political offenders of the laws and regulations prohibiting disorders
were sent before the justices of the peace or the correctional courts,
where they received small fines or brief prison terms. Some administrators hoped that frequent prosecutions would compensate for the weaknesses of juridical sanctions. Instead, their petty repression multiplied

---

[106] In national and local sources I have found reports of only five violent
clashes between small crowds of Reds and gendarmes or police commissioners in
the Hérault, one in the Gard, and none in the Basses-Alpes, the Gers, the Lot-et-
Garonne, the Nièvre, the Var, the Vaucluse, and the Yonne between Jan. 1 and
Dec. 2, 1851. Note, however, the incidents in the Ardèche and the Cher, described above.

[107] Thus, nonviolent disorders involving Republicans in bourgs and villages of
the Hérault reportedly increased from two in 1848 to seven in 1849, twenty-one
in 1850, and twenty-five in 1851. Sources cited in n. 104.

[108] Only one case reported in the Hérault in 1848-49, and thirty-two in 1850-51;
six cases reported in the Vaucluse, all during 1850-51 (ADV, 4M 47-52 bis).

[109] As the P-G at Montpellier wrote about a funeral procession of over 1,000
Republicans at Bédarieux in Oct. 1851, "This very calm, this convocation [of
various communes] and this gathering on a fixed day reveal an organization as
complete as it is extensive." Letter of Oct. 20, 1851, AN, BB[30] 394.

enemies of the government. Hundreds of men who had been convicted of minor political offenses during the Second Republic took arms after the coup d'état. Especially in the small towns and bourgs that spearheaded the insurrection, opposition to political repression was a leitmotif of insurgency in December 1851.[110]

The failure of police bureaucrats to intimidate subversives by prosecuting demonstrators can be shown clearly from data concerning the Hérault. In this department, where disorders apparently became more frequent with each passing year of the Second Republic, most seditious protests and demonstrations involving Republicans were actually small and nonviolent. Out of 197 such incidents mentioned in reports to Montpellier or Paris, only 30 resulted in damage to persons or property, of which only 6 had over five hundred participants. The most typical form of sedition in 1850-51 was the display of political symbols by a small group of less than 50 men (2 cases in 1848, 17 in 1849, 34 in 1850, and 41 in 1851). Alongside such trivial incidents, the only demonstrations that consistently drew large numbers of participants were funeral processions (32 cases in 1850-51, ranging in size from a few hundred to over one thousand persons).[111] Neither symbolic disorders nor funeral *cortèges* gave administrators much opportunity to crack down on the Montagnards. The former generally violated only local police regulations, and the latter remained legal unless officials imposed arbitrary limits on their size. Thus, although dozens of men in the *arrondissement* of Béziers were convicted of participating in minor disorders, almost none of them were still in prison when the coup d'état occurred. At least 73 of these political offenders joined the ranks of insurgency, sometimes in a leadership capacity.[112]

The case of two Republicans at Maraussan illustrates the contrast between administrative hopes and political realities. Arrested in June 1850 for singing Republican songs that "insulted" the Legitimist mayor, Pierre Balaman, surveyor, and Victor Robert, cooper, were sentenced to forty days in prison. The subprefect wrote enthusiastically, "This has improved the morale of the municipal administration and has inspired fear among the perturbators, who until now have enjoyed a kind of immunity in the commune. It is an excellent example for the entire *arrondissement*."[113] In fact, the incident almost brought about the resignation of the largely Legitimist municipal council and

---

[110] Around one in twenty of the 24,000 provincial residents sent before the MCs in 1852 were *repris de justice* for political offenses (72/1097, or 6.6% of a sample of every twentieth name in the general register). AN, F⁷ 2588-95.

[111] Sources cited in n. 104.

[112] Tabulation based on register of MC Hérault, AN, BB³⁰ 401.

[113] S-P Béziers, June 28, 1850, ADH, 39M 134.

stimulated the Republican faction in the village. When the "culprits" returned from prison, they led the local branch of the Montagnards and helped organize the village contingent of rebels in December 1851.[114] The positive correlation between disorder, petty repression, and insurgency can be seen from the fact that nearly half (25/54) of the communes in the Hérault where disorders occurred in 1850-51 took arms against the coup d'état, as compared with around one-tenth (35/277) of the quiescent communes.

This does not mean that the repression of disorder never aided the government cause in the Hérault. Officials in large towns such as Cette, Lodève, and Montpellier used military force to curtail violent protests in 1849 and to eliminate them in 1850. Aided by troop garrisons, they maintained order after the coup d'état.[115] The prefect launched a similar "clean up" of the political atmosphere at the smaller towns of Marsillargues and Mèze, where Republican crowds rioted in several instances against police commissioners and gendarmes.[116] Here, too, memories of rapid troop deployments may have helped deter rebels in December 1851.[117] Outside the towns, however, riots were too infrequent and troop deployments too rare for government retaliation to have much effect on Montagnard organizations. Only one violent protest in the entire *arrondissement* of Béziers gave magistrates an opportunity to arrest Montagnard leaders: a riot of 500-600 men and women at the bourg of Gabian on September 12, 1851. Most of the 16 men prosecuted for helping this crowd rescue a debtor from the gendarmes were notorious Reds, and they were still in prison when the coup d'état took place.[118] Yet even this successful repression had its negative aspect: Montagnards in the area around Gabian rebelled on December 3-4 and marched to Béziers, where they hoped to liberate the prisoners.[119]

The frustrations of administrators in rural communities of the Hé-

[114] Municipal correspondence in ADH, 17M 31; dossiers of Pr. Balaman, surveyor, and Victor Robert, cooper, in ADH, 39M 145, 157.

[115] Montpellier had 9 violent disorders in 1848-50, Lodève had 3, and Cette had 3, but none of these towns had any armed protest against the coup d'état.

[116] Disorders at Marseillargues in Nov.-Dec. 1849 culminated in the dispatch of 400 troops and the arrest of 18 Reds (all subsequently acquitted); those at Mèze in March 1851 also resulted in a temporary military occupation and 25 arrests (of whom 4 were sentenced to several months in prison). Reports of CPs and gendarmes, in ADH, 39M 132; and P-G Montpellier, Mar. 5, 1851, in AN, BB[30] 392A.

[117] Only a few men marched toward the Gard from Marseillargues, and around 150 demonstrators at Mèze stopped short of an armed mobilization, probably due to the temporary passage of artillery troops. See reports in ADH, 39M 142.

[118] Gendarmerie Béziers, Sept. 15, and S-P Béziers, Sept. 13, 15, 1851, ADH, 39M 134.

[119] Ints. Noel Benezech, cult. and Ant. Laurès, tailor, both at Pouzolles, ADH, 39M 145, 153.

rault can be illustrated by a curious event that occurred at the bourg of Capestang in February 1851. A private dancing society of married field laborers and artisans gathered on Ash Wednesday of that month to perform a traditional ceremony of *Carnaval* known as the "Drowning of the *Mannequin*." Armed with rifles, they marched in a double-file column through the bourg, carrying a tricolor flag and pulling a hearse. On top of the hearse was a whitewashed *mannequin* bearing the inscription, "They thought they were stronger. Long live the Republic!" The *cortège* of 60-80 men halted briefly at a Red café while a swordsman with a multicolored hat stepped forward. Solemnly he plunged the sword through the heart of the *mannequin*, which was then taken to the river and "drowned." During their march through the bourg, the demonstrators halted in front of a White café at the command of a former soldier named Gabriel Petit. They fired a few shots nearby, and later they opened fire again, this time in the vicinity of some wealthy ladies who were watching the spectacle from a garden terrace. One lady was reportedly injured slightly by buckshot, but the prominent citizens of the bourg were more fearful of the demonstrators' politics than of their gunfire. Several large landowners informed the subprefect at Béziers that "inconceivable anarchy" existed in the commune, and they obtained prompt repression. Twelve men were arrested and tried at Béziers, where 4 of them received jail sentences of from two to six months. To ensure order in the future, a brigade of gendarmes was stationed in the bourg. Yet this government support for the Legitimists provoked a backlash among the Montagnards, whose leaders had avoided being compromised in the demonstration. When news of the coup d'état reached Capestang, 400 men marched under Gabriel Petit's command to the *mairie*, where they opened fire on the gendarmes, wounding 2 of them. The result of political repression had been to redirect popular hostility from local rivals to agents of the state, compounding the risk of insurgency.[120]

Police regulations against disorders became a focal point of conflict in other conspiratorial districts of the nation, too. The *procureur* at Digne (Basses-Alpes) defended his policy after the insurrection by noting that only trivial sanctions had been imposed on seditious demonstrators: "I know, *Monsieur le Ministre*, that the insurrection of the Basses-Alpes has been blamed on the severe measures which I applied. This great severity consisted of edicts against political songs and red ties, and the repression amounted to fines of one franc."[121] It was pre-

---

[120] *Procès-verbal*, J. P. Capestang, Mar. 7, 1851, in ADH, 17M 33; P-G Montpellier, May 25, 1851, AN, BB³⁰ 392A; S-P Béziers, Mar. 9, 1851, ADH, 17M 33.
[121] *Proc.* Digne, Jan. 20, 1852, AN, BB³⁰ 397.

cisely the discrepancy between coercive ambitions and legal powers that stimulated mass opposition in departments such as the Basses-Alpes. At Forcalquier, for example, crowds demonstrated against the subprefect in July 1850 for prohibiting the singing of the Marseillaise and in February 1851 for prohibiting a dance to which "all the comrades (*frères*) of the demagogues in the *arrondissement* had been invited." The former protest, which involved the rescue of a prisoner from the gendarmes, led to a petition by a hundred citizens, including seven municipal councilors, which denounced the subprefect. He retaliated by prosecuting two leaders of the petition, but this only enabled "all the partisans of the suspects from neighboring communes" to attend the trial. Prosecutions also followed the demonstration of February 1851, but three of the five suspects turned up in December as leaders of the insurrection. Animosity toward the subprefect of Forcalquier had become so intense that he narrowly escaped being murdered by the rebels.[122]

Other small towns where petty repression undermined government authority include Apt in the Vaucluse, Mirande in the Gers, and St. Sauveur in the Yonne. At the subprefecture of Apt, the police commissioner was assaulted on October 26, 1851, when he tried to issue tickets against young men for wearing red ties in honor of a Red musical society. "The police are worthless! One hundred thousand men can't prevent us from wearing red ties!" shouted the son of a municipal councilor named Meritan. The subprefect then prohibited public gatherings of the musicians, but this only lost him further support within the municipal council. On December 7 his authority collapsed altogether and Meritan's son led a crowd that proclaimed a revolutionary commission, aided by several councilors. As for the police commissioner, he fled for his life.[123] At Mirande, the police commissioner was beaten up by a crowd on July 24, 1850 for trying to arrest a boy, and seven prominent Republicans were prosecuted on felony charges at Auch. They included a rich lawyer named Boussès and a veterinarian named Cantaloup. Even conservatives at Mirande blamed the commissioner and the subprefect for this political trial. After three months in prison, the suspects were all acquitted by the jury and they returned to Mirande, where crowds greeted them triumphantly. The political impact of this affair became clear in December 1851, when Cantaloup

122 P-G Aix, July 19, Aug. 14, 16, 1850, Mar. 4, 11, 1851, AN, BB³⁰ 358, 370; register of MC Basses-Alpes, entries Jn. Pr. Escoffier, watchmaker, Pr. Godefroi, cartwright, and Manuel, AN, BB³⁰ 398; Ténot, *La province*, pp. 163-67.
123 CP Apt, Oct. 27, 1851, and S-P Apt, Oct. 27, 1851, in ADV, 4M 52 bis; Int. E. Goddfrey, councilor, and Tems. H. Canavet, *manoeuvre*, J. Combe, CP Apt, and S-P Apt, in ADV, 4M 63, 76 (canton of Apt).

and Boussès organized an insurrection at Mirande. Like his counterpart at Forcalquier, the subprefect of Mirande was nearly killed in the uprising.[124] As for St. Sauveur, nine of its Montagnard activists were prosecuted in 1851 for "seditious songs," "insulting noise," "attacks on the respect due the law," or "planting liberty trees contrary to the orders of authority." They had been arrested after defying the justice of the peace and demonstrating around the liberty trees, which had been planted back in 1848 to symbolize the Republic. Sentenced in October to a few days in prison, they led a crowd at St. Sauveur, which demonstrated against the justice of the peace on December 6, and they organized the insurgent forces that marched toward Auxerre that night.[125]

Throughout the nation the issue of repression was most salient in the towns and bourgs that took rebel initiative after the coup d'état. It was here that the maintenance of public order had become synonymous with a vindictive spirit of political persecution. Rather than dismantling Montagnard societies and intimidating the Reds, officials in conspiratorial centers such as Apt, Forcalquier, and Mirande had undermined their own legitimacy in the eyes of the populace. Only in the prefectoral capitals and a few subprefectoral capitals where they had troop garrisons could they view the prospects of a political crisis without misgivings. Elsewhere, they ran the risk of becoming prime targets of mass uprisings on behalf of the "Democratic and Social Republic."

[124] P-G Agen, Nov. 4, 1851, AN, BB[30] 370; Dagnan, *Le Gers*, I, 266-67, II, 63-70; Ténot, *La province*, pp. 86-91.

[125] Report of gendarmerie St. Sauveur, Oct. 15, 1851, summarized in Forestier, *L'Yonne*, III, tome I, 166; ADY, III M[1] 156-57; Ints. Amédée Patasson, Jn. Landré, JM-1851, #285.

THE DYNAMICS OF ARMED MOBILIZATIONS

In the early morning hours of Tuesday, December 2, troops loyal to President Louis Napoleon occupied the premises of the National Assembly; police squads arrested over one hundred politicians in their homes; and agents of the Prefecture of Police posted a series of decrees and proclamations on the walls of Paris. The people of the city awoke to discover that the National Assembly had been dissolved, universal suffrage reestablished, the French people convoked to electoral bureaus in mid-December, and the state of siege decreed throughout the first military division. Thirty thousand troops were placed on alert to enforce this presidential coup d'état against the National Assembly. Around 1,200 Republicans took arms on the following two days, but their resistance was promptly smashed. Nearly 400 civilians were killed as soldiers used indiscriminate force to clear the streets of barricades and demonstrators. By nightfall on Thursday, December 4, the new regime was completely in control of the national capital.[1]

Yet the army had no sooner crushed opposition in Paris than alarming reports of provincial insurgency began to reach the Ministry of the Interior. The subprefectures of Béziers (Hérault), Poligny (Jura), and La Palisse (Allier) were invaded by rebel forces on Thursday morning; the prefectures of Agen (Lot-et-Garonne) and Auch (Gers) were threatened on the same day by large columns of insurgents from nearby towns and villages; and the prefecture of Draguignan (Var) was isolated by rebellions at Le Luc, La Garde Freinet, and Vidaubun. The government lost control of more subprefectures on Friday—Brignoles, Clamecy, Forcalquier, Marmande—and several more of its administrative centers soon became focal points of rebel columns—the prefectures of Auxerre, Digne, Mâcon, Nîmes, and Privas, and the subprefectures of Largentière and Montélimar. On Sunday large rebel forces occupied Digne, threatened Draguignan, assaulted Crest, and marched toward Avignon. For a brief moment, centralized authority seemed to be collapsing over widespread districts of the nation. Of course, the army quickly came to the rescue of the government. Mobile columns of troops occupied most insurgent towns without resistance,

---

[1] The first reliable account of the coup d'état in Paris was published by Eugène Ténot, *Paris en décembre 1851: Etude historique sur le coup d'état* (Paris, 1868). For a good modern history, see Henri Guillemin, *Le coup du 2 décembre* (Paris, 1951); for a concise analysis, see Maurice Agulhon, *1848*, pp. 162-73.

and they defeated the last rebel forces at Aups (Var) on Wednesday, the tenth. For the architects of the coup d'état, these military successes could not conceal the unexpected scale of provincial insurgency. They had anticipated trouble in Paris and other cities, where their military forces were concentrated. The uprisings of small towns and rural communities took them completely by surprise.[2]

If the new minister of the interior, the duc de Morny, did not anticipate serious resistance in the provinces, neither did most of the police bureaucrats who upheld presidential authority in rebel zones. Their successful measures against violent protest during the previous year had lulled them into a false sense of physical security. True, they still feared that subversion might result in electoral victories for the "demagogues" or "anarchists" in May 1852. As the *procureur-général* at Montpellier had written back in April 1851, the primary threat of the Republican underground was electoral: "This danger (of the secret societies) will be revealed entirely at the general elections next year. On that day we will see each decurion leading his disciplined squadron to the polls like a troop of old soldiers; and not one will be missing; not one will disobey the order given and received; and the counting of the ballots will reveal to the eyes of an astonished France, elected by compact majorities without the slightest dissidence, the most sadly celebrated names—all the heroes of demagoguery."[3] The very importance of these elections reduced the likelihood, however, of a premature insurrection. Montagnard leaders were determined to avoid pretexts for repression as the year 1852 approached. If they could triumph at the polls, why run the risk of fighting in the streets?

The coup d'état transformed these beliefs and expectations overnight. It precipitated a crisis of legitimacy whose outcome seemed uncertain even to "men of order." As the first telegraphic dispatches announcing the coup reached provincial towns on December 3, the ground rules of political action were abruptly changed. Louis Napoleon had violated the laws of the Republic. Would he be stripped of his powers, as Article 68 of the Constitution required? Was a new revolution about to begin? Or would he succeed in his audacious enterprise? Was the Republic about to be overthrown? Communications lagged by a day or more between Paris and southern France, so police bureaucrats and Republican leaders had to evaluate the situation on

---

[2] An essential aspect of the coup was the seizure of the Ministry of the Interior by le Duc de Morny. No advance instructions had been issued to the prefects, and some of them were fired or transferred on the eve of Morny's takeover. For a chronology and general account of provincial resistance to the coup, see Agulhon, *1848*, pp. 178-90.

[3] P-G Montpellier, April 9, 1851, AN, BB[30] 380.

the basis of incomplete and misleading information. Under these circumstances, preexisting political tensions assumed paramount importance. Where local populations were well organized into Montagnard societies and where their bureaucratic rivals were isolated and outnumbered, the climate of opinion favored insurgency. The Montagnard leaders who improvised regional mobilizations in such areas enjoyed massive popular support. Rumors of hasty and ill-judged measures of repression stimulated their ardor. The "authorities" could be swept aside with impunity. The rights of the people were about to triumph everywhere in France.

Government officials were naturally reluctant to emphasize the political context of armed mobilizations against the coup d'état. If they focused attention on the secret societies that coordinated the uprisings, it was not in order to explain the Republican convictions of peasant rebels but to denounce the "plots" of their leaders. Officials generally denied that most participants had any political loyalties whatsoever. Either they marched under duress, fearing to violate their initiation oaths, or they took arms to attack the rich. This latter motive responded to the folk memories of anti-Republican notables. At the sight of villagers carrying pitchforks and hunting rifles, they imagined that crops were about to be pillaged, men of property murdered, and towns invaded by mobs of hungry peasants. This social myth of a *jacquerie* conveniently deflected public attention from the issue of political legitimacy to that of social defense. Officials were encouraged to forward exaggerated and tendentious reports of popular violence to Paris. In the words of one subprefect, the insurgents in his area planned to "ransom" and "pillage" the towns. Their movement had "nothing" to do with politics; it was "social war in all its horror."[4]

This Bonapartist propaganda mingled two opposing images of peasant rebels: the passive recruit, fearful of Montagnard vengeance, and the rampaging barbarian, hateful of civilized society. The journalist Ténot tried to erase these negative images by describing Republican efforts to defend the Constitution, but recent historians have doubted whether most rebels had any interest in the issue of constitutional defense.[5] According to Vigier, "A majority of the peasants, even the artisans, who marched on Digne or Crest ignored this Constitution entire-

---

[4] S-P Die, Dec. 30, 1850, ADD, M 1297. As late as 1868, officials were still echoing this propaganda line. See the letters from the prefects of the Allier, the Basses-Alpes, the Hérault, the Loiret, and the Yonne, replying to a ministerial circulaire of Nov. 13, 1868, which asked them to evaluate the accuracy of Ténot's book, AN, F^{18} 308.

[5] Ténot notes in the preface to *Paris en décembre 1851* that he wrote *La province en décembre 1851* in order to destroy the legend of a "demagogic *jacquerie*."

ly, indeed, they knew nothing about politics in general." True, many insurgents were Montagnard initiates, but they took arms naively, some fearing to disobey their leaders, others hoping to obtain immediate relief from debts and taxes.[6] Agulhon interprets the social aspirations of peasants as an aspect of their political consciousness, but he discounts the role of Montagnard societies in the revolt. Villagers in Provence shared a popular psychology of "communal unanimity," and they mobilized in accordance with communal traditions of political and military action. In contrast to the localism of most recruits, only a thin stratum of leaders, drawn mainly from the artisanate, grasped the national significance of the political struggle unleashed by the coup d'état.[7]

Behind these differing interpretations is the assumption that a single type of collective action generated violence in 1851. *Either* peasants took arms as members of preexisting political organizations *or* they marched into battle as members of traditional rural communities. Following Tilly's theoretical map of collective violence in modern France, the insurrections were based on either specialized associations or communal groupings; and they were either "proactive" in their claims to new political power or "reactive" in their defense of communal autonomy against the state.[8] If Montagnard leaders planned and implemented these armed mobilizations, if they mustered large numbers of men over wide areas in a short span of time, and if they attempted to seize political power, then their collective actions would correspond to Tilly's definition of proactive conflict. If crowds formed excitedly at news of the coup d'état, if they derived strength from solidary relationships within the bourgs and villages, and if they attacked agents of the state who had oppressed them in earlier months, then the concept of reactive conflict would better characterize their actions. In the former instance, the insurrection of 1851 would take its place alongside political demonstrations, urban rebellions, and strikes as an essentially modern form of collective action. In the latter case, it would look backward to the reactionary protest movements that swept rural France during the first half of the nineteenth century.

In fact, the townsmen and villagers who rebelled in 1851 shared both proactive and reactive orientations to the nation-state, and they mobilized manpower on both an associational and a communal basis. Their collective actions are best interpreted as a transitional phenomenon in in the history of collective violence in modern France. The electoral

---

[6] Vigier, *La Seconde République*, II, 330, 319-36.
[7] Agulhon, *La République au village*, pp. 450-55, 463-67.
[8] Charles Tilly, et al., *The Rebellious Century*, pp. 48-55, 62-67.

and conspiratorial mobilizations of previous months had equipped them with new organizational resources and ideological impulses for confronting the nation-state; but they resided in small communities whose preexisting traditions of collective action shaped popular responses to the Montagnard call to arms. In most instances, conspiratorial organizations played a vital role in the preliminary phase of armed mobilizations: Montagnard leaders circulated messages from town to countryside, they mustered bands of devoted followers, and they provided ideological justifications for action. Once these bands appeared in public, however, a new phase of collective action began. Sometimes such public mobilizations were precipitated by threats of repression, sometimes by news of insurgency in a nearby town. In either case, crowds now imparted a distinctive momentum to the Montagnard cause, derived in part from traditional beliefs and expectations regarding territorial solidarity. After a large turnout of manpower had been generated, specifically military measures were undertaken in accordance with communal traditions. This third and final phase of local action involved the creation of military columns under the leadership of national-guard officers or former military men. Although high-ranking Montagnard leaders generally directed these military columns, decurions or section leaders of the underground often blended into the ranks. Communal military traditions and French army experience rather than Montagnard paramilitary hierarchies supported most of the rebel "companies," "battalions," or "phalanges" that confronted troops in 1851.

For purposes of exposition, the shift from Montagnard preparations to public mobilizations will be analyzed in this chapter, and the transformation of crowds into military columns will be discussed primarily in Chapter Twelve. While the political and communal forces behind the insurrection resulted in large-scale mobilizations, the military resources, leadership, and morale of the insurgents proved to be no match for the regular army of the nation-state. The uprisings of December 1851 often achieved temporary goals as political demonstrations, but they quickly failed as military operations.

Montagnard leadership networks provided regional channels for planning and decision making in response to news of the coup d'état. Just as Montagnard branches were more closely linked together within *arrondissements* and cantons than within entire departments, so the impetus for revolt generally came from these lesser levels of the administrative hierarchy. Small-town leaders did establish contact with prefectoral capitals before taking action in several departments, but they themselves were responsible for the "orders" that circulated in rural communities. From their central locations in routine marketing networks, messengers could rapidly circulate news of mobilizations to village militants. Sometimes urban leaders awaited the arrival of rural contingents before challenging the authorities, and sometimes they took arms first and then urged villagers to assist them in defending the town or marching elsewhere. In either case, they relied heavily on pre-existing political contacts within the underground, and their plans then shaped the deployment of rebel forces on a regional scale.

Even where centralized planning did exist at the prefectoral level, poor communications and administrative countermeasures limited the extent of concerted regional action. The largest mobilizations were not those preceded by the most careful planning, but those inspired by the example of a successful urban revolt. This can be seen by examining in some detail the circulation of messages and manpower in several rebel zones of the nation. The Gard, the Gers, and the Drôme have been chosen to illustrate the limitations on centralized departmental planning, and the Basses-Alpes, the Var, and the Nièvre to show the escalatory possibilities of successful uprisings outside the prefectoral capitals.

Nîmes was the only prefecture whose Montagnard leaders tried to organize a simultaneous mobilization throughout the department. They drew up a plan of action on Thursday, the fourth, which called for all the *arrondissements* to attack Nîmes from four different directions on Friday night. Indeed, Montagnards from widely scattered points did take arms that night. Yet most of these mobilizations were confined to small cantonal seats and nearby villages. Only one rebel force converged as planned on the prefecture of the Gard. This partial success was due to the energy of Montagnard leaders at the *arrondissement* center of Alais, who issued specific orders to several cantonal seats and who spearheaded the rebel column. In the words of an "appeal to arms" that they sent to St. Jean-du-Gard: "The rendezvous for the arrondissement is at le plan de la Fougasse (just north of Nîmes). You must be there at 1:00 a.m., take the brothers from Anduze. Don't fire any shots en route, no useless demonstrations. Lézan, Lédignan, Cassagnoles, and the other friends (e.g. friendly communes) will assist you en route. You must leave at 4:30 p.m. You have a long road to travel. But how great is your love for the Republic!"[9] Similar orders reached the Montagnard leaders at Anduze and Lédignan, who relayed them to surrounding villages.[10] The actual course of events depended even more on Alais. The leaders at St. Jean-du-Gard decided not to march,

[9] Copy cited by P-G Nîmes, Jan. 8, 1852, AN, BB³⁰ 397.
[10] Int. V. Gascual, schoolteacher at Anduze; tem. F. Barbe, harness maker at Cassagnoless; tem. Pr. Richard, cult. at Laval, ADG, 3U 5/1.

and those at Anduze were equally reluctant to take arms until they learned that "the men of Alais" were on the move. It was this urban example that triggered a general mobilization in the region, extending northeast to St. Ambroix, southwest to Anduze and Lasalle, and south to Vézénobres, Lédignan, and St. Chaptes. Several thousand men poured down the valley of the Gardon to reach the plan de la Fougasse at 3:00 a.m. According to one witness, they intended to seize the prefecture, the arsenal, and the town hall, and they expected to march onward to Marseille, Lyon, and Paris, aided by the army.[11] But the troops inside Nîmes were loyal to the government, and so were most of the national-guard units in the city. At the last minute, four leaders from Nîmes arrived at the rendezvous to call off the march. Their counterorders were promptly obeyed, and the rebel columns dispersed into the night.[12]

Planning in the Gers was ostensibly centralized at the prefecture of Auch, where several Montagnard editors of *l'Ami du Peuple* met with a series of "delegates" or "emissaries" from other towns on Wednesday evening, the third. Instead of drawing up a single plan of action, however, the leaders at Auch agreed to the conflicting proposals of their more militant counterparts elsewhere in the department. The delegates from the *arrondissement* center of Mirande wanted permission to seize local power, so they returned from Auch on Wednesday night with "orders" to take arms and arrest the authorities. Those from the cantonal seats of Vic-Fezensac and Jegun demanded a general mobilization and a coordinated march on the prefecture. They, too, received "orders" to implement their own plans. The Mirandais, who overthrew the subprefect on the morning of the fourth, spent the day appealing for rural manpower and barricading their town, while the men from Vic and Jegun were marching to Auch. These latter columns, which included many villagers whom urban militants had recruited during the morning, approached the northern suburbs of Auch in the late afternoon, numbering around 2,000 men. It was this initiative from Vic and Jegun that posed a serious threat to the prefecture. Montagnards in Auch itself had completely lost control of the situation during the day. One leader turned back a column from Mauvezin (to the east), another issued counterorders to a column from Masseube (to the south), others

---

[11] Tem. L. Mourq, *fermière* at le mas de la fougasse, ADG, 3U 5/3.

[12] For a general account of these events, see P-G Nîmes, Jan. 27, 1852, in AN, BB[30] 396. For an unusually precise account of mobilizations in one district, see J. P. St. Ambroix, Dec. 16, 1851, in ADG, 3U 5/1. Events throughout the department can be reconstructed in detail from the testimony of witnesses and the dossiers of prisoners, in ADG, 3U 5/1-13 and 4U 5/26, 306. For summary accounts see the register of MC Gard, AN, BB[30] 401.

tried in vain to obtain municipal authorization for the rearmament of the national guard, and a few even tried to persuade the rebels from Vic to withdraw a safe distance from town. Having undertaken their own march at their own initiative, these rebels were in no mood to disperse. It took a cavalry charge from the garrison at Auch to spread panic in their ranks. As a final commentary on the importance of cantonal as compared with departmental planning, townsmen at Mirande dispatched a column of 600 men on the following day to attack Auch. They retreated at news of the town's defenses, but they continued to occupy Mirande until Sunday, the seventh, when they learned that troop reinforcements were being sent to the department.[13]

Events in the Drôme provide another example of the role played by Montagnard leaders in lesser towns and bourgs. The president of the underground at the prefectoral town of Valence met on December 5 with leaders from other towns, and he agreed to order a general uprising. That night emissaries carried coded messages to the presidents of various branches, including Crest and Bourdeaux in the central Drôme. Rebel forces were supposed to converge on Valence, overthrow the prefect, and march northward to Lyon and Paris. In fact, urban leaders in the northern Drôme refused to implement the orders they received on the sixth, and that evening the president at Valence issued counterorders to halt all operations. In the meantime, however, villagers in the central Drôme had begun to execute specific plans that they had received from Montagnard leaders at Crest and Montélimar. Columns of insurgents, each numbering 500-600 men, advanced on Crest from both sides of the Drôme river during the afternoon, where they collided with a small troop garrison and then dispersed. That night over 1,000 rebels from eighteen bourgs and villages near Montélimar took arms, and around 600 of them joined together at Sauzet to march on the town. Near St. Marcel they clashed with a detachment of 100 soldiers from the urban garrison, and both sides fled in confusion. Meanwhile, Montagnard leaders at Dieulefit had responded to orders from Bourdeaux by organizing a march on Crest. First they undertook a coordinated mobilization of villagers and townsmen in their canton, culminating in the occupation of Dieulefit by around 900 insurgents at 1:00 a.m. on the seventh. News of this success was relayed north to Bourdeaux, where "orders" from Dieulefit were eagerly awaited by Montagnards in the bourg, aided by nearby villages. The men from Dieulefit and Bourdeaux marched northward to a general

[13] This interpretation of planning in the Gers uses evidence presented in a somewhat inconsistent manner by Dagnan, *Le Gers*, II, 2-89. See also Ténot, *La province*, pp. 71-96.

rendezvous at the village of Saou, and they approached the town of Crest on the afternoon of the seventh. At each stage of the route, they were joined by reinforcements under local Montagnard leadership. An artillery patrol from Crest retreated hastily in the face of a rebel force, which now numbered nearly 3,000 men from thirty-five communes. The insurgents tried in vain for the rest of the afternoon to cross the river Drôme and defeat the 250 soldiers inside the town. By nightfall the fighting had ceased, and they withdrew in disarray, leaving behind several dead comrades.[14]

In the only department where insurgents did succeed in capturing the prefecture—the Basses-Alpes—Montagnards in the southwestern *arrondissement* of Forcalquier planned and implemented its seizure entirely on their own initiative. Planning began at a farmhouse near Forcalquier, where several Montagnard leaders gathered on the fourth at news of the coup d'état. As Ailhaud de Volx, an ex-functionary from the bourg of Château-Arnoux, later testified: "We drew up a sort of proclamation, which was not printed but handwritten in several copies for distribution to the communes. The latter task was done. In this proclamation we announced what had happened, and we engaged our friends to be ready to take arms."[15] While Ailhaud de Volx carried the alert northward to the *arrondissement* of Sisteron, two leaders from Forcalquier retreated south to the bourg of Mane in order to avoid arrest. There they may have reached the decision to call for help in attacking Forcalquier, where a small troop detachment was in transit. Montagnards at the southernmost town of Manosque had already occupied their *mairie*, where they assembled manpower from nearby villages. The deployment of a large column from Manosque to Forcalquier on the morning of the fifth heralded a full-scale uprising. Joined by a column from Mane, the men of Manosque entered the *arrondissement* center at noontime, just a few hours after the troops had departed, and they rapidly seized the subprefecture. Flushed by this success, Montagnard leaders such as the *liquoriste* Buisson, from Manosque, and the watchmaker Escoffier, from Forcalquier, sent orders to other cantonal seats in the southern half of the department, calling for an immediate march to the prefecture of Digne. Three large columns streamed northward on the sixth from Forcalquier, Valensole, and Riez, each gathering support from all the bourgs and villages en route.

[14] For a detailed description of rebel plans, mobilizations, and confrontations with troops in the Drôme, based on archival sources, see Margadant, "The Insurrection of 1851," pp. 310-16, 317-411 *passim*, 450-75. See also Ténot, *La province*, pp. 189-210.

[15] Int. Ailhaud de Volx, forwarded to M. Justice by the Tribunal at Marseille, Dec. 30, 1851, AN, BB[30] 397-P463.

They occupied Digne without resistance on the following morning, numbering 7,000-8,000 men. Thanks to the success of Montagnards in the southwestern corner of the department, the rebellion now encompassed the better part of three *arrondissements*.[16]

The insurrection of the Var was organized by Montagnards in several small towns, including Le Luc, Brignoles, and Barjols. Two waves of rebel activity spread outward from these urban centers to rural branches of the underground: armed mobilizations to overthrow municipal authorities; and mobile columns to centralize manpower. Militants at Le Luc were the first to take arms: they held a tumultuous meeting on Wednesday night, the third, overruled the objections of cautious leaders, and established a provisional commission on Thursday morning to organize military resistance. Delegates from Le Luc urged nearby communes to follow their example, and La Garde Freinet and Vidaubun rebelled the same day. Brignoles entered the general current of armed resistance on Friday morning, guided by M. Constans and other Montagnard leaders. Constans first sent written orders to Montagnards in three nearby communes, obtaining their aid in occupying the town hall. He then assumed the title of provisional subprefect and issued orders for other communes in the *arrondissement* to imitate the *chef-lieu*. Aided by Montagnard leaders in cantonal seats such as Barjols and St. Maximin, these orders eventually reached at least twenty-six branches of the underground. Alongside the wave of municipal revolutions that thus began, leaders at Le Luc and Brignoles began circulating orders for a march on the prefecture of Draguignan. After nearly 1,500 men from the region of Le Luc and La Garde Freinet reached Vidaubun on the evening of the sixth, the rebel leaders changed the direction of their march. Instead of attacking Draguignan, they headed northwest for the Basses-Alpes, passing through Lorgues on the seventh and camping at Salernes that night. Constans and the Montagnard leaders at Barjols now conveyed new orders for reinforcements to march to Salernes. Around 1,000 men from sixteen communes in the *arrondissement* of Brignoles reached that rendezvous point, where they joined forces with around 3,000 men from the *arrondissement* of Draguignan. Several hundred more peasants joined this "army of the Var" at Aups on Tuesday, the ninth, but the end of the road was near. On Wednesday morning, 1,200 soldiers from the city of Toulon caught

---

[16] Only the general outline of events in the Basses-Alpes can be described, due to the loss of the archives of the MC. See Vigier, *La Seconde République*, II, 310-11, 317-19; Ténot, *La province*, pp. 161-79; register of MC Basses-Alpes, AN, BB[30] 398. For a dramatic novel about these events, see Luc Willette, *Et la Montagne fleurira* . . . (Paris, 1975).

up with the rebels and immediately attacked, overwhelmed, and dispersed them.[17]

The town of Clamecy gave the signal for the most extensive mobilization in central France. Its revolt was not planned in advance, however, by Montagnard leaders in conjunction with other towns. Decurions within the society had agreed to await further news from Paris, and their emissaries to Auxerre had not yet returned on Friday afternoon, the fifth, when rumors spread that the authorities intended to arrest the centurion, Eugène Millelot, and other leaders. Relatives and friends of the intended victims appealed for rural support, but before any villages had responded to their alert, Millelot and a few other decurions decided to rescue the political prisoners in the town jail. They aroused the *flotteurs* in the *faubourg de Bethleem* and led a column of 200 men into town at 8:00 p.m. This small rebel force broke into the jail, rang the tocsin, killed a gendarme, and occupied the town hall. Its success triggered a general mobilization throughout the hinterland of Clamecy. Around 1,000 men from fifteen bourgs and villages took arms at the instigation of urban emissaries or local leaders, and they marched to town during the night. The danger of spontaneity became apparent at 8:00 a.m., when the courier arrived from Auxerre with news that Paris had been pacified. Some leaders lost hope of victory and advised the peasants to return home, but others denied the news and talked of marching to Auxerre. When more peasant bands arrived later in the morning, three Montagnard leaders from town organized a march of several hundred rebels on the *caserne* of the gendarmes. One gendarme was killed and the others fled, but this victory against the local forces of order could not compensate for Clamecy's isolation from other towns. One final call to arms was issued on Sunday at word that troops were advancing from Nevers. Townsmen prepared to defend barricades, and bands from several villages started marching to their aid, but even the advocates of a last-ditch stand soon recognized the hopelessness of their position. After nightfall, they deserted the barricades, and troops occupied Clamecy without resistance on Monday, the eighth.[18]

[17] The circulation of orders from Brignoles and other cantonal seats in that *arr.* can be traced in detail from the prisoners' Ints., AD Var, 4M 19 1-5, 4M 26. For narratives of events in the Var, see Noël Blache, *Histoire de l'insurrection du Var en décembre 1851* (Paris, 1869); Charles Dupont, *Les Républicains et les Monarchistes dans le Var en décembre 1851* (Paris, 1883); Ténot, *La province*, pp. 126-60. Agulhon, *La République au village*, pp. 436-42. For an imaginative reconstruction, see the novel by Emile Zola, *La Fortune des Rougon* (ed. Garnier-Flammarion, Paris, 1969).

[18] Events at Clamecy can be pieced together from the dossiers of prisoners, ADN, U, Ins. Clamecy, and ADC, U83, CG Clamecy. See also S-P Clamecy to

Just as Montagnard leaders in the towns shaped regional patterns of mobilization, so their counterparts in the bourgs and villages imparted local momentum to the revolt. The men who had been most prominent in the underground as presidents, *chefs*, initiators, or centurions usually exerted the most influence over local mobilizations. These branch leaders communicated urban plans to rural militants, sometimes by contacting townsmen who urged them to take arms, sometimes by receiving messengers who brought orders to this effect. Generally speaking, they responded to mobilization orders by assembling Montagnard members in a local café, *chambrée*, or farmstead, or by alerting them to gather in arms at the *mairie* as soon as they heard the ringing of church bells (the tocsin) or the beating of the drum (the *générale*). This preparatory phase of action often lasted until local leaders of the underground were convinced that uprisings had already begun elsewhere in the region. Then they assumed responsibility for the decision to rebel, either by making a public appeal for armed support or by mustering a devoted band of followers and marching elsewhere secretly. Montagnard leaders were likely to use public techniques of mobilization such as the tocsin and the drum when they enjoyed substantial support within the community. They directed such public uprisings by ordering militants to sound the alarm, occupy the *mairie*, recruit laggards, and disarm opponents. Against hostile authorities, they served as spokesmen for the rebels, demanding their rights and sometimes seizing control of the symbols of municipal power—the mayor's sash and the tricolor flag. Once they had mustered all available manpower for the Republican cause, these same leaders helped organize military columns, which they guided toward urban destinations. At all stages of insurgency, high-ranking Montagnards received assistance from section leaders and other militant members of the underground. Having already created bonds of political loyalty through their conspiratorial activities, Montagnards were the foremost architects of resistance to the coup d'état in most bourgs and villages.

The rebel initiative of conspiratorial leaders was especially important in rural communities that were not immediately adjacent to an insurgent town. In such cases, Montagnards could not rely heavily on the "demonstration effect" of a successful urban uprising. Instead of being

M. Carlier, *commissaire extraordinaire*, Dec. 9, 1851, in AG, G9 186-87; *Compte rendu du Conseil de guerre siégant à Clamecy en 1852* (Paris, 1869); Ténot, *La province*, pp. 25-46; and A. Sonnié-Moret, "Récit des évenements de l'insurrection qui a éclaté à Clamecy les 5, 6 et 7 décembre 1851," manuscript dated July 20, 1874, reprinted in *Clamecy et le coup de 1851* (Clamecy, 1951), pp. 15-38. For good recent histories of events at Clamecy after the coup d'état, see Autenzio, "La Résistance dans la Nièvre," pp. 111-63, and Martinet, *Clamecy*, pp. 79-102.

swept into action by force of example, they had to make up their own minds whether to embark on the dangerous course of revolt. Especially good examples of rural leadership occurred in cantons such as Crest-sud and Marsanne (Drôme), Bonnieux and Gordes (Vaucluse), Cape-stang and Roujan (Hérault), Rians (Var), Lédignan (Gard), Courson (Yonne), Varzy (Nièvre), and Montesquiou (Gers). In all these districts only bourgs and villages rebelled: either the cantonal seat itself remained calm or it was only a bourg. The role of Montagnard leaders in such zones of rural insurgency can be illustrated by the cases of Puy-St. Martin and Roynac (Drôme), whose large-scale mobilizations typify the involvement of peasants in the struggle against Louis Napoleon's coup d'état.

Montagnards in the region of Crest improvised their plans without much assistance from the town, where troops arrived on December 4 to maintain order. Thus, Louis Comte, an owner-farmer whose ambitions as a grocer and as the mayor's secretary had been thwarted by business reversals and political repression, was the moving force behind the revolt at Puy-St. Martin, located ten miles south of Crest. This village of 505 inhabitants held several fairs and provided some artisanal and administrative services for the dispersed rural population of the area, which included 415 peasants who resided on farmsteads in the commune of Puy, and 623 peasants who lived in the neighboring commune of Roynac, whose *chef-lieu* was a hamlet (Les Girards) with only 93 inhabitants.[19] Aided by his central position in the hierarchy of agglomerations, Comte influenced not only Montagnard recruits in the farmsteads of his commune, but the leader of the Roynac branch of the underground, a master mason named Jean Antoine Jeune. When orders for a march to Crest first reached Roynac on December 5, Jeune sent a messenger to ask Comte "what time he plans to ring the tocsin." Communications with Crest broke down on the following day, due in part to repressive measures taken by military authorities inside the town, but rumors that "all the communes are going to Crest" spread to Roynac after nightfall on the sixth. Again Jeune sent messengers to Comte, this time to find out "if the men of Puy-St. Martin have left yet." Comte set 4:00 a.m. as the departure time for both communes and assigned a hamlet near Crest as a general rendezvous. It was by following this plan that Montagnards in the area brought several hundred reinforcements into the battle for Crest on December 7.[20]

Comte's orders brought a massive turnout at Puy-St. Martin, where

---

[19] Census lists, Puy-St. Martin and Roynac, 1851, ADD, 35M.
[20] Tems. Ant, Arnaud, *négociant*, next-door neighbor of Jeune; Pr. Arnaud, tenant farmer; L. Bénistand, cult., ADD, M 1355, dossier Roynac.

"a great number of peaceful ploughmen" mustered from the farmsteads during the night.[21] Through secret alerts and door-to-door recruitment, militants helped him gather sixty men on the village parade ground by 9:00 p.m. Shouts of "To Arms!" resounded in the streets, and soon the crowd advanced to the church square, singing the Marseillaise to the tune of the village band. Comte stepped forward to confront the mayor, who refused to hand over the keys to the bell tower: "*M. le maire*, I have always obeyed you and I respect you; we don't want to harm anyone, but the tocsin is ringing everywhere, and we must ring it here." The mayor's resistance to his former secretary was *pro forma*, and he stood aside while several men clambered up a ladder, through a window, and into the bell tower. For the next two hours the tocsin summoned forth recruits from the dispersed settlements. So well prepared was the mobilization that when Comte sent three militants to make the rounds of some farms, they found only one man who had not yet left for the village. Comte's authority over the peasants of Puy-St. Martin became even clearer when he gave them a speech before their departure. "My friends," he declared, "we must not steal, pillage, or burn, but we must preserve the Democratic and Social Republic." To his request that they remain faithful to their oaths and swear to die for the defense of their brothers, most of the insurgents replied "Yes! Yes!" When they marched northward at 4:00 a.m., commanded by the captain of their former national guard unit, the men of Puy-St. Martin comprised a voluntary force of 150-200 rebels.[22]

The mobilization in Roynac had a similar sequence of events—secret contacts, a preparatory gathering, the tocsin, recruitment bands, a political speech, and a military column. Jeune was the most prominent figure at each stage of operations. By nightfall he had assembled a large number of armed men inside a new schoolhouse he had been constructing at Les Girards. While he awaited the return of his messengers to Puy-St. Martin, some of the men went home with orders to return at the sound of the tocsin, and others gathered at a local inn that the Montagnards customarily used as a social center. As soon as Jeune learned of Comte's decision to mobilize, he headed a band of 20-30 men that tried to enter the church. Foiled for a moment by the priest, who had fled with the keys, Jeune ordered a few men to climb into the bell tower and sound the alert. As peasants arrived, he told them to go through the farmsteads, systematically recruiting the laggards. "Go in every direction to get everybody up," he ordered one band. "Don't

---

[21] Letter from the mayor, Dec. 28, 1851, ADD, M 1355, dossier Puy-St. Martin.
[22] Tems., P. Authon, innkeeper; B. Gaulheron, owner-farmer; D. Magnet, rural guard; A. Borle, owner-farmer; Et. Jeune, tailor, ADD, M-1355, dossier Puy-St. Martin.

harm anyone and don't damage the doors, but everybody must march."
Confronted at night by these armed bands, which numbered from 5 to
15 men, most of the peasants who stayed home now agreed to march.
As new recruits joined the main gathering at the schoolhouse, a militant wrote down their names on a roster. Some peasants complained
that the mayor was not leading them, but Jeune brushed aside their
doubts: "The mayor no longer counts. We are the masters, and everyone must leave." Shortly after 4:00 a.m. he gave a speech to the insurgents of Roynac, defending the legitimacy of their impending march:
"We don't intend to harm anyone," he announced. "We are marching
to deliver the (political) prisoners of Belleville (*sic*) and to restore
universal suffrage." Under his command, the rebels formed a double-
file column, recruited the mayor's son and the rural guard, and headed
for Crest, numbering 150-175 men.[23]

If Montagnard leaders often mobilized peasants for regional action,
they sometimes hesitated to obey orders from the towns. Their caution might prevent any public agitation, forestall linkage with rebel
forces elsewhere, or confine insurgency to the local level. The impact
of leadership decisions that contradicted urban plans can be seen at
Capestang, a cantonal seat nine miles west of Béziers. Despite its minor
administrative and market functions, Capestang was a typical winegrowing bourg of Mediterranean France, with several hundred agricultural laborers who resided alongside a hundred artisans and a few landlords.[24] The Montagnard society in the bourg was large and well
organized, and its president, Maxime Chambert, an owner-farmer and
grain dealer, had close contacts with leaders of the underground at
Béziers.[25] When news of the coup d'état reached Capestang on December 3, Chambert and other leaders decided to await orders from Béziers, although they did discuss occupying the *mairie* immediately.
Two townsmen arrived that night with written orders to march to Béziers at 5:00 a.m., but now Chambert opposed joining the urban rebels.
"We'd better stay at Capestang and seize the *mairie*," he told a midnight meeting of the executive commission. "Then we'll see." Everyone accepted his opinion as authoritative, and three centurions went
to alert the decurions, enjoining them to go with their men, arms and

[23] Tems. Ant. Pinard, farm servant; Jn. Ant. Bertrand, S. Gaulthier, and Aimé
Monier, owner-farmers; M. Plan, the mayor's son; Fr. Pouchoulin, mason, ADD,
M 1355, dossier Roynac.

[24] Capestang had 2,135 inhabitants in 1851, of whom 1,920 resided in the agglomeration; 174 were *journaliers*, 251 *journaliers-propriétaires*, 96 owner-farmers,
136 farm servants, 112 craftsmen and shopkeepers, and 25 landlords and professional
men. ADH, M, census lists for Capestang 1851.

[25] Ints. Jos. Cans, *journalier*, Fr. Méric, owner-farmer, and Pr. Pioch, *journalier-
prop.*, in ADH, 39M 147, 154, 156.

munitions to a field outside the bourg. "The 'Aunt' has arrived," one centurion told a decurion. "Take your rifles and munitions and march." Even as the mobilization was underway, Chambert had second thoughts. He decided to send two centuries to find out what was really happening at Béziers, and he suspended further operations at Capestang: the armed gathering at the rendezvous, which numbered 150 men at 3:00 a.m., dispersed until further orders.[26]

Popular excitement spread in the morning, as militants ordered the peasants not to leave for work in the fields. A large crowd on the road to Béziers hailed the centurions, who returned at nine o'clock with rumors that people had begun to seize the town hall. This news sparked an immediate mobilization. Men rushed home to get their weapons and over one hundred nonmembers of the society joined the military column that marched to the *mairie*, numbering 400 men. Chambert and the other Montagnard leaders accompanied the rebels, but they still hesitated to commit themselves. Instead of forcing their way into the town hall and declaring a revolutionary commission, they began arguing with the mayor, who insisted that someone accept written responsibility for occupying the municipal premises. When some peasants in the crowd on the town square opened fire moments later at the brigade of gendarmes, Chambert was appalled. Far from taking advantage of his opportunity, he marched everyone out of the bourg, had them form ranks, and ordered the decurions to call the roll of their men. With discipline restored, the Montagnards patrolled the bourg for another six days, helping the mayor preserve the peace instead of overthrowing him. Restrained by their leaders, the peasants of Capestang took arms, but they did not take power.[27]

Montagnard leaders derived much of their energy and determination from a complex blend of political loyalties and expectations, which they articulated during the insurrection. Most closely linked to their previous organizational experience in the underground was the argument from authority: they had received "orders" that initiates of the society must obey. This stress on authority relationships characterized rural *chefs* who were at the same time subordinate to urban leaders and dominant over local recruits. In organizing local branches of the underground, they had followed the initiative of townsmen, and they

[26] Ints. and Tems. in dossiers A. Bonnet, shoemaker, Jos. Cans, Jos. Dumas, *journalier-prop.*, A. Lamur, carpenter and owner-farmer, Pr. Lignon, *journalier-prop.*, Jn. Montaulieu, *journalier*, and M. Pech, café owner and barber, in ADH, 39M 140-60; Int. M. Chambert and Tem. Jq. Marcel, *journalier-prop.*, in CG Capestang.
[27] In addition to the above sources, see Ints. Jn. Augé, *journalier-prop.*, and Pr. Fabre, *journalier-prop.*, ADH, 39M 144, 150; Tem. Jos. Rouquier, *journalier*, CG Capestang; and Margadant, "Insurrection," pp. 435-37.

had come to anticipate the possibility of a general uprising. The arrival of "orders" signified that "the moment had come" to demonstrate in arms their commitment to the Democratic and Social Republic. At the same time, by presiding over initiation ceremonials that bound recruits to obey their commands, these branch leaders had established a claim to the exercise of authority. They were in a position to give orders as well as to receive them. The political organizations derived from Montagnard leadership hierarchies implied unquestioning obedience to such orders. Furthermore, militants who had acquired a special sense of purpose and prestige by participating in a *secret* society often responded eagerly to word that orders had arrived. Now they could display their inside information and local prominence by alerting friends and neighbors that the time had come to march. Not fear of disobedience but sectarian enthusiasm motivated the leaders and militants who used "orders" as a justification for taking arms in December 1851.[28]

The coup d'état gave Montagnards a second line of argument with which to mobilize popular support: defense of the Constitution and the Republic. According to Article 68 of the Constitution, if the president dissolved the National Assembly, he was guilty of high treason and must be stripped of his powers. All citizens were obligated to refuse him obedience, and Article 110 reaffirmed that "all Frenchmen" were entrusted with the defense of the Constitution.[29] In each rebel zone, a few urban leaders were sufficiently educated to grasp the fact that Louis Napoleon's coup d'état violated the Constitution and legitimized popular resistance. At Forcalquier, for example, the watchmaker Escoffier announced to the subprefect, "The Constitution has been violated, and we intend to defend it and march on Paris to defend our brothers." At Béziers, the shoemaker Baudoma clambered onto a table at the café Palot and declaimed before a gathering of centurions and decurions: "The Constitution has been violated, and we must defend it at the peril of our lives." The spokesman of the rebels at Dieulefit, a pharmacist named Darier, argued that "they wanted to maintain the Republic and preserve their rights and the Constitution."[30]

[28] Thus, rural militants in at least twenty-five communes of the central Drôme used "orders" as a justification for mobilizing manpower. See, for example, Tem. Fr. Masseron, owner-farmer at La-Roche-sur-Grane, ADD, M 1355, dossier La-Roche-sur-Grane; Tem. Jn. Brun, rural guard, in dossier Jn. Planel, tailor at Félines, ADD, M 1361; Int. Jos. Icard, sharecropper at Salettes, ADD, M 1363; and Int. Amédée Toutet, landlord at Sauzet, in ATML, Ins. 1851, dossier Toutet.

[29] For a clear statement of the constitutional grounds for resistance to the coup d'état, see the proclamation issued by opposition leaders of the National Assembly on Dec. 2, 1851, reprinted by Ténot, *Paris en décembre 1851*, p. 126.

[30] Ténot, *La province*, p. 165; Int. Jos. Tournès, in dossier P. Palot, café owner

Montagnard leaders in towns of the Var and the Nièvre, the Gers and the Lot-et-Garonne, used the same rhetoric of constitutional defense.[31] So did militants in a few bourgs and villages. According to one cultivator at Grane (Drôme), "Everyone was shouting that the Constitution had been violated and it was necessary to go defend it;" a villager who joined the rebels of Lavardac (Lot-et-Garonne) testified that "everyone was saying it was necessary to organize in order to defend the Constitution and march to Agen"; and three municipal councilors at Monoblet (Gard) told the mayor that "part of the population wanted to leave in order to defend the Constitution."[32] Although a majority of rural leaders were too unsophisticated to adopt the slogan of constitutional defense, they often shared with townsmen a vague awareness that the Republic was in danger. Their Republican loyalties encouraged a defensive reflex against the coup d'état. In the words of one peasant from Soyans (Drôme), "We were marching to defend the Republic; beyond that I don't know anything."[33]

A third justification for revolt against the government was popular sovereignty. In defiance of hostile officials, Montagnards argued that legitimate authority flowed from the popular will, not from the national government. They shared a generalized belief that police bureaucrats could be swept aside with impunity. Some leaders reasoned that just as Louis Napoleon had "dissolved" the National Assembly, so they could "dissolve" local authorities. "Because the President dissolved the Assembly, the People are sovereign," argued a militant at St. Félix-de-Palières (Gard). "In the name of the French people, you are dissolved," announced a Montagnard shoemaker at St. Sauveur to the mayor. "Withdraw, you're no longer anything. The *mairie* is ours."[34] Other Montagnards imagined that the coup d'état resembled earlier Parisian revolutions in its overthrow of constituted authority. The government was changing, and police bureaucrats no longer had any "authority." Thus did Montagnard spokesmen confront the jus-

---

at Béziers, ADH, 39M 156; Tem. Jos. Fr. Roman, *négociant* and *adjoint*, in ADD, M 1354, dossier Dieulefit.

[31] Letter from Giraud, a Montagnard *chef* at Brignoles, to Flayosc, *chef* at Bras, in AD Var, 4M 19; Int. Pr. Seroude, house painter and window maker at Clamecy, in CG Clamecy; order from Boussès, lawyer and provisional subprefect at Mirande, to rural communes, cited by Ténot, *La province*, p. 90; and Tem. Peyronni, retired military officer at Miramont, near Marmande, cited by Ténot, *La province*, p. 63.

[32] Int. Pr. Gilles, cult. at Grane, ADD, M 1362; Int. Jn. Marcade, at Vianne, AD L-G, 4U, Ins. 1851; Tem. mayor of Monoblet, ADG, 3U 5/2.

[33] Int. Jn. Pr. Marson, owner-farmer at Soyans, ADD, M 1365.

[34] Tem. F. Laurent, *prop.* at St. Félix-de-Palières, ADG, 3U 5/2; dossier J. Marion, shoemaker at St. Sauveur, JM-1851, #255.

tice of the peace at Masseube (Gers): "There is no more authority in France. You're no longer the justice of the peace. The people are sovereign. It is for the people to issue orders." When the mayor of Lédignan (Gard) asked the Montagnards in that bourg "by what right" they were gathered, their leader replied, "By the right of the people," and others shouted at the gendarmes, "There is no more authority, there are no more gendarmes."[35] Montagnards were especially likely to use the rhetoric of popular sovereignty when they not only defied opponents but installed themselves in office. "The people are sovereign, and we want our share of sovereignty," argued a fiddler on the village square of Caux (Hérault). His astonished interlocutor, a local landlord, was unable to prevent a ten-man commission from occupying the *mairie*. At Alignan-du-Vent (Hérault), the Montagnard initiator, a stonecutter named Lucien Fay, led a band to the mayor's house and announced, "We've come to demand the keys to the *mairie*, the communal seal, and the mayor's sash, because we are the people and the people govern."[36] The peasant leaders of a band at Forcalquieret (Var) pushed the logic of popular sovereignty to its extreme when they told the mayor, "We're the people, we've just made the elections, and we don't want you anymore." He pointed out that their band numbered only 20 in a commune with 120 voters, but they insisted, "We are the sovereign people." When 7 recruits began to waver in their opposition to the mayor, the brothers Guiot, both cultivators, shouted "You're chickens! You're cowards! No weakness now! Stick to your promise!" The mayor stepped aside, and "the people" of Forcalquieret placed their new mayor and municipal commission in office.[37]

The ideal of a "Social Republic" provided Montagnards with another justification for revolt. Surprisingly few leaders reportedly used this subversive term "Social" in appealing for support, but their previous propaganda had aroused popular expectations that a *new* Republic would triumph in 1852, bringing liberty and equality to the poor.[38] Rumors of revolution fostered a generalized belief that social justice would be realized immediately. Peasants in a few villages thought that the government had already changed: the real Republic—*La Rouge*,

---

[35] Words of Esquinance, miller, and Gachiès, music master, cited by Dagnan, *Le Gers*, II, 39-41; Tem. Et. Mendre, brigadier at Lédignan, ADG, 3U 5/1.

[36] Tem. S. Coustan, in dossier A. Calas, *fidelier* at Caux, and Tem. Eustache, mayor, in dossier L. Fay, stonecutter, ADH, 39M 147, 150.

[37] Report of the mayor of Forcalquieret, Dec. 15, 1851, AD Var, 4M 19.

[38] For an exceptional reference to the Social Republic, see Dossier Séré, barrel maker at Samazan. When asked what he meant, Séré replied, "It is dividing the sum of pleasures and pains as equally as possible; it is founding the new society on the ruins of the old." AD L-G, 4U, Ins. 1851, *arr.* Marmande.

La Belle—had arrived.[39] At La Garde Freinet (Var), the cork workers marched to overthrow the prefect, but their women urged them
to "bring back *La Bonne*," the authentic Republic.[40] Whether insurgents thought they were celebrating the advent of a new government
or overthrowing the present one, in either case they might expect the
prompt granting of their "rights" and "liberties." Popular pressure at
Digne resulted in a formal proclamation by the triumphant Montagnard committee of the Basses-Alpes, abolishing indirect taxes;[41] the
workers of Bédarieux tried to strike for higher wages in the aftermath
of their victory over the gendarmes;[42] peasants at St. Julien (Var)
thought they were marching to Draguignan in order to obtain their
rights of usage to communal lands;[43] Montagnard leaders at Beaumont
(Vaucluse) proclaimed the division of communal lands, the abolition
of municipal sales taxes, and the abolition of labor services for road
work;[44] militants in several villages of the Drôme tried to recruit farmers by promising them lower taxes or higher wages;[45] and a tailor at
Gargas (Vaucluse) talked of establishing a government at Apt "to sell
farm produce at better prices."[46] Although references to economic reforms were *not* common at the leadership level, the promises that
Montagnards had previously made to initiates continued to influence
popular motivation after the coup d'état.

   The issue of political repression imparted another dimension to

---

[39] "The Red has arrived," tem. A. Balmigière, *journalier-prop.* at Capestang, CG
Capestang; "The Republic has arrived," Int. Ant. Cros, cult. at Lespignan, in ADH,
39M 148; "People said that 'La Belle' had arrived," tem. Jq. Rocher, *prop.* at
Salavas, in ADA, 5M 18. At Sauzet (Drôme), this phrase "La Belle" definitely
referred to the refrain from a popular song, "And when 'La Belle' arrives, the
Republic of the peasants." See Int. E. Arnaud, *prop.*, cited by Vigier, *La Seconde
République*, II, 333.

[40] Agulhon, *La République au village*, pp. 465-66.

[41] Proclamation cited by Vigier, *La Seconde République*, II, 332. A crowd celebrated this abolition of indirect taxes by burning the registers in a bonfire on the
fairgrounds of Digne (sources cited by Vigier, *La Seconde République*, II, 317, n.
27).

[42] See Margadant, "Insurrection," pp. 428-31.

[43] Ints. S. Maraus, cult., and L. Berne, cult. AD Var, 4M 19, dossier St. Julien.

[44] Five leaders signed this proclamation. Tems. C. Riper, mayor, Jos. Archard,
innkeeper, and C. Roche, rural guard, in ADV, 4M 74, dossier Beaumont. An unsigned ten-point document, more radical in content (Article 1 called for the
abolition of usury) exists in the dossier for this commune, but it was not the basis
for the public proclamation, *contra* Vigier, who cites it at length in *La Seconde
République*, II, 332.

[45] Tems. Aimé Rouin, owner-farmer at La-Roche-sur-Grane, L. Eymery, owner-
farmer at Roynac, and Colombor, *dit* Brunet, *journalier* at Montclar. Out of some
2,000 testimonies and interrogations, however, these are the only references to
economic motives for insurgency in the central Drôme, ADD, M 1354-55.

[46] Int. D. Barthelemy, cult. at Gargas, citing the words of Salvan, tailor, ADV,
4M 64, #748.

Montagnard rhetoric about popular rights and liberties. Where Republican municipal officials had been revoked, new revolutionary commissions could justly claim to represent "the sovereign people."[47] Where political leaders had been imprisoned in distant towns, militants could invoke the memory of their martyrdom in order to stimulate opposition to the coup d'état.[48] And where they had been recently jailed in a nearby town or driven into hiding, their fate could become the overriding cause of insurgency. Montagnards demanded the release of political prisoners throughout the region of the central Drôme where political fugitives had evaded the army in previous months, and they marched with this same goal in mind from Lablachère (Ardèche), Corvol-l'Orgueilleux (Nièvre), and several villages to the north of Béziers.[49] Around Crest, men began gathering on the night of the fifth and they marched on the sixth to rescue prisoners who had just been taken inside the town. "We must go deliver our brothers," announced a former schoolteacher and rebel leader at Beaufort, in the valley of the Gervanne. "We are marching to reconquer our rights and deliver the prisoners," claimed the secretary of the mayor at Grane. From the cantonal seat of Marsanne, a column of 100 rebels headed for Montélimar on the evening of the sixth, led by a fugitive who told the justice of the peace, "We want the Democratic and Social Republic and we want to rescue our brothers in prison." Finally, from Mirmande and Cliousclat, 800 rebels marched toward Valence on the eighth, again demanding the release of political prisoners.[50] This latter contingent included several fugitives who had hurried home from the Ardèche at rumors of the fighting at Crest. When they reached Cliousclat, they went through the farmsteads, asking men to help them obtain their liberty.[51] For such fugitives, the word *liberty* had a concrete meaning indeed.

[47] A noteworthy example is La Garde Freinet, where the new commission installed itself "in the name of the Sovereign People." Agulhon, *La République au village*, p. 357.

[48] Agulhon discusses one such example of martyrdom at Le Luc, where the *confiseur* Méric was sentenced to prison for two years in the Plot of Lyon. *La République au village*, pp. 390-92.

[49] Witnesses or insurgents from thirteen communes in the central Drôme reported this objective, ADD, M 1353-71; Tem. L. Blachère, cult. at Lablachère, ADA, 5M 18; dossier Corvol-l'Orgueilleux, especially Belin, doctor, ADN, Ins. Clamecy; Ints. Michel Couderc, cult. at Gabian, G. Ganidel, carpenter at Puissalicon, Ant. Laurès, tailor at Pouzolles, and P. Pagès, cult. at Puimisson, in ADH, 39M 148, 151, 153, 156.

[50] Tem. Mouriquand, in dossier Jn. Pr. Oullier, cult. (ex-schoolteacher) at Beaufort, ADD, M 1367; Int. Pr. Gilles, cited in n. 32; Tem. Jos. Froment, clerk of J. P. Marsanne, ADD, M 1354, dossier Marsanne; Ints. E. Bérard, silk manufacturer, and Jn. L. Chamboncel, cult.-tilemaker at Mirmande, in ADD, M 1357, 1359.

[51] Tem. Jq. Pascal, potter, and Int. S. Monier, potter, ADD, M 1353 (dossier Cliousclat), 1366.

As political appeals and slogans were transmitted from bourgeois and artisanal leaders in the towns to peasants in the bourgs and villages, they merged with traditional beliefs and expectations. For example, the legal theory that the president of the Republic and subordinate officials who continued to obey him should be "stripped of their functions" became confused with longstanding anarchist impulses against the state: "There is no more authority!" The concept of popular sovereignty became synonymous with the will of the village community, not the French people as a whole. When asked by magistrates to define what he meant by "the People," a rebel leader at Cabrières d'Aigues (Vaucluse) replied, "What I call the People consists of the agglomeration of almost all the men in the area (*pays*)."[52] Instead of referring to the Constitution of the Republic, peasants talked of defending *le bon ordre*, a term which implied that the prevailing order was not just.[53] They personified the Republic—"La Belle," "La Bonne"—and they translated abstractions such as liberty into personal terms. "There would be more liberty in the Red Republic," thought one illiterate cultivator at Murs (Vaucluse)—"We would all be able to hunt without a permit."[54] Above all, peasant rebels imagined that their cause would triumph overnight. As villagers told a hostile landlord at Boisset et Gaujac (Gard), "Your time is finished, and ours begins."[55] This belief in instant success combined peasant perceptions of the recent political past—the sudden change of government in February 1848—with more deep-seated cultural attitudes toward time. In comparison with the seasonal rhythms of nature and the generational cycle of the family, political events were sudden and nonrecurrent. This gave them a dramatic impact analogous to monsters and miracles: the coup d'état might easily be translated into an apocalyptic vision of hope or terror. For the Montagnards it was naturally hope that abounded as orders circulated into the countryside and as leaders demanded the rights of the people. "What a beautiful day!" insurgents from Grane exclaimed as they marched to Crest. "How the good Lord is pleased by our Revolution."[56]

The fusion of political ideology and traditional beliefs suggests the

[52] Int. Alex. Jourdan, cult., revoked as *adjoint* in 1850 and named mayor by the rebels, ADV, 4M 58, #115.

[53] Examples of this popular objective—*le bon ordre*—include Tems. Pr. Eynard, owner-farmer at Plan-de-Baix; and A. Morin, owner-farmer at Soyans (ADD, M 1355, dossiers Plan-de-Baix and Soyans); Int. E. Maurel, cult. at Rustrel. (ADV, 4M 61, #435); and Int. A. Charbonnier, tailor at Lagorce, for whom *le bon ordre* included lower taxes (ADA, 5M 18).

[54] Int. T. Pascal, cult. at Murs, ADV, 4M 66, #901.

[55] Tem. D. Drille, *prop.* at Boisset-et-Gaujac, ADG, 3U 5/1.

[56] Words reported by the priest of Grane, cited by Vigier, *La Seconde République*, II, 333.

limits of an organizational interpretation of insurgency in 1851. However actively Montagnard leaders participated in the revolt, their plans, decisions and appeals for public support occurred within a traditional context of sociopolitical antagonisms and solidarities. In some communities, crowds reacted against police bureaucrats or "men of order," imparting a spontaneous element of popular violence to the revolt. Such hostile outbursts were especially typical of towns and bourgs that had experienced sporadic and ineffectual repression before the coup d'état. Villagers within the market radius of such leading centers of revolt tended to share the same "reactive" orientation toward the state: they formed crowds in response to news of rumors of fighting in nearby towns, and they hoped to escape from the repressive burden of centralized administration. Alongside this reactive dimension of protest was a widespread reliance on communal forms of collective action. At the sound of the tocsin or the beating of drums, entire communities took arms. Men marched as the members of agglomerated settlements or rural neighborhoods, and they derived support from communal traditions of unanimity. Coercive pressures often accompanied these imitative mobilizations. Once militant minorities had begun armed uprisings, the scale of popular participation depended less on political organization per se than on the merger of political loyalties with cohesive communities of artisans and peasants.

Crowd outbursts against police bureaucrats and "men of order" had an especially radicalizing impact on the scale and objectives of protest. At the town of Apt, for example, the revolt began as a spontaneous demonstration against the repressive measures of the subprefect. On the night of December 6, officials from Forcalquier had arrived in flight, and the subprefect had tried to organize a defensive force of gendarmes, forest guards, and civilians. Out of eighty men of order who responded, only five remained at the subprefecture by ten o'clock the following morning. The subprefect also sent an urgent request for aid to the nearby bourg of St. Saturnin, where the dominant faction was notoriously clerical and anti-Republican. When fifty-eight national guardsmen from St. Saturnin rushed to the rescue, accompanied by their priest, the townsmen of Apt exploded in anger. As the commander of the gendarmes later testified, "People demanded with a sort of fury that they be sent away; people said it was an insult to the inhabitants of Apt to have recourse to strangers."[57] The guardsmen of St. Saturnin made matters worse by threatening to open fire on the crowd, and when they reached the subprefecture, it was less to bolster the forces of order inside than to take refuge from the "exasperated

[57] Tem. A. Peyrand, *Maréchal des logis*, ADV, 4M 76, dossier Apt.

multitude," which now covered the square outside. The mayor of Apt and several Republican municipal councilors intervened to demand that the men of St. Saturnin be disarmed and expelled, and the subprefect, fearing a mob attack, agreed. After the village priest and his devoted parishioners ran the gauntlet of the crowd, protected by several prominent Republicans, townsmen stormed into the *mairie* and seized the weapons, which had been left behind. They emerged with rifles, a drum, and a red flag, and from the steps of the building the young Montagnard flaxcomber, Méritan, alias Barbès, named an insurrectionary committee to the acclamation of the crowd below. Other rebels broke into the prison and released a villager held for hunting illegally, and still others invaded the subprefecture, searching for more weapons. Despite the effort of moderate Republicans on the municipal council to restore order in cooperation with the members of the new committee, all of them Montagnards, it was the latter who now had the upper hand. Catapulted into power by the crowd, they proceeded to organize the regional force that marched toward Avignon on the following day.[58]

The threat of repression also precipitated armed mobilizations at Clamecy and Bédarieux. The Montagnards who decided to rescue political prisoners at Clamecy on the evening of the sixth had just learned that wealthy "men of order" were gathering with weapons at the town hall. "People were saying that bourgeois had gone in arms to the *mairie*," testified one rebel leader afterward. "We had to take arms ourselves in order to avoid a St. Barthélemy [massacre] and to defend our rights, which were being threatened."[59] According to another Montagnard, "Everyone agreed that if those Messieurs hadn't taken arms, nothing would have happened."[60] Exasperated by the military display of their class enemies, artisans began shouting "To arms!" and beating the drum in the *faubourg de Bethléem*, across the river from town.[61] This precipitate uprising developed a momentum of its own after the rebels captured the town. Their provisional mayor, a Montagnard *avoué*, had no control over the bands, which constructed barri-

[58] Among the many witnesses of these events at Apt, see especially Tems. Jn. Henri Emile Dévèze-Biron, president of the civil tribunal at Apt; Th. Bareau, S-P; Hip. Jaumard, watchmaker; Hip. Seymard, *secretaire en chef de la mairie*; and Ferry De Chenery, J. P., all in ADV, 4M 76, dossier Apt. Among those arrested, see especially Ints. André Seymard, carpenter; Crest d'Alencon, lawyer; Amédée Audibert, hatmaker; Elzéar Goffredy, lawyer; Jos. Archias, retired military officer and ex-*adjoint*; and H. Cavanet, *journalier*, in ADV, 4M 58, #128, #131; 4M 63, #631, #639; 4M 64, #729, #786.

[59] Int. Pr. Seroude, cited in n. 31.

[60] Int. G. Clement, *huissier*, ADN, U, Ins. Clamecy.

[61] Concerning this sudden formation of a crowd, see especially Int. Pr. Steau, *flotteur*, ADN, U, Clamecy.

cades, searched for weapons, and celebrated their victory. The ground-swell of revolt seemed to come from the lower depths of society: "The entire night passed in a terrible situation. Bands armed with rifles, sabers, hatchets, went through the streets by torchlight, clamoring at the top of their lungs and firing weapons into the air. Groups of peasants and workers entered the bourgeois houses, weapons in hand, and demanded arms and munitions. If they found none, the house was searched from top to bottom."[62] Compulsory disarmament of the bourgeois expressed the social resentments as well as the military requirements of the rebels. When Montagnard leaders tried to grant popular demands on the following day for a similar disarmament of the gendarmes, discipline broke down altogether, and a mob murdered one of the gendarmes. As Ténot writes, "The insurrection, without any real direction, floated as if by chance. No one even succeeded in creating a revolutionary commission."[63] On Sunday, after most of the peasants had gone home, rumors spread through town that troops were coming. Again "immense disorder" reigned, as drums and church bells called forth a "furious multitude." Nearly all the ranking Montagnards in town had abandoned the struggle, but obscure artisans mustered around a thousand men behind barricades. When the army commander decided to bivouac for the night instead of attacking immediately, this defensive reflex of the populace gave way to discouragement, futile attempts to arrange a negotiated surrender, and flight.[64] From start to finish, popular emotion governed the course of events at Clamecy.

A strong element of spontaneity also characterized events at Bédarieux, where Montagnards responded to emissaries from Béziers on December 4 by organizing an unarmed demonstration at the town hall. Many textile workers left their jobs at precisely 4:00 p.m. as if they were going on strike, and some of them did join the crowd in order to obtain higher wages.[65] The leader of the crowd, a watchmaker named Bonnal, hoped to occupy the *mairie* without violence, but the police commissioner and the brigade of gendarmes opposed him with a threat of force. As the gendarmes ostentatiously loaded their weapons in full view of the "furious multitude," men shouted "To arms!" and rushed home for their weapons.[66] They were in a fighting mood when they marched again on the town hall, organized this time into "platoons"

---

[62] Ténot, *La province*, p. 35. [63] Ibid., pp. 37-38.
[64] Ibid., pp. 39-41.
[65] Fifteen witnesses described a mass desertion of the textile workshops, ADH, 39M 144-60, scattered dossiers of suspects from Bédarieux. Among participants, see Ints. Jn. Boni, wool finisher; E. Gely, spinner; and J. Soques, weaver, ADH, 39M 146, 151, 158.
[66] Report of CP Bédarieux, ADH, 39M 142.

and brandishing rifles, sabers, skewers, daggers, knives, and pipes.[67] Their anger turned to joy when they found the premises undefended, and they celebrated their victory by proclaiming a revolutionary commission. That evening protest escalated dramatically when the "immense crowd" at the town hall learned that a worker had just been killed by the gendarmes, who had retreated to their barracks.[68] Cries of vengeance filled the air, and hundreds of men hurried to the scene of the crime. "Those without weapons were treated as laggards and criminals," one participant later claimed.[69] About a thousand men assaulted the barracks during the night, and three gendarmes died in the fray. This impassioned outburst against the gendarmes expressed a rough sense of popular justice rather than a deliberate decision of Montagnard leaders.

Crowds in several rebel centers, including Mirande, Le Luc, and Grane, took vengeance against hostile officials and wealthy men of order. At the town of Mirande, a public mobilization began at the instigation of Montagnard leaders on the morning of the fourth. Several militants went through the streets, crying "To arms!," a shoemaker rang the tocsin, two drummers beat *La générale*, and soon a crowd of 400 men invaded the square in front of the town hall. Spectators seem to have been more numerous than armed rebels, but an incident at the subprefecture quickly radicalized the crowd: a shot rang out during a dispute between the subprefect, M. Grabias, and a young lawyer, M. Terrail, who was trying to arrest him. Grabias was wounded and carried inside the building by his friends, but a rumor spread through the crowd that he had tried to shoot Terrail. However false the accusation, it harmonized with the popular view of Grabias' character—he had persecuted Republicans in the past—and a troop of furious men burst into the subprefecture to capture and punish him. Another Republican lawyer proclaimed himself subprefect in the tumult, perhaps so that he could restore order by evacuating the building, but Grabias' many enemies now searched the neighborhood for him. Apprehended by a carpenter, he was escorted to prison amidst shouts for his death. Only the protection of upper-class Republicans spared him from the mob. This example inspired militants to arrest several other officials, including the *procureur* and the tax collector. The rebels now turned to military matters, constructing barricades and seizing weapons from the subprefecture and from a few proprietors. Their impetuosity flared briefly that evening at word that troops were arriving from Auch. The

[67] Tem. Vernazobres-Lavit, acting mayor and wool manufacturer, CG Bédarieux.
[68] Ints. Jq. Fabre, weaver, and Ant. Fournier, landlord, in ADH, 39M 150. See also the CP's report, cited in n. 66.
[69] Int. Fr. Bouffard, tailor, CG Bédarieux.

battle cry, "To arms!" resounded through the streets again, and a crowd hurried to the barricades, compelling the small detachment of soldiers to retreat without a fight. Excitement rose again the next day when peasant bands marched into town, dragging several gendarmes, whom they had captured and bound in chains. These agents of the state quickly followed their predecessors into prison, where they were safe at least from popular violence. The upper-class Republicans who had begun the revolt managed to direct the turbulent energies of their recruits into further military preparations, and by Saturday evening popular enthusiasm had given way to fear of repression. After midnight, the leaders had all the barricades dismantled and the prisoners released. On Sunday they surrendered voluntarily to the same magistrates whose arrests they had sanctioned three days earlier.[70]

The rebels of Le Luc seized upper-class hostages and forced them to march. This harsh treatment of anti-Republican notables reflected the political animosities and social tensions that had accumulated in this Provençal town before the coup d'état. Insurgency began on December 4 when a provisional commission, chosen the previous night during a tumultuous meeting of "exasperated democrats," called the entire population to arms. A crowd shouted down the conservative mayor and replaced him with the former *adjoint*, a bourgeois Republican. Women and children joined the men in a victory celebration—*la fête de la liberté*—but joy turned to suspicion on the following morning, when a stableboy found a letter that the director of the postal service, a notorious anti-Republican, had tried to send the prefect. Great indignation followed this news of treachery, and the members of a Republican *chambrée* decided to arrest the postal director. This example of popular justice triggered a wave of arrests: five gendarmes, six functionaries (including a priest), six members and dependents of a noble family (the Colberts), five landlords, three peasants, and two artisans suffered imprisonment. Some were denounced for resisting disarmament, others for conspiring against the Republic, still others for being agents of the state. Popular feeling ran especially high against M. Colbert, a Legitimist *châtelain* in the neighboring commune of Le-Cannet-du-Luc. Public rumor accused him of mustering eighty servants in order to attack the Republicans. Rebel leaders agreed to all these arrests in order to neutralize the Whites and hold them hostage, but many insurgents harbored social resentments against their "bourgeois prisoners." When the hostages were forced to march with the column from Le Luc, bourgeois Republicans risked unpopularity in order to

70 This description of events at Mirande is based on Ténot, *La province*, pp. 86-94; and Dagnan, *Le Gers*, II, 62-88.

protect them from the "crude sentiments" of the poor. As Agulhon writes, "The problem of the prisoners was the main sign of the internal tension which existed throughout the insurrection, and which was at least as much a tension between bourgeois and workers as between leaders and simple militants."[71]

An outburst of gunfire between gendarmes and armed peasants triggered a massive uprising on December 6 at Grane (Drôme), where several political suspects had fled arrest earlier in the year, leaving behind embittered relatives and friends. Montagnard leaders had alerted peasants during the previous night that a march to Crest was about to begin, but they were still awaiting news from town when a crowd of recruits exchanged shots with mounted gendarmes a half-mile from the village. The gendarmes fled, someone rang the tocsin to muster reinforcements, and large numbers of men answered the call to arms. In the words of Antoine Portier, the son of an owner-farmer worth 40,000 francs, "At the sight of men running, I took my rifle and went to the square of Grane."[72] The mood of the crowd was impassioned. As one landless farmworker testified, "I fell into a considerable gathering, which seemed composed of madmen."[73] The first thought of militants was to seize the weapons of their adversaries, whom they denounced as Whites, *mouchards* (police spies), *aristos*, and *prétaille* (priest-lovers). Then they decided to march on Crest, where they hoped to rescue political prisoners, so they began arresting several priests and landlords as hostages. This compulsory recruitment was so thorough that nearly the entire adult male population joined the column of several hundred men which approached town at nightfall. Political fugitives ordered the priests and landlords to march in the front ranks, and several dozen other Whites were also disarmed and shoved forward. The entire community would brave the gunfire of the troops, its Montagnard rebels shielded by its reactionary hostages.[74]

If socioeconomic antagonisms precipitated armed mobilizations in

---

[71] Agulhon, *La République au village*, p. 399. This discussion of events at Le Luc is based on Blache, *L'Insurrection du Var*, pp. 57-68; and Agulhon, *La République au village*, pp. 391-403.

[72] Int. and dossier Ant. Portier, cult., ADD, M 1368. Twenty-seven of the men who were later interrogated said that they took arms as soon as they heard the tocsin, ADD, M 1356-71.

[73] Int. L. Pelissier, cult., ADD, M 1368.

[74] This narrative is based on the Ints. of suspects, in ADD, M 1356-71; Tems. of hostages, in ATML, Affair Grane; a letter from Pr. Ant. Charles, *adjoint*, Dec. 26, 1851, ADD, M 1354, dossier Grane; and published accounts by Paul Bècque, *curé*, "L'Insurrection de Crest en Dauphiné," in abbés Borges and Amodru, eds., *Souvenirs divers* (Valence, 1892), pp. 1-35; and l'*abbé* Forget, "L'Insurrection de décembre 1851 dans la Drôme," in *Semaine réligieuse de Valence* (1894), pp. 701-720. For more detailed references, see Margadant, "Insurrection," pp. 351-60.

some towns and bourgs, rumors of insurgency provided a comparable stimulus to collective action in many other communes. These rumors varied from imaginary accounts of general insurrection throughout France to exaggerated reports of mobilizations elsewhere in a department, false claims of fighting in nearby towns, and distorted news of uprisings in adjacent market centers. In the central Drôme, for example, villagers at St. Gervais heard that "everywhere in France people are gathering en masse to change the authorities"; rebels at Beaufort told a local notary that "Crest, Valence, and Lyon were in the power of the insurgents"; a political fugitive at Cliousclat boasted that "before dawn (on the eighth) 50,000 people would reach Loriol from the departments of the Drôme and the Ardèche"; the *habitués* of a Montagnard inn at La Coucourde took arms when a townsman burst into their deliberations, shouting, "Montélimar is in revolution!" villagers at Poët-Laval gathered at word that "there is fighting at Dieulefit"; and a rebel from the cantonal seat of Bourdeaux later testified, "I heard talk of fighting at Crest, and like the others, I left with the intention of helping the townsmen."[75] In fact, the only insurgents who reached Loriol were from Cliousclat and Mirmande; Montélimar remained calm; Dieulefit took arms without any fighting; and most townsmen at Crest abstained from revolt, while a few bourgeois helped the army disperse the rebels of Grane. In all these cases, false rumors stimulated widespread popular participation in the revolt. Comparable rumors circulated with the same effects in other rebel zones of the nation, such as the southwestern Yonne, the southern Ardèche, and the northwestern Gard.[76] These inaccurate and exaggerated accounts of insurgency were a natural concomitant of the oral communications networks through which villagers exchanged information with townsmen. By democraticizing their leadership to include semiliterate and illiterate peasants, and by renouncing written means of communication within the underground, Montagnard organizers had encouraged the circulation of unconfirmed rumors in the countryside. Many branch leaders were themselves unaccustomed to verifying political information in the newspapers. Instead of dominating the flow of news by virtue of their superior literacy, militants often shared with everyone else a penchant for numerical exaggeration, emotionalism, and wishful thinking. Bour-

[75] Tem. Louis Friot, schoolteacher, ADD, M 1355, dossier St. Gervais; Tem. Jn. Jq. Achard, notary, ADD, M 1353, dossier Beaufort; Tem. Ant. Clauzet, ATML, Ins. of 1851, Affair Cliousclat; Ints. Et. Battu, mason, and Jn. Pr. Berenger, shoemaker, commune of Lachamp, ADD, M 1357; Tem. L. Martin, baker, and Int. Hip. Rousset, cult., ADD, M 1355 (dossier Poët-Laval), M 1369; Int. E. Augier, tailor at Bourdeaux, ADD, M 1356.

[76] See, for example, Int. P. Pierre, tinsmith at Ouanne (Yonne) JM-1851, #252; Tem. F. Cachon, CP at Vallon, ADA, 5M 18; and Tem. F. Barbe, *journalier* at Cassagnolles, ADG, 3U 5/1.

geois Republicans in the towns might await precise, written news from Paris before deciding whether to support a *prise d'armes*, but artisans and peasants in the bourgs and villages often responded with enthusiasm to oral messages heralding a general uprising.

Accurate news of events in nearby towns and bourgs naturally encouraged rural mobilizations, too. Some peasants visited market centers on business, joined crowds of demonstrators, and then returned to impress fellow villagers with eyewitness accounts of rebellion. Others combined business with political curiosity in their travels, and they mingled with urban rebels instead of going back home. Militants from at least five villages near St. Sauveur (Yonne) happened to be attending a fair in that market bourg on December 6, when merchants from Clamecy arrived with news of its insurrection. They helped occupy the *mairie* at St. Sauveur and then carried impromptu orders for rural mobilizations back to their villages.[77] On the same day, a fair at Marmande attracted many villagers, who crowded into the cafés and appeared to lend support to the rebel town.[78] Several peasants from villages near Apt claimed they went to town on Sunday, the seventh, for business not politics: one "agriculturalist" intended to see a watchmaker, a tenant farmer had business with his landlord, and a tailor wanted "to buy raw material, which I do every Sunday." All alike stayed to march with the townsmen.[79] From Beaumont-d'Apt (Vaucluse) a rather numerous group of young men went to the fair of Manosque on the sixth and returned with news that the town was in full insurrection. After electing a five-man committee to replace the municipal council, they took arms that night in response to an appeal from another market town (Pertuis).[80]

Peasants also imitated rebels from neighboring villages. The tocsin sounded the alert throughout some rebel districts, such as the central Drôme and the southwestern Yonne. "It's ringing everywhere else, so let it ring here," said the mayor of one village in the valley of the Gervanne (Crest-nord); and the drummer in a nearby village started beating the call to arms as soon as he heard church bells ringing and drums beating elsewhere in the valley.[81] Signal fires and drums had a com-

---

[77] Int. Fr. Bernard, potter at Treigny; Int. Jq. Briot, potter at Moutiers; Int. Fr. Just, *laboureur* at St. Colombe; Int. Alfred Terrain, wheelwright at Saints; and dossier Jn. Bapt. Thiébault, veterinarian at Thury, JM-1851, #258.

[78] Letter from the mayor of Gaujache, Dec. 23, 1851, AD L-G, 4U, Ins., *arr.* Marmande.

[79] Ints. Hip. Sellier, *agriculteur* at Saignon; Jn. Bourgues, tenant farmer at Gargas; and Fr. Sauvan, tailor at Gargas, ADV, 4M 61, #458, #457, #448.

[80] Tem. V. Sauvan, sect. of the mayor, and Int. Fr. Blanc, owner-farmer and Montagnard *chef*, ADV, 4M 74, canton of Pertuis; 4M 57, #73.

[81] Tems. P. Beval, priest, and Jq. Eymery, owner-farmer and tilemaker, in ADD, M 1355, dossier Plan-de-Baix; Tem. Jn. Jos. Terret, *prop.*, ADD, M 1354, dossier Gigors.

parable effect in the northern Gard, where gendarmes reported that "the entire population was on foot, signal fires shone on all the mountains, and from every direction could be heard the sound of drums." As the schoolteacher in one of these villages later testified, "All the inhabitants of Colognac, men and women, were gathered on the square; people shouted that the drum was beating at Lasalle and we must go there."[82] Once rebel columns began marching, they carried the example of insurgency directly to other communities. For example, Boucoiran and Ners in the Gard, Leugny and Ouanne in the Yonne, Billy and Trucy in the Nièvre, Autichamp and Cobonne in the Drôme, Les Arcs and Salernes in the Var, Nézignan-l'Evêque and Laurens in the Hérault, all marched in response to the arrival of contingents from other communes. As one landowner from Nézignan-l'Evêque testified, "The foreman of my field laborers told me they didn't want to continue the day's work. Instead, they wanted to join the population of St. Thibéry, which had already arrived in our commune and which was gathered near the deputy mayor's house. They wanted to go together to Pézénas."[83] The disingenuous words of a Montagnard from Autichamp reflected the same phenomenon of contagion: "We spent the entire night in the houses or cabarets of Autichamp, awaiting the arrival of the contingents from Puy-St. Martin and Roynac—we'd decided in our commune that if the other communes didn't come to get us, we wouldn't march."[84] Success bred success, as rebel columns swelled with each passing village en route to their urban destinations.

However significant the example of rebel towns and mobile columns, the local pressures toward unanimity were what determined the large scale of mobilization in many rural communes. Aided by public alarms such as the tocsin and the drum, militants generated a contagious mood in the streets of many bourgs, village centers, and large hamlets. By force of example, everyone in the community was drawn into the general current of rebellion. Many insurgents later claimed that they had marched in order to imitate the other men of their commune. In the words of a merchant from Lespignan (Hérault) who denied belonging to the underground: "At 4:00 a.m. (on the fourth), I was awakened by shouts and drumbeats. I got up, and women in the streets told me that messengers from Béziers had come to get all the men of Lespignan to march in arms. I took my gun, like everyone else, and joined the large crowd."[85] Similar excuses by rebels in other districts show the

---

[82] *Rapport* gendarmerie, arr. Alais, Dec. 22, 1851, AG, F¹ 54; ADG, 3U 5/2 canton of Lasalle.
[83] Tem. I. Andrien, in dossier Jq. Benaud, *adjoint* of Nézignan-l'Evêque, ADH, 39M 145.
[84] Int. Louis Arbod, son of an owner-farmer, ADD, M 1356.
[85] Int. Fr. Merle, *marchand revendeur*, ADH, 39M 154.

contagious influence of territorial networks of male sociability, such as the commune, the village, the neighborhood, and the youth group: "I followed the example of the other inhabitants of the commune" (Francillon, Drôme); "I marched like many other people from the village, we marched like a flock of sheep" (Aigremont, Gard); "I left with my neighbors" (St. Martin-de-Castillon, Vaucluse); "Seeing all my comrades leave, I took my rifle and left with them" (Apt, Vaucluse); "I went with the young men of my commune" (Assions, Ardèche); "I followed the crowd, I saw many men in it who knew what they were about, and I believed I should do as they did" (Dornecy, Nièvre); "I marched with the entire population" (hamlet of Baugy, Nièvre); "I acted like everyone else" (Droiturier, Allier).[86] The example of "everyone else" reduced the abnormality and danger of revolt; it became both a justification for taking arms and a guarantee of success in the minds of the participants.

Thus, imitation was not only an individual motive for insurgency; it was a collective demand. The men who took arms often agreed that everyone in the community must share the risks of insurgency: "People said that since we were going, everyone must go," testified a day laborer at Thionne (Allier), and many rural crowds agreed.[87] Even women sometimes joined the chorus of voices against laggards: "A large number of women treated me as a weakling and a coward, and they said I'd be shot if I didn't leave," claimed a day laborer at Dornecy (Nièvre).[88] Such accusations of cowardice were difficult to refute. As a cultivator at Lablachère (Ardèche) testified, "I never wanted to join the movement, but Martin Brayasse, Malmuzat *fils*, baker, and Gilles *fils* kept telling me I was a coward, they would always despise me, I wasn't worthy of being from Lablachère, and they finished by winning me over."[89] Militants also rejected family responsibilities as a pretext for staying home: "I went to M. Angilbert's house to make him leave," a journeyman cobbler at St. Sauveur (Yonne) admitted. "I said to his wife, who was crying and holding him by the neck, 'I'm leaving my wife home, too. He has to do the same.' "[90] Threats of reprisal were the counterparts of moral pressures for unanimous participation. Some local militants invented "orders" to shoot the laggards, and crowds threatened that anyone who did not march would suffer

[86] Ints. Fr. Barral, shoemaker, ADD, M 1357; Fr. Froissac, ADG, 3U 5/1; H. Peysson, cult., ADV, 4M 65, #892; X. Monestier, 27, *peseur public*, ADV, 4M 61, #481; Victor Chabert, cult., ADA, 5M 18; Jn. Tissier, *manoeuvre*, ADN, Ins. Clamecy; Jn. Plancon, *manoeuvre*, ADN, Ins. Clamecy; Jn. Danton, stonecutter, AD Allier, M 1303.

[87] Int. Louis Rey, *journalier*, AD Allier, M 1300.

[88] Int. Jn. Saulge, *manoeuvre*, ADN, Ins. Clamecy.

[89] Tem. L. Blachère, cult., ADA, 5M 18.

[90] Int. L. Breton, JM-1851, #255.

in the future.[91] As a cultivator from Maruéjols (Gard) testified, "People insisted that those who didn't march would be treated roughly at the return." A cultivator at Comps (Drôme) echoed these words: "Many people in the village said that if someone didn't leave, people would come to get him tomorrow." Similarly, a tailor from Lagorce (Ardèche) reported hearing that "everyone is going to Largentière and those who don't march will be noticed and will repent later."[92] In the popular imagination, harm would befall anyone who shunned the general call to arms.

If threats symbolized the will to unanimity of crowds, they also expressed sociopolitical division within communities. In districts where many peasants lived in hamlets and farmsteads, such as the central Drôme, the southwestern Yonne, and the central Gers, rebels deployed bands in order to recruit laggards in the countryside. Of course, peasants who resided in dispersed settlements had reason to claim afterward that they had been forced to march by passing bands even if they had been eager to join everyone else at the time. As the mayor of one village in the Drôme commented about such excuses, "It is difficult to believe that so many men were intimidated by the appearance of such a small number of agitators."[93] Nonetheless, bands *did* intimidate peasants on isolated farmsteads in some communes. At Montboucher (Drôme), for example, where the Montagnards decided to recruit nonmembers of the underground, the spokesman of one band told a tenant farmer: "The entire population of Montboucher is leaving. You are being requisitioned. In the name of the law, march with us! We need your men, your weapons, and your munitions."[94] Similarly, at Soyans (Drôme) bands visited peasant households in the hamlets and farmsteads to force all the able-bodied men to march. One middle-aged peasant proprietor later denounced two men for telling him he had to march "by order of force," two more for leading a subsequent band to recruit him "on pain of death," and another three for finally succeeding in forcing him to march by hitting him with their weapons. Montagnards in this commune used force not only to maximize their manpower but to punish their enemies. According to one elderly owner-farmer, the *chef* of the rebels told him angrily, "If you hadn't denounced me last June, I wouldn't have been arrested and put in prison. Now it's my turn to

91 For examples of such "orders," see dossier Ad. Varennes, *cerclier* at Treigny (Yonne), JM-1851, #258; dossier Fr. Eynard, tailor at Plan-de-Baix, ADD, M 1361; and Tem. Eugène Truc, at Brue-Auriac, AD Var, 4M 19.
92 Tem. Et. Villaret, ADG, 3U 5/1; Tem. Jos. Broc, ADD, M 1354, dossier Comps; Int. A. Charbonnier, ADA, 5M 18.
93 Letter from the mayor of Beaufort, Dec. 26, 1851, ADD, M 1353, dossier Beaufort.
94 Tem. Pr. Ant. Roussin, *fermier*, ADD, M 1354, dossier Montboucher.

hold you prisoner. You must come with the rest of us." They may have also used bands to "liberate" younger sons from the authority of their landowning fathers. As a fifty-year-old owner-farmer from Soyans testified, "A troop of men came to my farm (*domaine*), asking for my two sons to make them go. At the sound of the tocsin. I'd hid them." His sons returned and went to the village, supposedly "fearful of ill treatment" while admittedly curious "to see what was happening."[95] Bands in the central Drôme also recruited sharecroppers and farm servants whose employers remained aloof from the movement. A middle-aged peasant proprietor at Montclar testified that when a band arrived, he offered them a glass of wine, "because three of them had worked for me." After a friendly exchange, "they consented to leave me alone, provided my two servants join them." He added that two flax combers who happened to be working for him were also "forced to march."[96] The sons and other dependants of proprietors who resided in the countryside might enter the ranks of the insurgents "by force" only because they were unable to disobey their parents and employers.

While forcible recruitment usually involved ordinary residents of the countryside, forcible disarmament reflected class cleavages in rural communities. The broad mass of the rural population was sharply differentiated from a thin stratum of landlords, professional men, and functionaries. Where political animosities sharpened the disunity between upper and lower echelons of the social hierarchy, insurgents were tempted to disarm their class enemies. In several villages and hamlets of the central Drôme, for example, crowds demanded weapons from prominent men of order, including fifteen landlords, three innkeepers, two food merchants, and a tax collector.[97] "It's about time to search his house," said rebels at the hamlet of Derbières (Savasse), as a crowd of 200 men disarmed the former mayor, a sixty-six-year-old landlord who had probably helped the gendarmes search *their* houses for weapons before the coup d'état. According to a sixty-eight-year-old landlord in the neighboring commune of Lachamp, a large number of men came to demand his son (the *adjoint*) and his son's rifle. "Go ahead now and get the gendarmes," they joked, alluding to the *adjoint's* use of gendarmes to help enforce closing hours in the cafés and inns of the commune.[98] A stronger undertone of social rather than po-

[95] Tems. R. Lantelme, 59, owner-farmer, Jn. Pr. Got, 62, owner-farmer, and Jq. Tavan, 50, owner-farmer, ADD, M 1355, dossier Soyans.
[96] Tem. Jn. Claude Terrail, 47, *prop.*, ADD, M 1354, dossier Montclar.
[97] Tabulation based on testimonies in dossiers Lachamp, Savasse, and Sauzet, ADD, M 1354, 1355.
[98] Tems. P. Chapon, priest, Jn. Ant. Sestier, *prop.*; Jn. Pr. Espenel, *prop.*, ADD, M 1354 (Lachamp), 1355 (Savasse).

litical antagonism appeared in some communes where anti-Republicans were disarmed. According to the Montagnard leader at St. Sauveur, lower-class rebels told him, "We want to go to the houses of all the bourgeois in order to take their weapons."[99] At the village of Pousseaux, a crowd of *flotteurs* tried to disarm the mayor, an elderly wood merchant, and someone shot him dead when he threatened to open fire from his second-story window.[100] Republican municipalities granted vociferous popular demands to disarm "the proprietors" at Besse (Var) and "the bourgeois" at Bessan (Hérault).[101]

In several villages peasants made a special trip to the nearby château, where they insisted on searching for weapons. Such visits betrayed a traditional pattern of popular action in time of food crises—requests (or demands) for bread and wine from the storehouse of the *châtelain*. One day laborer who accompanied a band to the château of M. Bandin, near St. Sauveur, later explained to magistrates: "Because I was tired and hungry, I just said that if they wanted to give me some wine, bread, and cheese, I'd be pleased."[102] The *fermier* of the château de Berardesc (Fox-Amphoul, Var) testified that a band of 150-200 men who searched the premises meticulously for arms and munitions also asked for and received wine in the courtyard. These rebels were careful not to "pillage" the château—they gave the *fermier* all the cash that they found on the premises—but their military operation was also a popular eruption into a forbidden storehouse of wealth, hence their ritual request for wine.[103] In the popular consciousness, disarmament of the rich symbolized the transfer of power to the poor; weapons and wine might be equally coveted.

Just as the rebels appealed for unanimous support in many villages, so they often adopted communal symbols of authority, such as the tricolor flag, and communal forms of collective action, such as the military parade. In the larger agglomerations, their occupancy of the *mairie* was generally the decisive public event. In the smaller villages, where a separate building for municipal affairs did not always exist, the mayor's house or the church often attracted the first public bands. In either case, political and military preparations followed customary patterns: crowds applauded the installation of new municipal authorities

[99] Int. Amédée Patasson, *musicien*, JM-1851, #255.
[100] Martinet, *Clamecy*, pp. 81-82; Tems. and Ints. in ADC, CG Clamecy.
[101] Int. Fr. Fabre, cult. at Besse, AD Var, 4M 19; and Int. Pr. Albert, *vigneron* at Bessan, ADH, 39M 144.
[102] Int. Jn. Cloutier, at St. Sauveur, JM-1851, #255.
[103] Tem. Et. Grégoire, *fermier*, in AD Var, 4M 19, dossier Fox-Amphoul. The only château where valuables were stolen by a peasant band was owned by the Legitimist mayor of Le Donjon (Allier). According to P-G Riom, insurgents broke the furniture and took away seven sets of silver (letter of Dec. 9, 1851, AN, BB^{30} 395).

at the *mairie*; militants distributed whatever national-guard weapons were deposited there; bands rang the tocsin or obtained the tricolor flag and the drum of the commune; and guards prevented anyone from leaving the village. Once all the inhabitants had been assembled, national-guard officers or former military men often stepped forward to arrange them in military ranks. Long lines of men then filed out of the commune, marching to the step of the village drummer. Sometimes a red flag fluttered above the column, but more commonly it was the tricolor flag of the Republic. In a few communes, mayors or *adjoints* lent their authority to these public events. At St. Médard (Gers), for example, the mayor convoked the inhabitants on the public square and ordered them to march: at Lussan (Gard), the mayor helped distribute the rifles of the national guard; at Moissac (Var), the *adjoint* pronounced the dissolution of the municipal council and named a new municipal commission, with himself as mayor: and at Marsanne (Drôme), the *adjoint* commanded the rebels once they had taken arms and formed a marching column.[104] However, most municipal officials remained detached from the Montagnard cause, as noted in Chapter Nine. Less than one-tenth of the rebel communes in the nation had the active support of a mayor or *adjoint*.[105] Yet insurgents in many communes behaved *as if* they had municipal authorization. It was not the leadership role of the mayor but the collective style of the populace which revealed the importance of communal traditions. Whether they were demonstrating in front of the *mairie*, displaying the flag, sounding the alarm, or marching in a column, the rural insurgents of 1851 were repeating traditional modes of behavior.

The Montagnards succeeded in obtaining nearly unanimous participation in many communal mobilizations. As one mayor in the central Drôme reported, "The male population of the commune, with the exception of a few old men, the sick, and the children, all departed; the commune was left in the hands of God."[106] Thirty-five communes in this region contributed overwhelming public support to the revolt. So did most of the villages near Anduze (Gard), Aups (Var), Clamecy (Nièvre), Lavardac (Lot-et-Garonne), St. Sauveur (Yonne), and Vallon (Ardèche), as well as some of those near Barjols (Var), Jaligny

---

[104] Dagnan, *Le Gers*, II, 75; ADG, 3U 5/3 canton of Lussan; Tem. C. Roux, AD Var, 4M 19, dossier Moissac; Ints. Denis Fare, *adjoint*, and Jos. Gauthier, *journalier*, ADD, M 1361, 1362.

[105] I have identified forty mayors and twenty-nine *adjoints* who helped the rebels in several hundred communes, located in eleven major zones of revolt. Municipal officials played a role in 5/52 rebel communes in *arr.* Béziers, 7/72 communes in the central Drôme, and 9/45 communes in *arr.* Brignoles (with a moderating influence in several cases, such as Besse).

[106] Report of the mayor of Cliousclat, Dec. 10, 1851, ADD, M 1353, dossier Cliousclat.

(Allier), Mirande (Gers), Pézénas (Hérault), and Poligny (Jura). The shift from secret preparations to public mobilizations brought about a redefinition of collective actors. Montagnard societies seemed to vanish into the social world of all adult males within the community. Significantly, observers tended to describe rebel columns as "the men" (*les gens*) or "the young men" (*les jeunes gens*) from such and such a commune. In the words of one witness at Vallon, "I saw the men of Lagorce arriving; they were marching in good order like soldiers, shouting and singing and making a great noise."[107] Even Montagnard leaders sometimes described their role in social rather than political terms: "I led the young men of St. Gervais," testified the vice-president of the Montagnard society in that village of the Drôme.[108] As Agulhon notes with respect to the Var, "Crowds often appear to be still formed (in large part) of entire villages, communal unanimities."[109] Thousands of rebels who took arms against the coup d'état saw themselves less as the affiliates of a political organization than as the residents of a community. It was by activating communal traditions that Montagnards brought so many rebels into the field against the forces of order in December 1851.

[107] Int. Pr. Massot, *portefaix*, ADA, 5M 18.
[108] Int. Prosper Chavanet, 29, shoemaker, ATML, Ins., Affair St. Gervais.
[109] Agulhon, *La République au village*, p. 452.

· II ·

COLLECTIVE VIOLENCE

At two o'clock on Saturday afternoon, December 6, the gendarmes of
Clamecy saw a crowd of men, women, and children advancing up the
hill toward their barracks in the center of town. A makeshift column
of 200 armed men led the march, shouting "Long live the Republic!"
Spokesmen soon arrived at the door to demand the disarmament of the
gendarmes. Inside the barracks, a few dozen government supporters,
including the subprefect, had also taken refuge after gunfire had driven
them from the town hall the previous evening. A gendarme and a
rebel had died in that earlier fray, and now the crowd was in an ugly
mood. Shouts of "Death!" greeted a compromise plan for the gendarmes
to keep their weapons after surrendering their munitions. The subprefect and the civilians fled out the back door, but the lieutenant and four
gendarmes continued to debate the terms of their disarmament. One
Montagnard leader, the hardware merchant Guerbet, tried desperately
to maintain discipline—"Don't fire!" he cried out. "Whoever opens
fire I'll have shot!" It was too late. A gendarme named Bidan suddenly
appeared at the door, carrying his carbine. Several rebels who had
clambered up the stairs began scuffling with him on the porch, trying
to take away the gun. One of them pulled him into full view of the
crowd below. "Kill him!" people shouted, and first one gunman, then
others, opened fire at close range. Their shots knocked him down the
stairs and into the street. Men swarmed around the fallen gendarme,
and a *flotteur* from Pousseaux beat on his head with a pickhammer.
Bidan made one last effort to rise. More bullets slammed into him. Unconscious and nearly dead, his body covered by fifty-four wounds
from over a dozen different weapons, the victim of the crowd's rage
was finally carried off to the hospital, where he expired soon afterward.[1]

This mob scene at Clamecy seemed to confirm upper-class fears of
popular violence, and assaults on gendarmes, which occurred in several
other towns as well, came to symbolize popular savagery in the eyes
of Bonapartist officials. Yet such outbursts of crowd vengeance were
exceptional rather than typical events in December 1851, and the mag-

[1] The most useful eyewitness accounts of this event were given by Jn. Bapt.
Cliqued, maître d'hôtel at Clamecy, Pr. Cuisinier, *flotteur* at Pousseaux, and
Maurice Davy, *médecin* at Dornecy, all in CG Clamecy; and S-P Clamecy to M.
Carlier, Dec. 9, 1851, in AG, G⁹ 186-87, Nièvre. See also Ténot, *La province*, pp.
36-37, based on newspaper reports of the *Counseil de Guerre*.

nitude of violence was surprisingly low in most rebel districts. Tens of thousands of men took arms and captured local power in nearly two hundred towns, bourgs, and villages, but they clashed violently with troops or gendarmes in only two dozen localities, and they killed only nine gendames, nine soldiers, and four civilians throughout the nation. As the *procureur-général* at Aix wrote of the typical protest movements in the Ardèche, the Gard, and the Vaucluse, "There have been none of the murders, the pillages, and all the horrors that one might so justly have expected. . . . A certain moderation, a certain legality (pardon the expression) characterized the actions and the speeches of the leaders."[2] Where rebel discipline did break down, it resulted more often in headlong flight than in anarchic violence. Despite the dramatic impact of events at Clamecy, it was the less obtrusive violence of the army—disciplined, rational, and systematic—which proved decisive. Indeed, military officers initiated most of the skirmishes that resulted in bloodshed. From the perspective of collective violence, the organizational capabilities of the army were a more potent cause of deaths and injuries then the passions of the rebels.

The rapid defeat of Montagnard demonstrators in 1851 underscores the importance of military organization in violent civil conflicts. The search for psychological origins of violence has misled some social scientists into assuming that casualties in rebellions are a function of the intensity of popular deprivation, frustration, and anger.[3] In fact, violence is often a contingent feature of group actions that are normally nonviolent, and its probability depends less on popular motivation than on government tactics of repression and accommodation. As Tilly has shown in his study of collective protest in modern France, violence characteristically erupts when police or troops intervene to break up demonstrations, and the well-armed forces of order usually inflict most of the casualties that occur in civil disorders. In the rare cases when opponents of a regime succeed in organizing a strong military force, army and police casualties may increase dramatically, but internal wars are likely to exact a much heavier price from the rebels themselves, as the June Days and the Paris Commune showed. On balance, the militarization of protest favors the agents of authority rather than the forces of dissent. Not surprisingly, "intrinsically nonviolent" forms of protest, such as the strike and the unarmed demonstration, have prevailed in modern France.[4]

[2] *Rapport* P-G Aix, Dec. 17, 1851, cited by Vigier, *La Seconde République*, II, 334.

[3] Thus, Gurr argues that "the greater the intensity of deprivation, the greater the magnitude of violence." Gurr, *Why Men Rebel*, p. 9.

[4] C. Tilly, et al., *The Rebellious Century*, pp. 16-24, 44-55, 84-86, 238-64.

It was the historic destiny of the Montagnards to prove that armed demonstrations had become an anachronistic form of political dissent in the French provinces by the mid-nineteenth century. In taking arms against the government, they appeared to engage in an intrinsically violent form of collective action, analogous to the tax revolts of earlier years. Yet unlike these "primitive" peasant movements against centralized authority, the insurrections of 1851 involved seizures of political power as well as threats of popular violence. By borrowing the military procession from a traditional repertoire of communal forms of action, leaders hoped to deploy their men in deliberate and controlled assertions of popular sovereignty. It was less the violent overtones than the organizational discipline of the armed demonstration that gave it such ascendancy as a form of collective action. Herein lay the irony of events: the armed political demonstration seemed relatively modern in comparison with the anarchic crowd, but as an instrument of military force, it was hopelessly outclassed by the French army. Instead of giving the Republicans serious leverage against the government, rebel columns succeeded mainly in galvanizing the repressive energies of the army. The disastrous outcome of insurgency in December 1851 proved that armed demonstrations had no future in France. Henceforth, the predominant form of collective action in rural confrontations with the state would become the *unarmed* demonstration, a development already foreshadowed by the unarmed protests against the coup d'état in many cities.

If the armed demonstration was the generic form of collective action in 1851, the *violent* demonstration was a more specialized form of interaction between dissidents and repressive agents of the state. Collective violence almost never occurred unless gendarmes or troops were present, and its intensity then depended primarily on the capacity of the rival military formations to inflict casualties on each other. Where armed crowds confronted small units of gendarmes, they either succeeded in intimidating these forces of order or assaulted them with relative impunity. Where the rebels confronted regular units of the army, the balance of power shifted in the other direction, and violence generally favored the state. Casualties often occurred accidentally, and neither side was usually motivated by uncontrollable anger. These generalizations can be confirmed by examining the full range of nonviolent and violent confrontations that occurred between rebels and local or centralized authorities after the coup d'état. For purposes of exposition, occupations of municipal premises will be discussed first, followed by clashes with gendarmes, and skirmishes with troops, in ascending order of violence.

Republicans undertook illegal occupations of around two hundred town halls or *mairies*, where they installed new municipal authorities or obtained weapons from national-guard depots.[5] Yet these seizures of political power and military equipment rarely encountered any resistance from local officials. In three-quarters of the cases, the mayors lacked any military force with which to oppose the demands of the Montagnards. Even in the fifty towns and bourgs where they had brigades of gendarmes at their disposal, municipal officials rarely tried to disperse demonstrators. At most, they assembled loyal supporters—"men of order"—at the *mairie*, hoping to intimidate the Montagnards. If this failed, they almost always abandoned the municipality without bloodshed. As for the Republicans, they often took precautions to avoid violence, too. Instead of breaking into the *mairies*, they generally tried first to obtain the keys from the mayor, and sometimes they asked him to open the doors for them. If they anticipated serious opposition, they sometimes obtained assistance from other communes before confronting the mayor, and in a few cases they marched toward the *mairie* in military formation. Yet unarmed crowds were just as likely as armed bands to initiate changes in municipal authority. It was by occupying the *mairies* that they often established their claim to military power, distributing the rifles on deposit and posting guards under the command of the new commissions. The respective caution of officials and demonstrators ensured that nearly all of these municipal resolutions occurred without deaths or injuries. Only at Capestang, Clamecy, and Cuers did insurgents open fire on gendarmes who were trying to protect the *mairies*: elsewhere, they occupied these symbols of communal authority against token opposition or none at all.

Most attempts to change local authorities were concentrated in six departments of southern France, with successes most frequent in the Var (48 communes), and the Hérault (19), followed by the Lot-et-Garonne (12), the Basses-Alpes (10), the Gers (9), and the Vaucluse (7). The factors that exerted the most influence on these municipal revolutions were political rather than military: (1) the examples of nearby towns; (2) the ambitions of Montagnard leaders; (3) the "communal" style of popular involvement in politics; and (4) the attitudes of local mayors. Both the form and outcome of local bids for power depended on whether these factors encouraged ceremonial displays of crowd solidarity, paramilitary seizures of municipal premises, or negotiations and withdrawals in the face of opposition. The range of out-

---

[5] I have tabulated 188 installations of new municipal officials and another 76 occupations of municipal premises (usually for weapons) in rebel districts. Sources for this tabulation include the registers of the Mixed Commissions, the interrogations of suspects, and the correspondence of local officials.

comes can be illustrated from five regions where some challenges to municipal authority occurred: the *arrondissements* of Béziers and Brignoles, where Montagnards often succeeded in proclaiming revolutionary commissions without encountering significant opposition; the *arrondissement* of Orange, where they attempted without much success to negotiate a share of municipal power; the *arrondissement* of Marmande, where they used military formations with varying success to intimidate local authorities, and the *arrondissement* of Condom, where they generally failed to overcome the opposition of local officials and men of order.

Montagnards challenged the authorities in sixteen communes of the *arrondissement* of Béziers, including three towns (Béziers, Bédarieux, and Pézénas) and four bourgs that served as cantonal seats (Capestang, Florensac, Roujan, and Servian). The most serious confrontation occurred between armed demonstrators and troops at Béziers, where fighting erupted at the initiative of the soldiers and resulted in disaster for the insurgents (see Chapter One). When the clashes between armed crowds and gendarmes at Bédarieux and Capestang are added to the roster of bloody incidents in the *arrondissement*, it would appear that Montagnards generally tried to conquer power by force of arms. Furthermore, their temporary successes in some communes brought a dramatic reversal in the social basis of municipal leadership. None of the forty-eight new municipal officials had been *censitaires* in 1847, as compared with thirty-two of the eighty-six deposed municipal councilors; and only one-quarter of them were proprietors, professional men, merchants, or owner-farmers, as compared with over nine-tenths of the previous officials. Reflecting the social composition of the Montagnard societies, artisans and agricultural laborers came to power in the new municipal commissions. From the perspective of police bureaucrats and wealthy men of order, this heralded a social as well as a political revolution.[6]

A closer examination of these local transfers of authority shows, however, that they were more common near Pézénas, where officials negotiated with demonstrators, than near Béziers and Bédarieux, where they resorted to force. Montagnards in bourgs and villages near Pézénas created five of the seven municipal commissions that briefly obtained public recognition in the *arrondissement*. It was the urban example of a *nonviolent* change in municipal personnel which inspired

---

[6] This analysis is based on the interrogations and dossiers of revolutionary municipal officials at Alignan-du-Vent, Boussagues-Latour, Caux, Faugères, Nézignan-l'Evêque, Quarante, Roujan, and St. Thibéry; the dossiers of municipal councilors from these communes; and the *Censitaire* lists for 1847-48. See ADH, *9M 42-45, 1847; 17M 30-32; and 39M 144-60.

them. Peasants in this area also revealed their moderation by gathering in large numbers without arms to accompany their Montagnard leaders to the *mairies*. After attending the ceremonial installation of the new authorities, they soon returned to work in the fields. These municipal "revolutions" provided Montagnards with an opportunity to acquire the dignity of office. They were community rituals, following a traditional script, in which lower-class militants enjoyed for a brief moment the public honor normally reserved for conservative landlords. However much the democratization of municipal personnel might appear to threaten the social and political order, its main impulse was to equalize prestige, not power or wealth.[7]

The *arrondissement* of Brignoles led the nation in municipal revolutions. Montagnards in twenty-four of its fifty-four communes established commissions, and those in another eight communes replaced mayors or *adjoints*.[8] Although armed demonstrators from several bourgs and villages helped townsmen overthrow the authorities at Brignoles and St. Maximin, most transfers of municipal power in the *arrondissement* occurred without the threat of force. Only a few mayors were swept aside by hostile demonstrators, and some were sympathetic to the Montagnards. Nor did "men of order" resist changes in municipal personnel. Only at Carcès did a small number of national guardsmen turn out to guard the *mairie*, and even these "bourgeois" did not object strongly when Montagnards held a large meeting to elect a new mayor and *adjoint* by acclamation.[9] Provençal cultural traditions imparted distinctive forms of collective action to the municipal changes in the region: the *farandole* dance, the civic procession (*promenade*), the honorific demonstration (*ovation*). Thus, peasants at Montmeyan danced the *farandole* and sang the Marseillaise to form the crowd that "elected" a twelve-man commission; villagers paraded through the streets of Camps to celebrate the proclamation of a new municipality; and a crowd at Tavernes held an honorific banquet (*ovation bachique*) on the public square after installing a new municipality in the town hall.[10] As for the armed men who paraded in some demonstrations, they, too, were imitating a traditional form of collective action: the *bravade*, or militia procession with honorific rifle fire in the air. "Why did you carry a weapon on Sunday, the seventh," magistrates asked a cultivator at Tourves, where a municipal commission

---

[7] For a detailed narrative of these events in the Hérault, see Margadant, "Insurrection," pp. 439-50.

[8] Tabulation based on Ints. of suspects and reports of J. P.s in *arr.* Brignoles, AD Var, 4M 19, 26; and register of MC Var, AN, BB[30] 398.

[9] Ints. Z. Mireur and Jos. Portal, AD Var, 4M 19, dossier Carcès.

[10] AD Var, 4M 19, dossiers Montmeyan, Camps, Tavernes.

took power that day. "It was to render honors to the authorities," he replied.[11] Of course, weaponry also had an explicit military purpose, especially in communes that deployed armed columns elsewhere, but above all it heralded Montagnard claims to the dignity of office. Most civic demonstrations in the *arrondissement* were pacific in tone, however bellicose their appearance.

Montagnards in several bourgs near the town of Orange tried to occupy their *mairies* on the pretext of defending order. Their maneuvers for civic recognition were inspired by two events at Orange: a crowd demonstration in front of the town hall on the evening of December 3; and a secret "committee" of Montagnard leaders, formed afterward in a local café. The demonstration, which threatened to erupt in violence when several hundred Republicans began insulting a small post of ten soldiers, ended peaceably when the mayor and the *adjoint* arranged a compromise: the *dragons* withdrew to the subprefecture, and citizens from the local fire brigade occupied the guard post.[12] Although the subprefect and the municipal authorities remained in office, Montagnard leaders formed a committee to organize resistance elsewhere in the *arrondissement*. It was the example of Orange that inspired Montagnards at Caderousse, Montdragon, Mornas, Sérignan, Valréas, and Uchaux to form their own committees and to gather at the *mairies*, where they hoped to post armed guards with the permission of the mayors. This subtle strategy worked temporarily at Mornas, where the Montagnards told the mayor that they wanted to keep him in office, while boasting to his secretary that now *they* were the masters. Yet none of these unarmed gatherings resulted in any real transfers of municipal power. Thus, at Caderousse and Montdragon, where small bands of 20-30 Montagnards faced armed men of order, they offered their services politely to the mayors and then withdrew, singing the Marseillaise; at Sérignan a crowd of 200 men abandoned its effort to obtain the keys to the *mairie* when the local authorities threatened to call in troops from Orange; and at Mornas the 50-60 occupants of the *mairie* stopped trying to obtain weapons when the mayor and the gendarmes pointed out that they were going to compromise themselves. Intrigue and caution rather than audacity and violence characterized the Montagnards who organized demonstrations in this region.[13]

[11] Int. Jos. Tochon, cult., AD Var, 4M 19, dossier Tourves.

[12] P-G Nîmes, Dec. 7, 1851, AN, BB[30] 395; Tem. L. Massart, gendarme, Tem. F. Tardieu, *adjoint*, and *Rapport* CP, Dec. 12, 1851, in ADV, 4M 53; Aimé Autrand, "Commemoration de la résistance vauclusienne au coup d'état du 2 décembre 1851," in *L'annuaire administratif et statistique du Vaucluse* (1951), pp. 314-16.

[13] For these events around Orange, see Tems. in ADV, 4M 53; and François Veyne, "L'insurrection républicaine dans le canton d'Orange lors du coup d'état du 2 décembre 1851," unpublished Mémoire de Maîtrise, Aix-en-Provence, 1970.

Military forms of collective action did play a role in the municipal revolutions near Marmande, where a provisional commission nominated the former cavalry officer Peyronni as "supreme commander of the national guards in the *arrondissement.*" Peyronni issued an order on December 5 for "the citizens in each commune to take arms." After organizing their "internal defense," all available citizens were supposed to march to the subprefecture.[14] This order became the pretext for Montagnards in a few bourgs and villages of the region to seize weapons and replace the municipal authorities. When 30 armed townsmen arrived at the cantonal seat of Bouglon, for example, "most of the inhabitants" joined them on the public square, brandishing farm implements as weapons. Their Montagnard leader claimed to exercise the "mandate" of the "newly constituted authority" at Marmande. In the words of one cultivator, "He showed us a printed proclamation by Peyronni, which I regarded as an order from higher authority." Some 200 men obtained from the mayor the national-guard rifles on deposit at the *mairie,* and they proclaimed a five-man commission. "We are in a revolution," people said, "so we must name revolutionaries."[15] Yet nowhere did rebels in this area actually back up a threat of force with violent action. Most rural communes remained quiescent, and several small bands withdrew in the face of resolute mayors. At Argenton, for example, a "troop" of 40 armed men tried to get the papers of the commune from the mayor, but they left as soon as he pulled two pistols on them and threatened to open fire.[16] Weight of numbers and force of personality were more important than weaponry and military organization in these Montagnard bids for local power.

Bourgeois Republicans at Condom led 500-600 armed men to seize the town hall on the evening of the fifth, but their revolutionary commission, which lasted for less than a day, had few imitators elsewhere in the *arrondissement.* Only at the bourg of Gondrin did a Montagnard *chef,* a building contractor named Blaise Mondin, muster enough popular support to replace the mayor and the municipal council with a commission of five Republican moderates. Aided by peasant bands from outlying hamlets and two neighboring communes, Mondin and his local affiliates then marched to Condom, numbering 150-200 men. By contrast, 50 Montagnards at the cantonal seat of Eauze occupied the *mairie* on the same day to seize the rifles of the national guard, but they exchanged insults with the conservative mayor and 30-40 men of

[14] Ténot, *La province,* pp. 63-64.

[15] Ints. Cyprien Blouin, cult., and Jq. Bergat, cult.-*carrier*; Tems. of eyewitnesses, in AD L-G, 4U, Ins., *arr.* Marmande, canton of Bouglon.

[16] Letter from Mayor of Argenton, in AD L-G, 4U, Ins., *arr.* Marmande, canton of Bouglon.

order instead of establishing a revolutionary commission or marching to Condom. "You don't even have the courage to take a gun," the mayor taunted one demonstrator, and the mayor's friends greeted with shouts of derision the proposal that a commission be formed. Although the men of order withdrew to the main public square, the Montagnards abandoned the *mairie* voluntarily a few hours later at news that order had been restored at Condom. Even temporary defiance of local opponents seemed too risky for Montagnards in other communes. The *reductio ad absurdum* of their timid claims to power occurred at the village of Larroque-sur-Losse, where 5 armed men tried to occupy the *mairie* and appealed for peasant support against the mayor and a dozen men of order, including a rich landlord of noble lineage. Despite angry words that "all nobles are rabble," and despite threats to return with 50 men from Condom, the minuscule band gained no recruits. Public agitation at Larroque came to a rapid end as the 5 intrepid Montagnards laid down their weapons and went home.[17]

Armed demonstrators took a higher risk of violence if they confronted gendarmes rather than civilian authorities. For one thing, a more explicit military conflict existed in such cases. Montagnards had reason to fear the military power of the gendarmes, and they took measures to neutralize these soldiers of order. Frequently, they attempted to disarm local brigades, an aggressive posture that threatened the honor as well as the safety of the gendarmes. A second reason for violent conflict between Montagnards and gendarmes was their prior history of political and social antagonism. Not only had some brigades tried to apprehend conspirators before the coup d'état but many units had enforced unpopular laws governing the closing hours of cafés, the singing of songs, and the hunting of game.[18] The hunting laws, which many gendarmes enforced with increasing rigor in 1850-51 as an aspect of gun control, aroused special bitterness among the peasantry. As the *procureur-général* of Aix wrote in November 1851, "The hunting law is excessively unpopular, and its result is to create an antagonism between the (peasant) proprietors and the gendarmerie."[19] Some of the men who joined the insurrection had been fined earlier for hunting without a permit, and their resentments added fuel to the

---

[17] For descriptions of these several events, see Dagnan, *Le Gers*, II, 114-68 *passim*; and P-G Agen, Jan. 28, 1852, in AN, BB[30] 396.

[18] As the subprefect of Apt commented about a protest against the enforcement of closing hours at a country inn in 1849, "The lower class of the people is all the more hostile toward the gendarmerie because it is fulfilling its duty with more devotion and more exactitude." Letter on Dec. 23, 1849, in ADV, 4M 49.

[19] P-G Aix, Nov. 16, 1851, AN, BB[30] 370.

political conflict between Montagnards and gendarmes.[20] Finally, the internal organization and esprit de corps of the gendarmerie made its units more likely than civilian authorities to answer force with force rather than to surrender, negotiate, or retreat. The gendarmes were members of a national military organization designed to minimize local influences in the performance of police duties. They might be stationed outside their region of origin, regardless of whether they understood the local dialect, and they resided with their families in special government lodgings, or *casernes*. The extent of social segregation varied from brigade to brigade—some gendarmes were native to the region, and others married into local families.[21] Nonetheless, their training and supervision discouraged fraternization with local population. They were supposed to embody the military and judicial authority of the centralized government, and they were duty-bound to preserve the honor of their corps and the law of the state in riotous situations. Some brigades did try to disperse armed rebels singlehandedly after the coup d'état, and others joined regular army units in pitched battles with insurgents. The divergent military impulses and soiopolitical orientations of Montagnards and gendarmes implied a serious potentiality for violence in their interactions.

Systematic analysis of all collective protests involving gendarmes shows, however, that violence was uncommon. At least 60 confrontations between armed demonstrators and gendarmes took place in the nation, but only 12 of these incidents resulted in deaths or serious injuries, and only three involved minor casualties. If we distinguish between confrontations in which rebels tried to disarm gendarmes (34 cases), and those in which gendarmes tried to disperse rebels (17 cases), we find that insurgents were less prone to attack than to defend themselves against attack. They killed or wounded gendarmes in 1 out of 6 cases (6/34) in which the issue of disarmament was of central importance, while they inflicted casualties in retaliation to nearly half the attempts of gendarmes to disperse them by force (7/17 cases). Violence erupted above all when aggressive gendarmes collided with large and well-armed rebel forces. If casualties were so often avoided, this was because the rebels either succeeded in disarming the gendarmes without resistance (20 cases), or because they allowed the gendarmes to remain inside government buildings or to retreat to safety (at least 20 cases). The balance of military power was so disproportionately

[20] But in my 5 percent sample of persons judged by the MCs, only 19/1,156 of those residing outside the Seine had been fined for violating the hunting law.

[21] The P-G at Aix complained, for example, about gendarmes in the Basses-Alpes who had been "inactive" during the revolt because they were *gens du pays*, employed due to their knowledge of the local language. Letter of Jan. 19, 1852, in AN, BB[30] 396.

weighted toward the insurgents that gendarmes often behaved passively despite their code of honor. It was in the minority of cases where their aggressive reflexes provoked popular retaliation that gendarmes were likely to suffer casualties.[22]

Clearly delineated boundaries between insurgents and gendarmes helped to reduce the danger of violence. Where an armed band or crowd tried to disarm gendarmes who had taken refuge in their *caserne*, the physical barrier of the doorway delayed a face-to-face confrontation between the two sides. If large numbers of demonstrators threatened to force their way into the barracks, gendarmes nearly always abandoned any thought of resistance and allowed themselves to be disarmed. At the town of Apt, for example, a band of 200 insurgents marched to the barracks before dawn on December 7, and their spokesman, an artisan named André Seymard, announced to the gendarmes, "Your weapons or prison!" Voices from the crowd shouted, "Or we'll burn down the *caserne*!" The previous afternoon, a crowd had rescued from prison a villager accused of resisting arrest while hunting illegally, and now the peasants wanted to punish the gendarmes for issuing *procès-verbaux* against them. According to Seymard, "The crowd wanted to drag them to prison or open fire on them." Yet when the gendarmes accepted his terms and handed over their weapons, they were left alone.[23] At the town of Cluny, where popular antagonism fo-

---

[22] These tabulations are based on the following cases: (1) insurgents attempt to disarm gendarmes, inflicting casualties, at Barcelonnette, Bonny-sur-Loire, Clamecy, Cuers, Manosque, Monclar, Volonne; (2) insurgents attempt to disarm gendarmes, no casualties, at Barjols, Apt, Banon, Cluny, Le Donjon, Figeac, Fleurance, Forcalquier, La Garde Freinet, Lédignan, Le Luc, Marciac, Marseillargues, Mauvezin, Miélan, Mirabeau, Mirande, Neuvy-sur-Loire, Pignans, Poligny, Quissac, St. Christaud, St. Maximin, Salernes, La Suze, Tournus, Vidaubun; gendarmes attempt to disperse insurgents, suffering casualties, at Bédarieux, Capestang, Clamecy, Ouvèze (near Privas), La Palisse, St. André-de-Corcy, St. Bazeille; (3) gendarmes attempt to disperse insurgents, no casualties, at Agen, Bourganeuf, Chagny, Grane, Lumières, Mézin, Rignac, Roquevaire, St. Gengoux, Tonneins; (4) gendarmes attempt to disperse unarmed demonstrators, with casualties, at Estagel, Hyères, Montargis, Nancy, Prades, Rodez, Thiers; (5) gendarmes attempt to disperse unarmed demonstrators. no casualties, at Bar-sur-Aube, Brioude, Chalabres, Châtillon-sur-Seine, Crest, Floirac, Jouet, Louhans, Loudéac, Mornas, Orange, Pamiers, Pertuis, Reims, Rennes, Tulle, Valréas; (6) gendarmes take refuge in *casernes, mairies*, no injuries, at Bourdeaux, Eauze, Millhau, Moissac, Nérac, Pézénas, Riez, Villefranche, Villeneuve-sur-Lot (also Barjols, Fleurance, Lédignan, Marciac, Mauvezin, Tournus, listed under heading No. 1); (7) gendarmes unaccounted for, ordered to larger towns, not used, etc., at Aignan, Bouglon, Brignoles, Chomérac, Condom, Derbières-Savasse, Dieulefit, Florensac, Lavardac, Lumières, Le-Mas-d'Agenais, Saulce-Mirmande, St. Chinian, St. Gengoux, Sisteron, Vallon. Sources include the reports of officers of the gendarmerie (AG, F^1 51-54); the letters of P-Gs to M. Justice (AN, BB^{30} 395-403); local administrative correspondence; and the dossiers of the Mixed Commissions in departmental archives.

[23] Int. A. Seymard, joiner, and Tem. N. Robert, gendarme, ADV, 4M 58, #128;

cused on the *brigadier*, several hundred men arrived at the barracks on the evening of December 5. They threatened to burn it down in order to force the *brigadier* to open the gate. When he did so, the rebels disarmed his men and debated whether to imprison him, force him to march, or shoot him. "You've been causing evil long enough, this time we've got you!" For all their hostility, they decided only to imprison him, and before taking him to jail, they carefully wrote up a receipt for the weapons, munitions, and horses of the brigade. An hour later the *brigadier* was released by the provisional mayor, who asked him "not to be so harsh on the Republicans in the future." Perhaps he took these words to heart, for in his testimony he admitted recognizing only two of the insurgents.[24]

Barracks also gave gendarmes some physical security if they tried to defy rebel demands. At Mirabeau (Vaucluse), for example, the brigade refused to march with an armed band of eighty men who "besieged" their *caserne* at daybreak, December 7. The main rebel contingent, which came from the nearby village of Beaumont, was organized into ranks, with a commander, a drummer, and a flag bearer. Joined by a small band from Mirabeau, the men of Beaumont approached the barracks, shouting and threatening the gendarmes. Their spokesman, the young peasant leader François Blanc, stepped forward to the door and delivered a remarkable speech. The *brigadier* later testified:

> He told us that a new government had just replaced the old one. He had been delegated by this new government to represent it in the commune of Beaumont, so we owed him the same obedience which we had believed ourselves obliged to give our former leaders. He ordered us by virtue of his powers to follow them and to march with them on Pertuis to help establish the new government in this town. Our comrades at Pertuis had been taken prisoner by the sovereign people, and we would do well to obey immediately if we didn't want to suffer the same fate. We had only two choices: either come with them voluntarily, or be constrained by force.[25]

At this point, a chorus of voices arose from the insurgents, "March with us, or we'll shoot you!" The *brigadier* retorted that he would take orders only from his hierarchial superiors, and the insurgents debated what to do. Blanc advised everyone to withdraw, but a militant from Mirabeau insisted that they must at least disarm their adversaries. This

and Tems. A. Peyrard, *Brigadier*, and E. Cellier, jailkeeper, in ADV, 4M 76, dossier Apt.

[24] Tem. Fr. Thevenin, *brigadier*, in AD S-L, U, Ins. of 1851, dossiers from Cluny.

[25] Tem. T. Maillot, *Brigadier*, in ADV, 4M 74, canton of Pertuis.

compromise, which the local mayor helped to arrange, proved acceptable to the gendarmes. In exchange for their carbines, they were left alone at the *caserne*.[26]

In several other communes, the gendarmes stayed in their barracks and refused to hand over their weapons. At Lédignan (Gard) and Tournus (Saône-et-Loire), small bands of twenty-five to thirty men withdrew when energetic *brigadiers* threatened to oppose them with force.[27] As the *brigadier* at Tournus later testified, "I replied that they would not have the weapons of the gendarmerie until I had ceased to live, along with all my gendarmes."[28] He pointed two pistols at them and slammed the door in their face. At Barjols (Var), Fleurance (Gers), and Miélan (Gers), larger numbers of demonstrators posted guards at the *casernes* after the gendarmes defied their demands for weapons.[29] The rebels of Fleurance, who numbered four hundred to five hundred townsmen and villagers on the morning of December 4, betrayed their preference for defense rather than attack by constructing two barricades, guarded by thirty gunmen, in front of the barracks. As soon as the subprefect of Lectoure learned of this revolt, he hurried to the scene, accompanied by the *procureur* and two brigades of gendarmes. His small expeditionary force confronted the main rebel gathering on the town square, where a revolutionary municipality had just been proclaimed. Neither side felt strong enough to attack, but the subprefect had the advantage of moral authority. In a prolonged discussion, he rejected all proposals for compromise or clemency, and then he broke the stalemate by going to the rescue of the gendarmes at the *caserne*. "You can kill me," he replied to the threats of the men on the barricades, "but you cannot kill the law and you will go to jail."[30] These courageous words had a prompt effect: the insurgents laid down their weapons and demolished their own barricades. Rebels who had been guarding another barricade, on the road to Auch, quickly imitated their example, and everyone dispersed. By noontime, when fifty cavalry arrived from Auch, the town was calm again.

Gendarmes were naturally more exposed to violence if they stumbled across insurgents in open country, or if they found themselves surrounded and threatened by armed crowds in towns and bourgs. Several

---

[26] Int. Fr. Blanc, *agriculteur*; Tems. Fr. Rouvet, mayor of Mirabeau, and J. Biton, rural guard, in ADV, 4M 57, #73; 4M 74, canton of Pertuis.

[27] For Lédignan, see Tem. Et. Mendre, *brigadier*, ADG, 3U 5/1; and supplement to *Rapport* P-G Nîmes, Jan. 27, 1852, in AN, BB[30] 396-P440.

[28] *Maréchal des logis* Tournus, Dec. 4, 1851, AG, F[1] 51.

[29] For Barjols, see N. Blache, *Histoire de l'insurrection du Var*, p. 142; for Fleurance and Miélan, see Dagnan, *Le Gers*, II, 76-78, 90-98, and P-G Agen, Jan. 28, 1852 in AN, BB[30] 396-P440.

[30] Cited by Dagnan, *Le Gers*, II, 96.

incidents outside the *casernes* resulted in the injury, death or capture of gendarmes. This was the case in the countryside near Volonne (Basses-Alpes), where a band of fifty insurgents opened fire on the brigade of gendarmes, wounding one man; near Mirande (Gers), where several hundred peasants captured four gendarmes, one of whom was grazed by a bullet; and near Lédignan (Gard), where around five hundred peasants surrounded two gendarmes from the cantonal brigade, threatened to execute them, and pulled them from their horses in order to seize their weapons.[31] Violence also occurred at Manosque (Basses-Alpes), where gendarmes returning from a *tournée* came under rifle fire, suffering one wounded, and fell into the hands of the victorious insurgents, who forced them to march to Digne. The gendarmes at Barcelonnette (Basses-Alpes) similarly entered town after three hundred to four hundred men had taken arms, though in this case they surrendered after a less dangerous struggle in which the only casualty was a slight bayonet wound inflicted on the *maréchal des logis*.[32] At Mirande (Gers), violence was also averted because the gendarmes, who had attempted to ride on horseback from the *caserne* to a cavalry unit on the outskirts of town, surrendered as soon as the rebels threatened to shoot them.[33] Finally, demonstrators with guns did kill gendarmes who resisted disarmament in the streets of Cuers (Var) and Bonny-sur-Loire (Loiret).

Despite the explosive atmosphere in these armed confrontations, most demonstrators avoided the use of deadly force. They combined verbal threats and violent gestures in such a manner that the gendarmes were more likely to be roughed up and humiliated than seriously injured or killed. Popular restraint mirrored the exercise of state authority: just as lawbreakers suffered disarmament and imprisonment at the hands of the gendarmes, so now the gendarmes were forced to hand over their weapons and were placed under guard. When a patrol near Mirande fell into the hands of armed peasants, for example, a poacher hit upon the fitting mode of retaliation for previous fines and arrests: "Chain them up! Not long ago they chased me right out of my clogs while I was hunting, but now I've got them."[34] As for the violent scenes at Bonny and Cuers, in both cases only one man shot a gendarme, while large crowds of armed demonstrators held their fire. The man accused of murder at Bonny had a good reputation as an artisan, and his gun,

---

[31] For Volonne, see P-G Aix, Jan. 19, 1852, in AN, BB^{30} 396-P440; for the villages near Mirande, see Dagnan, *Le Gers*, II, 79-81 and P-G Agen, cited in n. 29; for Massillargues (near Lédignan), see P-G Nîmes, cited in n. 27, and gendarmerie Alais, Dec. 22, 1851, in AG, F^1 54.

[32] P-G Aix, cited in n. 31; Ténot, *La province*, pp. 174-75.

[33] P-G Agen, cited in n. 29.   [34] Dagnan, *Le Gers*, II, 79.

which he was pointing at a mounted gendarme's chest, probably went off accidentally when the gendarme suddenly pulled back his reins and tried to shove the barrel aside.[35] At Cuers, where poor peasants were brawling with the gendarmes in front of the *mairie*, one or two shots suddenly rang out and the *brigadier* collapsed with a fatal head wound. Agulhon has reconstructed this scene in detail, and he shows that the atmosphere was brutal, but not murderous. People were shouting "*Zou! Zou!*" (not "*Feu,*" or "Open Fire") at the gendarmes, and in the midst of the general excitement, a young peasant pulled his gun trigger, perhaps intending to fire into the air.[36]

If most demonstrators avoided deadly violence in confrontations with gendarmes who were clearly on the defensive, they behaved more aggressively toward gendarmes whose own actions appeared to legitimize the use of countervailing force. At Montargis and Bédarieux, gendarmes lost their lives after clashes in which rebels also died; and at St. André-de-Corcy, La Palisse, and Ste. Bazeille, gendarmes suffered heavy casualties while trying to charge on horseback against well-defended rebel positions. In several other cases—Capestang, Ouvèze (near Privas), Grane, Lumières—they retreated in the face of superior numbers, drawing gunfire, but only at Capestang was one of them seriously wounded. It was where gendarmes inflicted the first casualties or launched reckless cavalry charges that they became most exposed to mob vengeance or rebel counterfire.

The deaths at Montargis occurred during a scuffle between a small band of fifty to sixty unarmed demonstrators and two brigades of gendarmes, but those at Bédarieux involved a thousand vengeful rebels, who set fire to the barracks and killed three gendarmes.[37] This ferocious struggle resulted in a celebrated court-martial afterward, at which stories of murder and castration scandalized newspaper readers elsewhere in the nation. Yet for the townspeople of Bédarieux, the assault on the gendarmes was a righteous act of collective retaliation for the unprovoked murder of a worker. As noted in the previous chapter, rebels had already occupied the *mairie* on the evening of December 4 when shots were heard in the direction of the *caserne*. The *brigadier*, Liotard, and another gendarme named Brugières had left their refuge to track down a rebel sentinel, and both men had opened fire on a passing youth. Liotard's bullet found its mark, and Brugières grabbed

[35] Ténot, *La province*, pp. 10-12; Tems. at trial of E. Mallet, *La Gazette des Tribunaux*, Jan. 31, 1852.
[36] Agulhon, *La République au village*, pp. 429-35.
[37] For events at Montargis, where the *brigadier* shot an unarmed demonstrator and then died of a wound from his own saber, see Ténot, *La province*, pp. 8-10, based on Tems. at CG Montargis, *La Gazette des Tribunaux*, Feb. 20, 1852.

the victim and shouted, "You're only wounded, pig, you're only wounded!" The boy cried out, "My friends, help me!" and the gendarmes stepped back into the barracks and locked the door.[38] Liotard's commanding officer had described him back in April 1851 as "a very mediocre subordinate officer, totally lacking in elementary education."[39] Together with Brugières, he had unwittingly triggered the riot that would destroy them both.

Men poured into the street from a nearby café, screaming, "The rabble! the rabble! If we can't get them, set the place on fire." An old worker named Cabrol was shot dead early in the fight, and the cry of worker solidarity against the gendarmes brought hundreds of men to the scene. They came with memories of an incident back in October, when twelve hundred to fifteen hundred people had attended the funeral of a young baker whom the gendarmes had chased down and captured for hunting illegally. When the youth had sickened and died, the populace of Bédarieux had blamed the gendarmes.[40] Now the assault on the barracks became a righteous crusade against murderers, whose deserved fate was death. A crowd of furious women added their voices to the chorus of hatred: "Kill them! Kill them!" Rebels directed a fusillade at the barracks from the streets and neighboring buildings, but the six gendarmes inside—Liotard, Brugières, Lamm, Cirq, Flocon, and Seller—defended themselves with desperation, firing bullet after bullet out of the second-story windows. Both sides were shooting blindly—the gendarmes wounded only three insurgents after killing Cabrol, and none of them were hit in turn (though a bullet did gravely injure Flocon's wife). Finally, the crowd set fire to the *caserne*, and well-organized bands carried firewood from nearby bakeries to fuel the flames. According to Madame Lamm, "All the bakers of the faubourg except one gave wood to the insurgents, who formed a chain of men to pass the logs which would burn us." With their ammunition exhausted and their lungs bursting from the smoke, the gendarmes decided to surrender. Liotard appeared at the window and shouted down to the insurgents, "We ask for mercy! The fire has disarmed us!" He fell back, wounded by a volley of shots. The mob in the streets below wanted blood.[41]

Next, Flocon tried to surrender. "Death! Death!" roared the crowd. Over twenty shots drove him to cover, wounded. Seller, an Alsatian who had been stationed at Bédarieux for only nine months, tried to

[38] Tem. Marie Reymond, spinner, cited by Ténot, *La province*, p. 114.
[39] *Chef d'escadron* Béziers, Apt. 25, 1851, ADH, 39M 140.
[40] S-P Béziers, Oct. 19, 1851, ADH, 39M 132.
[41] Quotes drawn from Tems. Marie Reymond, cited by Ténot, *La province*, p. 114; Ch. Mical, cooper, Mme. Lamm, and Ant. Seller, gendarme, in CG Bédarieux, #13, #12, #111.

follow his wife and children out the front door. He was about to be killed when an insurgent named Eugène Combes jumped forward and led him to safety. Liotard crawled up to the third floor of the *caserne* and hid in the back room. Cirq, Lamm, Flocon, and Brugières fled through a courtyard to the rear of the building. The first three made it over a fence to a neighboring house, but Brugières was too wounded to follow them. The door of the courtyard burst open and a band of rebels opened fire, sending a bullet through his brain. Combes entered the courtyard to rescue Seller's horse, but when he rode past the rebels, they mistook him for another fleeing gendarme and shot him through the heart.[42]

Some townsmen began operating the fire pumps to save the barracks, but others searched the neighborhood for the missing gendarmes. Cirq, Lamm, and Flocon had all taken refuge in a nearby house. One band appeared, led by a Montagnard activist. It searched the house and left. A half hour later, a second band found Lamm hiding behind some wine barrels in the cellar, a pistol in his hand. "So, *coquin*, you're the one who fined us for hunting," someone said. Lamm was nearly shot on the spot. Outside the house large numbers of people were gathering while a Montagnard leader, the *cafetier* Malaterre, had Lamm tied up to be taken to the *mairie*. "People were talking of throwing Lamm into the water and then shooting him. Others said, 'Kill him right here.' There were so many people it was like the buzzing of flies." Miners from the commune of Graissessac had joined the riot, and some of them shouted, "We're gonna beat on his fat belly."[43] When Lamm appeared at the door, someone shoved him into the street. He died almost instantly under a hail of bullets.[44] Although poachers were later blamed for the crime, only 4 of the 259 men subsequently prosecuted for insurrectionary activity at Bédarieux had ever been fined for hunting. Perhaps personal enemies did fire the shots, but the crowd greeted Lamm's murder with general approval. One insurgent probably expressed the prevailing mood when he replied to Madame Lamm's reproaches on the next day, "Well, don't the ones they killed have just as much a right to complain?"[45]

A continued search of the house uncovered Cirq hiding in a hayloft.

[42] Ténot, *La province*, p. 117, based on Tems, Lamm and Cirq, both gendarmes; autopsy report of G. Touzen, doctor, *Le Messager du Midi*, May 20, 1852.
[43] Quotes drawn from Tems. Flocon, gendarme, L. Nougier, shoemaker, and Jn. Mical, cooper, in CG Bédarieux, #8, #204, #14.
[44] Tem. Fr. Cirq, ex-gendarme, CG Bédarieux, #9. The autopsy found only two bullet wounds and a nose fracture on Lamm's body (n. 42).
[45] Tem. Cirq. See also Tem. Rose Mical, "On the day afterward, people boasted of what they had done; some even thought they had earned medals," CG Bédarieux, #122.

A general cry went up, "Kill him like the other one!" but Malaterre intervened to save him. "You did me a service once, it's my turn now" —Cirq had permitted Malaterre to attend the funeral of a Montagnard a few months earlier despite police regulations against it.[46] Now he was rescued and escorted to the *mairie*. Flocon also survived. He hid under a bed until the following day, when he was taken to the *mairie*. As for Liotard, he met a ghastly end. The fire in the barracks had already been doused when the cry "To arms!" was heard, followed by gunfire. A small band had stumbled across Liotard in the dark. After a ferocious hand-to-hand struggle, the rebels had finished him off with six bullets in the chest and head. Heat from the gunblasts singed the corpse, so they drenched it in urine. The final indignity was castration, performed by an unknown psychopath during the night.[47]

The populace awoke as if from a nightmare on December 5. Armed guards patrolled the town, and the factories and workshops were closed for the day. The revolutionary municipality issued a proclamation blaming the gendarmes for "the murder of several citizens," and over fifteen hundred people attended the funerals of Cabrol and Eugène Combes. As for the dead gendarmes, large numbers of men, women, and children flocked to see their bodies, but no one attended their burials later in the day. For most inhabitants of Bédarieux, the rebels, not the gendarmes, were on the side of right and justice.[48]

Gendarmes who tried to disperse rebels met with success only against small bands. By contrast, large rebel forces were emboldened to counterattack. Thus, three gendarmes from the brigade of Bonnieux (Vaucluse) had no trouble dispersing twenty rebels at the nearby bourg of Lacoste on December 7, or capturing five prisoners in a band of thirteen on the road to Apt the following day. A fearless gendarme had marched up to the first band's leader and had seized his saber, whereupon several of the armed peasants had begun to weep, so great had been their shame and terror.[49] Yet when the second band was followed by a column of three hundred men, the gendarmes promptly abandoned their prisoners and took flight, drawing rebel gunfire.[50]

---

[46] Tems. Cirq and Flocon.

[47] Ténot denies that Liotard was castrated, but the CP testified that he exhumed the body one week after the murder and discovered that it had been "completely" castrated, testimony that M. Cayrol, a rural guard, confirmed. The coroner did not report this, but he testified, "I didn't see Liotard's body in the nude." Ténot, *La province*, p. 120; CG Bédarieux, #3, #5, #27.

[48] Tem. B. Theron, sect. of mayor, CG Bédarieux, #58, cited by Ténot, *La province*, p. 121; Tems. L. Guiraud, *portefaix*, G. Touzen, doctor, and J. Bonnel, ex-J. P., CG Bédarieux, #83, #27, #10.

[49] Tem. J. Barau, gendarme, ADV, 4M 74, commune of Lacoste.

[50] Judicial report in the canton of Gordes, ADV, 4M 74.

Similarly, the brigade at Capestang expected to disperse the crowd in front of the *mairie* on December 4, but instead it suffered assault. "It's the gendarmes!" people shouted, as the intrepid *cavaliers* rode onto the square, and they pushed forward excitedly. The mayor intervened to avoid bloodshed, but just as the gendarmes were wheeling their horses around to return to their barracks. François Caumette, a day laborer, opened fire. "Everything exploded," as at least ten other peasants let loose with a volley of shots which wounded one gendarme seriously.[51]

Events at La Palisse (Allier) and Ste. Bazeille (Lot-et-Garonne) showed the danger of precipitate assaults by gendarmes on well-organized rebel formations. Wealthy Republicans at Le Donjon, a market bourg near La Palisse, led the insurrection in that area, seconded by artisans and shopkeepers. They were much less hostile toward the local gendarmes, whom they disarmed and confined to the *caserne*, than toward the Legitimist mayor and the justice of the peace, whom they chained in irons and carried to La Palisse. Just before reaching this subprefecture on the morning of December 4, the 250-300 rebels from Le Donjon and nearby villages organized themselves into several sections, or *peletons*, commanded by former military men. Antoine Raquin, a grocer from the village of Montaiguet, led the first section, whose ranks were composed of well-armed insurgents (they had found a stockpile of around fifty army muskets at the J.P.'s house). The subprefect and twenty national guardsmen from La Palisse tried to halt them on the outskirts of town, but Raquin ordered a bayonet charge. The Donjonnais advanced on the double and put their opponents to flight. A few minutes later, they captured the subprefect at the *mairie*, which they occupied in order to obtain the guns in its national guard depot. Some rebels went to the church on a corner of the square to ring the tocsin, and others improvised a barricade in front of the *mairie*. At the sound of horses, a few men on the church terrace looked around the corner and spied the gendarmes of La Palisse, trotting to the attack with a column of 25-35 national guardsmen. "To arms!" they shouted, and rebels took up positions along the terrace, on the steps of the *mairie*, and behind the barricade. The lieutenant ordered his men to charge before they reached the street corner. With sabers drawn, they galloped onto the square and ran straight into a fussilade. Raquin had shouted "Fire!" after hearing two or three shots, and his men had delivered a massive blow to the gendarmes. The *maréchal des logis*, his

[51] For eyewitness accounts of this event, see, especially, Ints. M. Chambert, owner-farmer, and André Raux, *prop.-journalier*, CG Capestang; Tems. Ant. Decor, shoemaker, and Ad. Saisset, ex-mayor, CG Capestang; Ints. Jos. Cans, *journalier*, Jos. Dumas, *prop-journalier*, Ant. Grand, *prop.-journalier*, and Marcel Lignon, *journalier*, ADH, 39M 147, 149, 151, 153.

body riddled by twenty-one bullets, died on the spot. Under two dead horses lay the gendarmes Jaillard and Busson, the former wounded by fifteen bullets, the latter by eight. The lieutenant and the other two gendarmes escaped with minor wounds, and the national guardsmen fled without firing a shot. This debacle left the town in the hands of the Donjonnais, who disarmed some national guardsmen and tried without much success to recruit support from the local Republicans. When the courier arrived early in the afternoon, they learned that the government was in control of Paris, and shortly afterward, they heard rumors that cavalry were approaching town from two directions. Discouraged by their isolation, the insurgents returned to Le Donjon, where they disbanded later in the day. When the *chasseurs* from Moulins did enter La Palisse at 4:00 p.m., led by the subprefect (who had escaped during the fray), they found the town completely evacuated.[52]

On the outskirts of the bourg of Ste. Bazeille, a fortuitous collision took place between over five hundred insurgents from Marmande and several brigades of gendarmes. The rebels were expecting to fight against an infantry column from Bordeaux, while the gendarmes, who knew that the troops were moving up-river by steamboat, hoped to protect their disembarkation near Ste. Bazeille. Coming from opposite directions, these disproportionate forces stumbled across each other just before dawn on December 8. The rebels, who covered the center of the road, quickly took up defensive positions along both its sides, too. As for the gendarmes, they charged recklessly ahead. The commander of the men from Marmande, the former cavalry officer Peyronni, reacted instinctively to the threat of attack:

> I heard the cavalry without seeing them, because of the fog. I shouted, "Who goes there!" A volley of shots, one of which went through my cap, was the only reply. I turned back to my men and I shouted, "Fire!" I was so hoarse that no one heard me. The drummers beat the charge. I fired my two pistols and I waved my saber, shouting "Fire! Shoot your guns!" This time the fusillade began. When the cloud of smoke lifted, I saw that what I had mistaken for a squadron (of cavalry) was only a detachment of gendarmes, now fleeing from us.[53]

[52] For printed accounts of this revolt at Le Donjon and La Palisse, see Ténot, *La province*, pp. 13-17; Rougeron, "La résistance au coup d'état dans l'Allier," pp. 346-50; Jean Cornillon, *Le Bourbonnais en décembre 1851* (Cusset, 1903), pp. 71-90; and Denys Bournatot, *Le Donjon*, pp. 209-17. For archival documents, including Tems. and Ints. of eyewitnesses, see AD Allier, M 1301, especially Tems. A. Berthon, gendarme at Le Donjon, Jn. Combal, lieutenant of the gendarmerie at La Palisse, and Ant. Parier, *chaudronnier*; and Ints. Georges Gallay, prop., and Ant. Raquin, grocer.

[53] Int. Peyronni, CG Bordeaux, *La Gazette des Tribunaux*, Jan. 13, 1852, cited by Ténot, *La province*, p. 68.

According to lieutenant Flayolle, the commander of the gendarmes, his men had scarcely begun their charge when the order "Fire!" unleashed "a terrible explosion, accompanied by shouts and drumbeats."[54] Eight horses were shot down, and several gendarmes were wounded, including the *maréchal des logis*, who narrowly escaped being murdered after the shoot-out. The lieutenant rallied a few of his men, and the insurgents withdrew to the village of Castelnau just before the infantry arrived at Ste. Bazeille. These troops marched onward to Marmande, which they found half-deserted. As for the rebels, they began straggling home during the day, and they dispersed altogether the following morning.[55] Their riposte to the gendarmes could not conceal the fundamental balance of power in the region, which turned decisively in favor of the government once regular army units arrived from Bordeaux.

If rebels usually gained the upper hand in confrontations with gendarmes, they nearly always failed to stand their ground in opposition to the army. A majority of the armed demonstrators in the nation dispersed without even attempting to defeat urban garrisons or mobile columns. Either they withdrew from the outskirts of well-defended towns (e.g. Auxerre, Nîmes), or they fled before troops arrived to restore order (e.g. Bédarieux, La Palisse). The relatively few cases of violent clashes with army units only demonstrated the military incompetence of the rebels. Apart from the Basses-Alpes, where insurgents did capture the prefecture of Digne, rebel columns that marched on garrison towns all failed in their endeavors. A few columns did gain a temporary advantage against small detachments of soldiers (e.g. Auch, Crest), but they dispersed without entering the towns that these troops were guarding. More commonly, rebels fled at the first exchange of gunfire with troops, losing a few dead or wounded. Those who did try to resist assaults by the army only exposed themselves to death or injury, as the men of Le Luc (Var) discovered in the battle of Aups, where attacking cavalry killed at least twelve of them. The numerical strength of the insurgents proved unavailing against the superior organization and morale of the army.[56]

In evaluating the military capabilities of the rebels, three factors need to be considered: the paramilitary preparations of Montagnards before the coup d'état; the participation of townsmen and peasants in national-

---

[54] *Rapport* of lieutenant at Mirmande on the events from Dec. 2-8, in AG, F¹ 52.

[55] Ténot, *La province*, pp. 68-69.

[56] Ténot describes most of these skirmished in detail, *La province, passim*. See also Décembre and Alonnier, *Histoire des Conseils de Guerre de 1852* (Paris, 1869), as well as regional and local monographs such as Blache on the Var and Dagnan on the Gers.

guard units; and the ingenuity of rebels in creating military forces during the insurrection itself. Although the respective importance of these three factors varied from region to region, Montagnard societies rarely made a substantial contribution to the military organization of the rebels, and national-guard units played a direct role in only a few clashes with troops. Rebels usually had to improvise their weaponry, leadership, and discipline on the spur of the moment.

Despite the paramilitary overtones of Montagnard societies, their leaders had no particular expertise in warfare, and their recruits obtained no specialized training as soldiers. Decurions or section leaders might be prepared to mobilize rank-and-file members secretly, but nowhere did they practice military maneuvers with these ten-man units before the coup d'état. Drill in the use of arms, the deployment of manpower, or the engagement of opposing forces was nonexistent. Even in the districts where Montagnards tried to stockpile weapons and munitions, their military strategy amounted to nothing more than a "descent into the streets." Around Béziers, for example, where affiliates had a prescribed uniform—a blue smock and a red belt—they purchased some weapons and manufactured some bullets and gunpowder before the coup d'état, but only afterward did they assemble in arms for the first time.[57] Similarly, Montagnards in the cantons of Brignoles and St. Maximin received bullets and gunpowder from their section leaders in the fall of 1851, but they had no specific plans for military action.[58] More typically, peasants were left to their own initiative in supplying themselves with arms and munitions. "We were told to get weapons for the moment when we must march," a cultivator at Assions (Ardèche) testified, and a leader at Sauzet explained that "each individual armed himself as best he could."[59] This was no easy task: muskets were expensive, and munitions were tightly controlled by the state. Peasants had especial difficulty obtaining gunpowder, whose sale was a state monopoly.[60] Although some contraband gunpowder circulated in the countryside, police raids were relatively effective in controlling its extent. Some contraband dealers were arrested in 1850-51, and so were

---

[57] Ints. Jn. Jos. Thibeyranc, cult. at Boujan, Fr. Meric, *prop.*-cult. at Capestang, and Pr. Pastre, *cantonnier* at Nissan, in ADH, 39M 159, 154, 156.

[58] According to T. Amiel, at Le Val, the gunpowder came from Marseille. AD Var, 4M 19, dossiers Brue-Auriac, Ollières, Pourrieux, Le Val.

[59] Ints. Jn. Bapt. Roche, cult., ADA, 5M 16; and Amédée Toutel, *prop.*, ATML, Ins. 1851.

[60] One Montagnard from the Gard bought a gun for 20 francs several days after his initiation, but the double-barreled guns taken from bourgeois at Poligny were evaluated at 80-150 francs each. (Tem. F. Barbe, at Cassagnolles, ADG, 3U/5-1; Register of persons disarmed at Poligny, ADJ, MIV 45, Ins. of Poligny.) Concerning state controls over firearms and munitions, see Dalloz, *Répertoire de Droit pénal et procédure pénale*, t. II (Paris, 1968), "Armes," "Explosifs."

a few Montagnards who tried to manufacture gunpowder in nocturnal workshops.[61] The call to arms in December 1851 would find many initiates reaching for their pitchforks and their staves, or carrying unloaded guns into the streets. The rudimentary preparations of the Montagnards for armed mobilizations fell far short of their military needs vis-à-vis the army.

In theory, the institution of the national guard provided civilian populations throughout France with military leadership, weaponry, and training. In fact, mass poverty, social conservatism, and political re-action placed narrow limits on the social base of recruitment to this territorial militia. Apart from brief periods of revolutionary excitement, when guard units became vehicles for mass political mobilization, workers in the towns and peasants in the bourgs and villages were either disqualified from membership or left without weapons and uni-forms. During the July Monarchy, the guard functioned primarily as an urban peacekeeping force, whose bourgeois officers and lower-middle-class recruits supplemented army garrisons in the defense of property. Most rural units existed only on paper, and even urban units tended to become moribund with the passage of time. The February Revolution triggered a brief mobilization of urban and rural popula-tions through a revitalized and expanded national guard, but social and political reaction soon brought another halt to military democratiza-tion.[62] In communities where class conflict between property owners and wage earners erupted in 1848, conservatives restored bourgeois control of the national guard by purging the workers. Hence, the guard was "reorganized" in a few dozen localities during the later months of 1848.[63] A somewhat different pattern of reaction occurred under the government of Louis Napoleon, when the Republican con-victions of guardsmen brought entire units under suspicion. Thus, police bureaucrats began issuing edicts to abolish the guard altogether

[61] For state repression of clandestine manufacture and sale of gunpowder before the coup d'état, see the large dossier on this topic, in AN, BB[30] 392[B]. For an ex-ample of a successful police raid on Montagnards who were producing gunpow-der illegally, see the case of Nissan in June 1851, reported by S-P Béziers, June 23, 1851, in ADH, 39M 134.

[62] Louis Girard, La Garde nationale, 1814-1871 (Paris, 1964), pp. 165-229, 287-340.

[63] According to a register of national-guard dissolutions from 1839 to 1852, units in twenty-seven communes were reorganized from June to Dec. 1848, including Paris, six suburbs of Paris, and fourteen other towns. (AN, F[9] 423). For a case study of the class alignments behind such reorganizations, see John M. Merriman, "Social Conflict in France and the Limoges Revolution of April 27, 1848," So-cietas—A Review of Social History, 4 (Winter 1974), 21-38; and Merriman, "Radicalization and Repression: A Study of the Demobilisation of the 'Dem-Socs' during the Second French Republic," in Roger Price, ed., Revolution and Reaction, pp. 221-22.

in specific communes: such dissolutions increased in frequency from 5 in 1848 to 60 in 1849, 77 in 1850, and 124 in the first eleven months of 1851. The prefects of Louis Napoleon also dissolved the guard partially in another 89 communes, a measure which implied that a substantial portion of the local citizenry could not be trusted with weapons.[64] Furthermore, prefects and military commanders disarmed the guard in many communes where it supposedly continued to exist.[65] By the eve of the coup d'état, government policy was to rely as little as possible on civilians for the protection of order. The less military organization small towns and villages in Republican districts of the nation possessed, the greater the security of the government.

How successful was this repressive policy? To begin with, few rural communes acquired an effective militia force even during the revolutionary phase of the Second Republic. Their elected officers might lead military parades during public festivals (a customary practice, for example, in Provence), but their recruits often lacked the most basic military equipment and training. A policy of studied neglect, coupled with selective disarmaments, ensured that most rural guardsmen remained ill-equipped and inexperienced from 1849 to 1851.[66] Next, dissolutions and disarmaments probably did reduce the military capability of Republicans in some small towns and market bourgs that rebelled against the coup d'état. At least fifteen guard units in such rebel centers were entirely dissolved before the coup d'état, including Apt, Barbaste, Clamecy, Manosque, Marmande, and Poligny. As the prefect of the Nièvre reported in January 1852, "The units in rebel communes had been dissolved or disarmed long before the coup d'état."[67] Although "ex-officers" of the guard sometimes helped organize resistance in such communes, they had to overcome serious deficiencies of armament and discipline as a result of the dissolutions. Finally, where repression had been incomplete, national-guard weapons did fall into rebel hands, and a few communal contingents of the guard did take arms under the leadership of their officers. In some bourgs and villages,

[64] Tabulations based on the register in AN, F⁹ 423.

[65] In the Gers, for example, 54 units were dissolved and disarmed before the coup d'état, but none of them were listed in the above register. Similarly, around 20 units in the Drôme were disarmed when the state of siege was introduced to that department in 1849, but none appear in the register. Dagnan, *Le Gers*, 1, 429-36; letters in ADD, M 1344. For some national evidence concerning the scale of disarmament, see the prefectoral reports on arms shipments in AN, F⁹ 423.

[66] In the Basses-Alpes, for example, less than 2,000 guns were distributed in 1848-49, and the weapons removed from six left-wing towns and bourgs in 1850 cost 4,891 francs to repair. Many of them were old guns used only for public festivals. Letters from the Prefect, Apr. 11, 1850 and Mar. 8, 1851, in AN, F⁹ 431, Basses-Alpes.

[67] Letter from the Prefect, Dec. 23, 1851, AN, F⁹ 423.

guardsmen had been ordered to deposit their guns at the *mairies* as a first step toward dissolution, but these stockpiles had not yet been transferred to state arsenals when news of the coup d'état arrived. This helps explain why insurgents in the Basses-Alpes, the Gard, the Gers, the Lot-et-Garonne, the Var, and the Yonne were often eager to occupy their municipal premises, while those in the Drôme, the Hérault, and the Vaucluse, where disarmament had been more systematic, were less oriented toward municipal power.[68] As for the direct entry of guard units into the revolt, this occurred in several cantonal seats, including Bourdeaux (Drôme) and Le Luc (Var).[69] In the words of the drummer of the guard at Bourdeaux, "I thought we were marching as the National Guard."[70] The rarity of such cases is further proof that government policy did have a negative impact on the military capabilities of Republican electorates.

Under these circumstances, rebels usually had to improvise their military organization. By virtue of their customary participation in village ceremonials, many peasants knew how to form ranks and march in step to the beat of the village drummer. Collective discipline emerged naturally from such military parades.[71] For the leadership of local columns, insurgents often drew on the experience of former soldiers as well as former national-guard officers or fire-brigade commanders. Ex-lieutenants and ex-sergeants became prominent leaders of some columns, while ex-privates led sections and commanded some village bands. It became especially important to designate military leaders once contingents from various communes came together in large regional gatherings. Thus, the rebel *chef* from St. Gengoux delegated former soldiers to lead sections after his column obtained reinforcements from Cluny and a few villages; the Montagnard leader from Dieulefit held a meeting of ex-military men on the outskirts of Crest to choose leaders of the combatants from each commune; and rebel commanders from Le Luc and other towns helped villagers choose military leaders at Salernes.[72] Regional gatherings also accentuated the need for military equipment, munitions, and food. Peasant bands might look

[68] According to Dagnan, for example, many guns on deposit in the *mairies* of the Gers fell into rebel hands. *Le Gers*, II, 436.

[69] At least two national-guard lieutenants helped lead the "battalion" from Bourdeaux, and the commander of the guard at Le Luc led its battalion. See dossiers Ch. Aimé Cavet, *prop.*, and Jos. L. Monier, baker, in ADD, M 1359, 1366; and Agulhon, *La république au village*, pp. 395-96.

[70] Int. Jos. Monier, cult., in ADD, M 1366.

[71] See Agulhon's discussion of this "diffuse communal militarism" in the Var, *La République au village*, pp. 453-54.

[72] Int. Casimir Roberjot, *clerc de notaire* at Cluny, AD S-L, U, Ins. of 1851, dossier #2; Ténot, *La province*, p. 201; Agulhon, *La République au village*, pp. 449-50; AD Var, 4M 19, especially dossier Varages.

intimidating to officials in nearby towns because they brandished hunting guns and barnyard tools, and they might carry enough food for the day's journey to such market centers. Once large columns hoped to attack garrison towns, however, they needed more serious logistical support. The rebels who marched on Digne seized funds from government tax collectors to pay their troops a daily wage, and they obtained large amounts of gunpowder from the garrison commander, who capitulated.[73] Elsewhere, logistical problems were confronted on an ad hoc basis. Guns and munitions were seized from private citizens or government depots, while food supplies were usually paid for by wealthy leaders, donated by local tradesmen, or purchased by rank-and-file recruits.[74] Only the towns had sufficient stores of weapons and food to provision large rebel forces. By controlling enough cantonal seats and subprefectures, insurgents hoped to develop the military capability to challenge government power in the prefectures. This strategy worked in the Basses-Alpes, and it guided most rebel efforts to improvise military forces in other departments.

Perceptive leaders doubted, however, whether their impromptu military organization could withstand the shock of combat with the army. Communications between the various communal contingents would be difficult if not impossible to maintain in a battle, and discipline at the communal level was often more apparent than real. As their numbers swelled, rebel formations became less manageable. Thus, one leader from Le Luc decried the arrival of peasant reinforcements at Salernes: "I would prefer to have only one thousand well-armed and resolute men than all these crowds which are arriving."[75] Guns and munitions remained in short supply, and no rebel forces had any artillery or cavalry, the most potent weapons of the army. To console themselves for such obvious military weaknesses, political militants spread rumors that garrison towns had already fallen into rebel hands, or that the army would fraternize with the people. As one participant from Vallon testified, "When we left, we were told that we wouldn't have to fire a single shot. Paris was in insurrection, Privas had been taken, and the entire department was going to march on Nîmes."[76] Leaders even urged everyone to hold their fire if confronted by troops.

---

[73] P-G Aix, Jan. 19, 1852, in AN, BB³⁰ 396-P440; AD B-A, 6M 88; Int. Ailhaud de Volx, ex-*garde générale des forêts*, in AN, BB³⁰ 397-P463. For similar funding of the rebels from St. Gengoux and Cluny, see Int. P. Thiers, *coutelier* at St. Gengoux, in AD S-L, U. Ins. of 1815, dossier #1.

[74] Food was requisitioned from wealthy landlords or shopkeepers in only a few communes, including a château near Sillons (Var). See letter from mayor of Sillons, Dec. 26, 1851, in AD Var, 4M 19.

[75] Cited by Ténot, *La province*, p. 147.

[76] Int. E. Pascal, *confiseur*, ADA, 5M 18.

"Citizens, fear nothing," announced a townsman to peasants near Montélimar. "The garrison is for us. The troops will fire into the air as soon as they see you. Shout 'Long live the line!' and then greet them as brothers. They will hand over their weapons."[77] If these rumors turned out to be false, demoralization threatened the rebel forces. "You are trying to get family men killed," recruits from St. Gengoux complained bitterly to their leader when they found out that Mâcon contained eight hundred soldiers. "Stop your column! You're leading it to slaughter!" exclaimed a municipal councilor to the Montagnard *chef* of Grane at word that soldiers inside Crest were ready to open fire.[78] Rebels hoped to triumph against the government, but they did not expect to risk their lives against the army.

From the perspective of civilian authorities, the best way to capitalize on the prestige of the army was to deploy troops as rapidly as possible to vulnerable subprefectures and cantonal seats. Indeed, some police bureaucrats urged military commanders before the coup d'état to establish small detachments of soldiers in left-wing towns and bourgs that lacked permanent garrisons.[79] The Ministry of War rarely granted such requests. Its strategy was to concentrate troops in the cities, and to deploy them in large mobile columns to suppress localized rebellions.[80] This strategy had three advantages. To begin with, it guarded against the risk of Republican uprisings in cities such as Lyon and Marseille, where workers had tried unsuccessfully to rebel earlier in the Second Republic. Second, it enabled military commanders to husband their resources until they knew precisely which small towns posed a military threat to the government. If they responded to each and every civilian plea for assistance, they risked scattering their troops inefficiently throughout a region. Finally, it maximized the military power of the army. Individual soldiers did not have a substantial military advantage over armed insurgents. They carried smooth-bore muskets rather than breech-loading rifles, and they needed to engage in close-order volley firing in order to make such slow and inaccurate guns effective on the battlefield.[81] Yet many soldiers on garrison duty

[77] Int. Toutel, cited in n. 59.
[78] Int. L. Pornon, plasterer at St. Gengoux, AD S-L, U, Ins. of 1851, dossier #1; Tem. Ferdinand Amoric, *prop.*, ATML, Ins. 1851.
[79] For example, civilian authorities in the Hérault tried unsuccessfully to obtain a garrison for the town of Bédarieux in the fall of 1851. See their correspondence in ADH, 39M 128, 129, 132.
[80] This strategy was affirmed by generals in the departments, such as De Castellanne at Lyon, De Rostolon at Montpellier, and Hecquet at Marseille. See De Rostolon to Prefect (Hérault), Nov. 17, 1851, in ADH, 39M 129; and Hecquet to M. War, Dec. 6, 1851, in AG, F¹ 52.
[81] Concerning the continued reliance of the French army on smooth-bore muskets until after the Crimean War, see Colonel H. L. Scott, *Military Dictionary*

were recent conscripts, still unskilled in such tactics.[82] It was by incorporating foot soldiers into battalion-sized formations of several hundred men that military commanders could best exploit their collective power vis-à-vis the rebels. Naturally, artillery and cavalry increased substantially the fighting ability of such infantry battalions. This was the logic behind the deployment of mobile columns, composed of one or two infantry battalions, a few cannon, and some cavalry. Anything less might not do the job of defeating large rebel forces.

The problem with a strategy of massive deployments from urban garrisons was that generals might react slowly to requests for troops to guard small towns. The more they emphasized the military advantages of concentration, the more they neglected the political advantages of dispersion. Unless troops moved quickly to endangered towns, rebels could broaden their territorial control substantially without encountering significant military opposition. This is what happened in southeastern France, where General Hecquet, in command of the Seventh Military Division at Marseille, wrote on December 6 to the minister of war that he was still refusing to deploy any troops from his garrisons at Marseille, Toulon, and Avignon to other towns. He wanted to be certain of maintaining control of these "strategic points" before forming any mobile columns. Meanwhile, insurgency was spreading unchecked through the Basses-Alpes and much of the Var. When General Hecquet finally ordered three columns into the field on December 8, he complained that he had only fifteen active battalions left at Marseille: "My columns are very weak as a result, and if one of them fails or simply doesn't succeed, I don't know what can be done to reinforce it."[83] General de Rostolan, the commander of the Eighth Division at Montpellier, had no reserves to spare for Marseille, nor did General de Castellane, in command of the Fifth and Sixth Divisions at Lyon.[84] One of General Hecquet's columns did suffer a reversal in the Basses-Alpes, but his fears were greatly exaggerated. Troops succeeded in occupying all the rebel subprefectures of southeastern France without resistance, and they occupied the prefecture of Digne after the rebels had evacuated it. Mobile columns *were* a formidable military weapon, and generals used them with similar success in central and southwestern France. Indeed, large columns of infantry, cavalry, and artillery rarely

---

(New York, 1864), "Rifled Ordinance," esp. p. 515; and P. E. Cleator, *Weapons of War* (New York, 1968), pp. 138-41.

[82] See the complaints of General Hecquet, letter cited in n. 80, and General Lapène, at Valence, Dec. 7, 1851, in AG, F¹ 52.

[83] General Hecquet, Dec. 6, 8, 1851, in AG, F¹ 52.

[84] General Hecquet, Dec. 8, and General De Castellane, Dec. 4, in AG, F¹ 51-52.

had to engage rebel forces in combat; the mere rumor of their movements usually sufficed to restore order.

Most of the violent clashes that did occur involved less than a battalion of troops. Not all military commanders in garrison towns waited until they could organize mobile columns before taking the initiative against rebel forces. Those at Auxerre and Valence reacted quickly to news of impending revolts in the southwestern Yonne and the central Drôme by dispatching small numbers of troops to Toucy and Crest; those at Limoges, Montélimar, and Privas responded to similar rumors of insurgency in the countryside by sending small detachments on reconnaissance missions; and those at Auch, Béziers, and Largentière relied on small units to disperse rebel columns. These military deployments, which usually took place at night, were high-risk operations, but in a majority of cases they succeeded in spreading panic among the rebels. Thus, a band of a few hundred peasants at Linards (Haute-Vienne) defied a patrol of gendarmes on the night of December 5-6, but they fled as soon as 50 cavalry and a few dozen gendarmes arrived from Limoges; two separate bands, each numbering around 200 men, tried to enter Toucy (Yonne) on the night of December 6, but they fled from the 25 soldiers who had arrived shortly beforehand to guard the town; several hundred rebels from the canton of Chomérac (Ardèche) forced a patrol of 35 gendarmes to retreat on the same night, but they dispersed as soon as the gendarmes returned from Privas with a company of infantry; and over 2,000 rebels from the southern Ardèche had no more success that night against a small infantry patrol from Largentière, whose sudden appearance in the darkness caused panic in their ranks. Nor did a column of 500-600 men from Grane stand and fight against 50 soldiers who attacked them at Crest on the evening of the sixth. In all these cases, soldiers killed or wounded a few insurgents and put the rest to flight. More serious fighting occurred at Auch just after sundown on December 4, where 90 cavalry tried to charge a mass of 2,000 rebels and suffered heavy casualties; at St. Marcel (Drôme) on the night of the sixth, where a company of 100 infantry from Montélimar retreated after stumbling across several hundred rebels; and at Divajeu (Drôme) on the afternoon of the seventh, where an artillery patrol from Crest barely escaped being overrun by nearly 3,000 rebels from the cantons of Crest-sud, Bourdeaux, and Dieulefit. As for mobile columns of battalion strength, they saw action against rebel forces only at Charnay-les-Mâcon (Saône-et-Loire), Aups (Var), and Les Mées (Basses-Alpes). A battalion of engineering troops in transit at Mâcon marched against several hundred men from St. Gengoux and Cluny on the morning of the sixth, and they swept the field as soon as gunfire broke out; two battalions of infantry, aided by cavalry, smashed the "army of the Var," which was preparing to leave Aups on the morning of the tenth; and one battalion tried unsuccessfully to dislodge several thousand rebels from well-defended positions at Les Mées on the ninth. Even this latter failure was only temporary: the rebel leaders dismissed their men shortly after the infantry retreated southward. Once it became clear that the army controlled the cities and intended to occupy the rebel districts, further thought of armed resistance became foolhardy.[85]

Although the army restored government authority throughout the nation within two weeks, its clashes with rebels varied in intensity and immediate outcome from area to area. The local balance of power between army units and rebel formations did not always favor the government. If soldiers dispersed rebels easily in most violent clashes, they ran into serious difficulties in a few localities. Examples of easy victories against panic-stricken rebels include Largentière, Charnay, and Aups. By contrast, the skirmishes at Auch, Les Mées, and Crest-Divajeu threatened army units with defeat, although insurgents proved unable to exploit their initial superiority. Soldiers in most localities used violence more deliberately and more effectively than the rebels, but only at Aups and Crest-Divajeu did they inflict more than a handful of casualties upon their opponents. Elsewhere, insurgents dispersed before many of them became exposed to deadly force. Brief descriptions of these six clashes will illustrate the extent to which violence was an accidental rather than an intrinsic feature of rebel interactions with the army.

Rebels from the southern Ardèche had a huge numerical advantage over the troops guarding the town of Largentière, but they panicked and fled in disarray. Spearheaded by insurgents from the canton of Vallon, they numbered well over two thousand men when they reached a bridge near town before dawn on December 7. Some of their leaders wanted to wait until daybreak before advancing, but urban militants persuaded them to enter town under cover of darkness. Supposedly, no one would see them, and they would be able to seize the town without any resistance from the understrength garrison of only forty soldiers. In fact, a sergeant with only four men succeeded in halt-

[85] For events at Linards, see Ténot, *La province*, p. 5; and Merriman, "Radicalization and Repression," p. 229. For Toucy, see Ténot, *La province*, p. 49; *Rapport* Prefect, Nov. 16, 1868, AN, F[18] 308; Mayor of Toucy, Dec. 7, 1851, in ADY, III M[1] 149; and Int. A. Patasson, JM-1851, #255. For events near Privas, see E. Reynier, *Histoire de Privas*, vol. 3 (Privas, 1951), 266-73; and Captain of gendarmerie Privas, Dec. 5, 1851, in AG, F[1] 51. For Grane and St. Marcel, see Margadant, "Insurrection," pp. 451-58, 461-63. The other skirmishes are described in more detail below.

ing them at the bridge. He later testified: "I shouted, 'Who goes there?!'
A voice replied, 'Who goes there?!' and I replied, 'France!' The same
voice asked, 'Which regiment?!' When I replied, 'The Twelfth Light Infantry,' he said, 'Advance to order!' 'Come and get it,' I answered, 'It's at
the end of my bayonet!' At this, the voice called out, 'Surrender your
arms!' and a multitude of other voices repeated this cry. But at almost
the same instant, I heard them shout, 'It's the troops! We must negotiate! We must negotiate!' An insurgent advanced toward the soldiers,
and I seized him."[86] Staring into the darkness, the rebels who were
massed on the road had no way of knowing how many soldiers were
on the bridge. They feared the worst, and when two shots rang out
from the direction of town, everyone scattered for safety. So great
was the panic that one man leaped into a ditch by the side of the road
and broke his leg. More troops arrived to pursue the fleeing rebels, injuring one or two of them and making twenty-four arrests. The debacle was complete.[87]

Many of the insurgents from St. Gengoux and Cluny had guns and
munitions, and they organized themselves into several platoons, each
divided into sections of around ten men, before advancing the last few
miles toward Mâcon. They were scarcely more numerous, however,
than the five hundred soldiers who marched against them from town.
A peasant woman at the village of Charnay cried out in alarm, "Boys,
don't go as far as Mâcon! Otherwise, you'll all be lost!" Some rebels
deserted at word of the army's presence in the town, and others
huddled together anxiously. According to a section leader from Cluny,
"When we reached Charnay, everything became confused, and there
were no more sections or men to lead them." Just beyond Charnay, at
the bottom of a hill, the lieutenant-colonel in command of the column
of army engineers came forward with two mounted sappers. Some
rebels, who had received explicit orders not to open fire, broke their
ranks and began shooting at the officer, but they missed. Three companies of engineers charged forward to the rescue, followed by two
columns of sappers. The rebel leader from St. Gengoux, a former
huissier named Dismier, tried to deploy his men in the vineyards, but
his frantic command, "Every man for himself! Fire from behind the
vines!" only increased their confusion. Their scattered gunfire did not
hit any soldiers, and most of them fled before they could be killed or

[86] Tem. Sergeant Ouarse, dossier Fortune Coulet, ex-notary at Vallon, ADA, 5M
18.
[87] Concerning this event, see also Ints. L. Bouchet, cult. at Vallon, Jean Eldin,
cult.-domestique at Lagorce, and A. Michel, cult. (ex-blacksmith) at Vallon, all in
ADA, 5M 18; and letters from the lieutenant of the gendarmerie and the general
at Largentière, both on Dec. 8, 1851, in AG, F¹ 52.

captured. Only two rebels died, one suffered serious injury, and twenty-five fell into the hands of the army.[88]

Military disaster struck the rebels of the Var who reached the small town of Aups on Tuesday evening, the ninth, and who gathered on the esplanade the following morning. Their commanding "general," a journalist from Marseille named Camille Duteil, had decided to avoid combat with an advancing column of troops from Brignoles by retreating northward to the Basses-Alpes. He had no idea that a second column was about to arrive from Draguignan, led by Colonel Trauers and the prefect, M. Pastouret. This column, which contained eleven companies of infantry and fifty mounted gendarmes, had put to flight the only insurgents on the road between Draguignan and Aups, a "battalion" assigned to guard the village of Tourtour. Colonel Trauer's initial plan had been to occupy Aups while the troops from Brignoles, commanded by Colonel de Sercey, took Barjols; the two columns would then converge on the town of Salernes, where the rebels were supposedly still encamped. His easy victory at Tourtour convinced him to launch an immediate assault as soon as he found the main rebel force at Aups.

Several companies of infantry advanced in a long line across the meadows south of the esplanade, while the rest of the column charged toward a gateway on the east side of its parapet. The rebels, whose numbers had declined during the night from over six thousand to around four thousand, were listening without much enthusiasm to a speech by Duteil, their backs turned to the parapet, when a voice cried out, "It's the soldiers!" The sight of troops less than four hundred feet away, maneuvering in battle formation, spread confusion among the poorly armed peasants. Duteil lost his nerve and ordered the well-organized contingent from La Garde Freinet to retreat northward. This order, which the corkworkers promptly obeyed to the sound of the drum, triggered chaos on the esplanade. Rumors spread through the crowd that Duteil had fled after shouting, "Every man for himself!" (*sauve qui peut*). Gunfire from the soldiers in the meadows increased the mood of panic.

Suddenly, the gendarmes galloped onto the parade ground. The "battalion" of Le Luc, led by its national-guard commander, tried to resist the cavalry charge, but its ranks disintegrated as men fell be-

---

[88] Quotes drawn from Ints. Pr. Thiers, *coutelier* at St. Gengoux, C. Roberjot, *clerc de notaire* at Cluny, and Jn. Guichon, *vigneron* at St. Gengoux, in AD S-L, Ins. of 1851, dossiers #1-2. See also Int. N. Fort, shoemaker at Cluny (same archives); *Rapport-general* of *Cour d'Appel* Dijon, Feb. 2, 1852, in AN, BB[30] 396; and letters from the troop commander, Dec. 5, and the acting Prefect, Dec. 6, 1851, in AG, F[1] 52.

neath the sabers of the gendarmes. Everyone fled in terror toward the roads leading west of town. The gendarmes, who were infuriated by the fact that some of their associates had been captured earlier and forced to march, killed as many defenseless rebels as they could. Their commander later boasted, "We succeeded in reaching around fifty of them, who were all killed with weapons in their hands."[89] In fact, some of the victims had thrown their weapons away, but still they died at the hands of the vengeful gendarmes.

As for the infantry, they stormed into town after killing a few dozen rebels, and they opened fire on the building where the hostages were being held, mortally wounding one of them. Some of the soldiers then tried to charge the insurgents from La Garde Freinet, who had taken position on a knoll behind town. The cork workers fought back effectively. They killed one soldier and wounded two officers and a few soldiers before retreating northward without any losses. Meanwhile, other infantrymen captured around eighty prisoners, whom they placed in chains a few hours later and took to Salernes. There, two of the prisoners were left behind to be executed (both survived their wounds), and another four were taken aside at Lorgues and murdered by a gendarme who had lost his eye in a skirmish. The civilian and military authorities in the department gave tacit approval to these summary executions, which demonstrated the will of the state to terrorize and punish the insurgents.[90]

The rebel columns from Vic-Fezensac and nearby bourgs and villages that marched to Auch on December 4 were completely unprepared for combat when cavalry from the town attacked them after nightfall. At their first appearance on the road into town, a small detachment of cavalry persuaded them to halt. Negotiations continued for a few hours, aided by Republican leaders from Auch who feared a collision at night. The *procureur* agreed to temporize as long as the insurgents, who greatly outnumbered the cavalry (3,000 to 90), camped outside of town. The municipality of Auch even had large quantities of bread carried to the *faubourg de l'oratoire*, where the tired and hungry marchers were strung out along the road for nearly a mile. Men were calmly eating by the roadside, their guns and pitchforks beside them, when shooting broke out at the head of the column. Colonel Courby de Cognord, the commander of the cavalry, had lost patience with the demonstrators, who were supposedly threatening his position. He first persuaded the *procureur* to order the insurgents to

[89] Captain of gendarmerie Var, Dec. 11, 1851, AG, F¹ 53.

[90] For detailed narratives of events at Aups, see Blache, *L'insurrection du Var*, pp. 177-94; and Ténot, *La province*, pp. 148-60.

withdraw, and when they continued to block the road, he decided to disperse them by force. The cavalry squadrons fired their carbines into the darkness and galloped into battle. Some townsmen from Vic-Fezensac took refuge on the banks of the road and opened fire, killing three of the cavalry and wounding twenty, but the peasants to the rear had not heard the *procureur* read the riot act. They fell over themselves in their haste to escape. The hussars emptied the road in their quarter-mile charge and returned to town, badly battered but victorious. One officer, whose horse carried him off the road, became the last victim of the fighting: he was shot in the back and killed as he tried to ride away from a band of fugitives. The heavy losses of the cavalry aroused grave concern among the authorities, and the general at Auch wrote to the minister of war that if he did not receive prompt reinforcements of infantry and artillery, his position would become untenable.[91] In fact, the shock of combat had broken the rebel will to resist, and the heroic cavalry had no further difficulty maintaining order in the town.[92]

Montagnards in the Basses-Alpes took advantage of rugged terrain near Les Mées to withstand a mobile column of infantry on Tuesday morning, the ninth. Around eight thousand rebels had occupied the prefecture of Digne the previous Sunday, where they had established a Committee of Resistance to govern the department. Having obtained fifteen hundred pounds of gunpowder and 15,000 francs from timid military and civilian authorities at Digne, the Committee decided to fight when it learned on Monday evening that troops were marching up the left bank of the Durance river from Marseille. Over five-thousand men promptly left for the village of Malijai, singing the Marseillaise. The harsh weather and the news of government victories elsewhere in France provoked some desertions en route, but nearly four thousand rebels camped overnight and moved forward to Les Mées in the morning. They occupied not only the bourg but the heights overlooking the gorge to the south, through which the soldiers had to pass. Colonel Parson, the commander of the battalion, ordered his men to attack when they drew gunfire from the direction of Les Mées, but they bogged down and halted at the entry to the gorge. Instead of counterattacking in overwhelming numbers, the rebels sent two members of the Committee of Resistance forward to negotiate. Both spokesmen were denounced as brigands and taken prisoner until a local official intervened to gain their release. Still determined to force a

[91] General Dupleix, Dec. 4, 1851, AG, F¹ 51.
[92] Ténot describes this event in detail, *La province*, pp. 79-84. See also Dagnan, *Le Gers*, II; P-G Agen, Jan. 28, 1852, in AN, BB³⁰ 396-P440; and *Rapport* Capt. Michel on the encounter of Dec. 4-5, 1851, in AG, F¹ 51.

passage through the defile, Colonel Parson ordered one of his companies to scale the heights by a footpath so they could attack the insurgents from the rear. This audacious maneuver only exposed the soldiers to assault: they fell into an ambush and fled, leaving behind twenty-two prisoners, including two officers. Many peasants also fled during the skirmishes for control of the gorge, although casualties on both sides were light. When the colonel decided to retreat southward and await reinforcements, the rebels nearly all disbanded. Their brief victory only exposed them to repression in the future, as hundreds of troops poured into the department from the Var, the Vaucluse, and the Hautes-Alpes.[93]

The only rebels who launched a serious attack on the army came from the region south of Crest. Numbering around three thousand men, they had enough military organization and weaponry to challenge the two hundred and fifty artillery troops and infantry that the commander of the state of siege in the Drôme had sent to guard the town. After reaching the commune of Divajeu, just south of Crest, on Sunday afternoon, their leaders began to select a deputation of ten men to negotiate with the urban authorities. Suddenly, a woman appeared on a hilltop which was blocking their view of the town. "You're lost!" she shouted. "There's the artillery!"[94] The *chef d'escadron*, Delamothe, commanding officer of the troops, was marching against them with a howitzer and a small escort of infantry and mounted *artilleurs*. Convinced that he could defeat any number of poorly armed and ill-disciplined peasants, Delamothe was taken by surprise when the insurgents came over the top of the hill, spread across the fields on either side of the road, and moved forward to outflank him. They shouted "Long live the artillery! Long live our brothers! Long live the Republic!" but Delamothe ordered the *obusier* to open fire. A cannonball crashed through tree limbs and blew off the head of Auguste Tariot, the son of an owner-farmer from Puy-St. Martin. The center and the left flank of the rebel line returned the fire, while the right flank, composed of men from Bourdeaux, charged forward under the command of a national-guard lieutenant, M. Cavet. Delamothe was in trouble. His cannoneer fired off two or three more shells and the patrol began a precipitate retreat. "Forward, forward my friends! The battle is won!" cried a leader from Bourdeaux.[95] The insurgents scrambled through fields and over fences in hot pursuit of the mounted

[93] Ténot, *La province*, pp. 175-80; Int. Ailhaud de Volx, AN, BB[30] 397-P463; P-G Aix, Jan. 19, 1852, AN, BB[30] 396-P440; the novel by Willette, *Et la Montagne fleurira*, greatly exaggerates the violence of this encounter, pp. 227-56.

[94] Ténot, *La province*, p. 201.

[95] Tem. Jos. Aug. Mège, *cafetier* at Puy-St. Martin, ATML, Ins. of 1851.

artillerymen. Vineyards slowed their progress, and the troops reached
town without serious injury, but the battle had just begun.[96]

The keystone of the town's defense was the bridge across the Drôme
river, where the troops had dispersed a rebel column from Grane the
previous evening. To cover the road southward, Delamothe placed his
howitzer across the river on the quai. He also had another artillery
piece, an eight-inch cannon, which he fortified at the barricade across
the bridge. To capture this position, the men of Bourdeaux volunteered
to lead a frontal assault, followed by the contingents from Dieulefit
and Crest-sud. Forming tight ranks to the rear of the column, they
burst forward, singing the Marseillaise, and ran straight for the bridge.
The cannoneer of the howitzer waited coolly until they came into full
view. Then he lobbed a shrapnel shell into their front line, killing or
wounding several men. Like a wave hitting an irresistible obstacle, the
column bunched together, hesitated for an instant, and scattered to the
sides of the road. A drummer continued to beat the charge; M. Cavet,
his uniform torn to tatters by the *mitraille*, still waved his saber in the
air; the mayor of Poët-Célard shouted from the road, "Let's go, boys!
One more effort! We've got 'em!" To no avail. The man fanned out
along the river bank and shot at the troops on the other side, but they
were not about to brave the howitzer again. A loosely structured
battle continued for a few hours, as the cannoneers exhausted their
shells trying to dislodge the rebels from the southern bank of the river.
Just before nightfall, around a hundred and fifty insurgents made one
last attempt to break through the army's defenses. Slipping along the
riverbank below the dikes, they made their way to the stone supports
of the bridge and emerged behind the barricade. This maneuver threatened to capture the cannon and open up the road into town, but a few
dozen cavalry charged the rebels immediately, killing or wounding
several and putting the rest to flight. This skirmish ended the fighting.
The rebels, who had lost six or seven dead and twenty or thirty
wounded, dispersed under cover of darkness. The artillery troops, who
had suffered only one killed and one wounded, were nearly out of
ammunition, but their cannon could now fall silent over the deserted
battlefield. Henceforth, the town was secure.[97]

[96] For accounts of this skirmish, see Ténot, *La province*, pp. 201-2; Ints. Charles
Baudon, *prop.-cult.* at Montjoux, and René Espagne, weaver at Dieulefit, in ADD,
M 1357, 1361; Int. Et. Alvier, former notary at Saou, in ATML, Ins. of 1851; letter
from Lieutenant Tricoche, Dec. 12, 1851, published in *Le Courrier de la Drôme*,
Dec. 16, 1851; and letter from General Lapène, Dec. 24, 1851, published in *Le
Moniteur*, Dec. 21-22, 1851.

[97] Ténot, *La province*, pp. 202-5; l'abbé Robin's narrative, in *Dieulefit en son
histoire*, ed. J. de Font-Réaulx, et al. (Dieulefit, 1950), pp. 262-63; sources cited in
n. 96. Military officers gave a body count of one hundred dead rebels, but Ténot

Mathieu François Alphonse Pommier, a retired army officer, predicted the general fate of rebellion in 1851 when he refused to take command of the Montagnards from his village: "I tried to make them understand all the mad temerity of their enterprise, their impotence against a regular army, the difficult position in which they would find themselves even if they won a battle."[98] Perceptive observers knew that the success or failure of the coup d'état would be determined in Paris and other cities. A guerilla strategy might have prolonged the struggle in the provinces, but the Montagnards believed in the myth of the people in arms. Their large-scale demonstrations were supposed to intimidate officials and neutralize the army. Instead, haphazard and ineffectual violence only brought the wrath of the government down upon their heads. The fighting in December did not amount to much, but the purge that followed it would be impressive, indeed.

---

and Robin correct such exaggerated estimates. A monument in the cemetery at Crest—"To the Victims of December 2, 1851"—names five combatants who were killed in this battle. From the archival records, I have identified thirteen who were wounded (one from Dieulefit, one from Bourdeaux, and the rest from seven villages). See Margadant, "Insurrection," pp. 472-73.

[98] Tem. Pommier, ADD, M 1354, dossier Mirande.

・ 12 ・

THE TRIUMPH OF COUNTERREVOLUTION

Military failure brought political disaster and personal ruin to the Montagnards. The very haste with which they fled from the army only stimulated the repressive zeal of military commanders, who treated the rebel zones as conquered territories. Armed with the powers of the state of siege, which the government extended to thirty-two departments, generals used mobile columns to terrorize the populations and to arrest large numbers of suspects. Magistrates helped direct their operations by interrogating captives and by questioning men whom the rebels had disarmed or forcibly recruited. Instead of anonymous denunciations or fragmentary rumors of conspiracy, judicial investigators now obtained sworn depositions identifying opponents of the government in hundreds of communities. Their documentation enabled the army and the police to dismantle most of the underground networks that had flourished in the countryside before the coup d'état. Alongside this deliberate, sustained, and massive purge of the Montagnards, administrators also took arbitrary measures against bourgeois Republicans, militant artisans, and petty criminals whose political beliefs or social dispositions allegedly threatened public security. The new minister of the interior, le duc de Morny, explicitly authorized the prefects on January 2, 1852, to arrest "any dangerous individuals or conspirators, even if the courts have released them for lack of legal evidence."[1] To regulate military, judicial and administrative measures against "subversives," the government established special administrative tribunals in February, each consisting of a prefect, a public prosecutor, and a general. These "Mixed Commissions" officially disposed of 26,884 cases in eighty-two departments. They sentenced nearly 10,000 persons to deportation to Algeria and placed another 10,000 under various police controls. Although presidential pardons soon reduced the intensity of this purge, its scale far exceeded any other police measures against political activists in the French provinces during the nineteenth century.[2]

[1] *Circulaire* from M. Int. to Prefects, Jan. 2, 1852, AN, BB[30] 296.
[2] For general studies of the purge, see Vincent Wright, "The Coup d'Etat of December 1851: Repression and the Limits to Repression," in Roger Price, ed., *Revolution and Reaction*, pp. 303-28; Howard C. Payne, *The Police State of Louis Napoleon Bonaparte*, pp. 34-72; Pierre de la Gorce, *Histoire du Second Empire*, vol. 1 (Paris, 1894), 1-85; Charles Seignobos, *La Révolution de 1848*, pp. 216-22; and

While police bureaucrats were arresting opponents of the government by the thousands, they were simultaneously establishing a highly authoritarian regime with populist overtones. The police state of Louis Napoleon Bonaparte derived many of its constitutional and administrative features from earlier regimes, but its fusion of centralized power and universal suffrage heralded a new type of political system: the "pseudodemocracy." In such a system, elections function to legitimize the regime in power by mobilizing public opinion on behalf of a single leader or a single political party.[3] Louis Napoleon's plebiscites of December 20-21, 1851, and November 20, 1852, as well as the legislative elections of February–March 1852, were dramatic examples of pseudodemocracy in action. The overwhelming majorities he received, either personally or by the proxy of "official candidates," seemed to prove that most Frenchmen supported the new regime enthusiastically. In fact, Republicans were prevented from competing in these elections, and even anti-Republicans were discouraged from undertaking public campaigns. In the immediate aftermath of the coup d'état, arbitrary arrests spread terror among the Republicans; police measures destroyed all their newspapers, mutual-benefit societies, and other meeting places, such as *chambrées*, cafés, and inns; and prefects removed large numbers of municipal officeholders. A series of decree laws then gave police bureaucrats institutional controls over all channels of political propaganda and influence. Henceforth, newspapers and printers, mutual-benefit societies and social clubs, cafés and country inns had to obtain government authorization, and they could be closed down if they fostered subversive ideas. As for the mayors and deputy mayors, they lost their independence and became electoral agents of the prefects, who regained the power to appoint them. By combining mass arrests with authoritarian political controls and plebiscitarian elections, the new regime succeeded not only in demobilizing its left-wing opponents but in remobilizing many of them as Bonapartist voters. Republicanism seemed to vanish from the small towns and rural communities where it had acquired mass support before the coup d'état. Only in the cities did it persist as a major electoral threat to the government.[4]

Maurice Agulhon, *1848*, pp. 198-223. Among regional studies, see, especially Dagnan, *Le Gers*, II, 186-382; and Vigier, *La Second République*, II, pp. 338-79.

[3] For contemporary analysis of comparable political systems, see S. E. Finer, *Comparative Government* (London, 1970), Chaps. 9-10; for analogies between the Second Empire and twentieth-century fascism, see J. Selwyn Schapiro, *Liberalism and the Challenge of Fascism* (New York, 1949), pp. ix, 316-21.

[4] For impressionistic surveys of these repressive measures, see de la Gorce, *Second Empire*, I, 43-52; and Seignobos, *La Révolution de 1848*, pp. 222-40. For an excellent analysis of their effects, see Agulhon, *1848*, pp. 205-10.

Despite the fact that police bureaucrats were simultaneously engaged in repression and electioneering, historians have doubted whether the purge played an indispensable role in consolidating the Second Empire. According to some scholars, Louis Napoleon was so popular, especially in the countryside, that repression was irrelevant or unnecessary. Zeldin scarcely mentions the purge in his study of the political system of the Second Empire. He assumes that Louis Napoleon had so much mass support that his major problem was how to obtain allies among the notables. The system of official candidates enabled bureaucrats to harness the oligarchical tendencies of the notables to the Bonapartist loyalties of the masses.[5] Historians with less sympathy for Louis Napoleon generally devote more attention to the purge, but they also question whether it helped strengthen the government. Thus, Seignobos concludes from a study of the Mixed Commissions that their arbitrary procedures and punitive measures created ineradicable hostility to the Empire. Although Louis Napoleon tried belatedly to limit the brutal repression by his subordinates, presidential pardons were no less arbitrary than the original sentences of the Mixed Commissions. The Terror of 1852 left such atrocious memories among Republicans that opposition to the Second Empire became unbreakable in the most democratic regions of France.[6] Payne analyzes the purge as a triumphant administrative campaign against secret societies, but Vigier and Wright agree with Seignobos that arbitrary arrests, deportations, and pardons created permanent animosity toward the regime.[7] As Wright concludes from his excellent study of the repression, "For the Republicans, the real significance of the coup d'état lies less in the event itself or in the resistance offered but in the repression which followed. Widespread, enduring, and intense persecution engendered a bitter hatred which could unite all sections of the Republican party."[8]

Unquestionably, the events of 1852 failed to extirpate Republicanism, and memories of the purge did influence the resurgence of provincial radicalism in the 1870s. Yet the repression after the coup d'état needs to be viewed less as an assault on Republicanism per se than as a

[5] Theodore Zeldin, *The Political System of Napoleon III* (New York, 1971), pp. 10-27.

[6] Seignobos, *La Révolution de 1848*, pp. 218-21; and Seignobos, "Les opérations des commissions mixtes en 1852," *La Revolution de 1848*, 6 (1909-10), 59-67.

[7] Payne, *Police State*, pp. 40-43; Vigier, *La Seconde République*, pp. 120-22; Wright, "The Coup d'Etat," pp. 303, 308-13, 326-28.

[8] Wright, ibid., p. 327. Other scholars who agree that repression was excessive and counterproductive include J. M. Thompson, *Louis Napoleon and the Second Empire* (Oxford, 1954), pp. 122-23; René Arnaud, *The Second Republic and Napoleon III*, trans. E. F. Buckley (London, 1923), pp. 57-58; and Frederick B. Artz, "Bonapartism and Dictatorship," *South Atlantic Quarterly*, 39 (1940), 40.

counteroffensive against the Montagnards. The bulk of the political prisoners in 1852 had been compromised in conspiratorial or insurrectionary opposition to the government, although some moderate Republicans were also rounded up by the police or driven into exile. If the purge failed to alter popular loyalties in the long run, it definitely succeeded in destroying the Montagnard movement. The arbitrary procedures of the Mixed Commissions and the selective pardons of Louis Napoleon worked effectively against left-wing militants, especially in small towns and rural communities. By combining the threat of deportation with the promise of pardons for the wayward and the repentant, administrators restored centralized political control over the very populations that had been most hostile to government authority in 1851.

It was precisely the arbitrariness of this process which guaranteed its success. As historians of crime and social control in eighteenth-century England have recently argued, an arbitrary system of justice strengthens informal but essential lines of dependency within a hierarchial society. If lower-class peasants and artisans need wealthy and powerful patrons to avoid severe punishment, social relationships of deference and dependency are reinforced.[9] Just as capital punishment increased the need for such patronage in England, so deportations performed the same function in mid-nineteenth-century France. Montagnards who had challenged the political influence of bureaucrats and conservative notables suddenly found themselves totally dependent on these very men for their freedom. Psychological resistance crumbled, as conspirators and rebels threw themselves on the mercy of officials and promised full and complete obedience to the government. Where police bureaucrats continued to fear the social resentments of the poor, they viewed such recantations with skepticism, but increasingly they recognized that conditional pardons were the natural sequel to arrests and deportations. Liberated prisoners were brought under a system of police surveillance that ensured political stability for the following decade. Few regimes in modern Europe have been more successful in maintaining order than the Second Empire of Louis Napoleon.

Each of the three phases of repression—arrests, deportations, and pardons—proceeded in accordance with national-policy guidelines, but officials in the departments retained discretionary authority over the timing of the shift from punitive to conciliatory measures. Generally speaking, military officers led the purge in rebel areas of the nation,

---

[9] Douglas Hay, "Property, Authority and the Criminal Law," in *Albion's Fatal Tree*, by Hay, et al. (New York, 1976), reviewed by Laurence Stone, "Whigs, Marxists, and Poachers," *The New York Review of Books*, Feb. 5, 1976, p. 25.

while the administrative and judicial police helped widen its scope considerably. The army, the prefectoral corps, and the magistrature determined the general outlines of the purge before the Mixed Commissions were established to regulate the fate of prisoners in February. Variations in the scale of arrests from department to department reflected government policies with respect to four overlapping categories of suspects: men who had taken arms after the coup d'état; members of Montagnard societies; socially "dangerous" elements of the population; and political rivals of conservative or Royalist notables. Insurgency, conspiracy, social agitation, and left-wing factionalism were the dominant targets of repressive operations in the departments.

Armed resistance was naturally the greatest stimulus to mass arrests. In most departments that had major uprisings, the civilian authorities had been worried, even badly frightened, at the height of the crisis. Once the army restored "physical order," their fears gave way to anger and a thirst for vengeance. "Striking examples will be made," wrote the subprefect of Béziers as soon as he felt confident enough to send troops into the countryside. "This country needs to be mastered by brute force," commented the *procureur* at Auch when a new general arrived to take command of the department.[10] Army officers were even more determined to punish the insurgents who had challenged gendarmes or troops. "The punishment must be terrible," wrote General de Geraudon from Auch. "Against such audacious endeavors, it can never be too harsh."[11] For General Pellion, whose timorous strategy of troop deployment had given the Montagnards of Clamecy an opportunity to rebel, "Repression must be as severe as possible. . . . The laws of the country and the rights of society have been violated too outrageously for any indulgence to be given." He wrote on December 19 that it was "indispensable" to produce "a great effect" at Clamecy by holding some public executions as soon as possible.[12] Officers of the gendarmerie were also zealous in repression. The captain in the Yonne reported on the thirteenth that his men "won't believe their mission is complete until they have purged the entire canton of St. Sauveur of all known participants in the insurrection." His counterpart at Nérac (Lot-et-Garonne) complained on the seventeenth that "an immense number" of rebels were still at large, much to the indignation of "respectable citizens," but he added proudly that "the anarchists have

[10] S-P Béziers, Dec. 6, 1851, ADH, 39M 142; *Proc.* Auch, Dec. 8, 1851, cited by Dagnan, *Le Gers*, II, 189.
[11] General de Geraudon, Dec. 11, 1851, AG, F¹ 53.
[12] General Pellion, Dec. 22, 1851, AG, F¹ 54, and Dec. 19, AG, G⁹ 186-87, Nièvre.

been struck down by the most profound terror at the thought of the punishment which awaits them."[13]

Most of the men who had taken arms *were* terrified of the army, and they fled by the hundreds from the mobile columns that swept through the rebel districts in December. These troops had explicit orders from the new minister of war, Saint-Arnaud, to kill anyone who resisted them.[14] Prisoners captured with weapons could be summarily executed, and fugitives could be shot on sight. Officers in the Basses-Alpes, the Nièvre, the Var, and the Vaucluse had troops execute around twenty prisoners, and patrols in the Hérault and the Nièvre killed around ten fugitives.[15] Rumors of these "exemplary punishments" spread terror among the populations. A captain who had five negotiators from Clamecy executed on December 8 wrote naively to his commanding officer: "All the villagers are in the most profound consternation. Many people have abandoned their houses and gone to sleep in the woods for fear of being murdered by these infamous brigands. We are viewed as messengers from God. . . . The women, the children, the old men weep with joy at our passage: they all throw themselves in front of us as we approach."[16] He would learn soon enough that the young men who had vanished from these villages were terrified of the army, nor the "brigands," and that the relatives whom they had left behind were weeping tears of fear. Within a few days the troops at Clamecy would be shooting at the fugitives in the woods and carrying peasants back to town in chains.[17]

The manhunts that officers organized in nearly all the rebel districts involved surprise raids on agglomerated settlements and systematic forays into the countryside. So many suspects were in flight that these operations took as long as two months to complete. The pace of arrests varied from region to region, depending on the terrain and settlement pattern of the countryside as well as on the size and tactics of the military forces. While nearly two thousand men were captured in the small towns and agglomerated villages of the Var during the month of December, many of the fugitives in dispersed settlements of the central Drôme and the central Gers evaded arrest until mid-January or even

[13] Gendarmerie Auxerre, Dec. 13, and Nérac, Dec. 17, in AG, F¹ 53.

[14] See his telegrams of Dec. 7 and 9, 1851, to the military commanders in the departments, cited by Dagnan, *Le Gers*, II, 187, ADD, M 1348.

[15] Ténot describes these summary executions and deadly pursuits of fugitives, *La province*, pp. 44-46, 48, 123-24, 155-60, 182, 185-86.

[16] Capt. Sajoux to his colonel, Dec. 8, 1851, in AG, F¹ 52. See also Carlier, special *commissaire*, to M. War, Dec. 8, and Capt. Aveline to General Pellion, Dec. 9, in AG, F¹ 52.

[17] Ténot, *La Province*, pp. 45-46.

February.[18] The army was relentless in their pursuit. Generals issued edicts to treat anyone who fed or sheltered fugitives as an accomplice in revolt, and they established networks of military posts in rural areas. Subordinate officers led persistent cavalry raids and organized night ambushes until their prey, isolated and half-starved, finally surrendered.[19] Some rebel leaders of independent means had fled to foreign countries in the aftermath of defeat, but most of the artisans and peasants who had been compromised had gone into hiding near their families. With few exceptions, their common fate was prison.

Statistical evidence concerning mass arrests of rebels can be inferred from the registers of the Mixed Commissions, which give the place of residence of each suspect and which often note the charges against him. I have drawn a random sample of every twentieth entry in a master register of 26,884 individuals whom the Mixed Commissions sentenced.[20] This sample contains 1,156 persons who resided in the provinces, of whom 536 (46%) were specifically accused of revolt, 602 (52%) were residents of rebel communes, and 794 (69%) were residents of one of the thirteen departments that had a major uprising of over 1,000 men.[21] Extrapolating from this data, around 12,000 prisoners were taken in rebel communes, and around 16,000 in departments with major revolts. The summary tabulations of the departmental registers confirm that 15,896 suspects resided in these thirteen departments.[22] These tabulations actually underestimate the numbers of arrests in rebel districts, because the authorities in some departments released prisoners whose names were not subsequently registered by the

---

[18] Agulhon, *La République au village*, p. 443; Margadant, "Insurrection," pp. 480-81, 484-85; Dagnan, *Le Gers*, II, 192-93, 195-97, 205.

[19] See the vivid reports of gendarmes operating in the central Drôme (ADD, M 1348), used by Vigier, *La Seconde République*, II, 350-52.

[20] This set of registers is in AN, F⁷ *2588, *Inculpés* in 1851-52. It contains the name, age, occupation, place of birth, place of residence, marital status, and number of children of each suspect, as well as the charges of the Mixed Commission, its sentence, and revisions of that sentence before Dec. 31, 1853; prisoners who were actually transported to Algeria and those who died in captivity are also noted. The 26,884 entries are in alphabetical order. Thirty of the sheets are missing from registers 2-4, with a total of 960 entries, so the random sample is actually based on 25,924 cases.

[21] A few of these suspects were probably fugitives at the time of sentencing (72, or 6%, had an incomplete *état civil*), but the vast majority had been taken prisoner.

[22] These tabulations consist of a breakdown of the decisions by department and occupation for the entire nation, and by occupation for each department. They were made by the statistical service of the army, on the basis of the master registers, and they comprise a separate register, filed in AN, BB³⁰ 424. Agulhon has published some of them in *1848*, pp. 235-37, and Tilly has analyzed the occupational distribution in "How Protest Modernized in France," pp. 235-42; see, also, the tables and analysis by Price, *The French Second Republic*, pp. 291-96, 301-4.

Mixed Commissions. Such liberations were especially common in several departments that had major uprisings, including the Gard (608 unregistered cases), the Gers (447), the Pyrénées-Orientales (around 300), and the Vaucluse (353).[23] More detailed analysis of the summary tabulations, as corrected by evidence concerning unregistered prisoners, shows that mass arrests were characteristic primarily of the few departments which had over 1,000 rebels: all but two of these departments had more than 800 suspects, and they averaged 1,389 cases per department, while all but two of the seventy-two other departments (excluding the Seine) had less than 800 suspects, and these departments averaged only 112 cases.

A more precise measure of the dependence of mass arrests on rebel activity can be calculated from this data. By treating the number of armed demonstrators and the number of suspects in each department as separate variables, we can calculate their correlation coefficient, r. It is very high ($r = .83$), showing a strong tendency for the magnitude of repression to increase in direct proportion to the scale of insurgency.[24]

The departments with major uprisings had the most *extensive* repression, as measured by the number of communes from which individuals were prosecuted. Around 2,000 communes in the nation as a whole had political arrests and prosecutions after the coup d'état, of which nearly 1,300 were located in the few departments with major uprisings. Prosecutions were most extensive in the Drôme (143 communes), followed by the Hérault (138), the Var (123), the Nièvre (122), the Basses-Alpes (116), the Lot-et-Garonne (99), the Pyrénées-Orientales (86), the Gers (84), and the Gard, the Saône-et-Loire, and the Yonne

---

[23] The confusion in some departments concerning the numbers of suspects stems from the fact that a ministerial *circulaire* of Jan. 29, 1852, authorized the prefects to release prisoners unconditionally. Because the Mixed Commissions were formed in the following week, these liberated suspects were sometimes entered into its registers and sometimes overlooked. In addition to the four departments noted in the text, the following estimates of such unregistered prisoners can be made: Hérault (245), Ille-et-Vilaine (18), Isère (20), Loir-et-Cher (91), Maine-et-Loire (30), Marne (120), Nièvre (158), Rhône (375), Saône-et-Loire (77), Haute-Vienne (107). These supplemental figures are included in the notes to Table 12.3, which list the numbers of suspects in each department. See Wright, "The Coup d'Etat," pp. 308-9, 329 (n. 15); P-G Nîmes, Mar. 25, 1852, in AN, BB³⁰ 401; letter from MC Pyrénées-Orientales, Feb. 27, 1852, cited by Horace Chauvet, *Histoire du parti républicain dans les Pyrénées-Orientales*; Dagnan, *Le Gers*, II, 270-71; Autrand, *La résistance vauclusienne*, pp. 357-60; *Procès-verbal* of MC, Hérault, Apr. 10, 1852, in ADH, 39M 161; list of prisoners released at Clamecy, ADN, U, Ins. Clamecy.

[24] To calculate r, I have used the estimated scale of armed mobilizations in each dept., given in Chapter One, Tables 1.1 and 1.2; and the estimated number of suspects in each dept., given in the notes to Table 12.3.

(around 75 each). Only five other departments had prosecutions in a large number of communes, and many departments had prosecutions in fewer than 10 communes.[25] Similarly, departments with major uprisings had the most *intensive* repression, especially in small towns and rural communities. Out of some 60 communes that had large-scale prosecutions (over 50 cases), 15 were located in the Hérault, 11 in the Var, 8 in the Nièvre, 4 in the Lot-et-Garonne, 4 in the Drôme, and 3 in the Basses-Alpes.[26] Mass arrests not only occurred at Clamecy (278 cases), Bédarieux (257), Béziers (246), Manosque (212), Le Luc (128), Cuers (123), and La Garde Freinet (117), but also in many lesser communes of these regions.[27] Indeed, the smaller the commune, the larger the proportion of the rebel population likely to be prosecuted: the participants in a small band were easier to accuse than those in a large crowd.[28] Over one-third of the rebels in many villages of the Var were arrested, and so were high proportions of those in many bourgs and villages of the Basses-Alpes, the Drôme, the Hérault, the Nièvre, and the Yonne.

Many police bureaucrats were convinced that "secret societies" had organized the revolts. For months they had been trying to prevent "anarchists" and "demagogues" from conspiring against the government. Now they discovered how completely they had failed to halt the spread of Montagnard societies. Magistrates who directed their attention to the political origins of the revolts began uncovering solid evidence that such societies *did* exist in many communities. Dagnan and Vigier have described the process by which investigative judges in the Gers and the Drôme first extracted confessions from tearful peasant recruits and then traced leadership networks to the towns and bourgs.[29] Similar investigations yielded abundant details about Monta-

---

[25] Allier (c. 75), Cher (c. 75), Jura (c. 75), Bouches-du-Rhône (c. 50), Loiret (c. 50). Tabulations based on the registers of the MCs, AN, BB[30] 398-402 (Pyrénées-Orientales and Yonne missing, but names of suspects from these depts. are listed in Chauvet, *Histoire du parti républicain*, pp. 124-50, and ADY, III M¹ 282).

[26] Others were located in the Allier (1), the Ardèche (1), the Bouches-du-Rhône (1), the Cher (2), the Gers (2), the Jura (1), the Pyrénées-Orientales (1), the Rhône (1), the Saône-et-Loire (1), the Vaucluse (2), and the Yonne (1). These include the rebel communes of Apt (75 cases), Cluny (60), Le Donjon (66), Mirande (50), Poligny (70), and Vallon (56), as well as the cities of Lyon, Marseille, and Peripignan.

[27] Tabulations based on the registers of MC Basses-Alpes, Hérault, Nièvre, and Var. AN, BB[30] 398, *399, 401.

[28] In bourgs and villages with less than 25 rebels, the rate of prosecutions (per number of rebels) was 52% in *arr.* Béziers and 40% in the central Drôme; in such communes with over 100 rebels, the rate was only 18% in the former region and 11% in the latter. Margadant, "Insurrection," p. 489.

[29] Dagnan, *Le Gers*, II, 197-98, 245-50; Vigier, *La Seconde République*, II, 320-26.

gnard societies in most departments where major uprisings had occurred. Disillusionment and fear spread to affiliates who had remained calm after the coup d'état, permitting diligent magistrates to widen the geographical scope of the purge. Prefects and public prosecutors urged them forward. "The destruction of secret societies has become one of the most imperative needs of our age," commented the *procureur-général* at Paris after receiving detailed information in January about Montagnard societies in villages of the Yonne. "It is absolutely imperative to track them down," wrote the prefect of the Drôme on January 19, after magistrates had obtained enough confessions to implicate many leaders of the underground. From the Hérault came exaggerated reports that 60,000 men were initiates in this department alone, and on January 20 the *procureur-général* at Montpellier wrote grimly: "At least a quarter of this number are essentially dangerous men, socialist fanatics, incessant propagandists who will stop at nothing. In my opinion it is absolutely indispensable to purge this element from the soil of France."[30]

To estimate the national dimensions of judicial and administrative operations against Montagnard affiliates, we can examine the registers of the Mixed Commissions. Although these administrative tribunals were not obliged to base accusations of secret-society membership on documented confessions, they often did have such evidence at hand. In the *arrondissement* of Béziers, for example, 517 prisoners admitted membership, and in the central Drôme, 166 prisoners and 62 witnesses confessed.[31] These Montagnards compromised still others who persisted in denying any knowledge of the underground, and the registers of the Mixed Commissions in the Hérault and the Drôme are usually accurate in their charges of conspiratorial leadership or affiliation. The same generalization holds for most other departmental registers.[32] If we consider our random sample of 1,156 suspects drawn from the master list of all the Mixed Commissions, we find that over nine-tenths (365/392) of those accused of belonging to a secret society resided in districts where magistrates had documentary proof that Montagnard societies existed. As we might expect, the largest number of leaders and affiliates in the sample resided in the Hérault (87), followed by

[30] P-G, Paris, Feb. 9, 1852, AN, BB[30] 396; Prefect Drôme, Jan. 19, 1852, ADD, M 1348; P-G Montpellier, Jan. 20, 1852, AN, BB[30] 397.
[31] Tabulations based on Ints. and Tems. in ADD, M 1354-71; ATML, Ins. of 1851; ADH, 39M 144-60; CG Bédarieux, Béziers, and Capestang.
[32] The major exception is the Allier, where evidence of affiliations was uncovered in only a few communes; nonetheless, the Commission accused bourgeois politicians throughout the department of being members. See Georges Rougeron, "Le terreur bonapartiste dans le département de l'Allier après le coup d'état," *La Révolution de 1848*, 34 (1937-38), 155-71.

the Nièvre (44), the Basses-Alpes (35), the Bouches-du-Rhône (24), the Yonne (24), the Drôme (22), the Cher (19), the Var (18), the Lot-et-Garonne (16), the Pyrénées-Orientales (16), and the Vaucluse (14), with lesser numbers in seven other departments where Montagnards confessed. In sharp contrast to the situation before the coup d'état, administrators now had enough political intelligence to identify and arrest upwards of 7,000 initiates in conspiratorial districts of the nation. Although a majority of these suspects had also been compromised in the revolt, a substantial number (158 in our sample) resided in communes where no one had taken arms. Arrests for conspiracy but not revolt were especially common in the *arrondissements* of Aix (Bouches-du-Rhône), Joigny (Yonne), Nevers (Nièvre), St. Amand (Cher), and St. Pons (Hérault).[33] Altogether, Montagnards who had not rebelled accounted for around 3,000 political prisoners in 1852.

Social defense against thieves, rapists, murderers—and Republicans— gave administrators a third justification for massive repression. They shared a counterrevolutionary mentality that attributed moral depravity and social subversion to their Republican opponents. Social democracy already conjured up images of disease, violence, and anarchy in the minds of prefects and public prosecutors before the coup d'état.[34] Now they could interpret the rebellions as proof of a gigantic plot against the social order. "You have just experienced in 1851 the social war which was to have broken out in 1852," wrote Morny to the prefects on December 10. "You will have recognized it by its typical features of murder, brigandage, and incendiarism."[35] Journalists stimulated this social myth of a *Jacquerie*, which fearful notables were only too willing to believe. While applauding the coup d'état, they printed tales of popular savagery that blackened the reputation of Republicans throughout France.[36] One such story, printed by *La Patrie*, accused insurgents at Clamecy of raping the wife of the subprefect, the daughter of the excise collector, and the servant of the president of the Tribunal.[37] Parisian gossip embellished this grotesque rumor with pornographic details: "The socialist bands which mastered Clamecy had themselves served dinner," wrote one *bon vivant*; "they forced thirty-eight of the prettiest and youngest wives and daughters of the locality

[33] See P-G Aix, Jan. 17, 1852, P-G Paris, Jan. 21, 1852, and *Proc.* St. Pons, Jan. 16, 1852, all in AN, BB[30] 396-97; and the *Diplômes* by Furet and Autenzio on the Cher and the Nièvre in 1851-52.

[34] See Forstenzer's discussion of their counterrevolutionary ideology, "Bureaucrats under Stress," pp. 481-503.

[35] Cited by Adrien Dansette, *Louis Napoleon à la conquête du pouvoir*, p. 366.

[36] See the examples cited by H. Magen, *Histoire du Second Empire* (Paris, 1878), p. 124; and those invented by De Maupas, the Paris Prefect of Police, in *The Story of the Coup d'Etat*, pp. 406-26.

[37] Cited by Ténot, *La province*, pp. 41-42.

to wait on them, completely in the nude. The poor unfortunates were raped on the public square."[38] Nor were police bureaucrats immune from fantasies of rape. The *procureur-général* at Montpellier wrote on February 1 to the prefect of the Hérault that the Montagnards had been "soiled with disgusting hopes." Their recruits had been promised "material enjoyments of every kind, all as rewards for the battle. Rape would be permitted to everyone, although the members did promise to spare one another's wives." The *procureur-général* feared leniency on the part of the central government, but he wrote happily at the end of the month that the region had been "purged, so to speak, of all the vicious and indisciplined elements which it contained." He voiced confidence that severe repression would hasten the advent of a "complete social regeneration."[39]

By disfiguring the economic aspirations of workers and peasants, by slandering their social ideals, and by denouncing their political convictions, police bureaucrats tried to equate opposition to their own authority with criminality. This confusion between Republican militants and common criminals was the basis of Morny's repressive strategy as minister of the interior. The definition of any unauthorized political associations or meetings as "secret societies"; the treatment of electoral propagandists as "dangerous agents" who "pervert" public opinion; the assimilation of these men to ex-convicts liable to deportation for breaking parole; and the arrest of Republicans on mere suspicion of conspiracy: such were the main elements of Morny's policy, which he urged upon the prefects in a series of peremptory *circulaires*.[40] He disguised a general offensive against Republicans as if it were a crusade against antisocial criminals. Around one-tenth of the 27,000 suspects in 1852 did have criminal records, but many of these "convicts" had been guilty only of minor political offenses, such as insulting the authorities. Others had been fined for hunting illegally, or jailed briefly for getting into fistfights. Very few had committed serious crimes against persons or property.[41] The suspension of legality did enable the

---

[38] Viel-Castel, cited by Dansette, *Louis Napoleon*, p. 366.

[39] P-G Montpellier, Feb. 1, 1852, ADH, 39M 141, and Feb. 26, 1852, AN, BB[30] 380.

[40] Dated Dec. 20, 1851, Jan. 2, Jan. 11, 1852, in AN, BB[30] 396. See Payne's analysis of how Morny first obtained a decree law from Louis Napoleon on Dec. 8 to deport secret-society members who were "recognized guilty," and then tried to extend it to members of any unauthorized political associations, in *Police State*, pp. 41-43.

[41] In the random sample of 1,156 suspects (outside the Seine) whom the MCs sentenced, 139 were *repris de justice*, of whom 58 had committed political offenses, 19 had been fined for hunting illegally, and 17 had served brief jail terms for getting into fights; 15 had been convicted of theft, one of attempted murder, and one of rape. See, also, Loubère, *Radicalism in Mediterranean France*, p. 77.

police to incarcerate local riffraff, such as a *vigneron* at Mesnay (Jura), who was "feared by all the respectable men, a very evil subject, a marauder and a looter"; or a day laborer at Montbéliard (Doubs), who was "dangerous, without political convictions, hoping for pillage and odious excesses in 1852."[42] Such petty thieves were far outnumbered, however, by men with clean records who had neither joined the underground nor resisted the coup d'état. In extending the purge to these "demagogues" and "socialists," police bureaucrats wanted, above all, to smash the Republican movement, however much they talked about saving society from the rabble.

Thus, counterrevolutionary rhetoric concealed political factionalism. Administrators allied themselves with "men of order," whose hostility to Republicans was often based on family rivalries or personal ambitions. In creating new opportunities for electoral competition, the Republic had threatened to displace notables who opposed social reforms with those who offered a populist program to lower-class voters. To counter the threat of electoral defeat, former Royalist politicians were quick to denounce prominent Republicans as subversives. They wanted the police to prevent their rivals from campaigning; the police wanted them to support Louis Napoleon. It was a marriage of convenience which the coup d'état consummated in many districts of the nation. Henceforth, Republican patrons and their lower-class clients were exposed to arrest and deportation, regardless of whether they had participated in the underground or the revolt.

Factionalism had a substantial influence on the social base of the purge. Many Republican landlords and professional men were denounced although they resided in towns and bourgs that remained calm after the coup d'état, and others were falsely accused of leading rebels whom they had advised to disperse. By contrast, the bulk of the cultivators and day laborers who were arrested had actually taken arms. If we compare the proportions of bourgeois politicians and peasants in our random sample of suspects, controlling for insurgency, we can estimate these variations. Table 12.1 shows the dramatic shift in the social base of the purge, as administrators turned their attention toward Republicans who had not resisted the coup d'état. Typically, they denounced bourgeois politicians as "socialist leaders" or "party chieftains" who had used their influence to pervert the population. Republican artisans and shopkeepers became "agents of demagoguery" and "propagandists." At every level of the movement, "evil subjects" and "fanatics" were at work.[43] These terms masked the simple fact that

---

[42] Suspects #1,480 and #18,860 in the master register, F⁷ *2588.

[43] For abundant examples of these denunciations, see the master register.

TABLE 12.1

Occupations of Suspects in Rebel and Nonrebel Communes

	Liberal Professions, Proprietors		Crafts and Commerce		Agriculture		Total
Rebel commune	40	(7%)	263	(47%)	260	(46%)	563
Nonrebel commune	92	(18%)	314	(62%)	99	(20%)	505

SOURCES: Random sample of every twentieth entry in the master register of the Mixed Commissions, AN, F⁷ *2588.

Republicans had tried to mobilize voters in electoral campaigns. For this offense alone, several thousand men were placed under "administrative arrest" after the coup d'état.[44]

The multiple waves of repression that swept through the nation threatened to engulf the prison system with enormous numbers of inmates, especially in districts where the army was operating against former rebels. Administrators crammed hundreds of suspects into makeshift jails at the Palace of the Popes in Avignon, the *Ecole Mutuelle* at Clamecy, the medieval Tower of Crest in the Drôme, and they watched anxiously for signs of epidemics in the overstuffed prisons of towns such as Auxerre and Forcalquier.[45] Having arrested thousands of "dangerous men," military commanders, prefects, and public prosecutors had to figure out how to dispose of them.

The army's plan was to deport large numbers of rebels. For this purpose, military commissions were established in the various departments governed by the state of siege. Their precedent was the rough justice dispensed by the army after the June Days in Paris. At that time, the terrified National Assembly had decreed that only the leaders of insurgency would be judged by military courts; ordinary combatants would be summarily deported without trial. Military officers had formed special commissions to perform the task of separating the innocent from the guilty: they had referred only a few hundred prisoners to court martials, while sentencing over four thousand to deportation and releasing around seven thousand.[46] This procedure, which expedited punishment by avoiding courtroom debates, inspired Louis Napoleon's new minister of war, Saint-Arnaud. On December 19 he

[44] Concerning this category of arrests, see Payne, *Police State*, p. 44.

[45] Vigier, *La Seconde République*, II, 354; A. Sonnié-Muret, *Clamecy et le coup d'état*, p. 34; Prefect (Yonne) to M. of General Police, Mar. 29, 1852, in Forestier, *L'Yonne*, II, 179.

[46] Seignobos, *La Révolution de 1848*, pp. 104-106; Charles Tilly and Lynn Lees, "The People of June, 1848," in Roger Price, ed., *Revolution and Reaction*, p. 188.

ordered the commanders of the state of siege to create military commissions whose officers would sort the prisoners into three categories: those implicated in crimes of violence, such as murder or pillage, would be sent before court martials; other rebels would be deported to Cayenne or Algeria, depending on the gravity of their offenses; and only the innocent would be freed. Saint-Arnaud's instructions took time to implement because the army relied on civilian magistrates to interrogate the prisoners; but by mid-January military commissions were functioning in the major rebel zones of southeastern, southwestern, and central France.[47]

Military justice quickly revealed its political shortcomings. It was both too severe in application and too limited in scope to meet the needs of the new regime. If the commissions operated on the crude assumption that prisoners were either guilty if they had rebelled, or innocent if they had not, then thousands of obscure peasants would be deported, while prominent Republicans in many districts would be spared. The former danger was great in departments such as the Var and the Basses-Alpes, where the commissions threatened literally to depopulate the countryside.[48] The opposite problem of inadequate repression existed wherever Republicans had abstained from insurgency. Whether nonrebels came under the jurisdiction of military commissions was uncertain, and, in any case, most of them resided in districts where no such commissions were operating. Saint-Arnaud's effort to widen the prerogatives of the commissions while moderating their sentences resulted in incoherence and confusion. On January 17 he informed General de Rostolan at Montpellier that he should arrest not only "all the men compromised by their participation in the recent insurrections," but also those who were "recognized as leaders of socialism, or identified as violently hostile to the government, or designated as being able to disturb public order in the department." Yet two days later, he urged all the military commissions to discriminate between "inveterate conspirators" and "imitative and flighty followers," as if only the former should be deported.[49] The commission in the Basses-

[47] Payne, *Police State*, pp. 62-63; Dagnan, *Le Gers*, II, 254-56; Vigier, *La Seconde République*, II, 355; Autrand, *La résistance vauclusienne*, pp. 354-57; the dossiers of the military commissions at Béziers and Clamecy, in ADH, 39M 144-60, and ADN, U, Ins. Clamecy.

[48] Report of Paton, investigative judge sent to review the operations of the military commissions in southern France: at Draguignan (Var), when he protested that the commission could not depopulate the country, he was told, "That is what it must come to in certain communes, and if the measure is not thorough, the evil will remain, nothing will be accomplished, and it will be necessary to start all over again." Feb. 12, 1852, in AN, BB[30] 397.

[49] Letters cited by Louis Puech, *Essai sur la candidature officielle en France depuis 1851* (Mende, 1922), p. 52; and Payne, *Police State*, pp. 63-64.

Alpes went ahead and sentenced all but thirty-five of eight hundred prisoners to deportation, and General Hecquet authorized the commission in the Vaucluse to begin sentencing secret-society "leaders" to deportation in Cayenne, and "simple affiliates" to deportation in Algeria.[50] Presumably, all were "inveterate conspirators." The *procureur-général* at Bourges had already voiced his anger at the way military officers in the Cher were implementing such a policy toward conspirators: after magistrates had extracted confessions from several dozen peasants at Meillant, in exchange for promises of leniency, the military commission had sentenced all but five of the naive souls to deportation![51] It was becoming increasingly doubtful whether the army was the most appropriate instrument for a national political purge.

Meanwhile, the prefects and the *procureurs* were developing alternative methods for "saving society." The prefects took their example from Morny, who extended Louis Napoleon's harsh treatment of Republican deputies to lesser leaders of the Democratic-Socialist movement. On January 9, five deputies were sentenced to deportation as rebels; sixty-five were expelled from France as "recognized leaders of socialism"; and eighteen were exiled temporarily because of their "violent hostility to the government."[52] Two days later, Morny ordered the prefects to sort all the suspects into these same categories of deportation, expulsion, and exile, to which he added a fourth category of exile from a department. The purpose of this new classification was to extend repressive measures from insurgents to other Republicans, who could be exiled because of their "constant preaching against the government," or because their presence in a department caused "troubles or uncertainty."[53] The minister of justice offered no advice of his own to the *procureurs*, but he encouraged them to recommend sanctions against political prisoners. Among their suggestions were conditional release, expulsion, "internment" in a fixed residence, and deportation.[54] If the military commissions had only the extremes of liberation or deportation to recommend, prefects and public prosecutors were prepared to apply an intermediate range of sanctions, applicable throughout the nation. Their participation in the sentencing of suspects was all the more desirable because of their political expertise. The prefects were now the main electoral managers for Louis Napoleon, and the justices of the peace, beneath the *procureurs* in the

[50] Vigier, *La Seconde République*, II, 355; Autrand, *La résistance vauclusienne*, pp. 355-56.

[51] P-G Bourges, Jan. 13, 1852, AN, BB[30] 374.

[52] Seignobos, *La Révolution de 1848*, p. 217.

[53] *Circulaire* of Jan. 11, 1852 to the Prefects, cited by Dagnan, *Le Gers*, II, 257.

[54] Payne, *Police State*, p. 62.

judicial hierarchy, had extensive political tasks, too. Military commissions needed civilian advice concerning the moral character and political antecedents of insurgents. Why not incorporate representatives of the administrative and judicial police directly into the organs of the purge?

The Mixed Commissions represented just such a solution to the problem of harmonizing military and civilian perspectives. These administrative tribunals also enabled the government to formalize repressive measures in departments where the state of siege had not been declared. The commanding general, the prefect, and a *procureur* in every department would exercise jointly the same discretionary authority to recommend measures of "general security" against moderate Republicans as well as Montagnards, electoral leaders and militants as well as conspirators and rebels. From the perspective of Paris, the Mixed Commissions would thus fulfill two quite distinct objectives: they would settle the fate of the thousands of insurgents who had been imprisoned; and they would impose a graduated scale of police controls on leaders and militants who had not compromised themselves in rebellion or bona fide conspiracy.

Initiated by the head of the newly created Ministry of Police on February 3, the commissions were expected to use political rather than legal criteria in their deliberations. They could refer suspects accused of murder or attempted murder to military courts (*Conseil de Guerre*, abbreviated *C.G.*), and those who had violated minor laws to civilian courts (*Police Correctionnelle*, or *P.C.*), but they could not inflict the normal judicial punishments of imprisonment, hard labor, or death. Instead, they were empowered to recommend severe or lenient administrative sanctions, depending on the insurgent role, political background, and "morality" of each suspect. At the severe end of the spectrum of police controls were deportation to Cayenne, reserved for "especially culpable" men with police records (*Cay.*); deportation to an Algerian penal colony (*Algerie plus*, or *A+*); or deportation to an Algerian town where the suspect would reside under police surveillance (*Algerie moins*, or *A−*). An intermediate range of sanctions included expulsion from France (*Exp.*); temporary exile (*Eloignement*, or *El.*); and forced residence under police surveillance in a French town assigned by the authorities (*Internement*, or *Int.*). The mildest sanction was police surveillance in a residence of one's own choosing (*Liberté en Surveillance*, or *L.S.*). Prisoners could also be liberated without any police controls (*L.*). The commissions were ordered to classify each suspect into one of these several categories, and to forward registers of their decisions to the three Ministries of War, Interior, and Justice. Speed and secrecy were of the essence: their deliberations, based on secret examinations of the prisoners' dossiers, must be completed by the end of February.[55]

As joint administrative bodies with extralegal powers, the Mixed Commissions had a precedent in the three-man commissions established by Napoleon Bonaparte during the Hundred Days to intern "conspirators."[56] Yet in the speed of their deliberations, the harshness of their sanctions, and the scale of their operations, they bore the stamp of another age, when massive repression had become the counterweight to insurrection. The severity of their recommendations varied from department to department in accordance with perceived threats of popular involvement in politics. Where large numbers of artisans and peasants had joined the underground and taken arms, deportations were proportionately high; elsewhere, the preferred sanctions were expulsion, internment, or police surveillance, in accordance with the lesser danger of mass protest. Individual commissions did vary widely in their categorization of suspects, but, taken in the aggregate, their decisions were considerably harsher in departments where the Montagnards had rebelled than elsewhere in the nation.

Table 12.2 compares the distribution of sentences in the thirteen departments with major revolts (type I), the seventeen departments with minor uprisings (type II), the fifty-five departments with no armed mobilizations (type III), and Paris (the Seine). If we combine all the severe sanctions (C.G., Cayenne, A+, A−) in each type of department, we find that the Mixed Commissions in type I imposed such sanctions on 7,496 suspects, 42% of all their cases; those in type II sentenced 1,172 suspects to deportation (or referred them to court-martials), 31% of their cases; and those in type III recommended that 955 persons be deported or court martialed, 19% of their cases. The Seine was a special case: its commission released half of the prisoners unconditionally, and referred one-quarter to the misdemeanor courts. If we examine the frequency distributions of severe sentences by type of department, as shown in Table 12.3, the same trend is confirmed. Most commissions in departments with major revolts sentenced over 400 persons to deportation, while only two of those in quiescent departments sentenced over 50 persons to deportation.

[55] Concerning the powers and operating procedures of the MCs, see Seignobos, "Les opérations des commissions mixtes," pp. 59-67; Wright, "The Coup d'Etat," pp. 305-7, 320-24; and Payne, Police State, pp. 64-66. For regional variations in their policies, see Vigier, La Seconde République, II, 355-59.

[56] Resnick alludes to these earlier three-man commissions, also consisting of the prefect, the commanding general, and a procureur in each department (The White Terror, p. 101).

TABLE 12.2

Severity of Sanctions Imposed by the Mixed Commissions

	CG	Cay.	A+	A−	Exp.	El.	P.C.	Int.	L.S.	L.	(*L)	Total
Type Iᵃ	212	128	3,433	3,723	363	354	261	1,680	2,645	2,857	2,398	18,054
	.01	.01	.19	.21	.02	.02	.01	.09	.15	.16	.13	
Type IIᵇ	42	36	532	562	170	84	65	527	976	658	107	3,759
	.01	.01	.14	.15	.05	.02	.02	.14	.26	.17	.03	
Type IIIᶜ	54	72	347	482	307	178	281	573	1,521	619	682	5,116
	.01	.01	.07	.09	.06	.04	.05	.11	.30	.12	.13	
Paris	7	3	237	265	140	24	712	47	52	1,475	...	2,962
(Seine)	...	...	.08	.09	.05	.01	.24	.02	.02	.50		
Total	315	239	4,549	5,032	980	640	1,319	2,827	5,194	5,609	3,187	29,891
	.01	.01	.15	.17	.03	.02	.04	.10	.17	.19	.11	

ᵃ Type I: The thirteen departments with armed mobilizations of over 1,000 men.
ᵇ Type II: The seventeen departments with smaller armed mobilizations.
ᶜ Type III: The fifty-five departments with no armed mobilizations (Mixed Commissions registered suspects in fifty-two of these departments).
SOURCES: Statistique of the repression of the insurrection of December 1851, Register, AN, BB³⁰ 424.
NOTE: The column headings refer to charges as described in the text, page 318. (*L) refers to prisoners liberated by the prefect, the general, or the Commission, but not entered in the registers.

The strongest measure that the Mixed Commissions could recommend was trial before a military court. Only men accused of murder or attempted murder were supposed to be sent before court-martials, but several commissions in departments where gendarmes or troops had been killed interpreted this to include rebel leaders, who were presumably accomplices in murder. Thus, the commissions in the Allier, the Drôme, the Gers, the Hérault, the Loiret, the Nièvre, and the Var referred anywhere from five to eighty-one suspects before military justice. Apart from the Rhône, where General Castellane had 67 ordinary political suspects transferred to the *Conseil de Guerre* at Lyon, nearly all the men placed in this category resided in communities where violence had erupted in December 1851.

Whether they were guilty as charged was quite another matter. The government's purpose in several of the trials was to publicize the collective violence of the rebels and to exact vengeance on as many culprits as possible. This was especially true in the Hérault and the Nièvre, where military courts tried six suspects from Pézénas, fourteen from Capestang, twenty-five from Béziers, thirty-four from Bédarieux, and

TABLE 12.3

Number of Severe Sentences, Rebel versus Nonrebel Departments

	Under 25	25-49	50-99	100-199	200-399	400-799	800 plus
Depts. with major uprisings[a]	0	0	0	2	2	5	4
Depts. with minor uprisings[b]	8	2	1	4	2	0	0
Depts. with no armed protest[c,d]	42	8	0	1	1	0	0

SOURCES: same as for Table 12.2.

[a] Basses-Alpes (998/1,669 sentences by the Mixed Commission), Ardèche (177/355), Drôme (532/1,614), Gard (200/380 + 608 liberated without being registered by the Mixed Commission), Gers (461/464 + 447 L.), Hérault (1,654/2,840 + 245 L.), Lot-et-Garonne (412/884), Nièvre (875/1,506 + 69 CG not registered by the Mixed Commission + 158 L.), Pyrénées-Orientales (450/692 + c. 300 L.), Saône-et-Loire (189/390 + 77 L.), Var (820/3,147), Vaucluse (285/680 + 353 L.), Yonne (443/1,167).

[b] Ain (22/65), Allier (289/512), Hautes-Alpes (19/144), Aveyron (108/156), Bouches-du-Rhône (121/777), Creuse (28/73), Jura (114/422), Haute-Loire (12/64), Loiret (234/566), Lot (43/124), Lozère (3/46), Nord (1/69), Puy-de-Dôme (101/197), Basses-Pyrénées (3/45), Sarthe (14/187), Tarn (48/73), Haute-Vienne (12/132 + 107 L.).

[c] At least 25 severe sentences: Aube (40/151), Cher (249/937), Côte-d'Or (28/131), Doubs (28/89), Gironde (27/80), Loir-et-Cher (26/46 + 91 L.), Oise (28/107), Rhône (193/465 + 375 L.), Seine-Inférieure (25/196), Seine-et-Marne (33/130).

[d] Under 25 severe sentences: Aisne (0/51), Ardennes (0/149), Ariège (5/19), Aude (17/251), Calvados (24/76), Cantal (0/4), Charente (3/28), Charente-Inférieure (1/22), Corrèze (0/17), Côtes-du-Nord (3/3), Dordogne (14/78), Eure (7/90), Eure-et-Loire (15/31), Haute-Garonne (23/95), Ille-et-Vilaine (0/0 + 18 L.), Indre (23/81), Indre-et-Loire (3/34), Isère (13/132 + 20 L.), Landes (1/34), Loire (21/114), Maine-et-Loire (4/32 + 30 L.), Manche (1/1), Marne (4/80 + 120 L.), Haute-Marne (7/109), Mayenne (2/23), Meurthe (9/56), Meuse (7/44), Morbihan (0/22), Moselle (0/20), Orne (0/3), Pas-de-Calais (0/22), Hautes-Pyrénées (0/37), Bas-Rhin (18/49), Haut-Rhin (0/43), Haute-Saône (0/31), Seine-et-Oise (15/25), Deux Sèvres (15/95), Somme (0/14), Tarn-et-Garonne (0/30), Vendée (1/9), Vienne (9/34), Vosges (11/56).

sixty-nine from Clamecy and nearby villages. Individual justice was rarely the point of these trials. The prosecution brought together Montagnard leaders, ordinary rebels, and men accused of specific acts of violence, all of whom were charged with capital crimes. Not a single witness confirmed the contradictory testimony of the state's main witness in the affair of Bédarieux, a plasterer named Cazals whom the police commissioner had blackmailed into denouncing several dozen rebels. Cazals gave a different list of names every time he was questioned, and his own sordid role in the murder and castration of Liotard became evident during the trial, a witness who had helped save the life of a gendarme testified that he had seen Cazals lurking about the *caserne* long after everyone else had gone home—with his trousers off, wearing a gendarme's underwear![57] To salvage its case, the prosecution announced at the end of the trial that anyone who had been at the *caserne* would be charged with murder, an offense that could now apply to any of a thousand rebels.[58] General de Rostolan wanted death penalties, not because the suspects were necessarily guilty, but because they had displayed too much "pride" in the courtroom.[59] The military judges obligingly returned sixteen death verdicts, which Louis Napoleon subsequently commuted to life imprisonment. The prosecution at Clamecy relied on the same kind of dishonest testimony to convict the Montagnard centurion and rebel leader, Eugène Millelot, of murdering the schoolteacher Mulon. A rumored police spy claimed he had seen Millelot kill Mulon twenty minutes after the shoot-out with the gendarmes on the town square. Yet three witnesses testified that Mulon fell immediately after the fusillade and was carried to his home within five or six minutes. The judges nonetheless condemned Millelot to death. Again Louis Napoleon commuted the sentence.[60]

Political pressures forestalled a similar correction of judicial "error" in the trial of several men from Béziers who were accused of murdering a bourgeois pedestrian during the revolt. Lawyers for a gardener named Vidal and a stonecutter named Cadelard had obtained witnesses on their behalf. When the first defense witness, one Bousquet, took the stand on March 25, he testified that Vidal had been home warming his feet at the time of the violence. The presiding judge intervened to squelch his testimony: "Tell the truth! Watch out, or you'll be sent to the galleys!" Bousquet replied, "Do what you will to me. I am telling the truth." The judge read to the witness the articles of the penal code relative to false testimony. The witness persisted. The police commissioner at Béziers testified that according to a tanner named Miquel, the witness was going to testify because he had been in the revolt and feared that he might be denounced. The witness denied the assertion. "The testimony of Bousquet being in contradiction with that of the previous witnesses," announced the judge, "we order his immediate arrest in order that he can be tried, if cause be found, for false testi-

---

[57] Tem. Ch. Mical, cooper, reprinted by Ténot, *La province*, note E in the appendix, pp. 220-21. Cazals had also stolen Liotard's pistol, which the CP found under his bed. For his garbled testimony, see CG Bédarieux, #22.

[58] Speech by Teissier, asst. *commissaire* of the govt., reprinted in *Le Messager du Midi*, June 20, 1852.

[59] General de Rostolan to M. War, June 1, 1852, AN, F⁷ 12, 711.

[60] See the trial transcript published by Ténot, *La province*, note A in the appendix, pp. 212-18. Six others were sentenced to death for murdering the gendarme Bidan, and two were executed at Clamecy on June 30, 1852. See A. Sonnié-Moret, *Clamecy et le coup d'état*, p. 36, no. 1.

mony." A gendarme advanced and led Bousquet out of the courtroom. Following this scene, the names of ten witnesses for the defense were called out. Not one person stepped forward to testify. Then Marie Blayac took the stand to defend Cadelard. The presiding judge threatened to arrest her; she persisted in her testimony; he ordered her arrested; she equivocated; he had her hustled out of the courtroom before she could complete her testimony. Cadelard's sister took the witness stand and confirmed Blayac's remarks. The judge expressed regret that he could not have her arrested because she had not taken the oath (being related by blood to the suspect). Finally, Marie Magence appeared in court with the same testimony on Cadelard's behalf. She was arrested on the spot. The last witness for the defense had been heard, and both Vidal and Cadelard were condemned to death, along with two other men.[61] "The interests of public morals and the security of good citizens absolutely demand vengeance," wrote the prefect to the minister of the interior on March 30. "The attitudes of people in the unhappy *arrondissement* of Béziers make these examples of high justice indispensable."[62] Louis Napoleon commuted only two of the death sentences. On August 13, Cadelard and another man were executed on the public square of Béziers.[63]

The sanction of deportation to Cayenne was nearly as severe as a court-martial, because this penal colony in French Guiana had a notorious reputation for harsh discipline, tropical disease, and high mortality. By stipulating that only men with previous police records should be exposed to the risk of death in Cayenne, the government moderated the policy of the military commissions, which had been assigning the most prominent rebels to this fate. The *procureur* at Auch complained, "This rule makes it necessary to punish the soldiers more severely than the leaders," and he persuaded his colleagues on the Mixed Commission of the Gers not to sentence anyone to Cayenne.[64] At the opposite extreme, the Mixed Commission of the Basses-Alpes imposed this penalty on 41 men, including 2 bourgeois leaders of the revolt who had clean records and some militants who had committed minor political offenses.[65] In the nation as a whole, condemnation to Cayenne was rare, although several commissions, including those at Bordeaux, Marseille, and Perpignan, tried to take the opportunity to cleanse society

[61] For the transcript of this courtroom scene, and the subsequent verdicts, see *Le Messager du Midi*, Mar. 26 and 30, 1852.
[62] AN, BB[30] 401.
[63] Appolis, "La Résistance au coup d'état," p. 501. Cadelard became a martyr for the poor of Béziers. See Ténot, *La province*, note G in the appendix, p. 223.
[64] Dagnan, *Le Gers*, ii, 266.
[65] Register of MC Basses-Alpes, Pr. Ailhaud, *sans profession* at Valensole, and Gustave Jourdan, lawyer at Gréoulx (joint entry, #619), AN, BB[30] 398.

of militants with a violent reputation. A total of only 239 individuals were sentenced to Cayenne.[66] Some of them did have serious criminal records, such as a carpenter at Allègre (Gard) who had served seven years for attempted murder.[67] Nonetheless, even among *repris de justice*, only a small proportion were destined for Cayenne: out of the 139 men in our random sample who had a police record, this was the fate of only 7.[68] Cayenne earned its fearful reputation for political persecution less because of the disreputable workers and peasants sent there by a few Mixed Commissions, than because of the Montagnard leaders transported there by the military courts after their trials. Bourgeois such as Casimir Peret, Alexandre Guerbet, and Ailhaud de Volx were condemned to penal servitude and shipped to Cayenne. All 3 men died in captivity, as did 43 others (out of 239) who had the misfortune of being transported to the tropics as convicted criminals in 1852.[69]

Just one week before the Mixed Commissions were created, a new minister of the interior, Persigny, announced publicly that all the "misguided men who were led into revolt only by weakness and ignorance" should immediately be released.[70] At the Ministry of War, Saint-Arnaud agreed that "numerous arrests in various parts of the country have been made on the basis of very incomplete and often erroneous information." To reduce the congestion in the prisons, he ordered the generals to liberate anyone whom the prefects decided should not be transported or further detained on political grounds.[71] Persigny's *circulaire* provoked such a storm of protest from disgruntled counterrevolutionaries that he issued new instructions to rearrest anyone who continued to endanger public security.[72] Nonetheless, Louis Napoleon's ministers in Paris expected that the prefects, the generals, and the *procureurs*, henceforth taking joint responsibility for emptying the jails, would deal more severely with leaders and militants than with passive recruits. Both social and political distinctions were implied in this contrast between militancy and passivity. The influential "demagogues"

---

[66] *Statistique* of the Insurrection, AN, BB³⁰ 424.

[67] Entry #10,640 in the master register, F⁷ *2588.

[68] Of these 7, 4 had been convicted only of insulting the authorities. In the sample a total of 11 men were sentenced to Cayenne, i.e. 4/11 had no police record.

[69] Adolphe Robert listed all the suspects who were deported to Cayenne, and he noted those who died there, in *Statistique pour servir à l'histoire du 2 décembre 1851* (Paris, 1869), pp. 28-263 *passim*. His list of 239 names is not identical with the original 239 sentenced by the MCs; some of the latter were not, in fact, transported to Cayenne.

[70] *Circulaire* published in *Le Moniteur*, Jan. 30, and cited by Payne, *Police State*, p. 64.

[71] Letter from Saint-Amand to the military commanders, quoted by Dagnan, *Le Gers*, ii, 268.

[72] *Circulaire* from Persigny to the prefects, Mar. 2, 1852, noted by Payne, *Police State*, p. 64.

and "socialists" presumably had a higher social position than the peasants whom they had seduced and misled. Thus, bourgeois Republicans and merchants, shopkeepers, and artisans in the towns and bourgs would be treated more harshly than cultivators. At the same time, many villagers had participated actively in the underground and the revolt. The more heavily they had been compromised in violent and conspiratorial resistance, the more severely they would be punished, regardless of their social position. The national government did not give its departmental authorities any guidelines concerning the relative importance of controlling socially influential propagandists and punishing lower-class activists. It left open the possibility of deporting the former and liberating the latter, or vice versa. Seignobos and other historians have concluded that the decisions of the Mixed Commissions failed to conform to any consistent political rationale.[73] On the contrary, analysis of these decisions, based on our 5 percent sample of suspects in the registers, indicates that social class and political activism both had a systematic influence on the severity of sanctions. However much individual commissions varied in their application of particular police controls, such as exile or internment, their decisions generally reflected the social and political bias of the national government.[74]

Table 12.4 compares the treatment of suspects drawn from each of the three basic social classes in small towns and rural communities of mid-nineteenth-century France: landlords and professional men; merchants, shopkeepers, and artisans, and cultivators, day laborers, and other agricultural workers.[75] The first section of the table groups resi-

[73] Seignobos, "Les opérations des commissions mixtes," pp. 65-66; Payne, *Police State*, pp. 65-66; Wright, "The Coup d'Etat," pp. 320-24. These historians focus attention on the wide variations in sanctions imposed by MCs in departments that did not have major uprisings, while I am comparing sentences in rebel and non-rebel districts.

[74] Variations *were* extreme from MC to MC concerning which of the intermediate range of sanctions to apply: expulsion, exile, internment, or police surveillance. Thus, within the thirteen departments with major uprisings, the MCs sentenced an average of 28 persons to expulsion, 27 to exile, 129 to internment, and 203 to police surveillance, but these averages conceal the fact that only three MCs expelled over 15 persons (the Var, with 158, the Pyrénées-Orientales, with 93, and the Hérault, with 34); only two sentenced over 12 persons to exile (the Var, with 163, and the Lot-et-Garonne, with 125); only three sentenced over 74 to internment (the Nièvre, with 551, the Var, with 506, and the Vaucluse, with 300); and the proportion of sentences to police surveillance ranged from 20% to 30% in five departments, from 8% to 17% in five departments, and from none to 3% in three departments. *Statistique* of the Insurrection, supplemented by evidence of unregistered liberations (n. 23).

[75] I have used Agulhon's categories of occupational analysis, *La République au village*, p. 448, where he reaches the same conclusions concerning severity toward bourgeois and leniency toward peasants. See, also, Price, *The French Second Republic*, pp. 291-95, 303; and Tilly, "How Protest Modernized in France," p. 240.

TABLE 12.4

Severity of Sentences, by Social Class

	A+, A—	Exp., El	Int., L.S.	L.	Total
	Departments with Major Uprising (rebel communes only)				
Liberal professions, proprietors	16 (42%)	8 (21%)	9 (24%)	5 (13%)	38
Crafts, commerce	113 (49%)	3 (1%)	92 (40%)	24 (10%)	232
Agriculture	84 (35%)	3 (1%)	96 (40%)	59 (24%)	242
	Other Departments (nonrebel communes only)				
Liberal professions, proprietors	13 (22%)	12 (20%)	29 (48%)	6 (10%)	60
Crafts, commerce	37 (21%)	10 (6%)	99 (55%)	32 (18%)	178
Agriculture	8 (14%)	1 (2%)	36 (62%)	13 (23%)	58

SOURCES: Random sample of every twentieth entry in the master register of suspects sentenced by the Mixed Commissions, AN, F⁷ *2588.

dents of insurgent communes in the thirteen departments that had large-scale uprisings: nearly all of these men had been compromised in the revolt, apart from a few bourgeois patrons who had tried to caution their Montagnard clients against violent protest. By contrast, the suspects classified in the second section of the table lived in non-rebel communes elsewhere in the nation: they had nearly all remained calm after the coup d'état, although a few were accused of public disorder or clandestine agitation. The table shows that while the proportions of all three social classes sentenced to deportation increased substantially in rebel districts, landlords and professional men were treated considerably more harshly than peasants and somewhat more so than shopkeepers and artisans, regardless of whether rebellions had taken place. These bourgeois were especially vulnerable to the sanctions of expulsion or temporary exile. As the Mixed Commission of the Pyré-nées-Orientales wrote concerning the fifty-seven men whom it sentenced to expulsion from France: "Political leaders of their communes —these individuals abused the influence given them by their position, their education, their fortune, to pervert the populations; they bear the main responsibility for the disorders which broke out." The Commission also noted that "they have some wealth or an industry which will permit them to live abroad," a consideration that influenced most Commissions in deciding whether to deport or merely to expel "dangerous" men.[76] While 32 percent of the lawyers and 26 percent of the doctors whom the various Mixed Commissions sentenced were either expelled or temporarily exiled, the same was true of only 4 percent of the shoemakers and 2 percent of the cultivators whom they judged.[77] As for peasants, they were more likely to be liberated unconditionally than were either artisans or bourgeois, showing that the Mixed Commissions generally attributed less militancy to them. In rebel districts, however, one-third of the peasant suspects were sentenced to deportation, alongside one-half of the artisans and shopkeepers. Here the lesser sanctions of internment or police surveillance were often felt to be insufficient, while elsewhere in the nation, these were the preferred methods of dealing with militant artisans and peasants.

For more precise analysis of how sanctions varied in accordance with the type and degree of political activism charged against suspects, we can classify the individuals in our sample along two axes of militancy: (1) their alleged participation in the insurrection, whether as leaders, conspicuous rebels, or mere recruits; and (2) their previous involvement in the left-wing movement, whether as secret-society leaders and propagandists, electoral leaders, secret-society members, or other militants. Table 12.5 compares the numbers of individuals along both these axes who were sentenced to deportation with the numbers who were placed under police surveillance within mainland France. It shows that rebel leadership was the single most important determinant of severe sanctions; that secret-society leadership and conspicuous involvement in the revolt were equally common grounds for deportation rather than surveillance; and that ordinary rebels were likely to be deported if they had other political accusations against them. By contrast, non-rebels were usually placed under police surveillance rather than shipped to Algeria, even if they were accused of secret-society membership or other militancy. This table confirms at the level of individuals what we inferred earlier from departmental analysis: the purge struck most harshly against men who were heavily compromised in the revolt.

If the Mixed Commissions reflected national policy in their sentenc-

[76] Letter from MC Pyrénées-Orientales, cited in n. 23.

[77] *Statistique* of the Insurrection, 72/225 *avocats*, 83/325 *médecins*, 48/1,107 *cordonniers*, and 105/5,423 *cultivateurs* sentenced to expulsion or exile. Tilly's data, cited in n. 75, show this same correlation between the professions (and finance) and the sanctions of expulsion or exile.

TABLE 12.5

Severity of Sanctions, by Political Role of Suspects

Previous Political Role[b]	Role during the Insurrection[a]											
	Rebel Leader		Other Conspicuous Rebel		Rebel Recruit		Part. in Disorder		Nonrebel		Totals	
	$A+Int.$	$A-L.S.$	$A+Int.$	$A-L.S.$	$A+Int.$	$A-L.S.$	$A+Int.$	$A-L.S.$	$A+Int.$	$A-L.S.$	$A+Int.$	$A-L.S.$
Secret-society leader or propagandist	19	1	16	1	22	1	6	0	40	21	103	24
Other political leader	9	0	9	3	7	3	5	5	14	43	40	54
Secret-society member	6	0	29	4	54	31	8	5	16	51	113	91
Other militant	4	0	8	5	14	4	10	7	8	43	44	59
No accusation re. political antecedents	21	0	50	24	28	27	12	13	2	30	111	94
Totals	59	1	112	37	127	66	41	30	91	188	430	322

SOURCES: Random sample of every twentieth entry in the master register of suspects sentenced by the Mixed Commissions, AN, F⁷ *2588.

[a] This classification of rebels is based on the fact that most of the Mixed Commissions noted whether suspects were accused of leading rebels; of playing other conspicuous roles, such as ringing the tocsin, forcing others to march, disarming gendarmes, etc.; or of merely participating. Where the registers do not provide any information about suspects, apart from the vague term "dangerous," I have excluded such individuals from the analysis.

[b] This classification is based on the terms of opprobrium used by the Mixed Commissions to denounce the political activism of suspects. It distinguishes between secret society leaders (chefs, propagandistes, affiliateurs de sociétés secrètes, etc.); other political leaders (chefs de parti, propagandistes, agents de la démagogie, meneurs socialistes, etc.); secret-society members (affiliés); and other militants (socialistes, démagogues, anarchistes, etc.). Of course, the registers are sometimes misleading or false in their charges, but they indicate what kinds of activism the Mixed Commissions perceived as warranting severe sanctions.

ing of leaders and militants, they also responded to local pressures for severity or indulgence toward the Montagnards. Factionalism and social fear generated demands for massive deportations, while communal solidarity and patron-client relationships encouraged leniency. At one extreme, vindictive justices of the peace, mayors, and police commissioners, allied to fearful "men of order," denounced the moral character and the political convictions of ordinary Montagnard recruits. Charges of immorality and fanaticism were especially common in the Hérault and the Nièvre, where workers and agricultural laborers had defied rich proprietors by supporting the Democratic and Social Republic.[78] At the other extreme, sympathetic local authorities praised the family background of many suspects, and they blamed rebellion on the misleading propaganda of outsiders or the contagious influence of passing bands. The efforts of mayors or municipal councilors to protect local residents often signaled that peasant proprietors or their sons had been compromised in the insurrection.[79] Local patronage also expressed the solidarity of rural communities vis-à-vis police bureaucrats in the towns. Protective networks were strongest in Protestant districts of southeastern France, where magistrates generally agreed that the rebels were "ignorant" rather than "evil."[80] In sharecropping districts of southwestern France, where some peasants had been drawn into the revolt at the instigation of bourgeois patrons, local officials also recommended leniency.[81] Similar pressures toward conciliation existed in Provence, but they were often countermanded by factional rivalries. Thus, prominent landowners in the Basses-Alpes who had lost control of their popular clients were nonetheless denounced by personal enemies and imprisoned. This slowed down the restoration of patron-client relationships at the local level and may have blocked the transmission to the Mixed Commission of favorable recommendations concerning some of the prisoners.[82]

As a result of variations in the scope and effectiveness of local patronage, some Mixed Commissions imposed severe sanctions on a majority of the prisoners who had taken arms, while others released most of those who had not played a conspicuous role in the revolt. Thus, 1,563 suspects were sentenced to *Algérie plus* or *Algérie moins* in the

---

[78] For example, MC Nièvre accused the Montagnard society at the mining community of La Machine of aiming for "the pillage and massacre of the rich" (entry #645, comment on Benoit Bardet, miner, register in AN, BB[30] *399). The prefect of the Hérault wrote of the Montagnards: "Murder, pillage, rape, such was their aim, such were their methods," letter of Feb. 2, 1852, in ADH, 39M 141.

[79] See the correspondence from municipal officials on behalf of landowning rebels in the central Drôme, in ADD, M 1353-71 (dossiers of prisoners).

[80] For example, see the sympathetic analysis of the peasant affiliates to the underground, most of them Protestant, by J. P. Dieulefit, letter of Dec. 23, 1851, in ADD, M 1347.

[81] Most of the peasants arrested in the Gers were released without being sentenced by the MC. See Dagnan, *Le Gers*, ii, 270-74.

[82] Vigier attributes the severity of MC Basses-Alpes to the arrival of a new prefect in mid-February, but he also notes the importance of factional rivalries. *La Seconde République*, ii, 358-59.

Hérault, 956 in the Basses-Alpes, and 803 in the Nièvre, as compared with only 496 in the Drôme, 455 in the Gers, and 197 in the Gard. Although the generals, prefects, and *procureurs* on the Mixed Commissions had their own social prejudices and political biases toward severity or leniency, they rarely operated at cross-purposes with their subordinates, who provided them with written evaluations of the prisoners.[83] In the Hérault, for example, police bureaucrats at Béziers believed just as firmly in the virtues of terror as General de Rostolan, M. Saint-Amand, and M. Durand, the three members of the Mixed Commission at Montpellier. When the prefect released a few prisoners in response to Persigny's *circulaire* of January 29, a veritable panic seized local authorities in the *arrondissement* of Béziers. Popular hopes of clemency were "evil, hateful, and vindictive passions," to be mastered by "fear and force," wrote the subprefect. His own subordinate, the mayor of Béziers, reported an impression of "general terror" at the thought of any liberations: "To live securely in the midst of these savages and cannibals, we will have to be on guard constantly, armed to the teeth."[84] By denouncing most of the insurgents as immoral and fanatical men, local officials in this region guaranteed that they would be shipped to Algeria. The Mixed Commission of the Hérault simply reviewed the negative moral and political comments in the dossiers of prisoners, translated them into a standard phrase—"evil morality, fanatical, armed band, secret society"—and slapped a sentence of A+ or A− (either would do) on the defenseless suspect, often an agricultural laborer. Yet in the minority of cases when local officials did recommend leniency, the commission usually decided against deportation.[85] Despite more careful procedures, the Mixed Commission in the Drôme followed similar criteria in its decisions. Here the magistrates who had investigated the insurrection often praised the respectability, good reputation, and morality of prisoners, especially in the villages. Mayors and priests also wrote letters to higher authorities, calling for the release of *all* the prisoners. Consequently, the Mixed Commission reserved harsh sentences for the men whom magistrates *did* denounce as political militants, conspicuous rebels, or "evil subjects." Everyone else they released as passive participants in the general movement.[86]

[83] Concerning the importance of personalities on the MCs, see Wright, "The Coup d'Etat," pp. 313-24.

[84] S-P Béziers, Feb. 2, and Mayor of Béziers, Feb. 10, 1852, in ADH, 39M 141.

[85] Among rebels in a sample of urban and rural communes in the Hérault, 237/253 (94%) of those who received negative moral or political evaluations from mayors, CPs, J. P.s, and other magistrates were sentenced to deportation, as compared with 25/138 (18%) of those who received positive evaluations. Margadant, "Insurrection," pp. 518-19.

[86] Among rebels in the cantons of Bourdeaux, Dieulefit, and Marsanne, 62/88

The use of moral and political evaluations of suspects underscored the arbitrary powers of the Mixed Commissions. In keeping with a long tradition of French criminal procedure, which enabled government prosecutors to shift attention from the specific actions of defendants to their general characters, Mixed Commissions often decided whether to deport or liberate suspects on the basis of judicial reports concerning their attitudes toward "authority." This opened the way for a more conciliatory policy once administrators decided to reward *changes* in attitudes. Magistrates were already recommending leniency toward the wayward and the repentant. Why not also release former militants who renounced their political convictions and submitted to the government? The relatives and friends of such prisoners were willing to vouch for their good behavior in the future. So were many municipal councilors, mayors, and priests. Protestations of loyalty were coupled with cries of distress in the correspondence that began to reach high levels of administration: many artisans and cultivators would leave behind impoverished wives and children if they were deported. The prisoners themselves addressed letters to the prefects, or even to Louis Napoleon, pleading ignorance and foreswearing any future involvement in politics. Alongside the pleas of lower-class militants were the intrigues of bourgeois politicians, who protested their innocence and mustered support within the entourage of Louis Napoleon. As patronage networks began to operate on behalf of men who had been sentenced to deportation, the stage was set for a reversal of government policy. Incorrigible opponents would still be banished from France, but militants who rallied to the government would be paroled under police surveillance or granted full and complete pardons.[87]

This new policy was inaugurated by Quentin-Bauchart, one of three special *commissaires* whom Louis Napoleon named on March 26 to exercise presidential powers of commutation or pardon in the departments.[88] Quentin-Bauchart and his fellow *commissaires*, Colonel Espinasse and General Canrobert, received no specific guidelines for their mission of clemency, but on the next day Louis Napoleon raised the state of siege, abolished extraordinary police measures, and dissolved

---

(71%) of those who received negative moral or political evaluations from local officials were sentenced to deportation, as compared with 15/140 (11%) of those who received favorable evaluations. Ibid., pp. 524-25.

[87] Abundant correspondence on behalf of men sentenced to deportation exists in departmental archives and the national archives. See, for example, ADH, 39M 143-47, 152, 162; ADD, M 1356-71; and AN, BB[22] 129-89.

[88] See Quentin-Bauchart's memoires, *Etudes et souvenirs sur la Deuxième République et le Second Empire (1848-1870)*, pp. 452-64; and Payne, *Police State*, pp. 68-70.

the Mixed Commissions.[89] The sequel to arbitrary arrests and deportations was to be arbitrary commutations and pardons. It was Quentin-Bauchart who used his presidential authority generously. While Colonel Espinasse recommended only 300 pardons and commutations in the Hérault and two neighboring departments, and while General Canrobert restricted presidential grace to 727 individuals in the center and the southwest. Quentin-Bauchart issued pardons or commutations to 2,424 suspects in southeastern France, including 1,377 who had been sentenced to deportation.[90] Unlike his military colleagues, who agreed with vengeful authorities in departments such as the Hérault and the Nièvre that mass deportations were indispensable, Quentin-Bauchart, as a liberal convert to Bonapartism, insisted on considering each prisoner individually. He recognized that many peasants and artisans would confess, repent, and submit to the government in order to be reunited with their families. By inviting the prefects to attend personal interviews with the suspects, he neutralized their objections to clemency. Each prisoner was brought forward, reminded of his sentence to deportation, informed of Quentin-Bauchart's mission on behalf of the prince-president, and asked to describe his role in the secret societies and the insurrection. "If his attitude was bad, if he concealed information, he was sent back to prison. If, on the contrary, he expressed repentance by the sincerity of his declarations and his regrets, I had him swear to respect the laws and never again to join any secret societies (and released him)."[91] Despite the anguished cries of counterrevolutionaries, Quentin-Bauchart succeeded in persuading the prefects and public prosecutors of southeastern France to adopt his policy as their own. He proved that conciliation could affirm the authority of the government in a time of calm, just as punitive measures had consolidated its power in a time of crisis.

Underlying Quentin-Bauchart's success was popular recognition that further struggle for the Democratic and Social Republic was hopeless. Most Montagnards were profoundly disillusioned by their defeat and imprisonment. "Politics only leaves the heart empty and draws persecution and impotence upon men," wrote a leader from Dieulefit to his father in January. "May my example serve all my friends and prevent them from suffering such a heavy fall."[92] Their dominant reaction was

[89] Decree of Mar. 27, 1852, cited by Payne, *Police State*, p. 70.

[90] Results published by Payne, *Police State*, p. 69. See Quentin-Bauchart's detailed report to Louis Napoleon, published in *Le Messager du Midi*, May 7, 1852, and compare with Colonel Espinasse's report, cited by Seignobos, *La Révolution de 1848*, p. 221.

[91] Quentin-Bauchart, *Souvenirs*, I, p. 456.

[92] Letter from Benjamin Laurie, Jan. 16, 1852, in dossier Laurie, ADD, M 1364.

to withdraw altogether from politics. "I will never talk about politics to anyone," promised one village militant in the Drôme. "I will never again belong to *any* political party, whatever it is and wherever it comes from," promised another.[93] With unconscious irony, Louis Bertrand Cherfils, a peasant leader from this region, voiced his new loyalty to the powers that be: "I promise full and entire submission to the government of Prince Louis Napoleon; I repent entirely for anything I may have done against his government; and I promise never again to involve myself in politics, and to resign myself entirely to all the decisions of the government, whatever they may be, knowing in advance that they can only be very wise and liberal."[94] There were still Montagnards who continued to defy the authorities, such as Maurice Aubanel, the pastor's son from Lasalle (Gard). Aubanel wrote to "the Tyrant Bonaparte," in August 1852, "It is with the greatest contempt that I saw in a newspaper my name among those who are authorized to return to France. . . . Of grace I want none! Of amnesty I want none!" But Aubanel was in exile, not in prison, and his boastful talk of "marching on the cadavers of all the enemies of the Republic" rang falsely in the France of 1852.[95] Far more typical were the words of Jean Galibert, a peasant from Béziers: "I was promised the right to work, prosperity, happiness; and now, all that remains is the right to misery and despair."[96]

Some prefects were slow to recognize the demoralization of the Montagnards, particularly in departments where social conflicts and factional rivalries had magnified the intensity of the purge. Around 6,000 of the 9,581 prisoners sentenced to deportation were actually transported to Algeria, where a few hundred of them died in penal colonies such as Douera.[97] "Brave and respectable men" in some districts of the nation threatened to withdraw their confidence from the government if such "anarchists" were allowed to return home.[98] Nonetheless, more and more police bureaucrats came to recognize that the authority of the new regime was so firm and unshakable that prisoners

[93] Letters from Villaret, mason at Poët-Laval, June 2 and from Jn. André Jala, baker at Saou, Feb. 24, 1852, in dossiers Villaret and Jala, ADD, M 1371, 1363.

[94] Letter from Cherfils, Mar. 3, 1852, in dossier Cherfils, ADD, M 1359.

[95] Letter from Aubanel, Aug. 17, 1852, AN, BB[30] 401, dossier #6.

[96] Letter from Galibert, May 16, 1852, ADH, 39M 143.

[97] According to Wright, 3,430 (36%) of the 9,581 persons sentenced to deportation in Algeria were not transported there ("The Coup d'Etat," pp. 324-26). In the random sample of suspects, 158/467 (34%) of those sentenced A+ or A− were not, in fact, transported, of whom 107 obtained a commutation of their sentence, and 51 presumably fled arrest.

[98] For example, see the prefect's complaint in the Yonne, May 22, 1853, in Forestier, *L'Yonne*, III, 468.

could be safely liberated. The electoral triumphs of Louis Napoleon, culminating in the plebiscite of November 1852, which founded the Second Empire, proved that even former Montagnards were willing to vote for the government.[99] As political objections to indulgence subsided, officials began to pay more attention to letters of recommendation on behalf of the prisoners. They also observed that public opinion favored equal treatment of lower-class militants and upper-class leaders. Once bourgeois suspects, who often had impressive patrons writing letters on their behalf, obtained release, then further punishment of artisans and peasants seemed unjust.[100] Selective commutations of sentences generated pressures for mass pardons. The prefects drew up lists of deportees who might be liberated, and Louis Napoleon issued large numbers of pardons on ceremonial occasions, such as the proclamation of the Empire in December 1852 and the marriage of the emperor on February 4, 1853.[101] By October 1853, only 3,006 sentences to deportation in Algeria had not yet been revised, and, taking account of fugitives who had escaped deportation, probably less than 2,000 political prisoners remained in Algeria. As for the 1,650 men who had been sentenced to expulsion or exile, all but 665 had been allowed to return to France by this date.[102] Not until August 16, 1859, did the government issue a general amnesty, but most of the 1,200 deportees still in Algeria at the end of the decade had refused to accept earlier offers of conditional pardon.[103] In contrast to these Republican loyalists, the bulk of the "men of December" had long since submitted to the regime.

Although the mass repression of 1852 left bitter memories, it also taught the populations of provincial France a brutal but effective lesson: conspiracy and rebellion did not pay. Victims of the purge might nourish private grudges against the local notables who had denounced them. They might continue to support a dissident faction at municipal or legislative elections. They might reaffirm their Republican loyalties

[99] This had been true in the plebiscite of Dec. 20-21, 1851, when rebel cantons of the southeast had fewer negative votes than some cantons that had not taken arms. See Vigier, *La Seconde République*, ii, map on p. 345; and letters from officials in the central Drôme to the Prefect (Léchelle, Dec. 21, and S-P Montélimar, Dec. 24, 1851), in ADD, M 1347.

[100] See, for example, J. P. Aillant (Yonne) to Prefect, May 29, 1852, and Aug. 4, 1853, in Forestier, *L'Yonne*, iii, 186-87, 471.

[101] Wright, "The Coup d'Etat," p. 325.

[102] Table of the decisions of the MCs, as revised before Sept. 30, 1853, published by Wright, "The Coup d'Etat," p. 326. In the random sample of suspects, 28% (86/309) of those actually transported to Algeria were still there on Dec. 31, 1853, 3% (15) had died in captivity, and the sentences of the rest (208) had been commuted to internment, police surveillance, or unconditional release.

[103] Ibid., p. 326.

when the repressive apparatus of the Second Empire collapsed. Never again, however, would they join secret societies or rebel against the government.[104] When the generation that resisted the coup d'état had a second opportunity to found the Republic in the 1870s, its leaders and militants in the provinces refused to adopt conspiratorial tactics. Strong elements of continuity existed between the regions that supported the Montagnards in 1851 and those that voted for Republicans in the 1870s, but the Radicals of the latter period no longer remembered the rituals of the Montagnards.[105] The purge had induced a kind of collective amnesia in their political consciousness. Conspiratorial networks had not only ceased to exist; they had been forgotten.[106] The democratic hopes and social aspirations of the Second Republic survived in the guise of Radicalism, but the Montagnard movement was dead.

[104] Police reports for the Second Empire are filled with unsubstantiated rumors of secret societies, but officials were nearly always mistaking factional alignments for conspiratorial networks. See, for example, the reactions of J. P. Toucy and J. P. Courson (Yonne) to the election of 1857, when a candidate patronized by ex-Montagnards won several hundred votes in the southwestern Yonne. Forestier, *L'Yonne*, III, 318-21.

[105] For evidence of such continuity in southeastern France, where Napoleon III encountered the strongest regional opposition to his plebiscite of May 4, 1870, and where some Radical candidates triumphed in the by-elections of July 2, 1872, see Jacques Gouault, *Comment la France est devenue républicaine* (Paris, 1954), maps on pp. 27, 132. Concerning the Radical style of electoral politics, see Loubère, *Radicalism in Mediterranean France*, pp. 96-154.

[106] Many Republicans denied that secret societies had existed, as Seignobos reflects in his treatment of the coup d'état, in *La Révolution de 1848*, pp. 201-21.

CONCLUSION

The insurrection of December 1851 is an anomaly in standard interpretations of nineteenth-century France. Its left-wing political orientation seems baffling in the context of its timing, its social base of support, and its outcome. The year 1851 would scarcely seem propitious
for the extreme left. Parisian revolutionaries had been decisively
crushed three years earlier during the June Days, and Louis Napoleon
Bonaparte was about to establish the Second Empire with overwhelming voter support. How could Republicans hope to reverse the tide of
history? All the more unlikely was their mobilization of peasant manpower against the coup d'état. Surely peasants had been less exposed
to the stresses and strains of modernization than the residents of cities.
Political passivity and social conservatism were the natural concomi-
tants of their isolation, backwardness, and low aspirations. Republicanism could not hope to survive without the support of modern sectors of French society. Indeed, it was the urban-industrial focus of the
Republican movement that gave it renewed momentum in the 1860s.
As for the countryside, its voters remained predominantly loyal to the
Second Empire until the debacle of 1870, and they subsequently converted to Republicanism partly in reaction against the extremism of
Royalist politicians. From this historical perspective of urban democracy and rural conservatism, the insurrection of 1851 is unintelligible
and irrelevant.

My analysis of peasant radicalization, conspiracy, and revolt implies
a different perspective on the history of the French left. Peasants were
an integral part of the Montagnard movement during the Second Republic, and despite their renunciation of political opposition during
the early years of the Second Empire, their struggle for a Democratic
and Social Republic foreshadowed the leftward drift of some rural
populations during the Third Republic. The triumphant coup d'état of
Louis Napoleon should not mislead historians into assuming that Republican hopes were destroyed in the June Days, or that democratic
impulses were confined to the cities until a much later time. The revolutionary cycle that opened in February 1848 entered a national phase
after the election of Louis Napoleon to the presidency in December,
and it did not come to a close until police bureaucrats succeeded in
destroying the Republican underground in the provinces. This success
was no forgone conclusion. The repressive apparatus of the state was
ill-adapted to the tasks of detecting and dismantling secret societies,

especially in small towns and villages. Conspiratorial networks not only survived but flourished in many districts of the southeast, and they also spread into some villages of the southwest and the center. It was the coup d'état and the insurrection that finally broke the cycle of repression and conspiracy by enabling prefects, police bureaucrats, and army officers to use their superior force against the Montagnards. Just as the police state of Louis Napoleon was born out of this protracted conflict with the Republican left, so its subsequent decline and collapse would remove the main obstacle to a revival of rural Republicanism. Henceforth, French peasants who voted on the left would be drawn into the orbits of successive urban political movements: first Radicalism, then Socialism, and finally Communism. This pattern of peasant responsiveness to urban militancy is what stimulated the repressive zeal of police bureaucrats during the Second Republic and culminated in the insurrection of December 1851.

To explain the general features and specific forms of rural Republicanism at mid-century, I have distinguished between the economic environment, the political setting, and the collective actions of rebels against the coup d'état. Insurgency is the obvious focus of my study, but it is a focus that requires more than one analytical lens. At the widest angle of vision are the economic relationships and market trends which facilitated peasant participation in the "Democratic-Socialist" coalition of the Second Republic. Although I have rejected the argument that an agrarian depression motivated peasants to rebel against the government, I have formulated a model of urban/rural dependency on market fluctuations which helps to explain peasant radicalization, especially in southern France. Moving toward the political factors which had a direct bearing on insurgency, I have argued that the authoritarian traditions of the French state were difficult to reconcile with a democratic electoral system. Police bureaucrats used repressive legislation to restrict as much as possible the electoral strength of Republican politicians, and their assault on political dissent generated the conflicts that erupted violently after the coup d'état.

In the foreground of these conflicts, I have placed the Montagnard secret societies, which infiltrated the countryside in 1850-51. Despite their unusual rituals of affiliation, these organizations derived much of their strength from prevailing socioeconomic, cultural, and political conditions in rural France. Thus, Montagnard leadership networks were adapted to the role of townsmen and rural craftsmen as mediators between villages and the outside world; their local sections utilized youth groups, voluntary associations, cafés, and other social centers within agglomerated settlements; and their militants translated factional rivalries into a national vocabulary of political struggle. At the same time, Montagnard societies imparted new organizational dynamism to the Republican cause by recruiting lower-class leaders in town and countryside alike, and they remained largely impervious to repression before the coup d'état. Once the Montagnards took arms, however, their organization lost its effectiveness: crowds dissolved into communal formations, and bands merged into makeshift military columns. By magnifying the details of typical scenes of revolt, I have shown how large-scale Montagnard demonstrations became ruinous military confrontations. The stage was set for the Bonapartist purge of 1852, whose shattering impact on rural political life has generally been underestimated by historians.

I have used the term "modernity" as a crude signpost leading from the Second Republic toward French society and politics in the Third Republic. This usage differs from that of historians who analyze the forces of continuity and change in nineteenth-century France from the standpoint of the later twentieth century, when urbanization and industrialization have greatly reduced the social weight and the political importance of the rural population. From such a vantage point, modernization implies the disappearance, not the transformation, of the peasantry as a significant force in French politics. I have presupposed, instead, that peasants could and did modernize before they began to vanish from the historical stage. By this I mean that they became increasingly integrated into a national economy, an urban society, and a centralized political system while continuing to form a substantial portion of the nation's population. Of course, elements of tradition persisted in rural communities long after peasants had been drawn into cash-crop agriculture and national politics. Poverty, ignorance, and localism did not vanish overnight, and I have analyzed the importance of traditional mentalities and modes of behavior within the insurrection. Nonetheless, the Montagnard movement succeeded in harnessing tradition to the political cause of the Republic, which has become synonymous with modern France. In like manner, its history illustrates general features of French political development in the modern period. Each analytical domain of my study—marketing, political organization, and collective action—can be extended from the mid-nineteenth century to subsequent time periods.

With respect to marketing, the gradual expansion of cash-crop agriculture, rural handicrafts, and small-town industry gave rural populations an increasing stake in large-scale commerce, as compared with local trade. As the sale of commodities for export became more important than the production of food for subsistence, rural prosperity came to depend on price fluctuations in distant markets rather than local variations in the size of the harvest. Instead of suffering from poor harvests and high food prices—a crisis of penury characteristic of the traditional economy—peasants became vulnerable to low prices for their marketable surpluses—a crisis of abundance, such as French agriculture was to experience several times during the Third Republic. The rural sector underwent just such a modern type of agrarian depression from 1848 to 1851, and some rural populations responded eagerly to Republican promises of government economic protection. No longer could food riots against grain exports meet the pressing needs of peasant smallholders, laborers, and craftsmen. Instead of direct action in the marketplace, the residents of country towns and villages turned to interest-group politics. Cheap credit, lower taxes, and higher wages were characteristic themes of Montagnard propaganda, and in all three respects converts to the movement looked to the Republic for remedies to their market difficulties. Henceforth, agrarian depressions would call forth similar Republican appeals to peasant economic interests. Not local defense against food shortages, but national protection of agricultural markets would become a central theme of rural Republicanism.

Montagnard propaganda had considerable success in some districts of southern France where the export sector reinforced local trade between towns and villages. The higher the price of cash crops such as wine, *eau de vie*, and raw silk, the greater the prosperity of all social groups within regions such as the Rhône river valley and the Mediterranean foothills. Economic interdependency facilitated social communications and political cooperation between townsmen and peasants. So did the agglomerated settlement pattern of the Midi, which brought landlords, artisans, and cultivators together in agro-towns, agricultural bourgs, and large villages. By contrast, the export of grain and textiles from districts of nothern France often distorted local trading networks between towns and villages. Commercialized agriculture bypassed small towns in its response to higher food prices in the cities, and putting-out industries created competition between urban and rural workers. Economic rivalries and social tensions between town and countryside discouraged urban-rural coalitions in the political sphere. So did the dispersal of the peasantry in small settlements. The distinction between towns and villages was more sharply drawn in the wheat plains of the north, where antiurban sentiment became widespread during the Second Republic, than in the vineyards of the Midi, where it was uncommon. The propertied elite of northern France succeeded in mobilizing landless agricultural laborers and unemployed rural artisans against working-class Republicans in Paris and other cities. Social reaction was less vigorous in the south, where middling elements of urban society carried the message of a Democratic and Social Republic to the peasantry. This progressive alliance of townsmen and villagers, which presupposed common economic interests and social ties, would become a characteristic feature of southern French politics during the Third Republic.

Alongside the problems of a market economy, peasants in many districts of the nation continued to suffer from traditional deficiencies in agriculture, such as the fragmentation of holdings, the low productivity of labor, and the shortage of cash. Nor had traditional remedies to rural poverty disappeared: subsistence plots, communal rights of usage, seasonal migration, and part-time handicrafts were characteristic features of peasant economic life, especially in mountainous regions. Although the abundant harvests of the Second Republic improved the food supply for marginal peasants, chronic poverty might easily foster social resentment and political discontent. Left-wing Republicans tried to fuse the traditional frustrations of the rural poor into a common front against the government. In some villages, they opposed legal restrictions on communal rights of usage, in others they promised to serve the common people rather than the rich, and everywhere they called for fiscal reform. They used the tax issue as a traditional weapon against the state and its wealthy allies within the landed elite: taxes should soak the rich and spare the poor, and public spending on the bureaucracy should be reduced. The demand for progressive taxation was democratic, but it was not particularly modern in origin. Poor peasants had always wanted tax exemption. Nor would Republicans in the future refrain from demagogic appeals to small peasants, artisans, and shopkeepers who believed that their lagging incomes would miraculously increase if only the government would tax other people instead of themselves.

Neither the difficulties of market-oriented farmers and craftsmen nor the grievances of the rural poor determined the success of Republican politicians. Economic issues were subordinated to social identities and political loyalties. Behind the divergent interests of rich and poor were varying degrees of solidarity or conflict, depending on religious traditions, factional alignments, forms of sociability, etc. Generally speaking, the Republican movement was strongest where it combined upper-class patronage with lower-class political organization. On the one hand, vertical lines of dependency between Republican notables and popular clienteles provided a local basis for regional electoral coalitions. On the other hand, horizontal lines of solidarity within lower-class organizations gave Republicans some immunity from government repression and encouraged them to adopt a more democratic style of leadership and propaganda. Patron-client relationships, which originated in factional rivalries for municipal office and historical traditions of anti-Legitimism and anticlericalism, achieved their fullest expression where mayors and assistant mayors participated in Republican electoral campaigns. Police bureaucrats retaliated by purging Republican officeholders, but their authority over rural mayors was restricted by the new system of municipal elections. The subsequent evolution of the relationship between mayors and the state—obedient appointees during the authoritarian Empire, increasingly independent officials during the Liberal Empire, moderate supporters of the Republican regime during the 1870s, and elected leaders of Republican municipal councils after 1883—would mark the gradual consolidation of Republican patronage through the institutions of local government. The uniformity of municipal administration, with its several hundred mayors and councils in each department, would give Republicans a natural base of electoral power. Their ability to control municipal councils in rural as well as urban communes would make possible the stabilization of the Third Republic as an electoral democracy.

If all Republican politicians tried to use municipal patronage against their Royalist enemies, the Montagnards specialized in the development of lower-class organizations. Their ritualistic societies were designed for undercover work within the broad mass of the population, and they fostered leadership opportunities for craftsmen, shopkeepers, and landowning peasants, who exerted social influence over neighbors and friends by virtue of their literacy and economic independence. Especially significant was the emergence of a younger generation to positions of political responsibility. Against the oligarchic gerontocracy of the July Monarchy, young beneficiaries of the literacy transition and of universal suffrage called for the rights of the people. Subsequent turning points in French political history, such as the socialist gains of the 1890s, would bring a comparable shift in the social background and generational identity of grass-roots political leaders. The "new strata" of rural Republicanism would include tradesmen and young peasants, more prosperous and more well-educated than their mid-century counterparts, but no less firmly implanted in local society.

Alongside bona fide secret societies, Montagnards worked through ostensibly nonpolitical clubs and taverns. The inspiration for such front organizations came naturally to the populations of towns and bourgs in the Midi, where formal institutions of male sociability were common. Electioneering in 1848-49 brought about some politicization of *cercles*, *chambrées*, *mutuelles*, and *sociétés*, and it also introduced political alignments to informal drinking groups in cafés and country inns. The Montagnards continued to use such centers of popular sociability as meeting places, and they created new front organizations on these preexisting models. The same process of politicization and organizational proliferation would take place during the Third Republic. Republican and Catholic *cercles* would compete for the allegiance of workers in the towns, and Red or White *chambrées*, *sociétés*, and cafés would mobilize rural voters, especially in the Midi. Socialist politicians would also succeed in mobilizing peasant *syndicats* in a few regions where the Montagnards had been active—lumbermen in the Nièvre, the Cher, and the Yonne, vineyard workers in the Hérault and the Gard. Until the Republicans finally legalized political associations in 1901, militants would concentrate much of their organizational efforts on voluntary associations and solidary groups. Indeed, the use of "nonpolitical" societies, *ligues*, and *syndicats* for political purposes would become a distinctive feature of right-wing as well as left-wing movements in the Third Republic.

Despite widespread popular support, Montagnard societies were hampered by poor communications, weak finances, and the localized character of voluntary associations in mid-nineteenth-century France. With respect to the flow of information, they used the oral networks that existed within peasant marketing areas. This reliance on oral communications enabled conspirators to evade police repression of written propaganda and to recruit illiterate peasants, but it also prevented them from creating interregional leadership hierarchies. In the absence of written communications, local leaders were susceptible to false rumor, wishful thinking, and impulsive action. Similarly, Montagnards tried to finance local branches by collecting dues, but they mirrored prevailing customs that discouraged the financing of regional or national organizations. Either peasants were too poor to pay regular dues, or they expected funds to be used exclusively for local purposes, such as mutual benefit. This localism was reflected in the voluntary associations that Montagnards used as vehicles for their secret propaganda. Although social clubs were influenced by regional culture and national legislation, most of them recruited their members exclusively from a single commune. Departmental or national federations of *cercles*, *chambrées*, or *mutuelles* were prohibited by law, and their regional development would have been restricted in any case by the high cost of transportation and communications. The same was true of trade unions and other specialized interest groups. The only front organizations that provided any departmental infrastructure for the Montagnards were Republican newspapers, and these public organs of propaganda often succumbed to police repression. Left-wing militants would have to await the triumph of the Third Republic, with its better communications, wealthier populace, and more tolerant government, before they could create effective national organizations.

Just as political party development in mid-nineteenth-century France was alternatively stimulated by national electoral institutions and obstructed by police centralization and sociocultural fragmentation, so collective action had both a national and a parochial dimension. The insurrection of December 1851 originated in a national political crisis whose protagonists affirmed vital features of modern French government: police bureaucrats demanded obedience to the lawful authority of the state, while Montagnard leaders demanded freedom for the citizens of the Republic. The ideological distortion of these principles into bureaucratic absolutism and Republican anarchy implied an irreconcilable conflict between Bonapartists and Montagnards. Indeed, the logic of the political situation before the coup d'état pointed toward a violent outcome, no less destructive of public liberties than twentieth-century counterrevolutions. It is from this vantage point that some scholars have detected in the police state of Louis Napoleon a precursor of modern fascism. At the same time, however, the armed uprisings of 1851 revealed traditional forms of collective action within rural France. Peasants shared political resentments and territorial loyalties, which accelerated the momentum of Montagnard societies in rebel districts of the nation. Their communal "unanimism" gave an anachronistic image to the entire movement. So did their makeshift weaponry, their threats of violence, and their precipitate flights from the army. The bands which assaulted gendarmes seemed to illustrate that the popular taste for vengeance far outweighed any ideological motives for insurgency. In the eyes of hostile officials, rural populations took arms because they were ignorant or perverse. Peasant committment to the Republic was a contradiction in terms.

These contrasting interpretations emphasize features of modern political organization and traditional communal solidarity which were simultaneously present during the insurrection. Many peasant rebels were members of the Republican underground, whose leadership, initiation rituals, and conflicts with the police set the stage for mass mobilizations against the coup d'état. But these rebels were also members of small, face-to-face communities, whose limited repertoire of collective actions included military displays against external enemies. The people in arms to defend the Republic were also villagers in arms against the state. It is the traditional dialectic of state repression and peasant reaction which explains the elements of continuity between 1851 and earlier peasant movements in French history. Just as the protests of rural taxpayers in 1848 were frequently directed against coercive police measures, such as arrests, fines, and distraints, so the armed mobilizations of 1851 were often stimulated by a previous history of police raids, arbitrary arrests, and political trials. The more vigorously the government opposed electoral freedoms and peaceful demonstrations, the greater was the temptation of Republicans to revert to traditional forms of armed protest. In this manner, rural populations followed a circuitous path from modern electoral politics backward to the collective threats of an earlier age.

The massive purge of 1852 brought to a close the long history of armed demonstrations in rural France. Henceforth, the military superiority of the state would be so obvious that peasants would abandon their pitchforks and their hunting rifles as instruments of collective protest. This is not to say that localized resistance to state repression would disappear, or that violence would cease to characterize interactions between demonstrators and police. Tumultuous demonstrations of miners and textile workers, anti-Semites and anti-Dreyfusards, Catholic parishioners and right-wing students would continue to challenge the authority of the government, and so would monster meetings of *vignerons* in the Midi. The student protests of 1968 can be placed within this same tradition of popular resistance to state centralization. The dialectic of crowd solidarity and police intervention would persist as the locus of collective action shifted from small towns to cities, and from communal groupings to specialized organizations. This trend toward organized urban protest the Montagnards of 1851 had been unable to sustain. Its revival in the Third Republic would herald the triumph of a more democratic regime within a more urbanized society.

BIBLIOGRAPHY

Primary Sources

This study draws upon disparate collections of primary sources in national and departmental archives. The most important documentation is derived from the judicial investigation of Montagnard societies and insurrectionary resistance to the coup d'état. Interrogations of suspects and testimonies of witnesses are scattered by the thousands through departmental archives, and hundreds more have come to rest in the military archives at Vincennes. The registers of the Mixed Commissions, located in the national archives and the military archives, provide a summary view of this voluminous documentation.

Administrative and judicial reports from 1848 to 1851 rarely provide accurate information about Montagnard societies, but they do reveal the conflict between left-wing Republicans and government officials. Of special value are the reports of the *procureurs-généraux* to the minister of justice (in the national archives), which describe repressive operations against associations, demonstrations, newspapers, etc. Political conflicts are documented in greater detail by the subprefects and police commissioners in their correspondence with the prefects. This local correspondence, which exists in the departmental archives, must be used selectively because of its sheer bulk and variety. I have drawn upon such local sources in the departmental archives of the Ardèche, the Drôme, the Hérault, and the Vaucluse.

Archival sources are less indispensable for the study of economic trends and social structures, because historians and social geographers have published excellent monographs on most of the districts where resistance to the coup d'état occurred. For systematic analysis, however, the national archives contain one very useful source, the *Enquête* concerning agricultural and industrial labor, carried out by the justices of the peace, often aided by cantonal commissions, in 1848. Similarly, the nominative lists for the census of 1851, drawn up household by household in each commune, provide a solid documentary base for analyzing the social background of political prisoners in 1852. Extant census lists are located in many departmental archives, and I have used those from some rebel districts in the Allier, the Drôme, the Hérault, the Lot-et-Garonne, the Vaucluse, and the Yonne.

The following archival inventories classify the most important documentary collections I have consulted. For more specialized primary sources which appear only once in the text, the reader is referred to the notes.

Archives Nationales (Paris)

BB¹⁸	1460-1502	General Correspondence of the Criminal Division of the Ministry of Justice, Feb. 1848–Dec. 1851.
	1460-61	Forest disorders in 1848
	1462	Protests against the 45-centimes tax, 1848-49.
	1472	Secret societies, 1832-50
	1474	Clubs and associations, 1848-50
	1485ᴬ	Secret societies in the Drôme, 1850-51
	1488	The plot of Lyon
BB³⁰	333-35, 358-405	Cabinet of the Ministry of Justice, 1848-52
	358-66	Letters from the *procureurs-généraux*, describing disorders in their appellate court jurisdictions, 1848-50
	370-88	Monthly reports of the *procureurs-généraux*, Nov. 1849-52
	391-97	Letters from the *procureurs-généraux*, describing Republican protests and other "disorders" and "troubles," Dec. 1850–Dec. 1851
	398	The Mixed Commissions of 1852, general dossiers, correspondence, registers, and other lists of prisoners from the appellate court jurisdictions of Agen (Gers, Lot, Lot-et-Garonne), Aix (Basses-Alpes, Var), Amiens, Angers, Besançon (Jura), Bordeaux, and Bourges (Cher)
	*399	Register of the Mixed Commission of the Nièvre
	400	The Mixed Commissions in the appellate court jurisdictions of Caen, Colmar, Dijon (Saône-et-Loire), Douai, and Grenoble
	*400	Register of the Mixed Commission of the Drôme
	401	The Mixed Commissions in the appellate court jurisdictions of Limoges (Haute-Vienne), Lyon, Metz, Montpellier (Hérault), Nancy, and Nîmes (Ardèche, Gard)
	*401²	Register of the Mixed Commission of the Vaucluse
	402	The Mixed Commissions in the appellate court jurisdictions of Orléans, Paris (no registers), Pau, Poitiers, Rennes, Riom (Allier), Rouen, and Toulouse

*402¹ ᵉᵗ ²		Registers of the Military Commission in the Allier
	424	*Statistique* of the repression of the insurrection of December 1851 (national and departmental tabulations)
C	944-69	*Enquête* on industrial and agricultural labor, 1848 (cantonal returns, classified by department)
C	977	Legislative proposals and statistics concerning communal administration, 1848-51
F⁷	2588-95	Master registers of the Mixed Commissions (alphabetical list)
F⁷	12,651	Report on resistance to the coup d'état in the Gard
F⁷	12,710-13	Correspondence on political prisoners after the coup d'état
F⁹	423	Correspondence about provincial national guard units, 1830-52
F¹⁸	308	Prefectoral reports on resistance to the coup d'état, written in 1868 in response to Ténot's book, *La province en décembre 1851*
F¹⁹	10,031	*Statistique* of Protestants, 1851

Archives de la Guerre (Vincennes)

F¹	51-54	Correspondence of provincial military commanders with the Ministry of War, December 1851 (many descriptions of insurrectionary events)
AA	G⁸ 186-87	Insurrection of 1851 in the department of the Nièvre
	G⁸ 189	Insurrection of 1851, prisoners and deportees
	G⁸ 190-93	Insurrection of 1851 in the departments of the south-west
	G⁸ 194-97	Military commissions in Paris and the departments

Justice Militaire—B, Insurrection of December 1851

250-59	Dossiers of political prisoners in the department of the Yonne
264-79	Correspondence and registers of the Mixed Commissions

347

Archives départmentales

Allier

M   1300-1305   Coup d'état and Insurrection of 1851 (official
                         correspondence, interrogations, and testi-
                         monies of suspects and witnesses, cantons of
                         Le Donjon, Jaligny, and La Palisse)

Ardèche

5M   10 and 13   Reports from the subprefect at Largentière,
                         1849-51

5M   14-20   Coup d'état, insurrectionary movement, Mixed
                         Commissions (interrogations and testimonies
                         from the canton of Vallon, in 5M 18)

Basses-Alpes

6M   88   Pillage of public funds, 1851-52 (the archives
                         of the Mixed Commission have disappeared)

Bouches-du-Rhône

14U 47-48 bis   Coup d'état of 1851 in the Basses-Alpes, corre-
                         spondence of magistrates

14U 53-54   Documents on the "Complot de Béziers" (May
                        1850)

Cher

3   RS, 4   Dossiers of the 2ᵉ *Conseil de Guerre*, which
                        judged rebels from Clamecy in 1852 (the
                        archives of the Mixed Commission of the
                        Cher are missing)

Drôme

M   1297, 1343-50   Political correspondence of police bureaucrats,
                        1848-52

M   1353-55   Reports of mayors and testimonies of witnesses
                        concerning the insurrection, arranged by
                        commune

M   1356-71   Alphabetical file of dossiers of suspects judged
                        by the Mixed Commission (many interroga-
                        tions)

Gard

3U/5 (1-3, 27)   Judicial investigation of political societies, 1851-
                        52 (many testimonies that also concern the
                        insurrection, classified by *arrondissement*)

3U/5 (4-13)   Alphabetical file of dossiers of suspects judged
                        by the Mixed Commission

Hérault

39M 126-35	Political correspondence of police bureaucrats, 1848-51
39M 138-42	Administrative documents concerning the insurrection and the purge
39M 144-60	Dossiers of suspects judged by the military commission at Béziers, filed alphabetically (many interrogations)
39M 194	Alphabetical list of persons sentenced by the Mixed Commission (list "A" missing)

Jura

MIV 40-59	Insurrection of December 1851 (testimonies and interrogations from the canton of Poligny, in MIV 45)

Lot-et-Garonne

4U	Insurrection of 1851, *arrondissements* of Marmande, Agen, Nérac
6U, 1-5	Coup d'état of 1851
Z	Victims of the coup d'état (dossiers of some suspects)

Nièvre

U	Dossiers on the secret societies and the insurrection, arranged by *arrondissement* (see, especially, the interrogations of prisoners at Clamecy and nearby communes)

Pyrénées-Orientales

3M¹ 91-93	Interrogations, testimonies, and reports concerning secret societies and armed mobilizations in December 1851

Rhône

Archives du tribunal du Rhône, dossiers #2-8 Interrogations, testimonies, and reports concerning disorders, secret societies, and insurgency in the Drôme, 1849–December 1851

Saône-et-Loire

U	Dossiers #1-9 Insurrection of 1851, dossiers of insurgents (testimonies and interrogations from the cantons of St. Gengoux and Cluny, in #1-2)

Var

4M 19-21   Insurrectionary movement, judicial reports and interrogations, classified by *arrondissement* and by commune (*arrondissement* Brignoles, in 4M 19)

4M 26-28   Interrogations of suspects who were released (classified by *arrondissement* and by commune)

Vaucluse

4M 48-53   Political correspondence of police bureaucrats, 1848-51, classified by month

4M 53   Testimonies concerning the insurrection in the *arrondissement* of Orange

4M 57-67   Dossiers of suspects judged by the Mixed Commission, filed alphabetically (#1-1035)

4M 74-76   Testimonies concerning the insurrection in the *arrondissement* of Apt, filed by canton and by commune

Yonne

III M¹ 149   Letters from mayors, describing the insurrection in the Puisaye

III M¹ 282   List of victims of the coup d'état (taken from the register of the Mixed Commission)

SECONDARY SOURCES

These sources are classified into two parts. The first section gives all books and articles that provide information or analysis of the insurrection and the purge. Of foremost importance are the studies by Agulhon, Dagnan, Loubère, Price, Tilly, and Vigier. The second section lists other works that I have found useful in preparing this study. While some general studies with a comparative or interdisciplinary perspective are included, very specialized articles in the political and social history of nineteenth-century France are not listed unless they have been cited twice in the notes.

Studies that Examine the Insurrection of December 1851 and/or the Subsequent Purge.

Agulhon, Maurice. *1848 ou l'apprentissage de la République, 1848-1852* (Nouvelle histoire de la France contemporaine, vol. 8). Paris: Editions du Seuil, 1973.

————. "Où en est l'histoire de l'insurrection de décembre 1851 en Provence." *Feuillets documentaires régionaux* (Marseille, C.R.D.P., 1966). Fasc. 6-7.

————. *La République au village.* Paris: Plon, 1970.

————. "La résistance au coup d'état en province; esquisse d'historiographie." *Revue d'histoire moderne et contemporaine,* 21 (1974), 18-26.

Ancourt, André. "Le coup d'état du 2 décembre 1851 et ses répercussions à Villefranche-de-Rouergue." *Revue du Rouergue,* 7 (1953), 56-73, 177-96.

Appolis, Emile. "La résistance au coup d'état du 2 décembre 1851 dans l'Hérault." *Congrès nationale des sociétés savantes, actes, section d'histoire,* tome 77 (1952), 487-504.

Armengaud, André. "A propos d'un centenaire: Coup d'état et plebiscite dans le département du Tarn." *Annales du Midi,* 64 (1952), 41-49.

Autenzio, Marc. "La résistance au coup d'état du 2 décembre 1851 dans la Nièvre." *Diplôme de Maîtrise,* University of Tours, 1970.

Autrand, Aimé. "Commemoration de la résistance vauclusienne au coup d'état du 2 décembre 1851." In *L'annuaire administratif et statistique du Vaucluse* (1951), 279-394.

Balent, André. "La résistance au coup d'état (Pyrénées-Orientales)." *Revue "Massana,"* 20 (1973).

Becque, Paul. "L'Insurrection de Crest en Dauphiné." In *abbés* Borges and Amodru, editors, *Souvenirs divers.* Valence, 1892. Pp. 1-35.

Belouino, Paul. *Histoire d'un coup d'état, décembre 1851,* Paris, 1852.

Bercé, Yves-Marie. *Croquants et nu-pieds: Les soulèvements paysans en France du XVIe au XIXe siècle.* Paris: Editions Gallimard/Julliard (Collection Archives), 1974.

Blache, Noël. *Histoire de l'insurrection du Var en décembre 1851.* Paris: Le Chevalier, 1869.

Blet, H. "La résistance au coup d'état du 2 décembre 1851 dans le département des Hautes-Alpes." *Procès-verbaux de la société dauphinoise d'ethnologie,* 209-11 (1951), 26-37.

Boudard, Jean. "La répression policière en Creuse au lendemain du coup d'état de 1851." *Mem. Soc. Creuse,* 31 (1953), 429-35.

Bourgin, Georges. "Les Préfets de Napoléon III, historiens du coup d'état." *Revue historique,* 166 (1939), 274-89.

Bournatot, Denys. *Un chef-lieu de canton du Bourbonnais: Le Donjon, son histoire.* Moulins: Imprimerie A. Pottier, 1963.

Broutet, F. "L'Insurrection de Poligny les 3 et 4 décembre 1851." *Le Pays Jurassien,* 3 (1948), 106-10.

Bremond, Alphonse. *Histoire du coup d'état dans le département de la Haute-Garonne.* Toulouse, 1871.

Bruchet, Max. "Le coup d'état de 1851 dans le département du Nord." *Revue du Nord,* 7 (May 1925).

Chauvet, Horace. *Histoire du parti républicain dans les Pyrénées-Orientales, 1830-1877.* Perpignan, 1909.

Cheron de Villiers, P. T. *Chapitre inédit de l'histoire du coup d'état: Limoges en 1851.* Paris, 1869.

Clemens, Jacques. "La 'marche' Republicain de Lavardac à Agen en décembre 1851." *Revue de l'Agenais,* 102 (1975), 377-83.

Corgne. "Le coup d'état du 2 décembre 1851 et le Morbihan." *Bulletin de la société polymathique du Morbihan* (1961), 44-45, 51-52.

Cornillon, Jean. *Le Bourbonnais en décembre, 1851: Le coup d'état.* Cusset, 1903.

Courant, Abbé L. "L'Anjou et le coup d'état du 2 décembre 1851." *Anjou historique,* 239 (1953), 29-44.

Dagnan, Jean. *Le Gers sous la Seconde République.* Vol. I, *La réaction conservatrice.* Vol. II, *Le coup d'état et la répression.* Auch, 1928-29.

Dansette, Adrien. *Du 2 décembre au 4 septembre.* Paris: Hachette, 1972.

———. *Louis Napoleon à la conquête du pouvoir.* Paris: Hachette, 1961.

Décembre and Alonnier. *Histoire des Conseils de Guerre de 1852.* Paris, 1869.

Delberge, Léo. "Le coup d'état du 2 décembre 1851 en Lot-et-Garonne, d'après Eugène Ténot, rédacteur du Siècle." *Revue Agenais,* 83 (1957), 91-101.

De Maupas. *The Story of the Coup d'Etat.* Translated by Albert D. Vandam. New York, 1884.

Deries, Léon. "Autour du coup d'état du deux décembre dans la Manche." *Notices et documents publiés par la société d'agriculture et d'archéologie de la Manche (Saint-Lô),* 41 (1929), 263-67.

Detretz, Alfred, editor. "Autour du coup d'état: Souvenirs d'un paysan." *La Révolution de 1848,* 32 (1909-10), 165-70.

Dindinaud, Geneviève. "Les sociétés secrètes dans le sud du département du Cher in 1852." Manuscript article in AD Cher.

Druard, H. *Une page de l'histoire du 2 décembre: Le coup d'état dans l'Ain.* Bourg, 1885.

Dupont, Charles. *Les Républicains et les Monarchistes dans le Var en décembre 1851.* Paris, 1883.

Duveau, Georges. *La vie ouvrière sous le Second Empire.* Paris: Gallimard, 1947.

Encrevé, A. "Protestantisme et politique: Les protestants du Midi en décembre 1851." In *Droit et Gauche de 1789 à nos jours* (Actes du Colloque de Montpellier, 9-10 juin 1973). Montpellier: Centre d'histoire contemporaine du Languedoc Méditerranéen et du Roussillon, 1975. Pp. 161-96.

Ferras, Robert. "Les suites du coup d'état du 2 décembre dans un village du Biterrois: Capestang." In Féderation Historique du Languedoc Méditerranéen et du Roussillon, XLIIIᵉ Congrès (Béziers, 30-31 mai 1970), *Béziers et le Biterrois*. Montpellier: Faculté des Lettres et Sciences Humaines, 1971.

Font-Réaulx, J. de, et al. *Dieulefit et son histoire*. Dieulefit, 1950.

Forget, l'abbé. "L'insurrection de décembre 1851 dans la Drôme." *La Semaine religieuse de Valence* (1894), 701-20.

Forstenzer, Thomas Robert. "Bureaucrats under Stress: French Attorneys General and Prefects and the Fall of the Second Republic (10 December 1848–2 December 1851)." Ph.D. dissertation, Stanford University, 1973.

Fournier, Victor. *Le coup d'état de 1851 dans le Var*. Draguignan: Olivier Joulian, 1928.

Fourniol, M. "Sur l'origine d'une tradition politique: La République de 1848 dans la Drôme." *Bulletin de la société d'histoire moderne*, 46 (1949), 5-8.

Francieschini. "Une episode du coup d'état du 2 décembre 1851, l'émeute de Poligny." *Revue hebdomodaire*, 16 (1907).

Furet, Michel H. "Le département du Cher sous la IIᵉ République; étude politique (1851–début 1852)." *Diplôme d'Etudes Supérieures*, University of Orléans–Tours, 1967.

Gandilhon, René. "Documents sur l'émeute survenue à Saint-Amand (Cher) le 3 décembre 1851." *La Révolution de 1848*, 33 (1936-37), 44-48.

La Gazette des Tribunaux, Paris, 1852.

Geywitz, Gisela. *Das Plebiszit von 1851 in Frankreich*. Tübingen: J.C.B. Mohr, 1965.

Godechot, Jacques, et al. *La Révolution de 1848 à Toulouse et dans la Haute-Garonne*. Toulouse: Préfecture de la Haute-Garonne, 1949.

Goirand, Jean, editor. *Documents pour servir à l'histoire du département du Gard contre le coup d'état*. Alais, 1883.

Gossez, Rémi. "Bibliographie critique de la littérature du coup d'état." *1848 et les Révolutions du XIXᵉ siècle*, 44 (1951), 153-58.

Goudin, L. *Livre d'Or des victimes du coup d'état de 1851 et de la loi de Sûrêté générale de 1858* [dans la Drôme]. Valence, 1883.

Guillemin, Henri. *Le coup du 2 décembre*. Paris: Gallimard, 1951.

L'Herbier-Montagnon, G. "L'insurrection du dimanche 7 décembre 1851 à Chavannes [Drôme]." *Bulletin de la société d'archéologie . . . de la Drôme*, 76 (1964), 69-71.

Jacotin, A. "Notes sur le coup d'état du 2 décembre 1851 en Côte-d'Or." *Annales de Bourgogne*, 13 (1941), 73-96.

Jeanjean, F. J. "Le coup d'état du 2 décembre 1851 dans le département de l'Aude." *La Révolution de 1848*, 21 (1924-25), 161-80.

La Gorce, Pierre de. *Histoire du Second Empire*. Vol. 1, Paris, 1894.

Lauribel, Guillaume. *Pézénas et le coup d'état de Louis Napoleon, décembre 1851*. Pézénas, 1960.

Le Clère, Bernard and Vincent Wright. *Les Préfets du Second Empire*. (Cahiers de la fondation nationale des sciences politiques, No. 187). Paris: Armand Colin, 1973.

Levy, Claude. "A Propos du coup d'état de 1851 dans l'Yonne, aux sources de l'opinion républicaine sous la IIe République." *Annales de Bourgogne*, 25 (1953), 185-93.

———. "Notes sur les fondements sociaux de l'insurrection de décembre 1851 en province." *Information historique*, 16 (1954), 142-45.

Loubère, Leo. "The Emergence of the Extreme Left in Lower Languedoc, 1848-1851: Social and Economic Factors in Politics." *American Historical Review*, 73 (1968), 1019-51.

———. *Radicalism in Mediterranean France, Its Rise and Decline, 1848-1914*. Albany, N.Y.: State University of New York Press, 1974.

McPhee, Peter. "The Seed-Time of the Republic: Society and Politics in the Pyrénées-Orientales, 1848-51." *Australian Journal of Politics and History*, 22 (1976), 196-213.

Magen, Hippolyte. *Histoire du Second Empire*. Paris, 1878.

———. *Histoire de la terreur bonapartiste*. Paris, 1872.

Marcilhacy, Christianne. "Les caractères de la crise sociale et politique de 1846 à 1852 dans le département du Loiret." *Revue d'histoire moderne et contemporaine*, 6 (1959), 5-59.

Marcoux, H. "L'insurrection républicaine toucyoise du 6 décembre 1851." *Actes du 39e congrès de l'association bourgignonne de sociétés savantes*. Toucy, 1968. Pp. 25-30.

Margadant, Ted. "The Insurrection of 1851 in Southern France: Two Case Studies." Ph.D. dissertation, Harvard University, 1972.

———. "Modernisation and Insurgency in December 1851: A Case Study of the Drôme." In Roger Price, editor, *Revolution and Reaction: 1848 and the Second French Republic*. London: Croom Helm, 1975. Pp. 254-79.

————. "Peasant Protest in the Second Republic." *Journal of Interdisciplinary History*, 5 (Summer 1974), 119-30.

Marlin, Roger. *L'épuration politique dans le Doubs à la suite du coup d'état du 2 décembre 1851*. Dôle, 1958.

Martin, Huguette. "Antour du coup d'état de 1851 dans l'Hérault." *Diplôme d'Etudes Supérieures*, University of Montpellier, 1958.

Martinet, Jean-Claude. *Clamecy et ses flotteurs de la Monarchie de Juillet à l'insurrection des "Marianne," 1830-1851*. La Charité-sur-Loire: Editions Delayance, 1975.

Marx, Karl. "The Eighteenth Brumaire of Louis Bonaparte." In Marx and Engels, *Selected Works*. Vol. I. Moscow: Foreign Languages Publishing House, 1962. Pp. 243-344.

Merriman, John. *The Agony of the Republic: Repression of the Left in Revolutionary France, 1848-1851*. New Haven: Yale University Press, 1978.

————. "Radicalization and Repression: A Study of the Demobilisation of the 'Dem-Socs' during the Second French Republic." In Roger Price, editor, *Revolution and Reaction: 1848 and the Second French Republic*. London: Croom Helm, 1975. Pp. 210-35.

Le Messager du Midi (Montpellier, 1852).

Millelot, Numa. "Notice rectificative à l'ouvrage de M. Ténot." In Eugène Ténot, *La province en décembre 1851*, 9th ed. (Harvard University holding).

Moisson, Roger. "1851-1951 [on the Basses-Alpes]," *Le Patriote basalpin*, articles from Apr. 30 to May 20, 1951.

Moreau, Christine. "La réaction de la population du Loir-et-Cher lors du coup d'état du 2 décembre 1851," *Bulletin de la Société d'Art et d'Archeologie du Sologne* (1972).

Muller, P. "Autour du coup d'état dans le Haut-Rhin." *La Révolution de 1848*, 6 (1909-10), 197-212.

Nési, Marcel. "La résistance au coup d'état du 2 décembre dans les Deux-Sèvres." *La Révolution française*, 34 (July 1914), 63-68.

Neuville, J. Alfred. *Le 2 décembre 1851; Proscriptions de Marmande*. Agen, 1882.

Papon, A. *La République et le coup d'état dans le département de l'Eure*. Paris, 1869.

Payne, Howard C. *The Police State of Louis Napoleon Bonaparte, 1851-1860*. Seattle: University of Washington Press, 1966.

————. "Preparation of a Coup D'Etat: Administrative Centralization and Police Powers in France, 1849-1851." In Frederich J. Cox, et al., *Studies in Modern European History in Honor of Franklin Charles Palm*. New York: Bookman Associates, 1956.

Pelloille, Ferdinand. "Le procès des Mariannes du département du Cher (1851-1852)." *Union des sociétés savantes de Bourges, Mémoires*, 8 (1959-60), 122-58.

Perreux, Gabriel. "Trois dates de l'histoire d'Arbois, 1830-1848-1851." *La Révolution de 1848*, 28 (1931), 193-216; 29 (1932), 34-50.

Piallou, Auguste. *Le coup d'état du 2 décembre en Limousin*. Limoges: Imprimerie nouvelle, 1968.

Portail, Simone. "Le coup d'état du 2 décembre 1851 (dans le Lot-et-Garonne)." Manuscript article in AD Lot-et-Garonne, M i 36 (R-1).

Prat, J. G. *Les exploits du Deux-Décembre (récits d'histoire contemporaine)* [on the Var]. Paris: Lachaud, 1873.

Price, Roger. *The French Second Republic: A Social History*. London: Batsford, 1972.

———, editor. *Revolution and Reaction: 1848 and the Second French Republic*. London: Croom Helm, 1975.

Puech, Louis. *Essai sur la candidature officielle en France depuis 1851*. Mende: H. Chaptal, 1922.

Quentin-Bauchart. *Etudes et souvenirs sur la Deuxième République et le Second Empire (1848-1870)*. 2 vols. Edited by his son. Paris, 1901.

Ravold, M. *Les transportés de la Meurthe en 1852*. Paris, 1872.

Reynier, Elie. *Histoire de Privas*. Vol. III, *Epoque contemporaine, 1798-1950*. Privas: Imprimerie Volle, 1951.

———. *La Seconde République dans l'Ardèche, 1848-1852*. Privas: Maison de l'enfance, F.O.L., 1948.

Robert, Adolphe. *Statistique pour servir à l'histoire du 2 décembre 1851*, Paris, 1869.

Rougeron, Georges. "La résistance au coup d'état dans le département de l'Allier." *La Révolution de 1848*, 32 (1935), 341-52.

———. "La terreur bonapartiste dans le département de l'Allier après le coup d'état." *La Révolution de 1848*, 34 (1937-38), 155-71.

Rougeron, Georges, et al. *La Révolution de 1848 à Moulins et dans le département de l'Allier*. Moulins: Préfecture de l'Allier, 1950.

Schoelcher, Victor. *Histoire des crimes du 2 décembre*. Bruxelles, 1852.

Seguin, Jean. "A propos de l'insurrection à Toucy et en Puisaye de décembre 1851." *Bulletin de l'association d'études, de recherches et de protection du vieux Toucy*, 2-3 (1962), 10-21, 32-35.

Seignobos, Charles. "Les opérations des commissions mixtes en 1852." *La Révolution de 1848*, 6 (1909-10), 59-67.

———. *La Révolution de 1848—Le Second Empire*. In Ernest Lavisse, editor, *Histoire de France contemporaine*. Vol. VI. Paris: Hachette, 1929.

Sonnié-Moret, A. "Récit des événements de l'insurrection qui a éclaté à Clamecy les 5, 6 et 7 décembre 1851." Manuscript dated July 20, 1874, reprinted in *Clamecy et le coup d'état de 1851*. Clamecy: Société scientifique et artistique de Clamecy, 1951.

Ténot, Eugène. *Paris en décembre 1851: Etude historique sur le coup d'état*. Paris, 1868.

————. *La province en décembre 1851*. 13th ed. Paris, 1869.

Thomas, Louis. "Montpellier en 1851." *Monspeliensia*, 1 (1933), 167-233.

Tilly, Charles. "The Changing Place of Collective Violence." In Melvin Richter, editor, *Essays in Theory and History: An Approach to the Social Sciences*. Cambridge, Mass.: Harvard University Press, 1970. Pp. 139-64.

————. "The Modernization of Political Conflict in France." In Edward B. Harvey, editor, *Perspectives on Modernization: Essays in Memory of Ian Weinberg*. Toronto: University of Toronto Press, 1972.

————. "How Protest Modernized in France, 1845-1855." In W. Aydelotte, et al., *The Dimensions of Quantitative Research in History*. Princeton: Princeton University Press, 1971. Pp. 192-255.

Tilly, Charles, Louise, and Richard. *The Rebellious Century, 1830-1930*. Cambridge, Mass.: Harvard University Press, 1975.

Valentin, Jacques. "En marge d'un centenaire: Quelques épisodes de l'histoire de Thiers sous la Seconde République." *Revue d'Auvergne*, 62 (1948), 49-67.

————. "Les répercussions du coup d'état du 2 décembre 1851 dans le département du Puy-de-Dôme." *Revue d'Auvergne*, 65 (1951), 145-62.

Vergez-Tricom, Mme. "Les evénéments de décembre 1851 à Lyon." *La Révolution de 1848*, 17 (1920-21), 226-53.

Veyne, François. "L'Insurrection républicaine dans le canton d'Orange lors du coup d'état du 2 décembre 1851," Unpublished *Mémoire de Maîtrise*, Aix-en-Provence, 1970.

Vigier, Philippe. "Un quart de siècle de recherches historiques sur la Province [chronique bibliographique, III]." *Annales historiques de la Révolution française*, 47 (1975), 622-45.

————. *La Seconde République*. (Collection "Que sais-je?"). Paris: Presses Universitaires de France, 1967.

————. *La Seconde République dans la région alpine*. 2 vols. Paris: Presses Universitaires de France, 1963.

Villemagne, M. *Evénements politiques à St. Thibéry (Hérault) en 1851-1852*. St. Pons, 1903.

Weill, Georges. *Histoire du parti républicaine en France, 1814-1870*. Rev. ed. Paris, 1928.

Wright, Vincent. "The Coup d'Etat of December 1851: Repression and the Limits to Repression." In Roger Price, editor, *Revolution and Reaction*. London: Croom Helm, 1975.

Zola, Emile. *La fortune des Rougon*. Paris: Garnier-Flammarion, 1969.

Other Books and Articles

Agulhon, Maurice. "Les chambrées en Basse-Provence: Histoire et ethnologie." *Revue historique*, 498 (1971), 337-68.

————. "La diffusion d'un journal montagnard, le *Démocrate du Var*, sous la deuxième République." *Provence historique*, 39 (1960), 11-27.

————. "L'enquête du Comité du travail de l'Assemblée constituante (1848): Etude critique de son execution dans deux départements du Midi." *Annales du Midi*, 70 (1958), 73-85.

————. "La notion de village en Basse-Provence vers la fin de l'ancien régime." *Congrès national des sociétés savantes, actes, section d'histoire*, 90, tome 1 (1965), 277-302.

————. *Pénitents et francs-maçons de l'ancienne Provence*. Paris: Fayard, 1968.

————. "La Seconde République, 1848-1852." In Georges Duby, editor, *Histoire de la France*, vol. II, pp. 393-421. Paris: Larousse, 1971.

————. *La via sociale en Provence intérieure au lendemain de la Révolution*. Paris: Société des Etudes Robespierristes, 1970.

Almond, Gabriel, and Sidney Verba. *The Civic Culture: Political Attitudes and Democracy in Five Nations*. Princeton: Princeton University Press, 1963.

Amann, Peter. "The Changing Outlines of 1848." *American Historical Review*, 68 (1963), 938-53.

————. "Recent Writings on the Second French Republic." *Journal of Modern History*, 34 (1962), 409-29.

————. *Revolution and Mass Democracy: The Paris Club Movement in 1848*. Princeton: Princeton University Press, 1975.

————. "Revolution: A Redefinition." *Political Science Quarterly*, 77 (1962), 36-53.

Anderson, Eugene and Pauline. *Political Institutions and Social Change in Continental Europe in the Nineteenth Century*. Berkeley: University of California Press, 1967.

Anderson, Robert T. and Gallatin. "The Indirect Social Structure of European Village Communities." *American Anthropologist*, 64 (1962), 1016-27.

Armengaud, André. *Les populations de l'Est-Aquitain au début de l'époque contemporaine (1848-1871)*. Paris: Mouton, 1961.

Arnaud, René. *The Second Republic and Napoleon III*. Translated by E. F. Buckley. London, 1923 (reprinted by AMS Press, New York, 1967).

Artz, Frederick B. "Bonapartism and Dictatorship." *South Atlantic Quarterly*, 39 (1940), 37-49.

Atlas historique de la France contemporaine, 1800-1965. (Collection U. Série "Histoire Contemporaine.") Paris: A. Colin, 1966.

Barbier, Bernard. *Villes et centres des Alpes du sud, étude de réseau urbain*. Gap: Editions Ophrys, 1969.

Bastid, Paul. *Institutions politiques de la monarchie parlementaire française (1814-1848)*. Paris: Sirey, 1954.

Bernard, Leon. "French Society and Popular Uprisings under Louis XIV." *French Historical Studies*, 3 (1964), 454-74.

Bertier de Sauvigny, Guillaume de. *The Bourbon Restoration*. Translated by Lynn M. Case. Philadelphia: University of Pennsylvania Press, 1966.

Bezucha, Robert J. *The Lyon Uprising of 1834: Social and Political Conflict in the Early July Monarchy*. Cambridge, Mass.: Harvard University Press, 1974.

Blanchard, Raoul. *Les Alpes occidentales*. Tome IV, *Les préalpes française du sud*. 3 vols. Grenoble: B. Arthaud, 1945.

Bloch, Marc. *French Rural History: An Essay on Its Basic Characteristics*. Translated by Janet Sondheimer. Berkeley: University of California Press, 1970.

Bouchard, Gabriel. *Le village immobile: Senneley-en-Sologne au XVIIIe siècle*. Paris: Plon, 1972.

Bouillon, Jacques. "Les démocrates-socialistes aux élections de 1849." *Revue française de sciences politiques*, 6 (1956), 71-77.

Boulard, Fernand, and Jean Remy. *Pratique réligieuse urbaine et régions culturelles*. Paris: Les Editions ouvrières, 1968.

Bozon, Pierre. *La vie rurale en Vivarais: Etude géographique*. Valence: Imprimeries réunies, 1961.

Brunet, Roger. *Les campagnes toulousaines*. (Publications de la Faculté des Lettres et Sciences humaines de Toulouse, Série B, tome I.) Toulouse: Association des Publications de la Faculté des Lettres et Sciences humaines, 1965.

Bury, J.P.T. *France, 1814-1940: A History*. London: Methuen, 1949.

Charles, Albert. *La Révolution de 1848 et la Seconde République dans le département de la Gironde*. Bordeaux: Delmas, 1945.

Charléty, S. *La Monarchie de Juillet (1830-1848)*. In Ernest Lavisse, editor, *Histoire de France contemporaine*, vol. V. Paris: Hachette, 1921.

Chevalier, Louis. "Les fondements économiques et sociaux de l'histoire politique de la région parisienne, 1848-1851." *Thèse de doctorat*, University of Paris, 1951.

Cholvy, Gérard. *Géographie réligieuse de l'Hérault contemporaine.* Paris: Presses Universitaires de France, 1968.

Christaller, Walter. *Central Places in Southern Germany.* Translated by C. W. Baskin. Englewood Cliffs, New Jersey: Prentice-Hall, 1966.

Clapham, J. H. *The Economic Development of France and Germany, 1815-1914.* 4th ed. Cambridge: Cambridge University Press, 1936.

Clarenc, Louis. "Le Code forestier de 1827 et les troubles forestiers dans les Pyrénées centrales au milieu du XIXe siècle." *Annales du Midi,* 77 (1965), 293-317.

———. "Riches et pauvres dans le conflit forestier des Pyrénées centrales vers le milieu du XIXe siècle." *Annales du Midi,* 69 (1967), 307-15.

Cobb, Richard. *Les armees révolutionnaires: Instrument de la Terreur dans les départements.* 2 vols. Paris: Mouton, 1961-63.

———. *The Police and the People: French Popular Protest, 1789-1820.* Oxford: Oxford University Press, 1970.

Cobban, Alfred. "Administrative Pressure in the Election of the French Constituent Assembly, April 1848." *Bulletin of the Institute of Historical Research* (London), 25 (1952), 133-59.

———. *A History of Modern France.* Vol. II, *From the First Empire to the Second Empire, 1799-1871.* Baltimore, Maryland: Penguin Books, 1961.

Collins, Irene. *The Government and the Newspaper Press in France, 1814-1881.* London: Oxford University Press, 1959.

Coquerelle, Suzanne. "L'armée et la répression dans les campagnes 1848." *Société d'histoire de la Révolution de 1848, Etudes,* 18 (1955) 121-59.

———. "Les droits collectifs et les troubles agraires dans les Pyrénées en 1848." *Congrès national des sociétés savantes, actes, section d'histoire,* 78 (1953), 345-64.

Corbin, Alain. *Archaïsme et modernité en Limousin au XIXe siècle, 1845-1880.* 2 vols. Paris: Riviere, 1975.

Corley, T.A.B. *Democratic Despot: A Life of Napoleon III.* London: Barrie and Rockliff, 1961.

Crouzet, François. "French Economic Growth in the Nineteenth Century Reconsidered." *History,* 59 (June 1974), 167-79.

Dautry, Jean. *1848 et la IIe République.* 2nd ed. Paris: Editions sociales, 1957.

Davies, James C. "Toward a Theory of Revolution." *American Sociological Review*, 27 (1962), 5-19.

Deffontaines, Pierre. *Les hommes et leurs travaux dans les pays de la moyenne Garonne-Agenais, Bas-Quercy*. Lille: S.I.L.I.C., Facultés catholiques, 1932.

De Luna, Frederick A. *The French Republic under Cavaignac, 1848*. Princeton: Princeton University Press, 1969.

Derruau-Bonniol, Simone. "Le socialisme dans l'Allier de 1848 à 1914." *Cahiers d'histoire*, 2 (1957), 115-61.

Dessal, Marcel. *Charles Delescluze, 1809-1871*. Paris: M. Rivière, 1952.

———. "Le complot de Lyon et la résistance au coup d'état dans les départements du sud-est." *Revue des révolutions contemporaines* (1951), 83-96.

Deutsch, Karl. "Social Mobilization and Political Development." *American Political Science Review*, 55 (1961), 493-507.

Drouin, Jean-Claude. *Les élections législatives du 13 mai 1849 dans l'Aquitaine occidentale*. Paris: Hachette, 1973.

Duby, Georges, editor. *Histoire de la France rurale*. Tome 3, *Apogée et crise de la civilisation paysanne, 1789-1914*, edited by Etienne Juillard. Paris: Editions du Seuil, 1976.

Dugrand, Raymond. *Villes et campagnes en Bas-Languedoc*. Paris: Presses Universitaires de France, 1963.

Dunham, Arthur L. *The Industrial Revolution in France, 1815-1848*. New York: Exposition Press, 1955.

Dupeux, Georges. *Aspects de l'histoire sociale et politique du Loir-et-Cher, 1848-1914*. Paris: Mouton, 1962.

Dutacq, F. "Notes et documents sur le complot du sud-est (1850-1851)." *La Révolution de 1848*, 11 (1925), 345-95, 12 (1926), 403-15, 442-52.

Duveau, Georges. *1848: The Making of a Revolution*. Translated by Anne Carter. New York: Vintage, 1968.

Duverger, Maurice. *Political Parties: Their Organization and Activity in the Modern State*. Translated by Barbara and Robert North. 2nd ed. New York: Wiley, 1959.

Eckstein, Harry. "On the Etiology of Internal Wars." In George Nadel, editor, *Studies in the Philosophy of History*. New York: Harper and Row, 1965.

Eisenstein, Elizabeth. *The First Professional Revolutionary: Filippo Michele Bounarroti (1761-1838)*. Cambridge, Mass.: Harvard University Press, 1959.

Fabre, Daniel, and Jacques Lacroix. *Les paysans du Languedoc au XIXᵉ siècle*. Paris: Hachette, 1973.

Fasel, Georges. "The French Election of April 23, 1848: Suggestions for a Revision." *French Historical Studies*, 5 (1968), 285-98.

———. "Urban Workers in Provincial France, February–June 1848." *International Review of Social History*, 17, pt. 3 (1972), 661-74.

———. "The Wrong Revolution: French Republicanism in 1848." *French Historical Studies*, 8 (Fall 1974), 654-77.

Faucher, Daniel. *Plaines et bassins du Rhône moyen entre Bas-Dauphiné et Provence: Etude géographique.* Paris: A. Colin, 1927.

Feral, P. "La liquidation du prolétariat rural en Gascogne lectouroise." *Congrès des sociétés savantes, actes, section d'histoire*, 78 (1953), 425-39.

Feraud, J.J.M. *Histoire, géographie et statistique du département des Basses-Alpes.* Digne, 1861.

Finer, Samuel Edward. *Comparative Government.* London: Allen Lane, 1970.

Forestier, Henri. *L'Yonne au XIXᵉ siècle.* 3 parts. Auxerre: Imprimerie l'Universelle, 1967.

Fox, Edward Whiting. *History in Geographic Perspective. The Other France.* New York: Norton, 1971.

Friedl, Ernestine. "Lagging Emulation in Post-Peasant Society: A Greek Case." In Jean Peristiany, editor, *Contributions to Mediterranean Sociology.* Paris: Mouton, 1968. Pp. 93-106.

Friedmann, Georges, editor. *Villes et campagnes. Civilisation urbaine et civilisation rurale en France.* Paris: A. Colin, 1953.

Furet, F., and W. Sachs. "La croissance de l'alphabétisation en France (XVIIIᵉ-XIXᵉ siècle)." *Annales (Economies, Sociétés, Civilisations)*, 29 (1974), 714-37.

Garrier, Gilbert. *Paysans de Beaujolais et du Lyonnais, 1800-1970.* 2 vols. Grenoble: Presses Universitaires de Grenoble, 1973.

George, Pierre. *La région du Bas-Rhône, étude de géographic régionale.* Paris: J. B. Baillière et fils, 1935.

Girard, Louis. *La Garde nationale, 1814-1871.* Paris: Plon, 1964.

———. *La Seconde République.* Paris: Calmann-Levy, 1968.

Godechot, Jacques. *Les institutions de la France sous la Révolution et l'Empire.* Paris: Presses Universitaires de France, 1951.

Gooch, G. P. *The Second Empire.* London: Longmans, 1960.

Gossez, Rémi. "La résistance à l'impôt: Les quarante-cinq centimes." *La Société d'histoire de la Révolution de 1848, Etudes*, 15 (1953), 89-132.

Goujon, Pierre. "Le Vignoble de Saône-et-Loire au XIXᵉ siècle (1815-1870)." *Thèse de doctorat de troisième cycle*, 2 vols., Lyon, 1968.

Guillaume, P. "La situation économique et sociale du département de la

Loire d'après l'enquête sur le travail . . . du mai 1848." *Congrès des sociétés savantes, actes, section d'histoire*, 86 (1961), 429-50.

Guillemin, Henri. *La Première résurrection de la République*. Paris: Gallimard, 1967.

Gurr, Ted R. "Psychological Factors in Civil Violence." *World Politics*, 20 (1968), 245-78.

———. "A Causal Model of Civil Strife: A Comparative Analysis Using New Indices." *American Political Science Review*, 62 (1968), 1104-24.

———. *Why Men Rebel*. Princeton: Princeton University Press, 1970.

Haggett, Peter. *Locational Analysis in Human Geography*. London: Edward Arnold, 1965.

Hay, Douglas, et al. *Albion's Fatal Tree: Crime and Society in Eighteenth-Century England*. New York: Pantheon, 1976.

Higonnet, Patrick. *Pont-de-Montvert: Social Structure and Politics in a French Village, 1700-1914*. Cambridge, Mass.: Harvard University Press, 1971.

Hobsbawm, Eric J. "Peasants and Politics." *Journal of Peasant Studies*, 1 (Oct. 1973), 3-22.

———. *Primitive Rebels: Studies in Archaic Forms of Social Movement in the 19th and 20th Centuries*. New York: Norton, 1959.

Hobsbawm, E. J., and George Rudé. *Captain Swing*. London: Lawrence and Wishart, 1969.

Hohenberg, Paul. "Change in Rural France in the Period of Industrialization, 1830-1914." *Journal of Economic History*, 32 (1972), 219-40.

Huard, R. "Montagne rouge et Montagne blanche en Languedoc-Roussillon sous la Seconde République." In *Droit et Gauche de 1789 à nos jours* (Actes du Colloque de Montpellier, 9-10 juin, 1973). Montpellier: Centre d'histoire contemporaine du Languedoc Méditérranéen et du Roussillon, 1975. Pp. 139-60.

Huntington, Samuel P. *Political Order in Changing Societies*. New Haven: Yale University Press, 1968.

Joanne, Adolphe. *Dictionnaire des Communes de la France*. Paris, 1864.

Johnson, Christopher H. "Some Recent French Village Studies." *Peasant Studies Newsletter*, 2 (Oct. 1973), 9-16.

———. *Utopian Communism in France: Cabet and the Icarians, 1839-1851*. Ithaca: Cornell University Press, 1974.

Judt, Tony R. "The Development of Socialism in France: The Example of the Var." *Historical Journal*, 18 (1975), 55-83.

———. "The Origins of Rural Socialism in Europe: Economic Change and the Provençal Peasantry, 1870-1914." *Social History*, 1 (1976), 45-65.

Juillard, Etienne. *La vie rurale dans la plaine de basse Alsace: Essai de géographie sociale*. Paris: Edition Le Roux, 1953.

Labrousse, Ernest. "Comment naissent les révolutions: 1848, 1830, 1789." *Actes du congrès historique du centenaire de la Révolution de 1848*. Paris: Presses Universitaires de France, 1948. Pp. 1-20.

———. "The Evolution of Peasant Society in France from the Eighteenth Century to the Present." Translated by David Landes. In Evelyn M. Acomb, and Marvin L. Brown, Jr., editors, *French Society and Culture since the Old Régime*. New York: Holt, Rinehart and Winston, 1966. Pp. 43-64.

———, editor. *Aspects de la crise et de la dépression de l'économie française au milieu du XIXᵉ siècle, 1846-1851*. (Bibliothèque de la Révolution de 1848, no. 19.) La-Roche-sur-Yon: Imprimerie centrale de l'ouest, 1956.

Labrousse, Ernest, Pierre Goubert, and Pierre Léon, *Histoire économique et sociale de la France*. Vol. II, *1660-1789*. Paris: Presses Universitaires de France, 1970.

La Hodde, Lucien de. *Histoire des sociétés secrètes et du mouvement républicain de 1830 à 1847*. Paris, 1850.

Landes, David. *The Unbound Prometheus: Technological Change and Industrial Development in Western Europe from 1750 to the Present*. Cambridge: Cambridge University Press, 1969.

Langer, William L. "The Pattern of Urban Revolution in 1848." In Evelyn M. Acomb and Marvin L. Brown, Jr., editors, *French Society and Culture since the Old Regime*. New York: Holt, Rinehart and Winston, 1966.

———. *Political and Social Upheaval, 1832-1852*. New York: Harper and Row, 1969.

Lefebvre, Georges. "The French Revolution and the Peasants." In *The Economic Origins of the French Revolution*. Edited by R. W. Greenlaw. Boston: Heath, 1958.

———. *The Great Fear*. Translated by Joan White. New York: Vintage, 1973.

Léon, Pierre. *La naissance de la grande industrie en Dauphiné (fin de dix-septième siècle-1869)*. 2 vols. Paris: Presses Universitaires de France, 1954.

Léon, Pierre, et al. *Histoire économique et sociale de la France*. Tome III, *L'avènement de l'ère industrielle (1789-années 1880)*. 2 volumes. Paris: Presses Universitaires de France, 1976.

Le Roy Ladurie, Emmanuel. "Révoltes et contestations rurales en France de 1675 à 1788." *Annales (Economies, Sociétés, Civilisations)*, 28 (1974), 6-22.

————. *Le territoire de l'historien.* Paris: Gallimard, 1973.

Levasseur, Emile. *Histoire des classes ouvrières et de l'industrie en France de 1789 à 1870.* 2 vols. 2nd ed. Paris: A. Rousseau, 1904.

————. *La population française.* 3 vols. Paris, 1889-92.

Lévy-Leboyer, Maurice. "La croissance économique en France au XIXe siècle, Résultats préliminaires." *Annales (Economies, Sociétés, Civilisations,* 23 (1968), 788-807.

Loeffler, Reinhold. "The Representative Mediator and the New Peasant." *American Anthropologist,* 73 (1971), 1077-91.

Marcilhacy, Christianne. *Le Diocèse d'Orléans au milieu du XIXe siècle: Les hommes et leurs mentalités.* Paris: Sirey, 1964.

Marlière, A. *Statistique de l'arrondissement de Clamecy.* Clamecy, 1859.

Marx, Karl. "The Class Struggles in France, 1848-1850." In Marx and Engels, *Selected Works.* Vol. 1. Moscow: Foreign Languages Publishing House, 1962. Pp. 118-242.

Merriman, John. "Social Conflict in France and the Limoges Revolution of April 27, 1848." *Societas—A Review of Social History,* 4 (Winter 1974), 21-38.

————. editor. *1830 in France.* New York: New Viewpoints, 1975.

Mendels, Frank. "Proto-Industrialization: The First Phase of the Industrialization Process." *Journal of Economic History,* 32 (1972), 241-61.

Moreau, Jean-Paul. *La vie rurale dans le sud-est du bassin parisien entre les vallées de l'Armançon et de la Loire; étude de géographie humaine.* Paris: Société les belles lettres, 1958.

Morel, Alain. "L'espace social d'un village picard." *Etudes rurales,* 45 (1972), 62-80.

Morineau, Michel. *Les faux-semblants d'un démarrage économique: Agriculture et démographie en France au XVIIIe siècle.* (Cahiers d'Annales, 30.) Paris: A. Colin, 1971.

Mousnier, Roland. *Peasant Uprisings in Seventeenth-Century France, Russia, and China.* Translated by Brian Pearce. New York: Harper and Row, 1970.

Newell, William H. "The Agricultural Revolution in Nineteenth-Century France." *The Journal of Economic History,* 33 (1973), 697-731.

Perreux, Gabriel. *Au temps des sociétés secrètes: La propagande républicaine au début de la Monarchie de Juillet (1830-1835).* Paris: Hachette, 1931.

Perrie, Maureen. "The Russian Peasant Movement of 1905-1907: Its Social Composition and Revolutionary Significance." *Past and Present,* 57 (Nov. 1972), 123-55.

Pinkney, David. *The French Revolution of 1830*. Princeton: Princeton University Press, 1972.

Pitt-Rivers, Julien A. "The Closed Community and Its Friends." *Kroeber Anthropological Society Papers*, 16 (1957), 5-15.

Ponteil, Félix. *Les institutions de la France de 1814 à 1870*. Paris: Presses Universitaires de France, 1966.

Porchnev, Boris. *Les soulèvements populaires en France de 1623 à 1648*. Paris: S.E.V.P.E.N., 1963.

Pouthas, Charles. *La population française pendant la première moitié du XIXe siècle*. (Cahier I.N.E.D., No. 25). Paris: Presses Universitaires de France, 1956.

Price, Roger. "Popular Disturbances in the French Provinces after the July Revolution of 1830." *European Studies Review*, 1 (1971), 323-50.

Rémond, René. *La vie politique en France*. Tome II, *1848-1879*. Collection U." Paris: A. Colin, 1969.

Resnick, Daniel. *The White Terror and the Political Reaction after Waterloo*. Cambridge, Mass.: Harvard University Press, 1966.

Rokkan, Stein. *Citizens, Elections, Parties: Approaches to the Comparative Study of the Processes of Development*. New York: McKay, 1970.

Roubin, Lucienne A. *Chambrettes des Provençaux: Une Maison des Hommes en Méditerranée septentrionale*. Paris: Plon, 1970.

———. "Espace masculin, espace féminin en communauté provençale." *Annales (Economies, Sociétés, Civilisations)*, 25 (1970), 537-60.

Rudé, George. *The Crowd in History, 1730-1848*. New York: Wiley, 1964.

———. *The Crowd in the French Revolution, 1787-1795*. Oxford: The University Press, 1959.

Sabean, David. "Markets, Uprisings and Leadership in Peasant Societies: Western Europe, 1381-1789." *Peasant Studies Newsletter*, 2 (July 1973), 17-19.

Schapiro, J. Selwyn. *Liberalism and the Challenge of Fascism: Social Forces in England and France (1815-1870)*. New York: McGraw-Hill, 1949.

Seignour, Paulette. *La vie économique du Vaucluse de 1815 à 1848*. Aix-en-Provence: La pensée universitaire, 1957.

Sencier, G. *Le Babouvisme après Babeuf: Sociétés secrètes et conspirations communistes (1830-1848)*. Paris, 1912.

Sewell, William H., Jr. "La classe ouvrière de Marseille sous la Seconde République: Structure sociale et comportement politique." *Le Mouvement social*, 76 (July–Sep. 1971), 27-65.

————. "Social Change and the Rise of Working-Class Politics in Nineteenth Century Marseille." *Past and Present*, 65 (Nov. 1974), 75-109.

Shanin, Theodor, editor. *Peasants and Peasant Society*. Baltimore: Penguin, 1971.

Simmel, George. "The Sociology of Secrecy and Secret Societies." *American Journal of Sociology*, 11 (January 1906), 441-98.

Skinner, William G. "Chinese Peasants and the Closed Community: An Open and Shut Case." *Comparative Studies in Society and History*, 13 (1971), 270-81.

Soboul, Albert. "The French Rural Community in the 18th and 19th Centuries." *Past and Present*, 10 (1956), 78-95.

————. *Paysans, sans-culottes et Jacobins*. Paris: Librairie Clavreuil, 1966.

Spitzer, Alan. "The Bureaucrat as Proconsul: The Restoration Prefect and the *Police Générale. Comparative Studies in Society and History*, 7 (1965), 371-92.

————. "The Good Napoleon." *French Historical Studies*, 2 (1961-62), 308-29.

————. *Old Hatreds and Young Hopes*. Cambridge, Mass.: Harvard University Press, 1971.

Stone, Laurence. "Whigs, Marxists, and Poachers." *New York Review of Books*, Feb. 5, 1976.

Tchernoff, I. *Associations et sociétés secrètes sous la Seconde République*. Paris, 1905.

————. *Le parti républicain au coup d'état et sous le Second Empire*. Paris, 1906.

————. *Le parti républicain sous la Monarchie de Juillet*. Paris, 1909.

Ténot, Eugène. *Le suffrage universel et les paysans*. Paris, 1865.

Thabault, Roger. *Education and Change in a Village Community: Mazières-en-Gâtine, 1848-1914*. Translated by Peter Tregear. New York: Schocken Books, 1971.

Thompson, E. P. *The Making of the English Working Class*. Rev. ed. New York: Vintage, 1966.

————. "The Moral Economy of the English Crowd in the Eighteenth Century." *Past and Present*, 50 (Feb. 1971), 76-136.

Thompson, J. M. *Louis Napoleon and the Second Empire*. Oxford: Basil Blackwood, 1954.

Tilly, Charles. "Collective Violence in European Perspective." In H. D. Graham and T. R. Gurr, editors, *Violence in America: Historical and Comparative Perspectives*. New York: Bantam Books, 1969.

————. *The Vendée: A Sociological Analysis of the Counterrevolution of 1793*. 2nd ed. New York: Wiley, 1967.

Tilly, Charles, and David Snyder. "Hardship and Collective Violence in France, 1830 to 1960." *American Sociological Review*, 37 (1972), 520-32.

Tilly, Louise. "The Food Riot as a Form of Political Conflict in France." *The Journal of Interdisciplinary History*, 2 (Summer 1971), 23-58.

Toutain, J. C. *Le produit de l'agriculture française de 1700 à 1958.* Vol. II, *La Croissance.* (Cahiers de l'Institut de science économique appliquée, No. 115 and supplément, Juillet 1961. Sér. AF. Histoire quantitative de l'économie française, 2.) Paris: I.S.E.A., 1961.

Tudesq, André-Jean. *L'election présidentielle de Louis Napoléon, 10 décembre 1848.* Paris: A. Colin, 1965.

———. *Les grands notables en France (1840-1849). Etude historique d'une psychologie sociale.* 2 vols. Paris: Presses Universitaires de France, 1964.

Vidalenc, Jean. "La province et les journées de juin." *Etudes d'histoire moderne et contemporaine*, 2 (1948), 83-144.

———. "La situation économique et sociale des Basses-Alpes en 1848." *Société d'histoire de la Révolution de 1848, Etudes*, 16 (1954), 121-59.

———. *La société française de 1815 à 1848.* Vol. I, *Le peuple des campagnes.* Vol. II, *Le peuple des villes et des bourgs.* Paris: Marcel Rivière, 1970 and 1973.

Vigier, Philippe. "Elections municipales et prise de conscience politique sous la Monarchie de Juillet." In *La France au XIXᵉ siècle, Mélanges C.-H. Pouthas.* Paris: Presses Universitaires de France, 1973. Pp. 276-86.

———. *Essai sur la répartition de la propriété foncière dans la région alpine. Son évolution des origines du cadastre à la fin du Second Empire.* Paris: S.E.V.P.E.N., 1963.

———. *La Monarchie de Juillet.* (Collection "Que sais-je?") Paris: Presses Universitaires de France, 1965.

———. "Les mouvements paysans dans le cadre de l'agriculture et de la société rurale traditionnelles." In *Enquête sur les mouvements paysans dans le monde contemporaine.* Congrès Internationale d'histoire at Moscow, 1970, tome I. Moscow, 1974. Pp. 33-59.

Weber, Eugen. *Peasants into Frenchmen: The Modernization of Rural France, 1870-1914.* Stanford, Calif.: Stanford University Press, 1976.

Wolf, Eric R. *Peasant Wars of the Twentieth Century.* New York: Harper and Row, 1969.

Woloch, Isser. *Jacobin Legacy: The Democratic Movement under the Directory.* Princeton: Princeton University Press, 1970.

Wright, Gordon. *France in Modern Times.* 2nd ed. Chicago: Rand McNally, 1974.

Wylie, Laurence. *Village in the Vaucluse.* 2nd ed. Cambridge, Mass.: Harvard University Press, 1964.

Zeldin, Theodore. "Government Policy in the French General Elections of 1849." *English Historical Review,* 74 (1959), 240-48.

———. *The Political System of Napoleon III.* New York: Norton edition, 1971.

———. *France, 1848-1945.* Vol. 1, *Ambition, Love and Politics.* Oxford, England: Oxford University Press, 1973.

Zevaes, Alexandre. "La Propagande socialiste dans la campagne en 1848." *La Révolution de 1848,* 31 (1934-35), 75-94.

Library of Congress Cataloging in Publication Data

Margadant, Ted W   1941-
  French peasants in revolt.

  Bibliography: p.
  Includes index.
  1. Peasant uprisings—France.   2. France—History—
Coup d'état, 1851.   I. Title.
DC274.5.M37   944.07   79-18971